Make It New

RESHAPING JAZZ IN THE 21ST CENTURY

Bill Beuttler

LEVER
PRESS

Lever Press (leverpress.org) is a publisher of pathbreaking scholarship. Supported by a consortium of liberal arts institutions focused on, and renowned for, excellence in both research and teaching, our press is grounded on three essential commitments: to be a digitally native press, to be a peer-reviewed, open access press that charges no fees to either authors or their institutions, and to be a press aligned with the ethos and mission of liberal arts colleges.

DOI: https://doi.org/10.3998/mpub.11469938
Print ISBN: 978-1-64315-005-5
Open access ISBN: 978-1-64315-006-2

Library of Congress Control Number: 2019944840

Published in the United States of America by Lever Press, in partnership with Amherst College Press and Michigan Publishing

Contents

Member Institution Acknowledgments

Lever Press is a joint venture. This work was made possible by the generous support of Lever Press member libraries from the following institutions:

Adrian College

Agnes Scott College

Allegheny College

Amherst College

Bard College

Berea College

Bowdoin College

Carleton College

Claremont Graduate University

Claremont McKenna College

Clark Atlanta University

Coe College

College of Saint Benedict / Saint John's University

The College of Wooster

Denison University

DePauw University

Earlham College

Furman University

Grinnell College

Hamilton College

Harvey Mudd College

Haverford College

Hollins University

Keck Graduate Institute

Kenyon College

Knox College

Lafayette College Library

Lake Forest College

Macalester College

Middlebury College

Morehouse College

Oberlin College

Pitzer College

Pomona College

Rollins College

Santa Clara University

Scripps College

Sewanee: The University of the South
Skidmore College
Smith College
Spelman College
St. Lawrence University
St. Olaf College
Susquehanna University
Swarthmore College
Trinity University

Union College
University of Puget Sound
Ursinus College
Vassar College
Washington and Lee University
Whitman College
Willamette University
Williams College

For my parents,
Will Beuttler and Joan Beuttler,
and my wife,
Kim Abrams Beuttler

INTRODUCTION

I'm not an isolationist, and I'm not obsessed with trying to do anything new. I feel as attached to history as my teachers might have been. I'm trying to do what they did—keep it free and open. I use their language and reshape it. The ones who have passed, when I meet them at the big gate they're going to ask me, "Did you take care of our music?"
                     —Jason Moran, as quoted in the *New Yorker*, March 11, 2013

The most important artist and the most important time is, like, right now. It's the people who are learning now, and creating new things right now. Idol worship doesn't help this music in any way.
                     —Esperanza Spalding, as quoted in the *New Yorker*, March 15, 2010

This book on jazz as it enters its second century is modeled on one published in 1965. *Jazz Masters of the 50s*, by Joe Goldberg, was the first of the six decade-oriented volumes of jazz history published by Macmillan Publishing Co. between 1965 and 1972. It's my favorite in the series (though pianist/composer Ethan Iverson makes a good case for Rex Stewart's *Jazz Masters of the 30s*, which like Iverson's own award-winning blog, *Do the Math*, has the advantage of being written by an accomplished musician), largely for its format, which devotes a chapter apiece to a dozen heroes from my early jazz-listening days, among them Miles Davis, John Coltrane, Charles Mingus, Thelonious Monk, Art Blakey, Ornette Coleman, Cecil Taylor, and Sonny Rollins.

The format enabled Goldberg, in what turned out to be his only book, to use his dozen profiles to provide a snapshot of where jazz stood as it entered the 1960s.

(He died in 2009, having written "a few hundred liner notes" and still contributing to *Billboard* and other publications.) My book attempts to give a similar sense of where jazz stands today, through the stories of several top artists (seven individuals and the trio the Bad Plus, which switched pianists as the book was being written) who rose to prominence in the jazz world around the year 2000 and afterward.

Organizing this book into chapters that read like magazine profiles makes it more digestible for readers and allows them to read the chapters in whichever order they prefer. Goldberg's book was structured that way, as was series editor Martin Williams's similarly readable *Jazz Masters of New Orleans* (1967). More challenging was deciding which artists to include. I made and remade lists of thirty or so possibilities as I began my research, and found that about half of them kept bubbling to the top as musicians whose work had the qualities I was looking for. I wanted people whose music was taking jazz places it hadn't been, as opposed to carrying on styles of jazz already being established when Goldberg's book was published. I wanted musicians whose work has both intellectual and visceral appeal, who neither pandered to audiences nor were indifferent to pleasing them—that is, musicians whose work had a chance to captivate listeners who weren't necessarily jazz aficionados. I wanted people who illustrated how significantly jazz had changed over the fifteen years between my leaving an editing job at *DownBeat* in October 1987 and starting to write weekly on jazz for the *Boston Globe* in late 2002.

The title *Make It New*, borrowed from Ezra Pound's modernist call to arms, reflects those changes. When I left *DownBeat*, jazz was in its neoclassical period—a time when Wynton Marsalis and others dubbed "young lions" were emphasizing a return to the principles of straight-ahead jazz of the 1950s and earlier, particularly the foundational elements of swing and the blues. The newer styles of jazz that had arisen in the 1960s and '70s didn't disappear, and other experimentation had continued throughout the peak neoclassical years, but the neoclassicists were better marketed, meaning they dominated what little attention jazz received from mainstream media and got the most work in clubs and concert halls. This had changed, however, by the time I began covering jazz for the *Globe*. The newer talents on the scene showed more interest in not only mastering the music that had preceded them, but also building on that foundation to create something new.[1]

A digression in a 2013 "Before and After" session in *JazzTimes* magazine succinctly summarized this evolution. The pianist Kenny Werner was discussing a track by the young trumpeter Ambrose Akinmusire when he said, "You know, the '70s were about creativity. The '80s became this neoclassicist thing. The bad thing was that people got hung up on what is and what isn't jazz. But the good thing is that musicians really trained themselves. When I began to dig it was in the mid-'90s, when I realized that musicians were better trained than we ever were, because we didn't have that discipline. But they were becoming creative again."

The 2010 DVD *Icons Among Us: Jazz in the Present Tense* focused more formally on jazz as it was evolving in the first years of the new century, and can be viewed as a sort of addendum (and perhaps rebuttal) to the Ken Burns series *Jazz* from ten years earlier, which surveyed jazz history with a point of view greatly influenced by Wynton Marsalis. Esperanza Spalding, Anat Cohen, and Robert Glasper are among the many musicians featured in the newer film, Glasper most provocatively, whose main point can be summarized with a line from Terence Blanchard: "There's a group of young musicians who have a new vision."

An intriguing but gloomier point is raised in the film by the Seattle journalist Paul de Barros, who doubts whether it is possible for jazz to recapture the relevance it had a half-century earlier.

"You think of more than music," de Barros explained to the camera. "You think of integration, the civil rights movement. You think of a kind of bohemian outsiderism. The problem that jazz faces right now is that if you say 'jazz' to somebody, they don't have something in the present culture they can connect it with. What is it actually saying? If you asked Lee Morgan and Sonny Rollins what their music was saying, they would say, 'Well, I'm a black person in a white society, and I have something to say, and I need it to be heard.' That was part of the message behind that music. That was the urgency of it. We understand that, and we understand the relationship between Charlie Parker, John Coltrane, and Ornette Coleman and black freedom. We do not understand what the relationship is between Bill Frisell and society."

The late saxophonist and producer Bob Belden said something similar to journalist Bill Milkowski for a *JazzTimes* profile in 2000: "Jazz does not reflect what's going on in society at all. Because musicians don't make music that tells a story. And for the most part it's because they don't have a story to tell, except the story of long hours practicing at Berklee."[2]

That began changing significantly with the killings that launched the Black Lives Matter movement, with jazz reclaiming some of its role as protest music that it had ceded to hip-hop in recent years—and had already begun sharing through the turbulent 1960s and afterward with folk, rock, soul, and R&B.[3] Robert Glasper (one of the jazz musicians who performed on Kendrick Lamar's important 2015 hip-hop album *To Pimp a Butterfly*) and Ambrose Akinmusire (who played on one track of that album) both released albums that had tracks that included the recitation of the names of victims of police violence. In 2015, Terence Blanchard released *Breathless*, named for Eric Garner dying in a police chokehold after telling arresting officers "I can't breathe"; three years later Blanchard's album *Live* was focused around concerts in or near the three cities where Tamir Rice (Cleveland), Philando Castile (suburban St. Paul), and five police officers (Dallas) had been shot to death.

The resurgence of jazz as protest music accelerated after the 2016 election of Donald Trump. Jazz has long been associated with protest: John Coltrane's "Alabama," Sonny Rollins's *Freedom Suite* (1958), *We Insist!: Max Roach's Freedom Now Suite* (1960), Charles Mingus's "Fables of Faubus," Billie Holiday's "Strange Fruit," and Nina Simone's "Mississippi Goddam" are a handful of works that spring to mind.

Today we have Samora Pinderhughes's *The Transformations Suite* (2016), a five-movement exploration of resistance and the African Diaspora, performed by an ensemble including his sister Elena Pinderhughes of Christian Scott aTunde Adjuah's band. Scott[4] has composed numerous pieces referencing political topics. Jason Moran updated "Fables of Faubus" in a project with vocalist Georgia Anne Muldrow, titled "New Fables: Muldrow, Moran, and Mingus." Esperanza Spalding has raised money, via tour merchandise sales and a high-profile benefit concert, for the advocacy group Free the Slaves, and recorded the music video "We Are America" demanding the closing of the US detention center at Guantanamo Bay. Two more artists featured in this book—Vijay Iyer and Rudresh Mahanthappa— were among the dozen or so musicians who participated in a New York concert billed as Musicians Against Fascism on the eve of Donald Trump's inauguration as president. And in spring 2018, Robert Glasper, Terrace Martin, Christian Scott, and others put out an album and began touring as the supergroup R+R=NOW (for Reflect + Respond = Now), the name derived from the Nina Simone quotation "An artist's duty, as far as I'm concerned, is to reflect the times." Sometimes, too, political points are made more subtly: Rudresh Mahanthappa and Oded Lev-Ari each suggested to me, in separate conversations, that performing jazz as a person of South Asian descent and an Israeli, respectively, illustrated the desirability of multiculturalism without a word needing to be spoken.

All this points up the heightened timeliness of this book. The Trump administration and other nationalist movements are pushing back hard against multiculturalism. Jazz, in stark contrast, has a long history of knocking down barriers between peoples. Benny Goodman integrated his music by hiring and playing alongside Teddy Wilson, Charlie Christian, and Lionel Hampton a full decade before Jackie Robinson broke the color line and became the first African American to play major league baseball. Dizzy Gillespie, Louis Armstrong, Duke Ellington, Dave Brubeck, and Benny Goodman were each recruited by the US Department of State for concert tours at the height of the Cold War. The idea of the Jazz Ambassadors program was to combat Soviet propaganda critical of the United States, in particular that which called attention to the abuse suffered by African Americans in a nation proclaiming itself a champion of freedom and equal rights.

The Jazz Ambassadors themselves sometimes pushed back against official US policy. Gillespie distributed free tickets to a concert in Turkey to people too poor to afford them. While negotiations were underway for Armstrong to visit the Soviet Union, he caused a national uproar by strongly denouncing the US government, due to President Eisenhower's initial reluctance to send federal troops to enforce the desegregation of Central High School in Little Rock, Arkansas. Armstrong later performed with Brubeck in Brubeck's satirical musical *The Real Ambassadors* (1962). But the musicians' interactions with the citizenry of the nations they toured created goodwill and enhanced cultural understanding. A less high-profile version of the program continued after the collapse of the Soviet Union, surviving into the early years of the twenty-first century in partnership with the Kennedy Center. In fact, Miguel Zenón's album *Oye!!!: Live in Puerto Rico* (2013) was recorded by a band first assembled for a 2003 tour of West Africa.

The leanings toward multiculturalism derive naturally from the jazz life. That was a notion sounded frequently by the great jazz and civil rights journalist Nat Hentoff, who died twelve days before the aforementioned Musicians Against Fascism concert. In his 1997 memoir, *Speaking Freely,* Hentoff put it this way: "For one thing, jazz players are often widely knowledgeable. Having traveled a lot, they are the least parochial of professionals—including secretaries of state, who do not get a chance to walk beyond the palaces or other grand meeting places. And by working with musicians from many parts of the world, jazz players become easily multicultural without having to take courses in cosmopolitanism."

This is all the more so in the twenty-first century, with the influx of jazz musicians and their native musics from every corner of the globe. Progressive US politics from fifty years ago helped that along, with the Immigration and Nationality Act of 1965 opening the doors to immigrants from Asia and Africa—among them the parents of Iyer and Mahanthappa. Likewise, feminism and the women's liberation movement of the 1960s and '70s opened doors to women; that progress made it inevitable that some of them—many of them, it turned out—would take up playing jazz and creative music. And, of course, the civil rights movement of that era greatly impacted both jazz and every other form of "Black American Music" then and to follow.

To tell the story of these twenty-first-century developments in jazz required the participation of people who believed in my project and were willing to make time to be interviewed for it. My *Globe* association helped. I wrote early profiles of Esperanza Spalding and Christian Scott, having encountered them both during their undergraduate years at the Berklee College of Music, and met (and reviewed) Julian Lage even before he began his studies there. I profiled Jason Moran in 2005 as he toured in support of his album released that year, *Same Mother*, whose title references the close relationship of jazz to the blues, and discovered that a blues pianist friend of mine from Chicago is a cousin of Jason's father. The first interview specifically for this book took place at Moran's home in spring 2012, the morning after he and his wife, the vocalist and composer Alicia Hall Moran, concluded their five-day residency at the 2012 Whitney Biennial. Their willingness to be included in the book turned out to be a selling point when I approached the others about doing so.

Colleagues and mentors of the featured artists also agreed to interviews. Fred Hersch has taught Ethan Iverson and played duo sets with Moran, Lage, Zenón, Anat Cohen, and Esperanza Spalding. Danilo Pérez was an early mentor of Zenón in Boston. The late Geri Allen, whom I interviewed two months prior to her unexpected death, and Terri Lyne Carrington paved the way for female instrumentalists like Cohen and Spalding, and Allen and Carrington had planned to tour with Spalding as a trio the spring and summer of Allen's passing. Joe Lovano was among Spalding's professors at the Berklee College of Music, and she later toured and recorded with him in his band Us Five; Lovano also served alongside Zenón in the first edition of the SFJAZZ Collective. Greg Osby hired Moran for his first tour of Europe, and later helped get him signed to Blue Note Records.

Because these musicians are brilliant, well-spoken people, I have quoted them extensively and feel justified in doing so. Nat Hentoff did likewise in his first books on jazz, and Studs Terkel constructed many excellent books from quotations derived from carefully edited interviews. My subjects expressed themselves so well that I was put in mind of something Saul Bellow had told the *New York Times* the week his breakthrough novel, *The Adventures of Augie March*, was published in 1953: "All I had to do was be there with buckets to catch it." My buckets of material became so full, in fact, that it became necessary to trim back from the dozen chapters I had projected to eight, with plans to still publish the others—Christian Scott, Julian Lage, Lionel Loueke, Pedrito Martinez—in a subsequent volume.

Christian McBride, a contemporary of some of the artists featured in the chapters but ineligible for having been too successful too fast, attracting high-profile sideman gigs and a Verve recording contract in the early 1990s, granted me an hour in June 2016 while in town for two nights of shows in Boston. I spent it confirming that the artists and ideas I was including rang true to him. McBride prides himself on keeping his ear to the ground regarding new developments in jazz, a necessity in his roles hosting NPR's *Jazz Night in America* and taking over for George Wein as artistic director for the Newport Jazz Festival. Besides keeping up with what's going on, McBride is receptive to all sorts of jazz. He's best-known for playing straight-ahead stuff himself but not averse to mixing some pop into his sets (I'd seen his trio play its version of the 1970s R&B hit "Car Wash" the night before we spoke) or participating in more cutting-edge projects (joining Craig Taborn and Tyshawn Sorey on a 2016 John Zorn trio project, *Flaga: The Book of Angels Volume 27*, for example, or stretching out with Moran and others on his own three-CD album, *Live at Tonic*).

That McBride liked my choices doesn't mean there aren't grounds for questioning some of them. I decided against including singers, ruling out such bright stars as Gregory Porter, José James, and Cécile McLorin Salvant—but *not* Esperanza Spalding, whom I knew first as a bassist and who continues to excel on that instrument along with being a gifted vocalist. And Norah Jones, for that matter, whose 2002 blockbuster release *Come Away with Me* put Blue Note Records on a stronger financial footing to champion more straightforward jazz people like Moran and Robert Glasper. (Glasper remembered running into Jones at jazz camps in their home state of Texas and thought I should include her.) I focused on small groups rather than big bands, thereby excluding important talents like Maria Schneider, Darcy James Argue, and Guillermo Klein. Kamasi Washington and Joey Alexander both made big splashes with debut albums in 2015, but I'd settled on my choices by then, and those choices all possessed more extensive track records.

Jason Moran and my wife both told me the book should include more women. McBride, however, was given the rule that I'd imposed on myself—to add someone to my existing list of twelve artists to be featured required specifying which of those already on it to take off—so he cut me more slack. "I could think of a few, but I'm not sure that they've had the impact and staying power of Anat," he told me, then rattled off three possibilities: tenor saxophonist Melissa Aldana, bassist Linda May Han Oh (whom the *Village Voice* would profile a few weeks later in a story about the difficulties of making a living playing jazz), and drummer Kim Thompson. Wadada Leo Smith had told me he hoped I'd include flutist Nicole Mitchell, and Mitchell did in fact top a list of other women I started out considering that included Aldana, Oh, violinist Jenny Scheinman, guitarist Mary Halvorson, and alto saxophonists Grace Kelly, Tia Fuller, and Matana Roberts. I was particularly keen to include Mitchell and/or Roberts for their connections to Chicago and the Association for the Advancement of Creative Musicians (AACM). But their work leans more toward the avant-garde, and I was looking for artists whose music seemed likelier to have broader appeal. "Which is why I'm glad you have Vijay in there," McBride told me. "Because he walks that fine line very well."

We could be wrong, of course. Mitchell's album *Aquarius* (2013) with her group Ice Crystal is very approachable, and she, cellist Tomeka Reid, and drummer Mike Reed enraptured a Sanders Theatre audience with music from *Artifacts* (2015), their AACM tribute album, when Iyer bought them to Harvard for a performance. As for Roberts, a young bartender at one of two bars in Puerto Rico to claim to have invented the piña colada nearly knocked me off my barstool when, on learning that I write about jazz, asked if I had ever heard of . . . Matana Roberts. It turned out a music service algorithm had guessed right in suggesting that if he liked Miles Davis, he might like her. He checked out one of her *Coin Coin*[5] albums and loved it.

The emergence of women instrumentalists is among the most notable and welcome developments in the jazz world over the past couple of decades. Many of jazz's greatest vocalists have been women, of course, and women have made important contributions as instrumentalists throughout jazz history as well. Lil Hardin Armstrong played piano on her husband Louis Armstrong's early Hot Five and Hot Seven recordings (her composition "Struttin' with Some Barbecue" was famously recorded by the Hot Five). The great pianist and composer Mary Lou Williams was a mentor to bebop legends Thelonious Monk, Bud Powell, Dizzy Gillespie, and Charlie Parker, and many years later to students at Duke University, where she became artist in residence in 1977. The annual Mary Lou William Jazz Festival at the Kennedy Center honors her legacy each spring with performances by leading female instrumentalists.

Marian McPartland was already an accomplished pianist when she was photographed chatting with Williams in the historic 1958 "Great Day in Harlem" photo Art Kane shot of fifty-seven jazz musicians gathered on and around a front stoop for *Esquire* magazine[6]; two decades later, McPartland launched her long-running syndicated National Public Radio show *Piano Jazz*. Toshiko Akiyoshi was a celebrated pianist, arranger/composer, and big band leader (and before that, the first Japanese student admitted to the Berklee College of Music), earning fourteen Grammy nominations between 1976 and 1994. Keyboardist Carla Bley is regarded as one of jazz's greatest composers. Alice Coltrane replaced pianist McCoy Tyner in her husband's band, and later also excelled as a harpist on the numerous spiritual recordings she made after John Coltrane's death. Pianists Dorothy Donegan and Joanne Brackeen are both National Endowment for the Arts Jazz Masters, as is the trombonist and arranger/composer Melba Liston.

Pianists Geri Allen, Michele Rosewoman, and Eliane Elias, guitarist Emily Remler, and drummer Terri Lyne Carrington were among the outstanding women instrumentalists to arrive in the 1980s, and the pace has accelerated since then. Where once the women in jazz were almost exclusively singers or pianists, today they're found playing virtually every instrument. The Diva Jazz Orchestra, in fact, is a big band composed entirely of women. Anat Cohen was still in its saxophone section when I saw the orchestra perform in Boston with vocalist Marlena Shaw in January 2005. "I remember I stole one of her lines," Cohen told me years later of playing with Shaw that night. "She said, 'The more you drink, the better we sound.' And when she said it, I was like, 'That's brilliant!' Sometimes I say it to the audience."

But the struggle for women's equality in jazz remains ongoing, and became especially visible in 2017 and early 2018. In February 2017, Robert Glasper made an infelicitous remark to Ethan Iverson during an interview for Iverson's blog that infuriated women who took it as another in a long line of insults regarding their presumed inability to understand jazz. The journalist Michelle Mercer wrote a scathing response for National Public Radio,[7] and that September the young vibraphonist Sasha Berliner posted "An Open Letter to Ethan Iverson (And the Rest of Jazz Patriarchy)" on her website that spelled out indignities she had been subjected to by men as a performer and music student. Not long after the #MeToo movement surfaced that October, the *Boston Globe* ran a story about the quiet dismissals of male Berklee College of Music faculty members in response to allegations of sexual misbehavior.

But more heartening developments arrived the next year. In January 2018, New York's Winter Jazzfest hosted a well-attended "Jazz and Gender" panel discussion led by Terri Lyne Carrington. That same week, Jazz at Lincoln Center and *JazzTimes* hosted their first Jazz Congress, which included its own "Gender and Jazz" panel discussion, this one moderated by Michelle Mercer (and with Carrington as one of its panelists), and Mercer also moderated a Jazz Journalists Association–hosted discussion of "Women in Jazz Journalism." In April, a group of sixteen musicians including Carrington, Oh, and Tia Fuller launched the We Have Voice Collective to prevent sexism in jazz. In June, women won an unprecedented thirteen of thirty-one categories in the annual Jazz Journalists Association Critics Poll.

Another prominent twenty-first-century development is how increasingly international jazz is becoming. Its interactions with Europe, Japan, and parts of Latin America (Cuba, Puerto Rico, Brazil) are long standing, well known, and too abundant to dig into in any depth here. In broad strokes, James Reese Europe introduced jazz to Europe during World War I. Django Reinhardt and Stéphane Grappelli were standouts among the Europeans playing jazz in the 1930s. American stars such as Kenny Clarke, Bud Powell, and Dexter Gordon relocated to Europe in the late 1950s and early 1960s to escape racism in the United States. Dave Holland and John McLaughlin both moved to New York from London in the late 1960s to work with Miles Davis. Many outstanding European jazz musicians chose to remain based in their native countries: Evan Parker, Tomasz Stańko, Enrico Rava, Albert Mangelsdorff, Willem Breuker, and Martial Solal, to name but a few.

The 1970s saw the rise of the Italian record label Black Saint/Soul Note—specializing in avant-garde and free jazz, primarily by American musicians, many of them associated with groups like the Chicago-based AACM—and the German behemoth ECM Records, which ignores genre and has a reputation for producing work that often has a pristine, classical chamber music-like feel to it. The Swiss label Intakt, founded in 1986, also specializes in more avant-garde jazz, with a catalogue containing a mix of American and European artists. Japan, like Europe, is known to be hospitable to jazz—even more so, it is sometimes claimed, than by audiences in the United States. There is a thriving scene of local musicians. Some international jazz stars to have originated in Japan include Toshiko Akiyoshi, Sadao Watanabe, Makoto Ozone, Tiger Okoshi, and, more recently, the pianist Hiromi and trumpeter Takuya Kuroda.

The big bang of Afro-Cuban jazz is generally said to have occurred on September 29, 1947, when Cuban congo virtuoso Chano Pozo joined Dizzy Gillespie's big band for a performance at Carnegie Hall. But Jelly Roll Morton had spoken of the "Spanish tinge" in his own early jazz, which had come to New Orleans from Cuba, and Mario Bauzá had already written "Tangá," the first song to mix jazz with clave, several years before introducing Gillespie to Pozo. In any case, the rise of Afro-Brazilian jazz followed roughly a decade later with the bossa nova craze of the late 1950s and early 1960s. Its best-known recording was *Getz/Gilberto* (1964). A collaboration of the American tenor saxophonist Stan Getz and the Brazilian guitarist João Gilberto, the album also featured pianist and composer Antônio Carlos Jobim, who wrote or cowrote most of the album's music, including the hit "The Girl from Ipanema." Jobim remains one of the composers most beloved by jazz musicians. Other Latin American jazz stars of the mid-twentieth century include the Cubans Bebo Valdés, Chico O'Farrill, and Mongo Santamaría; the Puerto Rican Juan Tizol (whose hits for Duke Ellington "Caravan" and "Perdito" preceded Latin jazz); and Eddie Palmieri and Tito Puente, both born in New York of Puerto Rican descent.

Other important jazz musicians emerged from Canada (Oscar Peterson, Maynard Ferguson, Kenny Wheeler) and South Africa (Hugh Masekela, Abdullah Ibrahim). The American pianist Randy Weston immersed himself in African music in the 1960s, settling in Tangier between 1967 and 1972. All of which is to say that jazz interacting with other nations and cultures is not new. It has been going on for at least half of its first century. But lately musicians have been coming to it from other places: Mexico (Antonio Sánchez), Chile (Melissa Aldana, Camila Meza), Argentina (Guillermo Klein), Venezuela (Luis Perdomo), Trinidad (Etienne Charles), Benin (Lionel Loueke), Israel (a wave launched in the 1990s by bassists Avishai Cohen and Omer Avital and now including Anat Cohen and her brothers Avishai and Yuval, Gilad Hekselman, Anat Fort, Eli Degibri, and others), Lebanon (Ibrahim Maalouf, whose family fled to and settled outside Paris during the Lebanese Civil War), Indonesia (Joey Alexander), Australia (Linda May Han Oh, Matt Baker), New Zealand (Matt Penman), Armenia (Tigran Hamasyan, Vardan Ovsepian), Azerbaijan (Shahin Novrasli), Pakistan (Rez Abbasi, whose family moved to California when he was four). In early 2018, there was much talk about a new wave of British jazz musicians, most prominent among them the saxophonist Shabaka Hutchings, who was raised primarily in Barbados, but also including the Bahrain-born trumpeter Yazz Ahmed.

Many of these newcomers inject jazz with music from their native countries. Some Americans tap into their parents' origins and do likewise. Rudresh Mahanthappa and Vijay Iyer have both explored Indian music and culture in some of their projects, as Amir ElSaffar has done with his Iraqi roots. Jen Shyu cast an especially wide net on her remarkable 2015 album *Songs & Cries of the World*, which included folkloric music from her parents' home countries, Taiwan and East Timor, as well as China, South Korea, and Indonesia. Her album wasn't what most people would call jazz, but the four musicians backing her on it are all leading lights on the current jazz scene.

Jazz has been crossing other boundaries as well. Jason Moran scored the music for the feature film *Selma* (2014), and Vijay Iyer collaborated with filmmaker Prashant Bhargava on the multimedia project *Radhe Radhe: Rites of Holi* (2014), but there have been many films involving jazz or jazz musicians through the years. Dance, too, has a history of overlapping with jazz that some artists in this book have added to: Mahanthappa's collaboration with Ragamala Dance Company on *Song of the Jasmine*, Moran employing dancers in his Fats Waller tribute performances, the Bad Plus performing in the orchestra pit at the Brooklyn Academy of Music while the Mark Morris Dance Company danced the trio's arrangement of *The Rite of Spring*. Spalding told me in May 2018 that she was planning a major theater-in-the-round project involving music and movement.

More novel are these artists' interactions with other art forms and influences. I saw Moran and Iyer perform within a few weeks of each other during their residencies at a pair of New York museums. Moran was recording a live solo piano album (with Henry Threadgill and Ethan Iverson in the audience) at the Park Avenue Armory. Iyer and Wadada Leo Smith were playing music from their duo album *A Cosmic Rhythm with Each Stroke* (2016), the last of the dozens of performances Iyer played in and/or curated during his residency at the Met Breuer.

The Iyer/Smith album began with the museum commissioning Iyer to write music honoring the late Indian visual artist Nasreen Mohamedi, whose work the museum was also exhibiting during Iyer's run there. But I've also seen Moran accompanying the artist Joan Jonas live at Boston's Museum of Fine Arts as she performed her multimedia piece *Reanimation*, a work based on the novel *Under the Glacier* (2005) by the Nobel Prize–winning Icelandic author Halldór Laxness. And literature has played roles in other of these artists' work. Miguel Zenón took a pause from exploring his Puerto Rican roots to honor the 1963 Julio Cortázar classic *Rayuela* (published three years later in English as *Hopscotch*) on the album of that name that he co-led with French pianist Laurent Coq. Iyer wrote and performed music inspired by his friend Teju Cole's novel *Open City* (Cole later made a separate spoken word contribution to Iyer's Met Breuer residency), and has also collaborated with the poets Amiri Baraka and Mike Ladd. And in 2018, Iyer and a small combo of improvising musicians began backing Cole as he read from *Blind Spot* (2017), Cole's innovative new book pairing his photographs with short essays. That same spring, Moran opened *The Last Jazz Fest*, a new art installation at Minneapolis's Walker Art Center that included his own visual works. And in March 2019, Moran and his wife, the vocalist and composer Alicia Hall Moran, were to perform their collaboration *Two Wings: The Music of Black Migration* at Carnegie Hall.

Less surprisingly, perhaps, the people featured in this book have incorporated other types of American music in their own work: soul, R&B, hip-hop, rock, pop, folk, bluegrass. Robert Glasper has even won a pair of R&B Grammys, and Esperanza Spalding was named best new artist at the 2011 Grammy Awards for an album that leaned more toward classical chamber music than jazz. The Bad Plus built its reputation on avant-garde jazz covers of improbable pop tunes, an approach the trio returned to on its 2016 release, *It's Hard.* But you can skim down the list of artists here and find Moran covering Björk and Afrika Bambaataa, Iyer covering Michael Jackson and John Lennon, Zenón with the SFJAZZ Collective covering Jackson and Stevie Wonder, Cohen covering Flying Lotus, Lionel Loueke covering the Bee Gees, and Pedrito Martinez covering the Jackson 5.

In his 2016 book *How to Listen to Jazz*, Ted Gioia is effusive about both this openness to other genres and to music from abroad:

> "And here's the beautiful part of the story: jazz musicians still beg, borrow, and steal, only now they do it on a global basis. Today we hear exciting jazz in the current moment that joins in intimate embrace with tango or salsa or the Carnatic music traditions of southern India. Or movie music, cartoon songs, the aleatory techniques of John Cage, hip-hop, electronica, country and western, folk ballads, and almost any other aural tradition you can name or conceive. All the original elements still flourish in the music—listeners still delight in the bent blues notes, those syncopated raggy phrases, the honking saxes and muted brass instruments, and that big bass drum that started out as a military tool but has evolved into the primal pulse of revelry and dance. Even in an age in which most music has gone virtual, abandoning the world at hand and descending into the realm of bits and bytes, jazz still rejoices in hand-made (and mouth-made) sound. When you think about it, we really aren't all that far from the music's roots back in New Orleans. We've just added more ingredients to the gumbo."

Such developments are now generally less controversial than they tended to be in times past. As Gioia notes in his next chapter, "The last two decades of jazz have seen a spirit of diversity and pluralism on the rise, a tolerance of different approaches unprecedented in the music's history."

Indeed, the musicians blurring all these boundaries rarely catch the grief their predecessors endured for similar explorations in the 1960s, '70s, and '80s—whether jazz-rock fusionists denounced as sellouts or avant-garde experimentalists decried for abandoning swing and otherwise straying from mainstream jazz. Wynton Marsalis emerged as a star in the early 1980s and soon became the loudest critic of such heresies, publicly quarreling with Miles Davis and Lester Bowie.

Marsalis's jazz neoconservatism arose alongside the political conservatism of the Reagan years, in reaction to a particularly challenging period for jazz. Reagan was just taking office when I encountered Marsalis for the first time, with Art Blakey and the Jazz Messengers at Chicago's Jazz Showcase in January 1981. At one point that night Blakey congratulated the audience for being hipper than most people just for being there watching live jazz. My recollection is that he then urged us to also "brush the dust off" the jazz albums at record stores and to purchase some of them in support of "this great American art form" and musicians like the then-nineteen-year-old trumpeter he was about to feature on a ballad.[8]

By the end of that decade, Marsalis had won Grammy Awards for both jazz and classical music, launched his own quintet, released acclaimed albums such as *Black Codes (From the Underground)* (1985) and *J Mood* (1986), and co-founded a jazz program at Lincoln Center in New York City that led to the creation of Jazz at Lincoln Center in 1996 and the opening of its Frederick P. Rose Hall in 2004. His example made jazz cool again, inspiring young people to master playing it and major record labels to sign so-called young lions—Wynton's brother Branford, Terence Blanchard, Donald Harrison, Wallace Roney, Roy Hargrove, James Carter, Nicholas Payton, Joshua Redman, Christian McBride, and others—to recording contracts. That flurry of "neo-bop" popularity eventually faded, but Marsalis's relentless touring and proselytizing for jazz never wavered. It helped earn jazz acceptance at elite institutions where it had long been rejected, from Lincoln Center and other classical venues to university music programs to Marsalis's own *Blood on the Fields* in 1997 becoming the first jazz composition to win the Pulitzer Prize for Music.

All of that builds a case for Marsalis being the most influential jazz musician of the post-Coltrane era, at least insofar as gaining jazz attention and respect from the wider culture. But Marsalis's influence since landing at Lincoln Center has largely involved honoring jazz history via devotion to classic jazz repertory. Others emphasize having their music reflect their own lives and time, more like the giants whose work Marsalis venerates had done. Marsalis's contemporary Steve Coleman and others associated with Coleman's M-Base Collective—Greg Osby, Geri Allen, and Cassandra Wilson among them—chose this approach, as have all of the artists in this book. Coleman in 2014 was awarded a MacArthur Foundation "genius grant," as Iyer, Zenón, and Jason Moran had all done before him. He has never been remotely as well known as Marsalis, but his influence on the new music being made today is arguably more profound. Iyer has called Coleman the most influential musician since Coltrane, and Zenón has said much the same thing.

That influence comes from Coleman's example of studying the masters who proceeded him and then using what he learned to create new art of his own. "I tried to *be* Charlie Parker, with the exception of the drugs," Coleman told Howard Mandel for Mandel's 1999 book *Future Jazz*. "He's still one of my biggest influences, musically speaking. I don't try to copy him, but I try to model a lot after him, because I feel cats of that period had the perfect balance between feeling, intellect, and trying to find themselves."

And why wouldn't musicians seek to find themselves and orient their music to the time in which they were making it? George E. Lewis, in *A Power Stronger Than Itself: The AACM and American Experimental Music*, his magisterial 2009 history of the AACM (another group of musicians that, like Coleman's M-Base cohort, bucked the neoclassical trend of the 1980s), dryly noted that "the transcribed orature of musicians endorsing the importance of exploration, discovery, and experiment is quite vast and easy to access; it spans virtually every era of jazz music, and includes nearly every improviser of canonical stature before the rise of Wynton Marsalis in the mid-1980s."

Coleman and Lewis were and remain crucial mentors to both Jason Moran and Vijay Iyer. Fred Hersch played a similar role for others. Ethan Iverson of the Bad Plus and Brad Mehldau both studied piano with him. (Mehldau, like McBride, isn't featured in this book because he attained prominence in the early 1990s, but he was an important influence to the musicians who followed him, pianists and non-pianists alike.) Julian Lage studied composition with Hersch, went on to record an album with him, and was the first of the several artists featured in this book I saw perform with him as a duo. As of this writing, the other four are Jason Moran, Anat Cohen, Miguel Zenón, and Esperanza Spalding.

The journalist, author, and Columbia University journalism professor David Hajdu made the case for Hersch's major contribution to jazz's twenty-first-century surge in creativity in his 2010 profile of Hersch for the *New York Times Sunday Magazine*: "A new movement in jazz has surfaced over the past few years—a wave of highly expressive music more concerned with emotion than with craft or virtuosity; a genre-blind music that casually mingles strains of pop, classical and folk musics from many cultures; an informal, elastic music unyielding to rigid conceptions of what jazz is supposed to be. It's fair to call it 'post-Marsalis,' in that it leaves behind the defensive, canon-oriented musical conservatism of '90s jazz (as both Branford and Wynton Marsalis themselves have done in their best work of the past decade). Among this music's most celebrated and duly admired practitioners are the pianists Brad Mehldau, Ethan Iverson (of the trio the Bad Plus), Jason Moran and Vijay Iyer. And singular among the trailblazers of their art, a largely unsung innovator of this borderless, individualistic jazz—a jazz for the 21st century—is the pianist and composer Fred Hersch."[9]

Others helped swing the pendulum away from neoclassicism. Henry Threadgill (whose *In for a Penny, In for a Pound* won the 2016 Pulitzer Prize for Music), Wadada Leo Smith, Muhal Richard Abrams, and other AACM elders have direct ties to Moran and Iyer. John Zorn, Don Byron, Dave Douglas, and Bill Frisell are among those besides Hersch who fueled jazz's renewed embrace of eclecticism. Cassandra Wilson helped with that too, her expanding the parameters for what constitutes jazz singing paving the way for vocalists such as Kate McGarry, Norah Jones, Gretchen Parlato, and Esperanza Spalding. Danilo Pérez, David Sánchez, Michele Rosewoman, and Arturo O'Farrill reshaped jazz's connection to Latin American music, inspiring people like Zenón, David Virelles, and Pedrito Martinez. The boldly forward-looking young musicians coalescing around the club Smalls in the 1990s—Omer Avital, Avishai Cohen, Jason Lindner, Guillermo Klein, Brad Mehldau, Mark Turner, Kurt Rosenwinkel, and others—were the immediate predecessors of the people in this book and significantly affected their approach to music. Avital and Cohen also sparked the new century's influx of Israeli jazz musicians. Superstars Herbie Hancock and Wayne Shorter, meanwhile, continued leading by example, making new music without worrying about whether it fit someone else's definition of jazz.

By the 1990s, the young lions were venturing beyond straight-ahead jazz. More recently, even Wynton Marsalis, while continuing to do valuable work celebrating iconic jazz, has permitted occasional infusions of other styles of music into his work with the Jazz at Lincoln Center Orchestra. Most notably, he explored the music of Cuba, including his collaboration with Pedrito Martinez on *Ochas*, music for big band and Afro-Cuban percussion that premiered at the opening of Jazz at Lincoln Center's 2014–2015 concert season. Marsalis and the orchestra have also done high-profile blues-oriented projects with Eric Clapton and Willie Nelson.

The pianist Aaron Goldberg considers the idea of jazz passing in and out of a neoclassical period an oversimplification, in many ways more a marketing phenomenon than an accurate gauge of what musicians were actually doing at the time.

"Wynton's early albums do not recreate the past," he told me. "His most famous early album, *Black Codes (From the Underground)*, is radical and innovative and interesting. And it's greatly effective on all the music that followed it, and doesn't particularly sound like anything that came before it. You can hear some influences of Miles's quintet in the '60s, but in the way that you hear influences of, I don't know, Clifford Brown and Freddie Hubbard, not in the way that is distinct from the way of all the great innovators that came before were also influenced by their predecessors. But it was pretty original-sounding music. And then Wynton entered a more classicist period where he decided that he had goals that were above and beyond music goals. He had societal goals to promote the cause of these great African American geniuses, like [Duke] Ellington and Louis Armstrong and [Thelonious] Monk, who were not getting their due, especially, from his perspective, in the white, elite, cultural circles of America. . . .

"Most of his classicist period was motivated—I know this because I played with him for seven months, touring, so I have had many conversations with him about it—by this idea of making a contribution to American culture, and creating a canon where African American genius was appreciated. And he succeeded beyond I think even his wildest dreams, and Jazz at Lincoln Center became super successfully institutionalized, and solid to the point where now it doesn't have a classicist program at all. It's everything, all kinds of stuff. And I think that Wynton himself kind of grew up in the sense that he realized, 'OK, I succeeded in this, let's let the musical program kind of take ascendance.' Even his own band, the Jazz Lincoln Center Orchestra, doesn't play repertory music anymore. Occasionally they do, but they mostly play original charts written by guys in the band."

Christian McBride sees history repeating itself. "From all the information that I've read and gathered from musicians I've played with—people like Chick Corea, John McLaughlin, Billy Hart—it almost seems to be the '70s all over again," he told me. McBride traced a history that had straight-ahead jazz dominant in the early 1960s, with Miles Davis's second great quintet and John Coltrane's quartet propelling things toward the ascension of avant-garde jazz at the end of the decade. "By the late '60s there wasn't a whole lot of classic straight-ahead swingin' goin' on anymore," he observed, "and by the '70s that completely blew open with all of the young guys coming on the scene wanting to fuse psychedelic rock and jazz—not so much classic straight-ahead jazz, more the avant-garde kind of jazz that was going on."

Marsalis and the first wave of young lions, along with still-active legends such as Benny Golson and George Coleman, had put straight-ahead jazz back in charge by the time McBride's generation—"young lions 2.0," he calls them—came along at the start of the 1990s. But it didn't last. As McBride notes, "By the late '90s there wasn't much of that going on anymore," said McBride. "And then the decade after that, which is where we are now—just out of that decade—now you have not a lot of classic straight-ahead swingin' goin' on. And it seems to have almost the same sort of time span of morphing as the early '60s through the mid-'70s did. That fifteen-year period is not too different from the period between 1990 and 2005. Of course, between 2005 and 2016, that's been very interesting because the music industry itself is so completely different now. For that reason alone it's hard to compare it with any other era. Which is ultimately not a bad thing. It's good to be able to be in uncomfortable terrain."

The upheaval in the music industry—largely brought on by music streaming undoing the recording industry and the income musicians used to derive from it—affects the business and marketing side of today's artists' careers. The rise of academic jazz programs and the decline of venues booking jazz means too many musicians for the available work, adding to the challenge of making a career of playing jazz. And so these musicians find ways to cope. Some put out their own recordings on their own private labels, and Cohen even has a small stable of artists on Anzic Records, the label she co-runs with Oded Lev-Ari.

The number of artists featured in this book with prestigious teaching appointments grew from three to five in 2016 when Ethan Iverson and Rudresh Mahanthappa were hired by New England Conservatory (NEC) and Princeton, respectively. Iyer runs the Banff International Workshop in Jazz and Creative Music in addition to his tenured professorship at Harvard. Moran succeeded Dr. Billy Taylor as artistic director for jazz at the Kennedy Center in Washington, DC, in addition to teaching at NEC, and in 2017 added distinguished artist-in-residence at Georgetown University to his portfolio. Zenón has taught at NEC since 2009. Esperanza Spalding taught briefly at the Berklee College of Music after her graduation from there, and in 2017 she joined Iyer on the music department faculty at Harvard with a half-time appointment as Professor of Practice. Robert Glasper co-taught a course with writer Ashley Kahn at New York University's Clive Davis Institute of Recording Music in fall 2016. Glasper has generally kept too busy performing and recording music to teach: collaborating with hip-hop and R&B big names and overseeing splashy projects like the music for the movie *Miles Ahead* (2016) and *Everything's Beautiful* (2016), the album he made using archival Miles Davis recordings.

Which raises a point I hadn't anticipated: Given the changes now taking place in the music, does it make sense to call the music these artists make "jazz"?

"A lot of times I prefer not even to say 'jazz,' because technically I do more than that," Glasper told Nate Chinen of the *New York Times* for a story pegged to the release of *Everything's Beautiful*.[10] A few years earlier, when I'd interviewed him for *JazzTimes* as his first R&B album, *Black Radio*, was about to come out, Glasper happily accepted the label but made clear that he identified with other types of music as well: "Yeah, I'm a jazz pianist. But I also like other things, like everyone else. I like chicken *and* I like beef. It's not that big of a deal."

Whether it's a big deal depends on whom you talk to. When I approached George Lewis, the trombonist, composer, Columbia professor, and author of the aforementioned history of the AACM, following a lecture he gave at Harvard, and asked if he would be willing to talk to me for this book, he agreed to do so, but he urged me to abandon the label *jazz* for the music being covered. Nicholas Payton is the most outspoken critic of the word these days, forcefully dispensing with the term in "On Why Jazz Isn't Cool Anymore"[11] and other blog posts and referring to his work as *Black American Music*. Ahmad Jamal once told me he dislikes the word *jazz* for the lewd associations to its origins in New Orleans brothels, preferring "American classical music." Steve Coleman, Henry Threadgill, and Gary Bartz are among many others of note who object to having their work called jazz.

Vijay Iyer reminded me that these sorts of objections have been around as long as the music itself. The greats have always balked at having their work hemmed in by what they view as an artificial designation. "I think we have to at least accept that as long as there's been this word floating around, there's also been intense critical examination of it from African Americans," he said, citing Duke Ellington, Charlie Parker, Miles Davis, John Coltrane, and Abbey Lincoln as historic figures who rejected the word. "That's basically the spirit in which most of my colleagues and I work."

Esperanza Spalding, when I caught her backstage at a Berklee event honoring retiring professor Hal Crook and reminded her that I wanted to talk to her for this book, wrinkled her nose in not entirely feigned disgust as she spat out the word *jazz*. But she was getting ready to tour her *Emily's D+Evolution* project at the time. The summer before I'd seen her playing bass in Tompkins Square Park, backing Joe Lovano at the annual Charlie Parker Festival, and she was the unnamed special guest performing with Noah Preminger at New York's Jazz Standard a few weeks after the Berklee event—so she hasn't rejected the music itself.

Christian Scott calls his music "stretch music" to account for the wide range of styles it incorporates, but doesn't hesitate to single out jazz by name as its primary component. Rudresh Mahanthappa is leery of the word because of its imprecision, given the numerous styles of jazz that have come and gone through the years and the negative associations that it can conjure for potential listeners. Rather than risk being tied to a type of jazz he wants nothing to do with when someone asks what sort of music he plays, Mahanthappa says he'd prefer responding, "Do you have ten minutes for me to explain it to you?"

Other musicians featured in these pages, however, have no qualms with having their work called jazz. They understand the misgivings others have, but those are outweighed by jazz's positive associations. The greatest jazz musicians are among the greatest musicians of the past century, period. They're heroic figures, capable of creating great, lasting art in the moment as well as composing it on paper.

Anat Cohen told me she likens authentic jazz musicians to knights. "To be a jazz musician, to me, is a certain way of living, it's a certain way of being open to music, it's a way of being ready for anything to be thrown at you at any given moment—to be interactive, to be respectful and listen, to know how to listen and converse with any person," she said. "Jazz musicians have that ability because we're trained to open our ears and our hearts. It's a highly respected term. And not everybody that plays jazz is a jazz musician. Some people like it more planned, and they only play what's safe. That's not, for me, what jazz musicians are."

Elder masters Herbie Hancock and Wayne Shorter both agree.

"What I'm thinking about is the purpose of jazz, the purpose of music, the purpose of improvisation," Hancock told me in an interview for *Esquire*. "It really is a vehicle for bringing people together. It's not just about playing notes. It's encouragement. It's hope. It's courage itself. Because we're improvising, we're in the moment, we don't know what we're going to play next. At its best, we are really fearlessly stretching out and trying things—and getting outside of the comfort zone."[12]

Shorter's definition of jazz is among the best. It's certainly the pithiest. "Jazz shouldn't have any mandates," he told NPR's *All Things Considered* in 2013. "Jazz is not supposed to be something that's required to *sound like jazz*. For me, the word 'jazz' means 'I dare you.' "[13]

The musicians collected in this book have all accepted Shorter's dare, and it's in that spirit that I'm going to go ahead and call what they play jazz. Their stories reveal the music to be in a period of creative ferment. There isn't much attention paid to it in the mainstream press beyond the *New York Times*, but there are signs that could change. The *New Yorker* has covered several of these artists at various lengths, including full-fledged profiles of Moran, Iyer, and Spalding. *Vanity Fair*, of all places, ran a photo feature in its December 2015 issue that included many of jazz's brightest young stars, Esperanza Spalding, Julian Lage, and Christian Scott among them. It noted that only artists born in 1981 (the year Wynton Marsalis released his eponymous debut album) and after were included, and name-checked Glasper, Zenón, Moran, and Cohen among those who would have been present otherwise. (That same age requirement also disqualified everyone else getting a chapter here.)

Whether that means these artists will someday be ranked alongside the legends in Joe Goldberg's book, of course, remains to be determined.

"We don't know how it's going to go either," Moran told me during that 2012 interview that began this project. "I'd say right now I'm entering my late thirties, Glasper's in his early thirties, Esperanza's in her mid-to-late twenties. So in fifteen years we'll really get to see what happened."

Please visit the open access version of Make It New *to see a video resource for Chapter One:* https://doi.org/10.3998/mpub.11469938.comp.1

CHAPTER ONE

JASON MORAN

I saw a lot of great music researching this book in 2016. Jason Moran recording a solo piano album at New York's Park Avenue Armory. Vijay Iyer and Wadada Leo Smith performing music from their duo album of that year, *A Cosmic Rhythm with Each Stroke,* at New York's Met Breuer Museum and again at Harvard. Anat Cohen unveiling her new Tentet at the Jazz Standard, where George Wein was also in the audience, and at Wein's Newport Jazz Festival. The Bad Plus and friends doing their version of Ornette Coleman's *Science Fiction* at Newport. An evening of the Bad Plus at the Blue Note followed by Julian Lage and Gyan Riley performing John Zorn bagatelles at the Village Vanguard. Moran and Robert Glasper as a piano duo, playing and telling funny stories at the Blue Note. Esperanza Spalding and company performing her *Emily's D+Evolution* at Boston's Shubert Theatre. Rudresh Mahanthappa leading a quartet through his *Bird Calls* tribute to Charlie Parker at Boston's Institute of Contemporary Art. Lage, Scott Colley, and Clarence Penn joining Miguel Zenón in Puerto Rico for a "Caravana Cultural" presentation of the music of Sonny Rollins.

I saw all that and more, and ranking them is something I'd generally avoid. But if forced to choose, my favorite jazz performance of that year was an afternoon trio set at the Charlie Parker Jazz Festival in New York's Tompkins Square Park. Jason Moran played acoustic grand piano and Fender Rhodes electric alongside two bona fide jazz masters, bassist Dave Holland (whose induction as a National Endowment for the Arts Jazz Master came the following April) and drummer Jack DeJohnette (who received the same honor in 2012). In keeping pace with these two great innovators, Moran erased any doubt that he is an artist worthy of their company—one, like others of his generation, as intent on expanding and updating jazz as Holland, DeJohnette, and their peers had been in the 1970s.

The park was already crowded when the trio came onstage on this pleasantly sunny August day. Three earlier groups had already performed, most notably the Donny McCaslin Quartet, whose profile had been boosted by backing David Bowie on his final album, released earlier that year. They came out dressed casually, Moran wearing a billed cap, gray shorts, and white sneakers, and started off abstractly, edging their way into Holland's "Four Winds," from his essential free-jazz album of 1973, *Conference of the Birds*.

Freedom rang throughout the set. If Moran was at all intimidated in such company, it didn't show. If anything, he appeared comfortably in charge. He smiled in admiration at what DeJohnette was doing on cymbals as they accompanied Holland's solo on the opener, and Holland in turn grinned at Moran and at what he was contributing harmonically.

Moran had played with each of them before: with DeJohnette on the Don Byron album *Ivey-Divey* (2004) and on the Rudresh Mahanthappa/Bunky Green collaboration *Apex* (2010); with Holland touring in the short-lived Overtone Quartet and, earlier, subbing for vibraphonist Steve Nelson on a Holland quintet tour. Holland and DeJohnette had worked together, too, most famously on the landmark Miles Davis fusion album *Bitches Brew*, whose 1970 release date preceded Moran's birth by five years. This was the first time the three of them had played together as a trio, though, and Moran clearly relished the opportunity.

"This is a dream come true to play with Jack DeJohnette and Dave Holland," he declared when they paused after the first tune for him to address the audience. "Let me just say that first off. We want to play a piece of music for Bobby Hutcherson, one of the greatest musicians ever in the world. We're gonna play a piece of his called 'Montara.' "

Hutcherson had died two weeks earlier, and the audience-friendly funk groove of his mid-1970s classic, accentuated by Moran's Rhodes, had an elegiac tinge to it as well as free-leaning improvisation from the trio. Then the freedom was ratcheted up fully for the set's highlight: a stretched-out medley of Juan Tizol's "Caravan," Duke Ellington's "Fleurette Africaine," and McCoy Tyner's "Inner Glimpse." Moran conjured both Tyner and Cecil Taylor as the trio roared through the latter, which culminated in a ferocious drum solo that left DeJohnette looking wrung out as they took their bows.

"Caravan" and "Fleurette Africaine" had an obvious link to a previous intergenerational trio, when Ellington had been teamed with Charles Mingus and Max Roach on the 1963 classic *Money Jungle*. But what Moran and company did with "Caravan" in particular and throughout their set put me more in mind of a double album recorded live in Paris in February 1971 by Circle, a quartet Holland and Chick Corea had assembled upon leaving Miles Davis's fusion band to explore the avant-garde. Joining them were Barry Altschul and Anthony Braxton, the latter having recently begun releasing influential albums of his own (both men would also join Holland on *Conference of the Birds*). I still own the copy of *Paris-Concert* I bought while in high school, and retain fond memories of first encountering how Circle took Wayne Shorter's "Nefertiti" uptempo and launched it into the stratosphere. What I saw in Tompkins Square Park that afternoon had a touch of déjà vu to it. These were artists whose devotion to jazz history compelled them to honor it by taking even classic works to radically new places.

I spotted two other such artists chatting together backstage as the set ended. One was Vijay Iyer, Moran's friendly rival in piling up various accolades from the jazz world and beyond, and, like Moran, someone whose work is inspired by visionary musicians with links to the M-Base Collective and the Association for the Advancement of Creative Musicians (AACM). I had seen Iyer perform those memorable sets with AACM icon Wadada Leo Smith twice that spring. Chatting with Iyer was Henry Threadgill, an early AACM member who had won the Pulitzer Prize for Music that April. Moran has called Threadgill his favorite composer, and performed with him on Threadgill's album *Old Locks and Irregular Verbs*, released the same month as Threadgill's Pulitzer honor.

Other acclaimed musicians of the Moran-Iyer generation and younger have similar ties to M-Base and/or the AACM. One of them, Matana Roberts, is related to Moran (I saw him back her one night during her January 2016 residency at The Stone). An album of hers, *The Chicago Project* (2008), was produced by Iyer. Others are AACM members (Nicole Mitchell, Tomeka Reid) or have earned academic degrees studying under AACM legends Braxton (Mary Halvorson, Tyshawn Sorey, Steve Lehman) and/or George Lewis (Sorey, Lehman, Courtney Bryan). But none of them has yet captured as much attention from the jazz press as Moran and Iyer have.

Moran that afternoon was in the midst of an especially productive period. A few weeks earlier I'd seen him perform at the Newport Jazz Festival as part of the Charles Lloyd New Quartet. In March had come his adventurous live solo piano recording at Park Avenue Armory (I'd spotted Threadgill in the audience there, too, seated near pianist Ethan Iverson of the Bad Plus), which he put out three months later as his first self-released recording since leaving Blue Note Records. Four days before *The Armory Concert* dropped, he joined fellow Houston native

Robert Glasper for a lively duo piano set at New York's Blue Note Jazz Club. His annual Thanksgiving run at the Village Vanguard a few months later with his longtime Bandwagon trio mates Tarus Mateen and Nasheet Waits also led to a live album, *Thanksgiving at the Vanguard*, released in April 2017. An October 2016 studio session with guitarist Halvorson and cornetist Ron Miles yielded *BANGS*, a collection of forward-looking chamber music, spacious and lyrical, to which all three musicians contributed compositions and which Moran put out via Bandcamp in May 2017.

Moran's duties as artistic director for jazz at the Kennedy Center in Washington, DC, led to a new project of his own, "Muldrow Meets Mingus," for which he recruited the visionary singer/rapper/producer Georgia Anne Muldrow to help him reimagine "Fables of Faubus," "Goodbye Porkpie Hat," and other Charles Mingus classics, which they premiered in January 2017.

Moran had told me about that Mingus project over dinner one night in Boston shortly after the Armory concert. His wife, the vocalist Alicia Hall Moran, had been at the Armory concert, too, where she suggested that the best way to get him to find time for an interview would be to share a meal with him. "He likes to eat," she noted, smiling. So he and I did so on his next trip to teach at New England Conservatory. The Mingus project came up when we found ourselves discussing the pros and cons of social media.

A mention of a recent *GQ* piece about Kamasi Washington, whose three-CD debut album, *The Epic*, had captured the music world's attention the year before, prompted me to bring up a rival saxophonist who had recently disparaged Washington's musicianship.

"Oh, tons of musicians do," Moran responded. "It's amazing. Like, c'mon. I know people you should be mad at. Believe me, this ain't the cat."

I asked if he'd gotten wind of a Facebook kerfuffle a few years earlier in which guitarist Kurt Rosenwinkel was dismissive of the high praise accorded Vijay Iyer, who had recently been awarded a MacArthur Foundation genius grant.

"Oh my God, that was a big one," replied Moran, who had received his own MacArthur in 2010. "Vijay and I went to breakfast not long after that. When I'm in New York, I would take people to breakfast at Sylvia's up in Harlem. I did like twenty, twenty-five of 'em, just friends over for breakfast. Just to hang out, just to talk. I figure I drop my kids off for school, I'm up—so who wants to have breakfast at 9, 9:30? Vijay and I talked about that for a while, because it was a fucked-up thing to have to go through."

Dustups between musicians are nothing new, Moran pointed out. "It's always been a thing between certain kinds of musicians—like Lester Bowie and Wynton [Marsalis], or Dizzy [Gillespie] and Louis Armstrong," he said. "The Internet makes it worse because those things become public. It's unfortunate when people have to deal with that shit. And everybody has to, to a degree. If you're online, somebody's going to come for you."

"Facebook can really alter reality for people," he said, pondering whether there were countervailing upsides to social media for musicians, beyond the obvious one of being able to publicize their performances and record releases for free. "I've watched it help the jazz scene because it keeps people up to date. Even pockets of scenes. I know a couple of cats on the West Coast. I would never call them to see what they're up to, but now I kind of know, passively. People in Chicago or Miami or Houston, people in DC, Philly, New York. I love that part of it. But it doesn't make it real. So if it I see a little ten-second clip of your gig where you play a drum solo, like, *it's a clip.*

"But at the other end of the spectrum," he continued, "I have totally been inspired by some things." He offered Muldrow as his example. "She's a genius. Ambrose [Akinmusire, trumpeter/composer whose acclaimed album *When the Heart Emerges Glistening* was co-produced by Moran] knows her, and Robert Glasper knows her. But she wrote this thing about Mingus on her Twitter page. I knew she comes from musicians, jazz musicians. She wrote this thing about Mingus, and I was like, 'What's up with that? Muldrow Meets Mingus.' Well, that's exactly what we're commissioning: we're commissioning her to write responses to Mingus's music."

"Did you ever see Mingus?" I asked, curious because I'd had the good luck to do so twice and not pausing to consider the unlikelihood of Moran having done so, given that Mingus's death occurred shortly before Moran's fourth birthday.

"No, I was too young," he answered. "My dad saw him. But I had Jaki Byard [as a professor], so that's the next best seat. I have a lot of affinity for those people. The neighborhood I grew up in in Houston is extremely political. Like, there was a church called Shrine of the Black Madonna that was kind of behind us. There were community centers that were very pro-black. The whole neighborhood kind of exuded this. 'Must have pride and know your heritage.' "

"That's weird for Texas, isn't it?" I asked.

"It sure is."

But it clearly helped shape Moran's worldview and art.

"I saw Bobby Seale[14] give a lecture in Houston when I was sixteen," he told me. "That's who was coming to our neighborhood. So learning music you were always learning it with that kind of stuff in mind. And it was also the same time that Public Enemy was out. So I had something that was kind of jazz being like some historical music dealing with that shit, and then Public Enemy with the contemporary focus dealing with the same thing."

Moran was taking on racial issues in his own career before "Muldrow Meets Mingus." The most widely known project in that regard to which he contributed has to be scoring the 2014 feature film *Selma* for director Ava DuVernay, with whom Moran also subsequently collaborated on her award-winning 2016 documentary *13th*, which draws a direct line from slavery and Jim Crow to the current state of the US prison system.

But composers of film scores often escape the notice of theatergoers. Moran's own most overt and wide-ranging project exploring race was his and his wife's five-day residency at the 2012 Whitney Biennial, titled *Bleed*, in part for its radical bleeding of music together with performance art, dance, conversation, journalism, and a variety of visual arts. I managed to catch the final day of performances.

By then I'd already had a taste of Moran's expansive view of how a jazz performance might differ from how they're typically staged in nightclubs. A few months earlier, I'd seen him and the Bandwagon in a double bill with Geri Allen at the 92nd Street Y in Tribeca. Their set contained freewheeling takes on some of their familiar fare—Duke Ellington's "Wig Wise," the standard "Body and Soul," and Moran's own "RFK in the Land of Apartheid," composed for a documentary with that title.

At one point the trio broke for a mid-set listening session, cuing up a recording of Gladys Knight singing "No One Could Love You More." The three of them sat back and chatted casually as the tune played, as if doing so were the most natural thing in the world. What they were driving at wasn't specified. A reference to Allen's Motown roots? A reminder of the comprehensiveness of Black American Music? But somehow the break made sense intuitively without its purpose being made explicit. The trio resumed playing to finish out the set, and Moran then brought out a couple of big boxes of gourmet cupcakes as a treat for the audience.

I saw Alicia Hall Moran perform around that time, too, as a cast member during the Broadway production of *The Gershwins' Porgy and Bess*. (She also occasionally appeared as Bess, in her role as understudy to Audra McDonald.) But my introduction to her work had been a performance of her Motown Project the year before at the Regattabar jazz club in Cambridge, Massachusetts, where she demonstrated that she is as much an outside-the-box thinker as her husband. Jason accompanied her on piano with Mateen on bass, joined by classical guitarist Thomas Flippin and taiko drummer Kaoru Watanabe, as she and baritone Steven Herring sang operatic arrangements of Motown hits, including "Signed, Sealed, Delivered I'm Yours," "(Love Is Like a) Heat Wave," and "Papa Was a Rollin' Stone."

The Motown Project was presented during *Bleed*, as was an astonishing array of artistic collaborations, nearly all of which involved one or both of the Morans. These even included Alicia undergoing acupuncture to musical accompaniment, and both Jason and Alicia exploring Alexander Technique—a method of using mindful movement to reduce physical tension, also practiced by Julian Lage and other musicians—with a pair of instructors. "Alicia did it," Moran told me during our dinner in Boston, "and then she helped me get in touch with it just for posture at the piano."

On Sunday, two live presentations involving the Bandwagon (with Jamire Williams subbing for Nasheet Waits on drums) stood out. The first, "Live:Time," was an hourlong work inspired by the famous quilts of Gee's Bend, Alabama, with Alicia joining the band on vocals and Bill Frisell on guitar. The piece's mood changed remarkably as it shifted from one portion to the next, from a taste of Moran's trademark Gangsterism series to guitar groove to spiritual to a climax of the Bandwagon at full throttle—all interspersed with readings, including Frisell reading from a letter he had sent Moran on how to locate the isolated hamlet where the quilts were born. Later that afternoon came "Rain," originally commissioned by Jazz at Lincoln Center. During this performance, trumpeter Ralph Alessi slowly circled the room as he played, signifying the ring shouts brought to America by African slaves. The music built in intensity and freedom as it progressed, with Abdou M'Boup on kora and Marvin Sewell on blues-infused guitar.

There were also video installations to check out between the live events. The three most memorable had racial themes. *Threshold*, by art critic Maurice Berger, was inspired by conversations with the Morans about what they planned for *Bleed*. It showed African American characters crossing thresholds in popular films and television shows, metaphors for a people's transcendence of barriers meant to hold them down. Glenn Ligon's *The Death of Tom* showed blurry images from a scene he had recreated from an early film adaption of the novel *Uncle Tom's Cabin*, Moran's recorded piano accompanying the flickering imagery with a score Moran based on the Bert Williams song "Nobody." Most haunting of all was Kara Walker's use of wire and cut-paper figures to create a slow-moving, shadowy enactment of newly freed slaves being raped and murdered by an angry white mob, set to original music by the Morans.

The first interview specifically for this book took place the next day at the Moran's home in Harlem. My wife and I had a train to catch right afterward, so she accompanied me to the interview and hung out with the family's four-year-old twins near the grand piano while Jason and I talked at the opposite end of the spacious room.

It wasn't long before the conversation touched on race. "I can't imagine the built-up pressure of centuries that then allows [African American] musicians to get instruments, and how they quickly learn these instruments and decide this is the way to use them," Moran told me at one point, describing the early evolution of jazz.

"Like that we get to Charlie Parker from Scott Joplin in thirty or forty years. It kind of just goes really quickly." And then it keeps spawning other genres Moran adores and taps into in his own work. "I always hate when they say that jazz is America's greatest contribution," he continued. "What is blues? What is Motown? What is hip-hop? What is funk? What is jazz? How dare we think that jazz is more important than James Brown? This is nuts!"

Moran, like the others featured in this book, knows and respects jazz history but wants to move beyond merely preserving it. These musicians see the need for jazz to keep evolving to reflect the current times, as music did through the emergence of those other genres and as jazz's own most important figures had all done to earn their places in the canon.

"It always weighs on me when I hear stuff like that," Moran went on, "because I know jazz is great and its importance within the lineage is great. There's two approaches. Because it has to have a canon and people have to promote the canon. That's why there's still a metropolitan opera." He talked about how little new material gets staged at the Met. "They're doing occasional new pieces or new productions of old pieces, but that's me doing Fats Waller. I'm doing new production on old pieces. I'm actually changing the music, too. They're not changing the music so much. The conductor might have some new ideas about what to cut, but they're just adding different context."

That, generally speaking, has also been Jazz at Lincoln Center's approach to jazz. It isn't Moran's, but he values it. Years after the Whitney residency, during our dinner conversation, he told me that Wynton Marsalis had asked him to join his band shortly after he graduated from the Manhattan School of Music. Moran declined. "That doesn't seem like you," I said. "No," he agreed. "It was never going to happen. Ever. But when I got the Kennedy Center job the first person I called was him. I was like, 'We need to have breakfast.' I went in his neighborhood, and he sat me down and gave me a long talking to about what it is like in that world. It was so helpful."

"For me, music needs Jazz at Lincoln Center," he said. "It needs somebody that goes up there and says, 'This is that old stuff and we really spent a lot of time practicing it.' But on the other hand, you need people who are gonna say, 'I'm gonna dig in this dirt, and I'm looking for something, not even sure if there's anything down there. Just keep digging for stuff.' Its relationship to social strife, it's relevant.

"But the thing is, you can never assume what a person's private social strife is. And it's quite an assumption to think that nobody's thinking of anything because you don't hear it. What a person like Fred Hersch battles with, kind of on an epidemic level within his body, as a homosexual within the jazz community, which is totally misogynistic. What that even feels like. Or even race from his point of view.

Those discussions are had, typically, very privately. Fred and I, or Ethan Iverson and I, Mary Halvorson and I, talking about stuff. Putting stuff on the table. I talk very freely with them about race, because I trust that they understand how this functions. And they do, too. They are not naïve."

He then demonstrated how this can play out by describing some of the *Bleed* programming that I'd missed.

"The 'wake' Alicia curated Friday was these powerful women, one writer from the blog *Colorlines* read two pieces, one about Trayvon Martin and one about misogyny in hip-hop. Another writer read a piece about how hip-hop mistreated women in general and how it was affecting her daughter. After that Joan Jonas comes up and plays this very abstract piece with the Bandwagon—we do like thirty, forty minutes. After that Kara Walker comes and gives, as usual, a very bold performance, which has the image of Condoleezza Rice at a piano while she's reading transcripts from Abu Ghraib—you know, it's really rough. Then it turns into 'Brown Sugar,' Rolling Stones. And the people who saw that see that this is the conversation. These are the conversations I'm constantly having with people that inform the music to a degree.

"And after that Esperanza Spalding comes up and plays a solo bass set. It was like through all that toiling of the dirt . . ." He let the thought hang a moment. "Because that's Esperanza Spalding. You don't think Spalding's not having these conversations either? You think it's just some passé beautiful music full of technique? No, it's not. This is just how people manifest their work."

Moran's unwillingness to be hamstrung by jazz tradition was evident from my first contact with him, which came when I interviewed him for the *Boston Globe* in 2005 before a Boston performance touting his album *Same Mother*. Blue Note Records sent me a copy of the CD with a press release that I kept and filed away. It explained that the album's title came from Alicia watching Savion Glover and observing that dance movement in jazz, blues, and hip-hop all come "from the same mother," offering my first hint of the artistic collaboration the couple shares.

The press release also contained a quote from Moran that referenced his interest in art forms beyond music to explain his desire to absorb jazz history without permitting it to constrain his own art later: "I saw [Jean-Michel] Basquiat's work while in high school and I'd never seen anything so raw and comprehensible. There was something rare and strange about his color scheme, multiple perspectives, line and textures. Very functional too—if a piece was too big he put hinges on it so it would fit through the door. Yet he still wanted to prove that he could 'really draw.' I came up through jazz education, came to New York to study at Manhattan School of Music, but I think a lot of my schoolmates took the rules too seriously. Therefore their personality was put on a backburner. I knew that was not the correct route. People like Jaki Byard taught me that you could learn the tradition, adhere to the rules just so much, and the music will never imprison you."

What caught my eye most of all, though, was the press release noting that two cousins of Moran's father used to stop by their home in Houston when touring with blues great Albert King. One of them had taught young Jason piano licks. I'd had a friend Tony in Chicago who played keyboards in King's band and knew that his brother had played drums in it as well. It seemed unlikely that two sets of brothers would have toured with King, so the first thing I did when I spoke with Jason was to ask if the cousins in question were Tony and Michael Llorens. "Yes!" he replied, and suddenly we had a family connection. He put me back in touch with Tony, who had relocated to Los Angeles at some point after I left Chicago, and I wound up quoting him in my *Globe* article about what he thought of Moran's *Same Mother* cover of King's "I'll Play the Blues for You": "When he took his solo he played all these tremolos on it. He told me I taught him to play that. Ain't that something? You never know what a child picks up."[15]

Moran had then just turned thirty, a rising star with his sixth album as a leader after several years as a sideman to Greg Osby. His third, *Black Stars* (2001), on which he and his Bandwagon trio mates were joined by the septuagenarian master Sam Rivers on saxophone and flute (as well as introducing the track "Sound It Out" on piano, before Moran slides onto the bench beside him and takes over), had already been an important breakthrough for him four years earlier. Ben Ratliff tapped it as the final entry in his *The New York Times Essential Library* book *Jazz: A Critic's Guide to the 100 Most Important Recordings* (2002). Gary Giddins, reviewing both the album and a New York performance for the *Village Voice*, praised it effusively and noted that Moran's teacher Jaki Byard had played on Rivers's great album *Fuchsia Swing Song* (1964). "The more Moran looks backward the more certain he is in moving forward," Giddins concluded. "At 26, he is good news for jazz's future."[16]

Moran's career really began blossoming in the years to follow. In 2010, he received both his MacArthur Foundation genius grant and a teaching appointment at New England Conservatory, the latter requiring traveling to Boston several times a year from his home in Harlem to coach student ensembles and teach master classes. The next year he was hired to replace the late Dr. Billy Taylor in overseeing jazz at the Kennedy Center. His promotion to Taylor's old title, artistic director for jazz, followed in 2014.

His move beyond music into multimedia projects began in those years as well. A few months before seeing *Bleed* at the Whitney, I'd reviewed a performance of Moran's *In My Mind: Monk at Town Hall, 1959* at NEC's Jordan Hall. Commissioned several years earlier to celebrate the ninetieth anniversary of Thelonious Monk's birth year, Moran went well beyond performing music from that concert. He teamed with videographer David Dempewolf to create a project mixing music (played by "the Big Bandwagon"—his trio augmented by horns) with, among other things, a trove of historical photographs and conversations recorded during the original Town Hall rehearsals. Moran, in the accompanying program notes, explained that taking this multimedia approach "allows me to ruminate on African-American slavery, jazz history, the piano, my life and religion."

I was able to see two similarly expansive projects involving Moran when they came to Boston. His Fats Waller Dance Party, commissioned by Harlem Stage, was brought to the Berklee Performance Center in April 2014 by the Celebrity Series of Boston. Once again he went beyond simply making a night of performing Waller's hits. He and Meshell Ndegeocello radically updated much of the music, modernizing it, and Moran spent a significant portion of his time performing it wearing a huge papier-mâché Fats Waller mask. The cast included professional dancers, and the audience was encouraged to dance along. Seven months later, at Boston's Museum of Fine Arts, Moran accompanied Joan Jonas on piano as she performed *Reanimation*, an absorbing blend of visual and performance art inspired by Icelandic Nobel laureate Halldór Laxness's novel *Under the* Glacier.

Another museum project I wish I'd seen was *Staged* (2015), for which Moran brought reproductions of New York jazz venues (the Savory Ballroom and the Three Deuces) to Brooklyn's Luhring Augustine Museum, where the Bandwagon gave two days of performances, and charcoal-on-paper artwork by Moran was also on display. The Luhring Augustine connection also led to the debut of *LOOP* in 2016, Moran's magazine of pieces by and interviews with jazz musicians. A second issue was scheduled for summer 2017.

Moran's "Looks of a Lot," a commissioned piece that he and the Bandwagon debuted at Chicago's Symphony Center with saxophonist Ken Vandermark and the Kenwood Academy Jazz Band in 2014, with a stage set by Chicago artist Theaster Gates, is one I particularly wish I'd seen. It not only happened in my hometown, it also called attention to the city's history of racial segregation and how that iniquity continues manifesting itself in the surge of gun violence there.

I did view a documentary by Radiclani Clytus on the making of the piece when he brought it to Boston. (Clytus was also at work on a documentary on Moran.) One moment from the performance that stood out involved high school musicians walking slowly past a makeshift casket in what was meant to resemble a funeral procession. Moran's piece had been intended to address gun violence, a scourge that the band itself fell victim to less than two weeks before the concert, when fifteen-year-old band member Aaron Rushing was shot dead a few blocks from his school. A second performance was held at the Kennedy Center in 2017, and that summer Moran recorded the project with the students for release on his record label.

Moran's purely musical busyness only continued to ramp up after our first meeting. When I talked to him about *Same Mother*, he hadn't had much sideman work since leaving Osby and launching his own trio, with the notable exception of Don Byron's *Ivey-Divey* project the year before. We speculated that other musicians might have assumed he was unavailable because of his Bandwagon commitments. But that soon began changing, with Moran appearing in rapid succession on albums with violinist Jenny Scheinman (*Crossing the Field*, 2008), a remarkably fresh standards album with vocalist Cassandra Wilson (*Loverly*, 2008), and a Rudresh Mahanthappa/Bunky Green collaboration (*Apex*, 2010). He also began a long, fruitful association with Charles Lloyd, as a member of Lloyd's New Quartet with Ruben Rogers and Eric Harland and as a recording partner on their 2013 duo album, *Hagar's Song*.

Holland and Threadgill are two other jazz legends who liked what they saw in Moran and eventually worked with him, Holland in his short-lived and unrecorded Overtone Quartet and Threadgill in his two-piano Ensemble Double Up.

"I knew Jason on the scene when he was starting to record his trio, the only trio records I was interested in," Dave Holland told me when I had a chance to ask him about Moran several months after the Tompkins Square performance.

"Tracing the roots, eh?" Holland responded when I brought up Moran's family connection to a pair of onetime Albert King sidemen. "Well, Jason's got all of that in his music. That's what I think is an incredible strength of what he does: there's all the tradition of the music, and then there's the whole performance art aspect to what he does as well—the multimedia thing. He's a real visionary for me, in many, many ways, and an extraordinary musician, of course. And very articulate. We both give classes at the New England Conservatory from time to time, and occasionally we'll be up there the same week. We've done a class together, and it's just so much fun, sharing ideas back and forth and then doing a little playing. He's wonderful with the students, and really makes them think about some other ways of looking at the music and the reference points and so on."

Henry Threadgill met Moran long before hiring him for his Ensemble Double Up. He told me he thinks it was Gene Lake who first told him about Moran, who would have been an undergraduate at the time. "He said, 'There's this one guy who is really crazy about your music,' " Threadgill recalled. "This was a long time ago. A little bit after Very Very Circus, maybe. After I met him, we ran into each other much later. I went to hear Bandwagon—a concert at Rose Hall, at Lincoln Center—and I caught him at a couple other places. Things just started to develop from there."

Prominent among the attributes Threadgill admires about Moran is his willingness to take risks. "He's open-minded, open-ended, you know?" Threadgill explained. "Because I can't really work with musicians that are stuffy. Period. That's fine, but you can't go anywhere with me. 'Cause you're stuck. I'm going over here, and you're stuck right there. I'm saying, 'Look here, we're jumping off this bridge without parachutes.' You got a parachute, I can't go." He laughed. "Only people without parachutes can go with me."

Musicians younger than Moran are similarly impressed.

"Jason Moran is the father of a lot of this shit, man," Christian Scott told me. "People are not saying that. But that Bandwagon band. Not *that* they're experimenting, but *how* they're experimenting. That's the shit. But no, Jason Moran is the father of what's going on conceptually. Anyone that says anything different from that is a fuckin' liar."

Robert Glasper arrived at Houston's High School for the Performing and Visual Arts the year after Moran's graduation from there, and went on to success of his own in both the jazz world and beyond, winning Grammy Awards for his own R&B projects and collaborating with high-wattage hip-hop stars including Mos Def, Kendrick Lamar, and Common. Glasper told Ethan Iverson, in a 2017 interview for Iverson's *Do the Math* blog, that he heard a recording the high school put out on which Moran played Tyner's "Inner Glimpse" and Kenny Kirkland's "Dienda." Moran as a high schooler sounded just like Kirkland, according to Glasper.

"He knows the whole lineage of jazz piano," Glasper told Iverson. "There are a lot of guys that dwell in that fine arts or 'go get the grant' world who can't really play. They found a crack in the door and get in there but I don't have a whole lot of respect for them.... Jason dwells in that world too but the fact that he came up the way he came up proves he's not skating, he's doing exactly what he wants to do."

Glasper, like Christian Scott, is also a big fan of Moran's trio.

"Bandwagon has their own sound," he told me when I caught up with him a few months after Iverson's interview. "They don't sound like anybody else. They sound like them. That's what's so dope about it. What's dope about it, too, is Tarus is one of the best hip-hop bass players out, but most people don't know that. I met Tarus Mateen at a Roots jam session. The Roots used to do jam sessions in New York every week. And Tarus was playing bass with them a lot. So I met him at the jam session playing bass. It was incredible. Tarus was throwing some Q-Tip shit out there....

"Tarus is an amazing hip-hop bass player. All of them just know a lot of music. They studied it, they know it, and they can play it with respect to the genre, to what it is. And authentic, really authentic. That's how they all are. Nasheet and Tarus and Jason. They're the tightest band I've probably ever seen. As far as just, like, the trust they have and where they go. And how they come back, when they come back, if they come back. It's incredible to watch."

How Moran came to make music like that is a story in itself, with a life-defining moment in his early teens that determined the artist he would become. He grew up middle class, the middle son of Andrew Moran, who worked in investment banking, and an educator mother, Mary Lou Moran, who also spent several years running a bakery from home. He began Suzuki-method lessons in classical piano at age six, which he didn't always appreciate. His piece "Cradle Song" on the album *Artist in Residence* (2006) has the sound of pencil scratching in the background, meant to convey his mother taking notes as he practiced. When I interviewed him at his home he offered to show me the potpourri still stuck inside his childhood upright piano, which he'd flung there in irritation many years before.

The idea that piano playing could be fun came along later, implanted by the boogie-woogie and other hipper styles that Moran's father's cousin would demonstrate for him on visits. "Tony would sit at that piano and play stuff, and I would be shocked. Because it never sounded like that when I played. I wanted to play like that. He always was having fun when he played the piano, and I was not. Then as I got better and better, I would check in with him to see what he was thinking. And then, I guess the biggest compliment, he heard 'I Will Play the Blues for You' from my version on the radio in LA. And he says, 'Who's this? They doing this shit right.' And then he heard it was me."

Moran's musical tastes early on ran toward hip-hop, though there was a middle-school flirtation with hardcore bands like the Dead Kennedys and Suicidal Tendencies, until he became "a little too obsessed" with them and his parents put an end to it. "I was still able to listen to Run DMC," he recalled. "Run DMC wasn't talking about that garbage. '*Suicidal Tendencies*.' I mean, the title. *Jeez*. I definitely shouldn't have been listening to them, but my brother was skating a lot. He was already in high school, and he was the one bringing those records."

Moran took up skateboarding, too, and much later managed to create a project that had the Bandwagon providing musical accompaniment to a group of San Francisco skateboarders. Tennis, golf, and family trips to museums and concert halls were also regular experiences for him growing up.

His interest in jazz began in August 1989, when he witnessed his parents mourning the death of a friend, Texas Congressman Mickey Leland.[17] Leland, forty-four, a prominent black legislator known for his dedication to ending hunger, had just perished in a plane crash in Ethiopia, and they were grieving his loss by listening to Thelonious Monk playing "Round Midnight."

Moran has often told this story of his birth as a jazz musician. "They were watching the television, there was no sound," is a version he told me. "This is what I remember, so it might not be true. I remember walking in that room. Such passion—they're watching TV, no sound—they were listening to Thelonious Monk. So I went to look at the record. 'What is this?' Just listen to it over and over again. Made a tape. Tried to go downstairs and figure it out. All the time, from that point on, it was just Thelonious Monk."

That the superb Monk documentary *Thelonious Monk: Straight No Chaser* (1988), with jazz fan Clint Eastwood as its executive producer, was released about this time validated Monk's impact on the teenager. "Clint Eastwood is a huge star, and he's focusing on Monk," Moran explained. "You don't think about those films in that way, but they're actually influential to kids who might have just stumbled onto a path, and then they say, 'Oh, that's a good path to be on. It's not a traditional one, but it's a good one to be on.'"

Moran was fourteen at the time, about to enter high school. He spent a year at a public school and then transferred to HSPVA, graduating in 1993. Monk was, and remains, his lodestar, but Glasper is right about Moran having thoroughly immersed himself in the history of jazz piano. In his case, that meant the dominant figures studied by most aspiring jazz pianists as well as certain lesser known masters to whom Moran found himself especially drawn.

"I studied a whole lot of Bill Evans and a whole lot of Herbie Hancock, a whole lot of McCoy Tyner—like really was clones of them when I was in high school," Moran had told me the first time I talked to him. "And when I met McCoy Tyner in high school I thought, 'Man, I can go ahead and pass away, I've met the god.' And they are [gods]: What they've contributed to the history is amazing. And they are equal to my people like Andrew Hill and Herbie Nichols.

"But it all started with Thelonious Monk. That was the person I decided to base everyone else on. So it wasn't Art Tatum, or it wasn't Wynton Kelly or Red Garland or Oscar Peterson. It was Monk. When you're first learning something, that's what you're gonna consider is right. And so Monk to me was all that was right within music, within jazz and within composition, and everything else had to measure up to Monk for it to be viable. And so of course I studied a lot of those other piano players, know a lot of their solos. But also people like Herbie Nichols. It's also a lot of my peers were playing those styles so much . . ."

"It got boring?" I suggested.

"Well, you felt that you were always hearing that," Moran replied. "And I just knew that there was so much out there for me to focus on, trying to play like Herbie—Hancock—I could also focus on playing like Herbie Nichols and see what those two produce as something that I ingested, rather than just Herbie Hancock. And so everything that I'm playing is still like a mixture of all these really fine pianists. And I still see all the traces that I've taken from Bill Evans or from Herbie Nichols or from Cecil Taylor."

Two additional key developments occurred during Moran's HSPVA years. First, attending a high school dedicated to an array of performing and visual arts made collaborations among divergent art forms come naturally to him as an adult. He had already worked with other types of aspiring artists as a teenager, including having his best friend design the poster for his senior recital.

Second, Moran met an upperclassman named Eddy Hobizal, who was awarded third place at the 1989 Thelonious Monk Institute of Jazz International Piano Competition during Moran's freshman year. "He had this pantheon approach to piano in high school," said Moran of Hobizal. "I didn't know anything and he was about to graduate, so I was intimidated—like any jazz jock. I would ask him to give me stuff to listen to. He would be, like, 'Art Tatum.' "

Thus came Moran's introduction to stride piano, which proved especially useful when he chose the Manhattan School of Music for college specifically to study with Jaki Byard.

"By the time I was here studying with Jaki Byard, I knew that [Byard] was into that, so I really started listening," Moran said. "I thought it would do me some good to be kind of comfortable with it before I got up here to school. So I was sitting in front of him at my first lesson and he said, 'Oh.' I didn't play it well, but he knew I was going for it.

"Also Thelonious Monk: He's the perfect cat to listen to that deals with modernism and tradition at the same time. So he's dealing with the stride stuff, it's very spare, and he's dealing with all these angular lines and melodies. So he was the perfect one. You could pivot: tip it a little bit and then he'd be dealing with Ellington; tip it another way and then he's pushing John Coltrane to another level.

"But yeah, I knew being with Jaki Byard that I would have to get into it. And I might say that to a degree it was just to please Jaki, because who wants to be studying with a teacher who doesn't get what they're into."

There were lessons where Moran didn't feel like playing, and so he and Byard would talk, mostly about social issues like integration. They talked about Byard being with Kenny Clarke in the Army, fighting with Mingus, traveling through the South, being on the road and meeting Teddy Wilson, loving Earl Hines, teaching at New England Conservatory, then teaching at the Manhattan School, and the difference between schools. Those life lessons Moran considers at least as critical to his development as the technical ones. But Byard's impact on Moran's approach to the piano itself was extraordinary.

"I knew I was gonna learn a lot of history at the piano, and how to make that current," he told me. "When I was studying with him he was showing me all this—the

Erroll Garner thing or the Earl Hines thing or the Art Tatum thing—and how he modified it. So he would do a stride piano, but what he was doing with his right hand would sound like they were from two different planets.

"He was constantly challenging those bounds of what could be possible with traditional elements. And that gave me a great respect for tradition from him, and how important it was to study and how important it was to be really knowledgeable about it—and still feel like you're making your contribution today. Because I'll never be able to play as good as Earl Hines at all. And what pianists used to do back then is extremely more technically savvy than people are doing today. And so I just thought that a lot of the techniques that the pianists were using you could use today and it would sound like it was new, but it was really, really old."

Moran got his chance to put what he learned from Byard to use when he joined Greg Osby's quartet for a European tour during his senior year of college, having been recommended to Osby by his HSPVA and Manhattan School classmate Eric Harland, who was already the drummer in Osby's quartet. It was Moran's first important tour, but the Osby connection proved essential for other reasons as well.

Then in his mid-thirties, Osby was associated with the M-Base Collective, an association of like-minded, Brooklyn-based musicians that included fellow saxophonists Steve Coleman (the musician most closely identified with the M-Base concept) and Gary Thomas, vocalist Cassandra Wilson, pianist Geri Allen, cornetist Graham Haynes, guitarist David Gilmore, drummer Marvin "Smitty" Smith, and others. These artists respected jazz tradition while rejecting being confined by it; they wanted their music to reflect their own experiences rather than imitating the work of their predecessors, the knock on Wynton Marsalis and subsequent "young lions" who rose to prominence in the late 1980s and early 1990s by taking a neoclassical approach to jazz.

Osby was an innovator, and in 1997 he was having trouble finding a pianist who could keep up with the music he envisioned. So much so that he decided to risk hiring Moran for that European tour before hearing him play piano, based largely on a lengthy phone interview. "I was going through several different pianists, well-established pianists in New York," Osby told me, "none of whom fit the requirements of my music and just my particulars as a composer. So Eric Harland, who was in the band at the time, he realized my frustration. He recommended Jason, whom he'd grown up with, and they had a lot of history together—they were also classmates at Manhattan School of Music. He said he would fit my music like hand in glove. So Jason came down to witness my band at Sweet Basil in New York. And he was really enthusiastic: 'Man, I'll do the gig right now!'

"But of course I couldn't fire the guy who was on the gig at that point. So that night, Jason and I, we had a marathon conversation on the phone for about three or four hours. He gave me a detailing of his aspirations as a young artist. He made a great deal of really important and striking references, which really, I think that was the selling point. Because he made references to pianists that a lot of people of this generation *didn't*. And he was very, very descriptive, very definitive, very, very solid with his outreach. And it impressed me, you know, the conversation. And my conclusion was that if he was one tenth as good as what he's talking about, well then he would certainly be my guy. He talked about all of my favorite people. And it wasn't just the normal list of go-to people. He talked about a lot of peripheral characters, a lot of the less-heralded figures in the music, innovators whom I considered just as or more important than the ones who are most often talked about.

"So yeah, the first time that I actually heard him, after we were on the road, was on the bandstand in Vienna, Austria. So he played, and I felt a great deal of comfort as he played and a great deal of security and familiarity. But I really got to hear him after I stopped playing, and I stood off to the side of the bandstand, and I could hear him play. That was his audition, as they say: trial by fire."

By the time I heard Osby's version of the story, I had already heard Moran tell a roomful of New England Conservatory students his side of it. Saying to himself before the Vienna gig, "Jason, this is it. All your years studying with Jaki Byard, all these things you think you know . . . now's your chance. No friends here, just Eric and the band and a bunch of Austrians. They don't know nothing about you. Twenty-one years old. So I played, and I—you can turn on that part that says, 'I'm in it, I'm invested in every moment'—and I turned it on then. I don't think it sounded that great, but at the end of the gig, Greg said, 'Damn, that was all right. That's good enough for me.' He gave me like $500. Like, whoa! Man! Oh my God! I just sat in my room looking at the money like, 'Damn! This is the dream. I'm playing music, getting cash. Oh man!'"

Shortly thereafter, Moran said, at a tour stop in Germany, Osby decided he didn't feel like playing an encore, so he sent Moran out to play one leading a trio.

"I think I finally played 'Have You Met Miss Jones?' or something like that," Moran told the students. "Because I couldn't think. I got through it, and then I had to make an assessment of myself. It was clear in that moment that I could assess myself: That was nothing, that was just nothing. I was very honest with myself. I recorded, I listened back: There was no magic in that. But then I was like, 'You know what? I'm going to find it, though!' And on that tour he kept letting me search for it. You want to be in an environment where a person wants to promote what you have to say. 'Go ahead, the stage is yours.' And through over and over getting that opportunity, that's when I started to find what I had to say. It took a while. And you'll know when you have something to say because someone else will come up to you and say, 'I heard you. I heard you.' And it will be someone you don't know. 'I heard you.' And for me that's enough: $500 a night just to have someone say, 'I heard you.'"

Osby was an immediate and enthusiastic champion of his young protégé.

"From the very onset we connected both musically and personally," Osby confirmed. "And I set the wheels in motion to present him as a front man, as an artist. Very early on during this tenure we had, I gave him feature status—it was 'The Greg Osby Four, featuring Jason Moran'—which is never done. But I endeavored to present him to the world, because he was a class find as far as I was concerned. He was, basically, as they say, exactly what the doctor ordered. He fit the description stylistically, conceptually, supportively, artistically. In every possible way, he was the answer. He was like Allen Iverson on piano."

Osby chuckled at his basketball metaphor. But he was serious about the star potential he recognized in Moran.

"My music, as it's written and composed and presented, is very, very specific," he elaborated. "And it takes somebody who is a cut above just your standard proficient young player. Somebody who had a lot more vision, a lot more scope, and is not reaching for a reference. And somebody who was completely open to these alternative approaches. Jason, you know, he never blinked, he never winced, he never recoiled in horror. He was always *game*. And that was what I needed also. Because I had been encountering a great deal of resistance, and also, I won't say incompetence, but I will say people who failed to measure up to my expectations. Even though, like I said, they were accomplished players. He was very young, he was a diamond in the rough, there were some things that were quite unrefined, there was a bit of wildness. But I really embraced his spirit and his ability to deliver."

Moran wound up performing on seven Osby albums over the next five years. Osby also introduced Moran to Andrew Hill and Muhal Richard Abrams, two of the off-the-beaten-path pianists Moran cited in the conversation that caused Osby to hire him. Osby had worked as a sideman to both of them, and thought it important that Moran have direct contact with them rather than merely studying them from afar.

"Jason embodied the spirit of these people," Osby explained. "He was kind of a hybrid of all of these players, you know? Herbie Nichols, Andrew Hill, Muhal Richard Abrams, Thelonious Monk, McCoy Tyner—he had all of these particulars at hand. And he could very easily shift or play a direct facsimile of their playing, or an extension of that. He possessed all of those characterizations. So I took it upon myself to make the introduction. I thought it was important that he get the information directly from the sources, these sage innovators and icons, as I would classify them. And they also embraced him and took to him as well. Because Jason, of course, is very personable. He also listens. He's kind of like a musical sponge—he absorbs that information, and he knows how to process it and incorporate it into his work."

Hill and Abrams both became important mentors to Moran.

"These two people, again, they rest on the periphery of the scene," said Osby. "You wouldn't find a lot of young players who would even know who they are, much less refer to them and seek them out. But Jason did, and I said, 'Wow, you know Muhal? You know about Andrew?' He couldn't have been any more than nineteen to twenty years old. So I thought it was essential that he meet these people direct."

Osby also helped land Moran a recording contract with Blue Note Records, the major label which Osby had been with since 1990.

"I almost put my recording contract in jeopardy by trying to force the hand," Osby recalled. "I went to the then-president of Blue Note Records, Bruce Lundvall. I went to his office, and I said, 'I have a young guy in my band, I think you should check him out.' I had brought people to the label before that, but nothing like this. To me, this was like a rare find, and I was really excited about it. We were doing a week in New York, and I said, 'You should come check him out.'

"Bruce was apprehensive. He said, 'I just signed another player, another pianist, and I really don't have any more room on the roster.' And I said, 'This guy is leagues beyond what that guy is capable of,' whom I also knew well. And he said, 'Well, I don't know . . .' So I kind of slapped his desk and said, 'Listen man, I'm telling you! I'm telling you!' I was very adamant, very insistent. He reared back, because he was a little bit shocked—he'd never seen me that animated, I guess. I don't know how he read it, but he was like, 'Man, what's going on with this guy?'

"So he actually came down to the club, and after the first set, he approached Jason and he said, 'Young man, you're remarkable. And I'm willing to sign you on the spot. Come to my office tomorrow.' It was that immediate. . . . Jason was the 'it' guy at that point."

Osby appeared on Moran's debut album as a leader, *Soundtrack to Human Motion* (1999), as did Harland, the brilliant vibraphonist/composer Stefon Harris (Moran's college roommate, who in 2017 was named associate dean and director of jazz arts at their alma mater), and bassist Lonnie Plaxico. Moran's sophomore release, *Facing Left* (2000), came the next year and introduced his Bandwagon trio. Osby had a hand in forming that unit as well, Moran having first played with bassist Tarus Mateen and drummer Nasheet Waits in the Osby-led Blue Note supergroup New Directions.

"That's when I guess he really found his people who could serve his purposes more efficiently, more accurately," Osby noted. "He found kindred spirits. They all have that . . . they're mining for what's next. I saw it happen, in fact. They were connected so patently that I had to make an adjustment. I'd played with all of them individually, but together they created this vortex, this whirlwind of sounds. It was unstable at times. I had to rely on every bit of access that I had in order to stay afloat. And I said, 'Wow. This is the birth of something very special.' "

Twenty years on, Moran is imparting wisdom to students of his own. I observed him doing so at a handful of New England Conservatory master classes in 2015 and 2016. One class focused on music's relation to death. He screened several YouTube clips: Son House performing "Death Letter," whose place in the pantheon of great music, he said, was driven home by Cassandra Wilson when they played the same song while he was touring in her band. John Coltrane's "Alabama," written for the four schoolgirls who died in the infamous church bombing. Ambrose Akinmusire. Leontyne Price. Jessye Norman. Scenes from the films *Alexander Nevsky* and *The Godfather: Part II* (Moran not bothering to mention that Bandwagon interpretations of the music accompanying those scenes appeared on his albums *Same Mother* and *Facing Left*, respectively).

He spoke of performing at funerals: With Henry Threadgill at Ornette Coleman's. With Greg Osby at mentor Andrew Hill's. With his wife at his own mother's, after she succumbed to leukemia. "It was a difficult position to be put in, to maintain composure to get through a song," he said of playing for his mother. "Especially if you're a musician in a family, it's like, 'OK, of course he's going to play.' " Alicia got him through the spiritual they chose, "Give Me Jesus."

The focus throughout was on the meaning that informs great music.

"In the past five years," Moran told the students, "I've been asked to make music for some of the most harrowing sides of history in films, and in videos by artists. How do you make music for the rape of young girls by a gang of angry white men? What sound accompanies that? The murder of the family and the rape of a young girl by a mob of angry white men. What sound have we learned in school that preps us for that?

"You don't know what your music is actually going to require. You might just think it's a gig to make a hundred dollars or something like that, but for me in the last 10 years it has been less and less about that, and more about: How does music begin to be a balm for society, a healing balm? And how does it agitate society?"

Music, for Moran, isn't merely about playing beautiful notes. It's about conveying genuine emotion rooted in one's understanding of the wider world.

"I think I was asking the question to my teacher, 'What is the right time for me to play shows and be ready?' " Moran said. "And he was like, 'Well, what do you have to say? That's when you'll know what to write.' I had never thought about that. I just thought about my songs, that I transcribe, and that was supposed to be enough. Shit. You travel the world, you get off these planes and show up to these venues and you meet people you don't know—you'd better know every emotion that comes out of your instrument. You'd better really know: Know every song, and know it in yourself."

That teacher, of course, was Jaki Byard, the focus of another master class of Moran's that I attended. This time Moran showed *Anything for Jazz*,[18] a short 1980 documentary on Byard, directed by Dan Algrant and available on YouTube, that included Ron Carter and Bill Evans commenting on how certain great musicians— meaning Byard, though neither named him—never get their due. Byard's inability to achieve greater renown, Moran suggested, may have fueled his skepticism toward competitions and awards, and toward a widely adored pianist or two whose fame had eclipsed his.

Moran's lecture on Byard was far-ranging and, he told the students, concerned matters he generally kept to himself. "He was the reason I am the type of musician I am," he said. "Everything I think I invented, he actually already invented, a very long time ago."

He talked about listening to recordings of Charles Mingus's great band with Byard and Eric Dolphy while in high school, and choosing the Manhattan School despite being offered better financial packages elsewhere so that he could study with Byard.

"What I thought made them one of the best bands in the history of music is how they treated their own compositions," Moran told the students. "The textures that they used, the amounts of dips and dives that they would make, dynamics, the variety of language within one group—meaning people speaking different languages. Sonic languages. And how political they were, too. They seemed to be able to combine all that much in the way that Ellington also combined excellence with political activism. Jaki Byard was a pianist who was making a lot of this stuff work. His regard for piano history."

Moran's lecture covered a lot of ground. He demonstrated keyboard exercises Byard assigned for enlarging the span and flexibility of his hands, played samples of Byard's music, highlighted the importance he placed on being able to discuss history and social issues with Byard alongside his weekly private piano sessions. He talked about other professors with a more hidebound approach to jazz, who rejected the very things that Byard had been teaching him about how to go about accompanying other musicians.

"Literally when I went into my improvisation class and started playing that stuff," Moran recalled, "the teacher said to me, 'You can't play like that in here. You'll never work. You'll never earn $20 for playing like that.' I was a senior. Those kind of teachers were at the school at the same time I was learning from Jaki Byard. . . .

"I've always liked people like Jaki," he continued. "Those are my heroes. Herbie and McCoy, too. But one-on-one, Jaki's got the more weird stuff that I really need in my playing. He's got the thing that it's going to take some time to figure out how to massage it into place, and into how I want to play."

Andrew Hill, the subject of the other master class I witnessed, is another of those people Moran likes who are less known than they deserve to be—a fact Moran mentioned a couple of times during the lecture, recounting how he once described Hill as "unsung," to which Hill angrily shot back, "I'm not 'unsung.' I'm under-promoted."

The lecture had begun with Moran playing along to a recording of Hill's.

"That song is called 'Smoke Stack,'" he said afterward, "and when I heard it the first time I thought I had never heard anything so messy in my life. So beautifully messy. Every person in the ensemble was part of putting their finger in the paint. It's gorgeous. Just gorgeous to me. And I aimed to work with people who enjoyed putting their finger in the paint. Even if they did it very slowly and deliberately, still they put their fingers in the paint. And Andrew Hill, for me, is the one who does that. The way he blurs reality. Really think about it like that. The way he plays melodies. He doesn't treat the melody as a piece of fact, either. It's a feeling that can change."

Hill also, Moran said, "was to a degree my first impetus for composing. I really kind of followed some of the things that he laid out in his compositions—well, I felt like I did—and so I got struck by how a musician could play in a way that would confuse people but seem so right for me."

Much of the lecture focused on the need for a musician to have a personal pantheon. Hill's own had included people he encountered coming up in Chicago, among them Albert Ammons, Earl Hines, and the classical composer Paul Hindemith. Hill urged Moran to find a pantheon of his own.

"I stayed close to Andrew up until he was gone," Moran said. "He for me is pantheon. Him and his connection to Earl Hines. Jaki Byard—*his* connection to Earl Hines. So I'm fourth-generation Earl Hines. By virtue of that fact alone, I'm fourth-generation Earl Hines. By having two teachers who spent so much time with him. That gives me the lifeblood. And you hear it, you *hear* your tribe in the music that you like. You actually hear them. They call you."

When the class began to wind down, the topic turned to what to do with your pantheon once you'd found one.

"All that to say, I wish more people knew about Andrew Hill," Moran said, wrapping up. "But also, that's a tribe thing. It's like, and *all* my people, that's just the tribe that I roll with. My tribe is not the one that's like out there like that. Henry

Threadgill, Muhal Richard Abrams, Jaki Byard. Andrew Hill. Steve Coleman. Greg Osby. That tribe's not really [widely known], and that's who I am. It circulates kind of like on another wavelength. And it's cool right there. That's just where we are.

"Now, compare that to who? Josh Redman. Dave Holland. Esperanza Spalding. That's another tribe. That's my tribe, too, but in a very different way. You know what I mean? I think about all that. There are ways that people function within the jazz world. And Andrew's way is seen as very difficult. . . .

"What Andrew figured out was that maybe he wouldn't have to circulate on this popularity contest thing, but he could circulate in a lane that would allow him to keep making work. So one thing he said to me was, 'Jason, you have to find your benefactor.' The fuck was that? They don't talk about that at Manhattan School of Music. They sure should, though. Like who's gonna help you make this stuff? That sometimes you're just gonna need help doing it. Who's gonna do it? And he really woke that part of me up, too. And I will say that, my tribe, they know how to do that. All the people I mentioned, they kind of know how to do that. Find the people to help them make a thing. They're not trapped by that. They do make those things. And they get help to make them. I mean financial help to make it.

"Any other questions?"

One student, a guitarist, asked for advice about how an aspiring musician should go about assembling a personal canon of influences. Moran asked him to name three guitarists he likes.

"My three would probably be Django Reinhardt, Jim Hall, and then I listen to a lot of piano players," was his answer. "But a third guitarist . . . Julian Lage, I would say."

"That's cool," said Moran. "Do you hear something similar in all of them?"

"Yes."

"What is it?"

"The shapes of their gestures, I would say. There's something that's very directional and intuitive about it. But I've also been hearing, in sort of a shape-wise way, Andrew Hill—that's part of what's been bringing me in."

"Did you hear the album with Jim Hall and Andrew Hill?" Moran asked. "It's a Greg Osby record, called *The Invisible Hand*. That's a beautiful record. Terri Lyne Carrington plays drums. Andrew and Jim Hall were on there together. I probably have videotape of these sessions. It's beautiful, because there is something about their version of modernism that I might say that I hear in people that you mentioned. And Julian is a fairly new wunderkind that seems to have been embraced by the *entire* guitar community, from Nels Cline to Gene Bertoncini. That whole pantheon, he's trying to develop a way to work with them."

That led Moran back to his own story and how musicians must strive to take what they borrow and move beyond their influences.

"Something that I think made me gravitate towards Andrew was because the first person I heard was Monk. I mean, I didn't have any taste for jazz, and hearing Monk—so that's my base level. That's a pretty odd base level to start with. As a pianist, as a composer, this is the one I'm starting with. I'm starting with this right out of the blocks. And so when I hear Andrew Hill or Herbie Nichols, the people who I think were really giving me so much more energy off of that tree, then it made sense that he was the one before."

Moran told a story about his own fascination with pianists that had influenced Monk. He named Herman Chittison as one, a pianist few remember but whose recording of "Embraceable You," Moran said, reveals an obvious link to Monk. "You hear really clearly people that are stealing from places whether they say it or not," he noted. The trick is to use such technical borrowings to forge unique art of one's own.

"OK, so that's just the music part," Moran explained. "That's only half as important as the context you're gonna put the music in. So [a musician's influences] only give you enough to get to the door. They don't tell you what to say once you get inside the door. And that part, they wouldn't talk about it in school either. I just had to learn that later. Still learning it now. So what is the context, and to set up groups that help you achieve it.

"I tell this story about playing pool with Ornette Coleman. He breaks, the balls go everywhere. And I shoot. Then it's his shot. And he just takes his pool cue and goes *whooooosh*. All the balls all over the table. And then he takes one and the cue ball, and he puts the ball in front of the hole and he shoots. And takes another one, does the same thing. About an hour and a half we just did that. And that was, like, 'Set up your game.' You know? And that is the baddest fuckin' music lesson I ever saw."

Moran laughed.

"You have control to set up the rules. And if you think you're supposed to get up here and solo the way [Charlie] Parker did or any of these people, *psssh*. That ain't it. I can't do that the way Andrew Hill did. That's a different time, different brain, different setup. So that's not what I'm supposed to do. My context is not the same, and it's changing dramatically. In the past ten years it's changed so much. So you have the opportunity to see, 'How can I reconfigure all this?' And then *that's* when your voice comes through. 'Cause only you can see that."

And with that Moran thanked his audience for listening and dismissed class.

Moran has had his share of important mentors. But his wife's influence has also been key, a point he acknowledges in the 2017 book *The Meaning of Michelle: 16 Writers on the Iconic First Lady and How Her Journey Inspires Our Own*, edited by

Veronica Chambers. In one chapter, excerpted in *The Daily Beast*, Alicia and Jason discuss Michelle Obama's influence on them and the culture at large. The chapter is titled "The Composer and the Brain: A Conversation about Music, Marriage, Power, Creativity, Partnership . . . and the Obamas," and in it Jason spells out to whom "the Brain" refers:

> *The Brain is pretty literal. I met Alicia as she graduated from Barnard. What she brought into my life was an intellectual component that was totally absent. None of my friends were discussing music in a way that brought in place and the landscapes that the music emerges from, what are the codes and meanings. She had this amazingly rigorous comprehension of not only Black music, but German music and French music and what it means to culture and society.*
>
> *I was learning how to do the music, but I wasn't necessarily concerned with why I was making it. Alicia is the one who said, "You need to turn that around. If you turn this around sooner, you'll be ahead of nearly everyone else because it's clear that none of your friends are thinking about this."*

That made me want to know more. I emailed Jason to ask whether Alicia would be willing to talk to me. "Alicia is up for talking," he emailed back. "And you are right, I can't really be where I am without her help."

In his Andrew Hill lecture, Moran had quoted Hill telling him, "Jason, you have to align yourself with the pantheon."

"So who's the pantheon?" Moran had asked. "My wife is part of the pantheon, because of who her parents are. And that becomes a very important decision, who becomes your partner in your life. And how do they help you reflect, how do they shine up your mirror every once in a while. 'I see it's a little rough around the edge. Let me shine you off.' "

Alicia Hall was raised in New York City and Connecticut in a family of overachievers. She is the great grandniece of arranger-composer Hall Johnson, renowned for tracking down and transcribing slave songs and orchestrating them for choirs. "In the '30s he was scoring films with his choir, the Hall Johnson Choir," Moran had told the students during his lecture on music's relation to death, setting up the story of performing with Alicia at his mother's funeral. "Those singers that I played, Leontyne Price and Jessye Norman, all knew Hall Johnson, because you had to come see him if you were going to sing a Negro spiritual. He was the expert in New York City for years."

Alicia's parents weren't musicians but both had comparably successful careers. Her father, Ira D. Hall, retired as CEO of the Wall Street firm Utendahl Capital Management in 2004 after having held key posts at Texaco, IBM, and elsewhere, and has served as a director on a variety of corporate boards, including twenty years with the Jackie Robinson Foundation and, beginning with the 2017–2018 season, as chairman of the Adrienne Arsht Center for the Performing Arts of Miami-Dade County. Her mother, Carole Hall, taught high school English in northern California (both she and Alicia's father are graduates of Stanford University) before launching a career in book publishing.

"She was one of a handful of editors during one of the heydays of publishing, in the '80s, when Toni Morrison was still in editing," Alicia told me shortly after I got her on the phone, explaining her own moment of language-obsessed riffing on the word *stereotype* and its relationship to jazz musicians. "So they shared ideas. My mother is an equal to Toni Morrison. I've never said that out loud. She's not an equal writer or author; my mom's not a writer at all. But the idea that we kind of . . ."

She caught herself digressing and switched the subject back to her relationship with Jason.

They met at the Manhattan School of Music, where Alicia studied classical music after completing her Barnard degree. She told me she arrived at the Manhattan School, "a school that had such a high-powered jazz program," without knowing any young people who played jazz.

"I didn't know it was a profession that one could decide that they wanted to undertake at age eighteen," she said. "This was a revelation for me, that this is even possible. I went to Manhattan School of Music for classical training, and I did have some inkling that those things were possible from a young age for classical musicians. But the stereotype of jazz musicians is that they are an old man with a saxophone who is struggling to make ends meet. Then, when you have an interface with all these young, cool people, male and female, people who you find interesting and who find you equally interesting and exotic in your way, that's life-changing. So I got to tell them things that other people think about jazz. What people say about you."

She told a story about how once, early in their relationship, she and Jason had gone to an upscale restaurant together. "The type that you might find in a movie, a fantasy version," she said, describing a place filled primarily with black clientele. "You know, they're playing hip-hop and R&B on the radio but the chicken is like $25 per plate. I said, 'The thing about jazz, nobody in here can name a jazz musician. Not one of 'em. And these are your black people. And if they can, they will be dead. And if they are dead, they won't know what instrument they play.'

"He was beside himself, with a kind of jocular, 'Alicia, get out of here.' But we went down the bar. I said, 'Jason, nobody knows what instrument Miles Davis played, if they have even heard of Thelonious Monk.' And so we went down the bar. I think it was that nobody knew that Miles Davis played trumpet. We got a lot of saxophone, because of what I told you."

Alicia helps ensure that Jason continues casting his eyes outside any particular jazz or artistic bubble.

"I've also been helpful to him in a generative sense, in terms of finding the artists between genres," she explained. "He has a friendly island for everybody, no matter what kind of music you're making out here. If you are truly out here with good intentions, he can make an intellectual home for the music that you're coming from, and see your legacy. That's why he's a great teacher. . . . If you're New Orleans-based, and you're young and you meet Jason at the airport and you're talking about some very local ideas about music, he can talk to you like that is the center of the world. Because he gets it: that for you, it is. We regard people who play from the center of their world in high esteem, whether they are relatively ignorant and just starting out or blazing up the major festivals.

"I think that I've been helpful to him. I gave him kind of this ability to compartmentalize his experience and passion in other people. . . . He doesn't feel the need to downgrade [other people's] experience, or upgrade. It's just a real, literal, 'What am I looking at? And who are you talking about? And what have you to say? What is that feeling like with you?' So, with him, I think I've been able to slow down his process of receiving information, and that makes him an institutional gem.

"But I'm just explaining something that was very organic," she added. "Something that was very helpful for me was reading books. At Columbia I got to take a class with Mark Tucker[19] on just Duke Ellington. Changed my life. And taught me how to talk to Jason when I would meet him, which was about two years later."

I told her about how she had come up a few times in his master classes. How she had gotten him through their performing a spiritual, whose title he'd forgotten as he recounted the story, at his mother's funeral. ("Give Me Jesus," she said, supplying the missing title.)

How he considers her his best critic. "One person wrote the review 'Jason Moran was a pointless noodler,' " he'd said. "It's still her favorite line. She'd hear me and she'd go, 'Jason, pointless noodling, pointless noodling.' " Alicia laughed when I read her the quote. "Yeah, he never forgets that one review. 'Pointless noodling.' "

How it had taken him years to compose a song for her, a fact she'd kept reminding him of until it finally happened: "He was playing a song one day and I was like, 'That's my song.' I said, 'Does it have a name?' He said no. I said, 'We know what the name of that song is, right?' He said, 'Yup, we do.' We'd been saying that for ten years, but that one, it really was. It jumped at me, and I loved it. And sure enough, on the album he had named it 'Alicia.' "

How at the Manhattan School he'd occasionally had her accompany him to his private classes with Jaki Byard, and how he had followed Alicia to her classes as well. "For us culturally it was really important for us to have African American teachers, because we wanted to see who we wanted to be," he'd confided during his Byard lecture. "I needed to see, hear it from his mouth, and I needed to hear it from her teacher Hilda Harris's mouth—one of the first African Americans to sing with the Metropolitan Opera. I needed to hear her say what it felt like, and then come back to these institutions and want to share it with us. I needed to have them be my definition of excellence."

That story resonated with Alicia as exemplifying their relationship. "I have to say that's almost 100 percent right there," she said. "Like, who dates—who *knows* any person, forget 'dates'—who knows a person and then follows that person into their conservatory lesson with the teacher at their regularly appointed time? A regular lesson. This is not a workshop, it's not a parents' visiting day. It's not a special commission, it's not a mock performance, it's not a dress rehearsal."

I laughed and asked, "Which of the two of you had the bright idea to do that first?"

"Oh, I'm sure it was Jason," she said. "I can't imagine myself saying, 'I'd like to watch your piano lesson.' Never would do that. It wouldn't occur to me."

"You don't seem like a shrinking violet, though," I said, "so that's why I asked."

"No, why would I? That's a personal thing. That to me is a sacred relationship, and I would not project myself onto it. And I think that's a big secret of my involvement with Jason. As deeply as I will go in where I'm not invited, I have the utmost grace in his presence. And respect. It seems sometimes like I'm ripping his head off, but only about the things he will allow me. And I just have a sense for what those things are.

"I don't touch the artist nerve, like that thing in his brain," she clarified. "That's a beautiful place in him. And I have my own artist space, you know? There's some places you go in and get a dialogue and some places that the dogs just go *'argh!'* I'm not afraid of the bark, but I do enjoy being his friend and his partner in it. I think people are shocked by how aggressive you can be with a lover. But play them on their side. I'm on his side. It's not a scrimmage. It's like: we're on the same team, tackling, and on the outside it looks like, *Wow, she don't have no respect for his opinions.* It's just the opposite. It's that I'm feeding the other part of his brain. If I feel that it wants to come out, we go in, we throw down. I'm not fighting him; we're fighting with the idea, and we do that very well. It's one of the most exciting things."

"He comes back at you with his critiques?"

"Yeah, he tries," she said. "He's not as verbal as me, so he can't. He's got to play it out, and that is some amazing magic."

"That's where we want to be," she added. "It's always an emotional place. It's never a musical conversation; it's a color. I know about eleven hundred shades of Jason Moran. I just do. Also, because we both are petrified of being bored, so we know a million places in the other that are flammable. I'm a Leo, and my parents are Leos, so I'm a Leo among Leos who will be heard. I really know how to get up on a chair and scream it out if I need to. And I've done it. It's never graceful, but you have to fight for your artist husband sometimes. In himself. Not with other people. Oh, my God. In private. It's fun."

A Facebook acquaintance of mine, a well-known writer on politics, emailed me a few years ago to inquire for a perspective student about the journalism program at the college where I teach. While he was at it, he asked for recommendations of musicians on the current jazz scene that he should check out. He had been a jazz fan when younger, before work and family became his focus, and was now curious about what had happened to it while he had been away.

I suggested he start with Moran and either of two albums: *Ten* (2010), because it was then the most recent Bandwagon album, a celebration of the trio's decade together that gave a good sense of the variety of their work, including pleasing takes on pieces by both Byard ("To Bob Vatel of Paris") and Monk ("Crepuscule with Nellie"). Or *Modernistic* (2002), Moran's first solo piano album, because, as Alicia writes in her liner notes, "in it you will hear his life." No Monk or Byard pieces this time, but stride via James P. Johnson's "You've Got to Be Modernistic," Moran wresting something new and worthy from perhaps the most covered standard of all ("Body and Soul"), hip-hop (Afrika Bambaataa's "Planet Rock"), Muhal Richard Abrams ("Time Into Space Into Time"), two additions to Moran's Basquiat-inspired Gangsterism series, Schumann ("Auf Einer Burg/In a Fortress"), and a stately, set-closing tribute to his family roots ("Gentle Shifts South").

Those two still rank high in the Moran oeuvre. But I now might also name his first few albums since leaving Blue Note to create his own label and issue his recordings via Bandcamp.

"I just thought, 'Well, I don't need this label anymore,'" he told me, explaining that decision. "Maybe it was my ego, but I was like, 'I'm doing y'all a favor now.' Anytime you think that's what's happening, you probably should leave. And Bruce Lundvall [Blue Note's late president] died, and he's the reason I stayed with them, because he was such a supporter. He passed away. Also I just thought, the way that record sales go now, I'd rather just own my material, me personally."

Thanksgiving at the Vanguard (2017) shows the Bandwagon in a familiar live setting, seven years beyond *Ten* in their shared evolution, with tributes to Monk and Byard (the latter performed solo by Moran), yet another Gangsterism excursion, compositions by Alicia ("Blessing the Boats") and Waits ("Between Nothingness and Infinity"), and one composition of Moran's from his second solo piano album ("South Side Digging") among its offerings.

The newer solo album is essential: *Modernistic* had revealed the roots of Moran's approach to the piano; *The Armory Concert* shows him stretching those roots even further, his playing grown freer and less bound to the music of others. His album with Ron Miles and Mary Halvorson, *BANGS*, also moves beyond jazz into the more expansive realm that the AACM founders had christened "creative music." Like *Cane*, the four-part suite he had composed earlier for the classical wind quartet Imani Winds, *BANGS* showed Moran flexing modern chamber music muscles.

When I talked to Henry Threadgill about Moran, he was familiar with *The Armory Concert*, having been there the night it was recorded. "A really great concert," he called it. He hadn't heard about *BANGS* but said my description of it sounded interesting and that he'd make a point of having Jason send him a copy.

Threadgill had just been discussing his own habit of moving from one method of making music to new ones. "I'm about moving forward," he explained. "It's hard to do that when you become a stylist. You don't need to look over here to go forward, because you keep refining what you've got. That's what stylists do: they keep refining what they've got. To their credit, you know? I don't fall in that category. I don't have that talent. I'm happy and good with what I do."

"Do you think Jason takes that same approach?" I asked.

"I think so," Threadgill answered. "Right now he does. He's still got a lot of time in front of him. I hope he keeps moving forward like this."

It seems likely that he will. Jaki Byard, like Monk and the other rebellious elders who shaped and reshaped the jazz canon, taught Moran to keep taking risks and to discover his own true artistic self.

"You figure out who you are and what statement you want to make," Moran had said at the conclusion of his NEC master class on Byard. "I wasn't going to be an obvious player, you know what I mean? It's like a thing that I champion to players now. Because there are ways to make it work, you know? Most of us don't want to go into that fire, but they really laid out a lot of ground for us to walk on. Unfortunately, most of us don't. We're too scared. We are *too scared*. We are too scared. We are too scared! I'm telling you right now! We too scared! We don't want nobody to say no shit to us. We too scared. You're too scared! You're too scared."

Those words about being scared, Moran altering the emphasis with each pass, rang like a challenge—issued both to Moran himself and to everyone else in the room.

"Especially to sound 'ugly,' " he added, keeping it personal. "I think Jaki made it OK for me to sound ugly. I think he plays ugly sometimes. And that's good. So I can be ugly, too. I can put on my new tuxedo and still play ugly. I can use that to rub, you know what I mean? Somehow Jaki does that.

"So I'm thankful for all the students who got to study with him," Moran said, wrapping up, "because I think everybody got something different. You ask Fred Hersch about him, he'll tell you something totally different, you know?[20] But these are parts of the things he enabled in me. As a student, it would be my only job to try to act on the lessons that he gave me, which weren't so obvious all the time. But years later, I'm positive how each one changed the trajectory of my personal career. To hear him say that shit about the awards makes me question every award I get. Because I hear his voice. Like, 'That's cool, but . . .' " Moran laughed. "I'm very aware of him."

Please visit the open access version of Make It New *to see a video resource for Chapter One:* https://doi.org/10.3998/mpub.11469938.comp.1

CHAPTER TWO

VIJAY IYER

A key performance at the 2017 Newport Jazz Festival was "Flying Toward the Sound: For Geri, with Love," a tribute to the great and beloved pianist, composer, and educator Geri Allen, whose unexpected death from cancer earlier that summer at age sixty had shocked and saddened the jazz world. Allen had been scheduled to perform a Newport set with the ACS Trio, the recently reassembled unit she shared with drummer Terri Lyne Carrington and bassist Esperanza Spalding.

Instead, Carrington and Spalding celebrated Allen's life and work with Christian Sands, Vijay Iyer, and Jason Moran taking turns on piano.

Sands, a generation younger than Iyer and Moran, went first, offering spirited versions of the Allen compositions "Unconditional Love" (Spalding featured on both bass and wordless vocals) and "Feed the Fire," Iyer and Moran chatting amiably as they watched from the side of the stage.

Iyer's two pieces were next and came from an earlier, more experimental period of Allen's career: "I'm All Smiles," a standard recorded with her formidable late 1980s trio partners Charlie Haden and Paul Motian, and "Drummer's Song," an Allen original dating back a pinch further to her M-Base association with Steve Coleman, who would later hire Iyer to tour with him.

The trombonist Josh Roseman leaned over to me as Iyer's segment ended and said, "I could hear him dropping some Geri-isms."

"They'll all tell you they came from her," I replied, mindful of the many encomiums from musicians that appeared on social media and elsewhere at the news of her passing. The *Pittsburgh Post-Gazette* published a number of them gathered from Allen's website, including contributions from Iyer and Moran. (Allen had been an associate professor at the University of Pittsburgh, where she directed the jazz studies program.)

When Moran's turn came, he played inspired takes on the sort of progressive arrangements of standards that Allen, Carrington, and Spalding had specialized in when working as a trio. His pair—Leonard Bernstein's "Lucky to Be Me" and Bob Dorough's "Nothing Like You"—were well chosen for their titles as well as their musical content. The legendary bebop pianist Bud Powell's son, Earl John Powell,[21] was among those watching from beside the stage. We had just been introduced by Roy Haynes's nephew Kenneth Haynes, a Boston friend I'd met when we shared a table at a Robert Glasper Experiment performance, and as Moran dug hard into those two classics, Powell turned to me and repeated something Moran once told him: that Moran always takes the stage "with a vengeance" to honor Jaki Byard.

The Allen set concluded with another standard, "Beautiful Friendship," with the three pianists each taking a couple of turns sliding on and off the piano bench to play in Allen's stead. As the piece concluded, Spalding looked toward the sky and repeated "Thank you, Geri" four times over her microphone. And then the five musicians exited the stage so it could be made ready for a rare performance by Henry Threadgill and his band Zooid.

Carrington's and Spalding's festival work was confined to that one set, but it was a busy weekend for the three pianists. Sands had led a quartet on Friday, and played with festival artistic director Christian McBride's big band earlier Saturday afternoon. Moran and vocalist Lisa E. Harris would have a main stage crowd up and dancing for his Fats Waller Dance Party on Sunday, with Roseman and alto saxophonist Tia Fuller added to his announced lineup of musicians.

Iyer had already led or co-led two other sets. Earlier that day, his sextet had played music from its debut album to be released later that month, *Far from Over*. Both Saturday sets displayed Iyer's jazz side—progressive in the M-Base vein, with a good dose of groove and funk keeping the sextet's complex horn lines grounded if not altogether danceable. The new material was forward looking but still recognizably jazz, despite Iyer's strong misgivings toward the word *jazz* and the notion of genres in general. The performance also reconfirmed that Tyshawn Sorey, who would be announced as a MacArthur Foundation grant winner a few weeks later, is a ferociously talented drummer in addition to being an outstanding composer. On Friday, Iyer and trumpeter/composer Wadada Leo Smith had performed music from their 2016 duo project *A Cosmic Rhythm with Each Stroke*, before which they were presented with a pair of awards from the Jazz Journalists Association—the two of them jointly for "Trio or Duo of the Year" and Smith as "Musician of the Year."

A few months after Newport, *Far from Over* would win the 2017 NPR Jazz Critics Poll as the year's best album. Iyer's biggest accomplishment of 2017, however, was serving as music director for the 2017 Ojai Music Festival that June, a role in which he introduced an audience more oriented toward contemporary classical music to a startling array of creative musicians. Iyer performed in a variety of contexts: leading his sextet; in a duo with Wadada Leo Smith; in a quartet with tabla master Zakir Hussain, saxophonist Rudresh Mahanthappa, and vocalist Aruna Sairam; and with the Brentano Quartet, ICE (International Contemporary Ensemble), and others. He also had compositions of his performed by others, most notably violinist Jennifer Koh, ICE, the Oberlin Contemporary Music Ensemble, and conductor Steven Schick joining forces for the world premiere of *Trouble*. Among the many others who performed over the four days of the festival were the trio of AACM legends Muhal Richard Abrams, Roscoe Mitchell, and George Lewis (whose *Afterward, an opera* also got its West Coast premiere); the flutist/composers Nicole Mitchell and Claire Chase; and composer/drummer/conductor Tyshawn Sorey.

Christian McBride, who in his new role as artistic director of the Newport Jazz Festival had booked Iyer's three performances there, also featured Iyer and the Ojai festival on an episode of *Jazz Night in America*, the weekend program he hosts on National Public Radio.[22] The Ojai festival has an association with classical music dating back to the late 1940s. Previous music directors include Aaron Copland, Pierre Boulez, and Igor Stravinsky. But Iyer, early in the broadcast, makes clear that such categories had little impact on the choices he made as music director. "It doesn't have anything to do with genre," he declares. "You know, genre is an invention of the twentieth century anyway."

"Vijay doesn't believe in genres," McBride tells his radio listeners, "but let's face it, genres are still a thing. Which is why a jazz musician serving as this year's music director made some waves."

Ojai artistic director Thomas W. Morris, a guest on the episode, then explains his decision to tap Iyer as the year's music director. "I think what's unique about him is what he stands for," says Morris. "His deep and vocal advocacy of a borderless music world is also what's happening today. The possibilities are completely boundless, but you need people to help show the way. And I suspect he's leading part of that change."

McBride goes on to explain that Morris, a self-described refugee from the symphony orchestra world, "has a freer hand at Ojai, working with artists along music's cutting edge. But this year he was ready to really bust out of the frame. And when he appointed Vijay as this year's music director, he was betting the rest of the classical world was ready, too."

"What intrigued me about Vijay initially was the breadth of his thinking," Morris says, "which in fact would push the festival in a particular direction that it hadn't gone before. A direction towards far greater emphasis on improvisation, an emphasis on artists who really have not been associated with Ojai."

"That's the only guiding force that I've ever had to make the choices I make as an artist, or as a person," Iyer adds in his next soundbite. " 'Well, this feels important. Let's move toward it, let's embrace it.' "

High up on the list of important things embraced by Iyer is *creative music*, the catch-all, genre-defying term he borrows from the AACM to describe experimental art music. He rejects the idea of genre, but Iyer's own work ranges into areas others categorize as jazz, classical (both the Western variety and the Carnatic music of his parents' native India), hip-hop (he has worked with Das Racist and other groups in addition to his politically charged collaborations with the poet and rapper Mike Ladd), and pop (recreations of work by Michael Jackson, Stevie Wonder, Flying Lotus, MIA, Heatwave). His trio's cover of "Mystic Brew," on the 2009 album *Historicity*, may owe as much to A Tribe Called Quest, the hip-hop group that sampled it on their tune "Electric Relaxation," as it does to its soul-jazz origin on a 1972 Blue Note album by organist Ronnie Foster, or so suggested writer Ben Gray in a 2013 post on Nextbop.com.[23] And John Murph, in his 2009 NPR review "Vijay Iyer Trio: Jazz at Its Finest and Friskiest," added hints of New Orleans second-line rhythms and M-Base syncopations to the mix as well.[24]

Iyer embraces other art forms as well as art as a platform for protest and civil rights advocacy. He was the 2015–2016 artist in residence at New York's Metropolitan Museum of Art, which included his curating, and usually participating in, an array of musical performances at the Met's newly acquired Met Breuer building. The highlight of these was the premiere performances of his collaboration with the trumpeter and composer Wadada Leo Smith, *A Cosmic Rhythm with Each Stroke*, a suite commissioned by the museum to honor the Indian modernist artist Nasreen Mohamedi, whose abstract drawings and photographs the Met Breuer was exhibiting at the time.

Another of Iyer's many collaborators at the Met Breuer was the Nigerian American novelist and essayist Teju Cole, whose celebrated novel *Open City* (2011) had already inspired Iyer's commissioned work of the same title, performed by an eighteen-piece ensemble at Montclair State University in October 2013. That performance included Cole reading excerpts from his book; the rapper Heems (formerly of the hip-hop group Das Racist); guitarist Rafiq Bhatia; bassist Harish

Raghavan; Rajna Swaminathan on mridangam (Carnatic hand percussion instrument); drummer Marcus Gilmore; Iyer's early employer and mentor Steve Coleman on alto saxophone; trumpeter Ambrose Akinmusire; trombonist Josh Roseman; cellist Okkyung Lee; violinist Mat Maneri; the rising teen talents Adam O'Farrill and Elena Pinderhughes on trumpet and flute, respectively; and three members of Iyer's then still unrecorded sextet, Graham Haynes (cornet), Mark Shim (tenor saxophone), and Tyshawn Sorey (percussion).

Yet another collaboration with Cole occurred at Boston's Institute of Contemporary Art in February 2018. It was called "Blind Spot," after Cole's 2017 book of that title, an unorthodox collection of photographs by Cole, each accompanied by his brief, essayistic reflections. Cole, who was battling the flu that night, read excerpts from the book as the corresponding images were screened above the stage. A quartet of Iyer, Okkyung Lee, Stephan Crump, and vibraphonist/marimbist Patricia Brennan performed brilliantly empathetic incidental music. A moment I found particularly striking was linked to the John Coltrane song "Alabama." The image was of the Sixteenth Street Baptist Church in Birmingham, where four black children were murdered by a bomb set by white supremacists in 1963. Cole's words described how Coltrane's saxophone had paraphrased the eulogy by Dr. Martin Luther King Jr. The accompanying music swelled, Iyer contributing deep rumbling chords. "McCoy Tyner's piano weeps," Cole intoned, as the segment concluded. "Jimmy Garrison on bass. Elvin Jones on drums. These children."

In his focus on creative art music and its integration with other art forms, Iyer shares much in common with his friend and contemporary Jason Moran.[25]

Both men have been recipients of MacArthur Foundation fellowships, commonly known as "genius grants," Moran in 2010 and Iyer in 2013. Both have composed for classical ensembles, including each of them having written music for the chamber ensemble Imani Winds; both have incorporated hip-hop and other modern pop music in their work as well. Both have held museum residencies and have curated concert series there and at other venues. Both are important educators: Moran at New England Conservatory, Georgetown, and as head of the Betty Carter's Jazz Ahead summer residencies at the Kennedy Center. Iyer became the Franklin D. and Florence Rosenblatt Professor of the Arts at Harvard University in January 2014, having taught previously at a handful of colleges and conservatories in New York, and in 2013 became director of the Banff International Workshop in Jazz and Creative Music. (Iyer's colleague Tyshawn Sorey would join him as Banff's co-artistic director in summer 2018.) Moran and Iyer both live with their families in Harlem and commute to Boston and Cambridge for their teaching jobs; they occasionally spot each other on Amtrak trains traveling to and from New York.

Iyer, like Moran, has composed music to accompany films. In Iyer's case, these include co-creating the score for Haile Gerima's *Teza* (2008) and his collaboration with filmmaker Prashant Bhargava, *Radhe Radhe: Rites of Holi* (2014), a colorful celebration of the centenary of Igor Stravinsky's The Rite of Spring, for which Bhargava traveled to the northern Indian city of Mathura and shot spectacular scenes from its annual eight-day Holi festival celebrating the love of Krishna and the Hindu goddess Radhe.

Each musician also has close ties with artists in the AACM and the M-Base Collective. Iyer's first tour of Europe came as a member of Steve Coleman's band; Moran's came with Coleman's M-Base associate Greg Osby. Both are in frequent contact with George Lewis, who besides being an early member of the AACM wrote the definitive history of the organization, *A Power Stronger Than Itself: The AACM and American Experimental Music* (Chicago, 2008); Lewis served on the committee overseeing Iyer's doctoral dissertation from the University of California at Berkeley, and he and Steve Coleman both appeared on Iyer's debut album as a leader, *Memorophilia* (1995). Two other key figures in the AACM, Roscoe Mitchell and Wadada Leo Smith, hired Iyer for their bands early in his career. And the AACM's principal founder and lifelong guiding light, the late pianist and composer Muhal Richard Abrams,[26] had been an important mentor to both Moran and Iyer.

Abrams and Andrew Hill were among several pianist-composers Moran and Iyer share as influences. Duke Ellington and Cecil Taylor are two more. Another is Geri Allen. Several months after participating in that tribute to her at the Newport Jazz Festival, Iyer and Moran participated in a two-day "festival/symposium" honoring Allen at Harvard University. The event, which took place in February 2018, was organized by Iyer, his Harvard music department colleagues Ingrid Monson and Esperanza Spalding, and Terri Lyne Carrington of the Berklee College of Music. Iyer himself moderated two roundtable discussions—one on "Geri Allen and the Piano," with Moran, Craig Taborn, and Kris Davis; the other on "Geri Allen and the Experimental," with Oliver Lake and Kris Davis. He served as a panelist on a third, moderated by Monson, "Geri Allen's Place in History," with Don Byron and Dwight Andrews. Iyer also performed both nights: the first night was a series of solo and duo piano improvisations involving every possible configuration of Iyer, Moran, Taborn, and Davis, and on the second night Iyer performed with Spalding, Carrington, and other symposium guests in various combinations.

A few days after the Harvard event, Iyer granted me a lengthy telephone interview, during which I mentioned what Josh Roseman had said about the "Geri-isms" he had heard in Iyer's playing at Newport.

"It's funny," he replied, "because both Esperanza and Terri said that to me after Saturday's concert. We played the same tune, which is [the Geri Allen composition]

'Drummer's Song.' Mostly I was just trying to play the song, which is really hard. It's a lot of counterpoint, and the rhythms are really tricky, actually. But then, she's been an influence on my playing since I was sixteen. That's thirty years. And an ongoing influence: I mentioned it the other day [at the Harvard symposium], one time I was out with my trio, with Marcus [Gilmore] and Stephan [Crump], and we were at Stephan's car, and I cued up *Etudes*.[27] They were like, 'When did you play with Charlie Haden?' " He laughed. "They thought it was me. So, I was like, 'Yes, the secret is out.'

"To me, it's always been in my playing, since before I made records. My first album came out when I was twenty-three, and I'm talking about seven years even before that. More than a quarter of my life would have been in the wake of Geri's influence by the time I made my first album, and I think if you listen to that one—I don't know if you've heard it, but it's really apparent on there the way early Geri Allen influenced early me. It's very directly: a sense of space and a way of building the control over dynamics. Even in what might seem like a volatile context, you can be expressive with tone. It was more of an intuitive connection for me; I hadn't really examined it—it's just that it was what I heard happening with her."

Iyer noted that people tend to overlook Allen's influence on him, as well as that of some of the other, less familiar piano giants whom he holds dearest.

"What often happens to me in critical discourse is that people say I don't sound like anybody," he said, "and that's partly a compliment, and it's also partly just like a fucking blind spot. Like, why don't you know that I sound like Geri Allen? Or like Andrew Hill, or even like Monk, in any remote way? Why wouldn't you make that point of contact between those people? To me, it's obvious. I mean, I've even played their music. I've recorded Andrew Hill's tune 'Smoke Stack' on *Historicity*. If you have studied their music, then it's obvious. But I think it's a couple of different things. I think some of it is the master narrative about jazz piano leaves some of those people out. People love to talk about Oscar Peterson or [Art] Tatum, Bud Powell, and then Herbie [Hancock] and Chick [Corea] and Keith [Jarrett] and Brad [Mehldau] and Bill Evans. The usual suspects, you know? And I'm certainly influenced by all of them, in different ways. But the ones that resonate most with me are the ones who brought that composerly quality and that expansive quality, and that to me is Duke Ellington, Thelonious Monk, Bud Powell certainly, Randy Weston, Andrew Hill, Herbie Nichols, Cecil Taylor, Sun Ra, and then Geri Allen. To me that's a direct line, and it makes complete sense when you hear them all in a row."[28]

A bit later in our conversation, I mentioned something the younger pianist Robert Glasper had told me about visiting Moran at his home shortly after moving to New York and being introduced to the Duke Ellington album *Money Jungle* while they ate fried chicken. This prompted a similar story from Iyer involving Moran and again, indirectly, Geri Allen.

"That's funny," he said, "because I remember Jason came over to my place—I moved to New York in '98, so it was after that—it was sometime in December of '99. He came over and I played him some things. I played him *Home Grown*, Geri's solo album, and he had never heard it before. He was floored. He was like, 'Can I borrow this?' And I was like, 'No, nobody can borrow this. It took me so long to find this record, I don't let it out of my house.' He was like, 'No, listen. I'll just run home and I'll rip it into my computer and I'll come right back.' I lived on 116th and Broadway; he lived in the same building where he lives now. So I said, 'OK, you can have it for a half-hour.' And he did, he brought it back. Then later I was over to his place, and he made me fried chicken."

The most profound piano influence on both men, however, was Thelonious Monk. Iyer told me of his early encounter with Monk's music the first time we spoke for this book, in April 2015, seated at the kitchen table of the sparsely furnished apartment he keeps in Cambridge for his weekly trips to Harvard during the school year. The day before, I'd attended an event at Harvard's Holden Chapel, at which he and his trio mates, bassist Stephan Crump and drummer Marcus Gilmore, had explained to a small audience how they work together. That same evening, I'd seen them perform a set at the nearby Regattabar. At his apartment the next day, Iyer mentioned two Monk albums that he had listened to early on in his jazz education, both from the twilight of Monk's career: *Monk Live in Tokyo* (1973) and an all-star album titled *The Giants of Jazz* (1971), on which Monk's bandmates include Dizzy Gillespie, Art Blakey, Sonny Stitt, Kai Winding, and Al McKibbon.

"I had already kind of started to study the music," Iyer recalled, spreading peanut butter on a piece of bread, "but hearing him play it, it seemed to go against everything that you're conventionally told to do in this music. But he was apparently a foundational figure in the music, so I couldn't really make sense of that: the fact that, on the one hand, there's this stock way of playing; on the other hand, the music came from people like him who didn't do anything like that at all. Every sound he made was so specific, so unique, and there's all this emptiness in the music. But like space in the music—silence or gaps, I guess you could say. Not silence. It's basically the sound of listening. I guess that's what it is. When he's not playing, others are, and so he's letting them kind of fill in the spaces. I just remember being mystified by it. I guess when I have that kind of experience it makes me want to lean in and try to understand it more, to pay more attention to it.

"So that's sort of what happened. Then not long after that, I think maybe a year or two later, is when that film *Straight No Chaser*[29] came out. This was, of course, long before YouTube or anything like that, so that was my first time seeing any footage of him. That definitely hit me like a lightning bolt, not because it was wacky or funny, but because it felt so true. It felt so honest and authentic, it was so expressive. It sort of resonated with me to see how he approached the instrument. It was his own personal relationship to the instrument. It had a lot of spontaneity in it; it was very organic and true to him. So that somehow, I think at least in retrospect, that's what I would say sent me on a certain path in relation to my understanding of what he did.

"He's still a source of inspiration, and I think when you heard us last night we played one of his tunes. I think about him all the time, and everything about what he does has influence: a sense of time, his rigor, his experimentalism, his playfulness, *loyalty,* and intensity. There's intensity and the sensation of sound that may lead you somewhere."

What led Iyer to Monk had been his own curiosity. Like Moran, Iyer began Suzuki musical instruction at a very young age—three, in Iyer's case. But Iyer's first instrument was violin, which he continued to study until age eighteen. His elder sister, Pratima, studied piano, however. Iyer found himself gravitating to the family's upright and learning how to play it on his own. He was doing all this in Fairport, New York, a suburb of Rochester that proclaims itself the Crown Jewel of the Erie Canal. Iyer's father, Raghu,[30] had come to the United States from India in the mid-1960s to pursue a PhD in pharmacology at the University of Florida; his wife (Vijay's mother), Sita, joined him in Florida a year later. Raghu's doctorate led to jobs in Albany, New York, where Vijay was born in 1971, and soon thereafter in Rochester, which brought the family to Fairport when Vijay was two.

"My parents moved specifically to that suburb because it had good schools," Iyer told me, "and that meant it also had a good music program."

By the time Iyer got to high school in the 1980s, many public schools were scaling back or even eliminating their music curricula. But not in Fairport, where Iyer eventually became the pianist for his high school jazz band and played violin in the Rochester Philharmonic Youth Orchestra. The music he favored early on, though, was the familiar American pop fare of those years: Michael Jackson, Prince, the Police. He liked the Beatles, too, and his playing in a rock band while in high school led him to Led Zeppelin and Jimi Hendrix. He told the Indian news website *The Wire* that the first record he owned was Eddy Grant's hit single "Electric Avenue" (from Grant's 1982 album *Killer on the Rampage*) and that his sister's had been *Saturday Night Fever*.[31] Iyer's interest in jazz came along a bit later, after he joined the high school jazz band.

"I mean, I had been exposed to the music kind of intermittently through my childhood, just like "anyone else," he told me. "Suddenly Dizzy Gillespie would show up on *Sesame Street*, or I remember Dr. Billy Taylor had a segment still on the [CBS] *Sunday Morning* show. So I used to see a lot of music there, and at Eastman School of Music [in Rochester] they have, and have had for some time, a serious program in jazz. That meant that there were great artists around there, but it wasn't so much on my radar. By the time I was in high school I was taking music theory courses at Eastman, and then sort of the natural next step was jazz theory, jazz improvisation, and courses like that.

"So I was in the high school jazz ensemble, and then I did these summer programs at Eastman. But around then was when Wynton [Marsalis] was becoming a very visible force. Basically, you'd see him on TV. I remember seeing him on *Saturday Night Live* with his band."

Iyer also recalled seeing Marsalis perform at an outdoor jazz festival held at the Finger Lakes Performing Arts Center, near Rochester.

"I remember seeing Kenny G and Wynton on the same stage," he said. "They were both just young whippersnappers back then." He laughed, then returned to his early experience seeing Marsalis on *Saturday Night Live*, which he decided must have been about the time Marsalis's album *J Mood* (1986) was current.[32] "I just remember being really mystified by the way they dealt with time, with rhythm. I think it must have been with [pianist] Marcus Roberts and [bassist] Bob Hurst. It all seemed synchronized, but I couldn't parse it yet. It was just that sort of thing where I wanted to understand it."

His understanding of both jazz and jazz piano began in his early teens, and built on the improvising he had always done on the piano.

"When I was led into the jazz ensemble I was going into the eleventh grade, and I had skipped a grade, so I was fourteen," Iyer explained. "See, I had been playing piano my whole life, just by ear, just with messing around on it. My primary instrument was violin, so the piano was kind of just a release for me. It wasn't guided by anybody. So when I was fourteen, and I auditioned for the jazz ensemble, I was an improviser, but I didn't really have any grounding in the language of the music. So the director referred me to this pianist in Rochester, his name is Andy Calabrese. He's still there; he's a local jazz musician."

Iyer took a few lessons from Calabrese. "He mainly showed me basic voicings, and he'd lend me some records. The rest of it, I just sort of followed my nose. And it was also that I had friends who were getting into the music at the same time. There was a saxophone player, there was a bassist, and there was a drummer. So we all played together."

Iyer set aside his musical ambitions somewhat when he arrived at Yale College, a couple of months before turning seventeen. He majored in math and physics. A

2016 *New Yorker* profile by staff writer Alec Wilkinson reported that he auditioned for the college symphony but didn't get in, after which his interest in the violin waned. He began playing piano in his dining hall, joined by a classmate, Jeff Brock, who played bass and went on to chair the mathematics department at Brown. Iyer took a workshop on Billy Strayhorn from Willie Ruff, a Yale alumnus who played French horn and bass. Ruff had been the subject of a *New Yorker* piece himself, titled "Shanghai Blues," in which writer William Zinsser described Ruff and pianist Dwike Mitchell introducing Chinese conservatory students to jazz in 1981, just five years after the horrors of Mao's Cultural Revolution. Zinsser, best known for his 1980 classic *On Writing Well* (a result of his having taught writing at Yale in the 1970s), fleshed out the material from the article in his 1984 book *Willie and Dwike: An American Profile*. Iyer also took a course on post–World War II jazz, taught by anthropology professor John Szwed.[33] Szwed would invite top-flight musicians from the city to speak to his class, and this was how Iyer met Allen for the first time.

Iyer's next stop was graduate school at the University of California, Berkeley, where his studies also appeared to be on a more conventional academic path as he arrived to pursue a doctorate in physics. But that changed. Iyer found an apartment in north Oakland, on 47th and Telegraph Avenue, across the street from a little dive of a jazz club called the Bird Kage. He began dropping by for Sunday jam sessions, and became the house pianist when the band leader realized Iyer owned a keyboard he could bring with him to play in place of the club's battered piano.

"Anyway, through that I ended up working with elders from the African American community in Oakland," Iyer recalled. "It wasn't like I was on some safari or anthropological mission. I just felt kind of embraced, like you said. It was just a very warm and nurturing kind of space. We were basically playing standards. There was a guy who would come in, he would be fitted in this amazing suit, and he had shades on. He'd show up with some beautiful woman next to him and his horn. It was like an event to him arriving, and then he'd take his horn out, and it was like, 'Wow, what's this guy going to sound like?' And he sounded like *Albert Ayler*. He was sort of like a gruffer, maybe slightly softer version of that, but it was basically energy music. But over a ballad, or over 'Invitation.'

"So stuff like that would happen. Or Pharoah Sanders used to come through. I got to play a bunch with him. Not like gigs, but he would sit in. We played 'Polka Dots and Moonbeams.' One time we played 'When Lights Are Low.' Many times we would just play blues, and he would get the whole room shaking."

Iyer also played in bands led by two veteran drummers living in the area. One was Donald Bailey, best known for his lengthy stint with organist Jimmy Smith. "Actually, there's an interview with Roy Haynes in the late '50s," Iyer noted, "where he says that Donald Bailey is his favorite young drummer, and there was a time when Trane was going to hire him. Anyway, he was a bad dude and passed away a year or two ago." The other, E. W. Wainwright, had played with McCoy Tyner in the 1970s. "He had been a student of Elvin's, so he had that kind of intensity and fire. So all this was happening. No one has heard any of it, and that was like my education. It was basically in that same period that I met Steve."

Steve being Steve Coleman, the alto saxophonist, composer, bandleader, and central figure in M-Base Collective that came together in Brooklyn in the 1980s, a circle that also included Greg Osby, Geri Allen, and Cassandra Wilson, among others.

"He came out to Yoshi's to play in Oakland in '93," Iyer told me, referring to Coleman, "and then he came back in '94. I went to, I think, all the sets those times, because it was mind blowing. I'd never heard anything like it. It was, again, like I had no idea how they were doing what they were doing. I mean, it was getting that sense of mystery and possibility. There was so much rigor and detail. They were so expressive and so loose. It must have been what it was like to see Bird and Diz and Max Roach. You just walk into this room, and suddenly there's stuff that you couldn't even imagine possible, like the highest level of ensemble synchrony. It was so expressive. It seemed to be exploding with information, with soul and wit and humor, just searing with intensity. That's sort of what it felt like to see Steve's band in the early '90s. This is around the time of [Coleman's albums] *Drop Kick* and *The Tao of Mad Phat*."

Coleman picked the younger musician's brain about other places to perform in the Bay Area. "What he was actually doing," Iyer explained, "was setting up this grassroots residency where he would bring his band, rent a house, and just kind of be playing in little corner spots and community centers, and doing a bunch of underground stuff. So I got kind of involved in that. I helped him a little bit with the organization, and then I went to almost everything he did, which was, for almost six weeks, he played several nights a week, and then he had the house where they were rehearsing all day, searching and stuff. So over the course of that I started sitting in with him. His presence had a huge impact on many of us in the Bay Area. But then a couple weeks after he left, he called me up and asked me to go to Europe. So that was it. Then I was like, 'Oh, I thought I was going to be a physicist, but something else is going on right now,' So things started to change around then, and that was '94 and '95."

Iyer spent the next several years, off and on, in Coleman's band. "That was like my bootcamp," he said. "Basically '95 to 2000. I'm on several albums of his, and we did a lot of tours and a lot of concerts. I remember feeling like an oddball even in that band. First of all, for a while I had imposter syndrome or something like that: 'At some point they will realize I shouldn't be here and my fifteen minutes will be over.'" He laughed. "Steve was very generous. I was really green. I had certain things together, but there was a lot I had to work on, too. And he just gave me a chance to do it in public, basically. How to play with a drummer like Gene Lake or Sean Rickman. But it was a real education, because his music is of course some of the hardest music in the world to play.

"But a concert would have a real spectrum," Iyer added. "I would have to say that what you saw us do last night, with that sort of organic flow from one piece to another, things suddenly shifting into a different energy—I leaned that from him. I mean, that's what he does. He doesn't play with a set list either. He taps into intuition and makes that the guide of the concert."

I mentioned that yet another Coleman acolyte, Miguel Zenón, had told me that Coleman was the most influential living artist on his generation of jazz musicians. "I've been quoted saying that, too," Iyer responded. "I think I was quoted saying he's the most influential musician since Coltrane, and I think that's true. In terms of the music itself: I mean, it could be argued that Wynton's the most influential musician in this area, but I wouldn't say he's influenced the music. I mean, he did. I guess you could debate it."

Coleman also introduced Iyer to another musician with Indian roots, Rudresh Mahanthappa, at the Stanford Jazz Workshop in summer 1995, suggesting that they work together. They became fast friends and frequent collaborators, touring extensively together and performing on each other's albums for more than a decade. Mahanthappa had finished his master's degree at DePaul University when they first met, and he was living and working in Chicago. Iyer had decided to discontinue his doctoral work in physics, but he had not abandoned graduate school. Instead, he switched to a self-designed interdisciplinary PhD program in Technology and the Arts, focused on music cognition. His 1998 dissertation, *Microstructures of Feel, Macrostructures of Sound: Embodied Cognition in West African and African-American Musics*, made the case for music perception and cognition being embodied activities more than purely cerebral and linguistic ones, and that "these sonic traces of bodily motion can be appreciated as such, and even aesthetically privileged in certain cultures, while neglected or suppressed in others."[34] And it applied this idea to electronic music, from the drum sampling and record scratching of hip-hop to the computer music experiments of his graduate adviser David Wessel and dissertation committee member George Lewis.[35]

Lewis, renowned trombonist, composer, scholar, and author (and 2002 MacArthur genius grant recipient), was on the faculty at the University of California, San Diego, at the time, but did a residency at Mills College in Oakland in fall 1994. He and Iyer had already performed music together when he joined Iyer's thesis committee.

"He literally went over every word in my dissertation," said Iyer. "I had a committee of five professors, but he was the one who really made me justify every word of it. Other professors maybe focused on an individual chapter, that was their thing. But he saw the whole project as something important and worthy. Because I never turned it into a book, I felt like maybe I let him down or something. But I did publish quite a bit after that, and I've continued to sort of develop those ideas both as an artist and as a teacher."

I told him about having overheard Jason Moran telling a couple of NEC students that both he and Vijay make a point of checking in with "George," who I realized must have been George Lewis, when undertaking their various projects, and I asked how that typically worked. Iyer offered an example.

"I had a piece commissioned by American Composers Orchestra in 2007," he said. "I remember when the news broke about that the previous year, he pulled me aside. He was like, 'Look, a lot of so-called jazz people, when they get the orchestra gig, they're sort of doomed to fail, because they haven't really kept up with the times.' Checked out what one can do with orchestration, with timbre, with time, with an ensemble of that scale. Usually they have the strings play a bunch of long tones while they blow, you know? That sort of thing.

"It was true. A lot of jazz people's main points of reference for classical music are Stravinsky and older. *The Rite of Spring* was more than a hundred years ago. If that's the most contemporary that anyone gets, then we're not really taking full advantage of what's at hand. So he loaned me a bunch of scores, he put me onto some orchestration textbooks, he just hit me with a bunch of stuff. It was basically like, 'They want you to fail, so this is how you essentially defy their expectations, by knowing more than they expect you to know.'"

Iyer doesn't so much seek advice from Lewis on his projects, he said. But he has followed Lewis's scholarly path.

"The whole AACM book was born in the time that I have known him," noted Iyer. "I had met him in '94, and that was just starting to become a twinkle in his eye back then." Iyer mentioned a couple of Lewis's related scholarly articles from those years as well, "Experimental Music in Black and White: The AACM in New York, 1970–1985" and "Improvised Music since 1950: Afrological and Eurological Perspectives," and that Iyer had contributed an article to a two-volume scholarly work Lewis edited, *The Oxford Handbook of Critical Improvisation Studies*.

"In a lot of ways, we're on similar trajectories," said Iyer. "I'm kind of in a space that's like a junior version of him. I was even interviewed for his old job at UCSD [University of California San Diego]. The fact that I am out in the world as an artist, a published scholar, whose work has had a certain amount of influence in the field, and that I'm moving across different musical communities, writing for contemporary classical performers as well as somehow showing up on the creative music circuit—it's a pretty clear echo of the sort of profile that he attained."

That Iyer didn't rework his dissertation for publication as a book was because he was too busy making music. His first recording as a leader, *Memorophilia*, was released in 1995 on the San Francisco-based Asian Improv Records label. Both Steve Coleman and George Lewis made guest appearances on it. Coleman joined Iyer's acoustic trio—with Iyer's former Yale classmate Jeff Brock (who was now also studying for his PhD at UC Berkeley) on bass and Brad Hargreaves on drums—for a couple of cuts on alto sax. Lewis and his trombone were on two other tracks with a separate quintet, Spirit Complex, with tenor saxophonist (and Asian Improv co-founder) Francis Wong, cellist Kash Killion, and drummer Elliot Humberto Kavee. Yet another group on the album included Liberty Ellman on guitar, Jeff Bilmes on electric bass, and Kavee on drums. In a 2014 master class with Jason Moran at New England Conservatory, Iyer acknowledged having taken a kitchen-sink approach to his debut.[36] "It was almost as if I thought it was going to be my last album," he said. "I was twenty-three, 1995, and I just sort of put everything in it, because I figured I'd never do this again. . . . It was sort of like, This is my message to the world, because I might never get to make another thing like this."

As things actually played out, his second album, *Architextures*, appeared in 1998, the same year Iyer completed his PhD and moved to New York. It, too, was on Asian Improv, consisted entirely of Iyer compositions, and featured the acoustic trio with Brock and Hargreaves on half of its tracks. The remaining tracks were performed by an octet that included Rudresh Mahanthappa, who had moved to New York from Chicago the previous year. In New York, Iyer and Mahanthappa forged a partnership that, over the next decade, saw them building their reputations among the jazz cognoscenti while establishing a place for themselves within the music as Indian Americans. Mahanthappa appeared on Iyer's quartet albums *Panoptic Modes* (2001), *Blood Sutra* (2003), *Reimagining* (2005), and *Tragicomic* (2008); Iyer appeared on Mahanthappa's *Black Water* (2002), *Mother Tongue* (2004), and *Codebook* (2006); and the pair made a piano/alto sax duo album together titled *Raw Materials* (2006).

Meanwhile, Iyer stayed busy with an array of side projects. He formed an experimental trio called Fieldwork with alto saxophonist Steve Lehman and, on drums, first Elliot Humberto Kavee and later Tyshawn Sorey. He began collaborating with the poet, producer, and performance artist Mike Ladd on a series of politically charged projects, having first encountered Ladd in a late-1990s double bill at the House of Blues in Cambridge, where Iyer was playing keyboards in the San Francisco hip-hop group Midnight Voices. Iyer appeared on several albums with Burnt Sugar, an Afrofuturist ensemble founded by writer and guitarist Greg Tate, who used the "conduction" technique originated by Butch Morris[37] to lead a revolving cast of band members in free improvisations. Iyer produced an album, *The Chicago Project* (2008), for a fellow Burnt Sugar alum and onetime AACM member, the saxophonist, composer, and visual artist Matana Roberts. And he performed in Blue Arc, a band led by the poet, critic, and author Amiri Baraka.[38]

Most significantly, Iyer in those years joined the bands of two AACM elders. He began playing with Roscoe Mitchell, a founding member of the Art Ensemble of Chicago, around 2001, as a last-minute substitute for a European tour. After a troubling start—Mitchell repeatedly asked Iyer to stop playing during their first several performances together—Iyer realized that Mitchell wanted him to contribute something more of his own to how the musicians were interacting, rather than merely following the others. The experience profoundly altered Iyer's approach to making music.

Iyer explained this change in his approach during an onstage interview and listening session that preceded his four-night residency at the SFJAZZ Center in February 2017. "I used to record these gigs," Iyer told the audience, "and when I got home I played it for my friends—for Rudresh, people I'd been playing with for years by then. I said, 'Guess who this is.' And they said, 'I don't know. Marylin Crispell? Or maybe Cecil [Taylor]? No, it's not Cecil. Is it Mal Waldron? No. Who is it?' They didn't recognize me. It didn't sound like the me from before. It was the new me. . . .

"I've come to hate that sound of imitative playing," he added. "Actually what you want to do is make space for them to be fully present. But not by just laying out, but by finding your own path in music. And you can only do that by listening. You can't do that by not listening. So it's not about not listening. It's about not forcing the conversation, but actually just riding it, and stepping back from it so that the interaction reveals itself as this kind of beautiful braided lattice of counterpoint."

Iyer stayed on in Mitchell's two-piano Note Factory band for several years, recording two albums with Mitchell, fellow pianist Craig Taborn, and the rest of the nine-piece ensemble. He also joined the second iteration of trumpeter and composer Wadada Leo Smith's Golden Quartet, which Smith completely reconstituted after the death in 2004 of bassist Malachi Favors. Smith thought the new group, with John Lindberg on bass and Ronald Shannon Jackson on drums, was even better than the original, which had also included Anthony Davis on piano and Jack DeJohnette on drums. "Let's say the other quartet was like John the Baptist," Smith told me, in a 2005 interview for the *Boston Globe*. "This quartet is like Jesus Christ. I mean, if I can use a metaphor like that."[39] Eleven years later, in another piece for the same newspaper, Smith summarized for me what had caused him to hire Iyer: "He played the complete range. His hands were large enough to play chords that I would write, which have five or six pitches and cover more than an octave or two. He could play lyrical, he could play all kinds of energetic, jagged stuff. And he also could play anything anybody else thought that he could play."[40]

That second conversation took place after Smith's *Ten Freedom Summers* had been a finalist for the 2013 Pulitzer Prize for Music and Smith had entered a period of extraordinary productivity. *A Cosmic Rhythm with Each Stroke* was newly released, and Smith and Iyer were about to play music from it to open the Iyer-curated 2016 Fromm Concerts at Harvard. Titled "Creative Music Convergences," the two nights of concerts included performances by Nicole Mitchell, Craig Taborn, the Steve Lehman Octet, and Tyshawn Sorey and his double trio, among others.[41] I asked Iyer whether he could describe what he had learned from his years of working with Smith in terms non-musicians could understand.

"It's probably his wisdom in the moment," Iyer answered. "What you learn from working with an elder who's been making creative music for more decades than you have: you learn how to make choices and how to respond to certain situations. Observing that has been so educational. Also, the way he talks about music in human terms. In a lot of ways, music is this mysterious process, maybe even a mysterious substance or something. He doesn't let go of that. He has a way of describing it, encapsulating it, in a way that both embraces the mystery and elucidates. Because it doesn't get bogged down with technical language. As rigorous as his process is and his compositional language is, it's something that really anybody can enter into.

"That wisdom about how to communicate, I think, comes partly from his spiritual practice, which has evolved and transformed over the years. His way of cutting to the heart of things, or seeing the truth of a situation. Seeing the essence of a person and embracing it. He's a welcoming and nurturing kind of person without sacrificing his own ideals and aesthetics. He also has very strong opinions, as you would want from any artist. He has an amazing amount of knowledge—so it's not just wisdom, it's a lot of information he has at his fingertips. He's studied Duke Ellington, Miles Davis, Louis Armstrong, and Michael Jackson. The civil rights movement, Rastafarianism, Sufi teachings. He knows about basically anything you can think of. He's very astute about politics. He can talk about basketball. He's one of those Chicago cats. That's kind of how it is."

Iyer did not bring up another key thing he learned from Smith, because it hadn't happened yet. But I observed him recounting it in the same online broadcast of the SFJAZZ Center interview in which Iyer had spoken of touring with Roscoe Mitchell.

"Not long ago, we were on the road in Europe," Iyer told the audience, "and one day someone asked [Smith] about the word *cool*. I've used that word, I think, my whole life. And he said something about it that shook me, and I'm still thinking about it constantly. It actually kind of redefined it for me. And I mention that he comes from a lineage of resistance and a lifelong path of revolutionary art making. He said that this word *cool*—that everyone associates with jazz, right?—what it actually means, not just to him but what it has always meant, is not just being easygoing. Actually it's about retaining your composure in the face of ugliness and refusing to be bothered by the smallness of another person. So if someone says, 'You can't come in this door,' and I say, 'Cool,' that doesn't mean *that's* cool. It means *I'm* cool, no matter what you say. And that means it's actually a method of resistance. Think about that. *Birth of the Cool.* 'Cool jazz.' Whenever you think of that word in relation to that music, think of it as a method of resistance, of every day how you get through it. Think about that.

"OK, so this is this piece called 'Passage,' " Iyer continued, introducing a track from *A Cosmic Rhythm with Each Stroke.* "And I'll tell you another thing about—I'm talking too much, this is a listening party—one last thing I'll say about it is, I wrote this piece, and then later when we were doing an interview, [Smith] told me what the piece was about. I said, 'Oh my God, you're right. I'd never thought about that.' He said the word *passage* refers to the right of every human being to move freely across this planet, which means it's actually about the refugee crisis. So think about that, too."

The night after that listening session, Iyer played separate duo performances with both Smith and Rudresh Mahanthappa. His working with Mahanthappa, after roughly a decade of playing in each other's bands, had by that point become a rarity. Iyer became focused on developing his trio with Stephan Crump on bass and Marcus Gilmore on drums. Mahanthappa was left off of five of twelve tracks on Iyer's 2008 quartet album *Tragicomic.* Mahanthappa, meanwhile, was gravitating toward projects involving guitar rather than piano. In both cases, the shift in focus paid dividends. Mahanthappa's two releases that same year, *Kinsmen* and *Apti*, increased the saxophonist's visibility considerably, leading to coverage in the *New Yorker* and an appearance on *Fresh Air* with Terry Gross. *Kinsmen*, in particular, attracted notice for making its Indian influences more blatant than on his past projects.

Iyer, too, took a turn in that direction in those years, forming a trio with two outstanding Indian musicians who had settled in the United States, guitarist Prasanna and tabla virtuoso Nitin Mitta, when Iyer was asked in 2007 to perform a concert to commemorate sixty years of Indian independence. The collaboration led to Iyer's 2011 album *Tirtha* (the sanskrit word for "crossing") four years later. The album was the most direct engagement of Carnatic and Hindustani influences yet recorded by Iyer. But, like Mahanthappa, he had been subtly embedding them in his music all along.

"All the rhythmic stuff that's been in my music since the early or mid-'90s has borne a trace of that influence, and continues to up until now," he told me. "The first piece on the sextet album is dealing with that rhythm, rhythms that can be traced to Carnatic music. My version of 'The Star of a Story' has a rhythmic element in it that I learned from hearing mridangam players. So it's been in there the entire time, from record one to—whatever it is—record twenty-three or twenty-four. It's been there literally the entire time."

The decision to work with Prasanna and Mitta had been inspired by a similar project undertaken by one of his piano heroes. "I had wanted to basically play the tabla-type rhythms and figures and grooves on the piano, and the reason I wanted to do that was because of Randy Weston," Iyer explained. "Because I saw Randy Weston's African Rhythms Trio in the mid-'90s and had a sort of revelation, because it was like hand drums and piano, and the tactile element that kind of unified it was exactly sort of what I was seeking in my trying to bring together these various Indian rhythmic forms and techniques and structures with the piano. I saw him doing something similar with African drumming and the piano, that made sense at some level. I've told him this, and he totally hears it. He hears it in what I do. He's on board with it.

"But the fact that my playing is compatible with a tabla player is because I've studied what tabla players do, and what mridangam players do, and also the fact that it's compatible with someone who's playing ragas and gamakas is because I studied that, and thought about, not how to do that on the piano, but how to do something that would work with it. And *Tirtha* isn't the only example; it's just the one that made it onto an album that someone thought they could sell. But there are plenty of other examples out there."[42]

Tirtha was one of four profile-raising albums Iyer put out with the German label ACT Music between 2009 and 2012. Another was *Solo* (2010), which is Iyer by himself on a mix of originals and interpretations of Ellington, Monk, Steve Coleman, the standard "Darn That Dream," and the Michael Jackson hit "Human Nature." It had been the label's idea for Iyer to record a solo album, and he said that he would do it differently if he could. But the album led to a series of solo performances afterward that proved invaluable to his development as an artist.

"I learned much more about what's at stake, what's involved, after making that album," Iyer told me. "It changed me, actually." He described one concert in particular, at the Beethoven House in Bonn, Germany. "That piano that they have there, it's a Steinway D," he said. "That still remains the best piano I've ever played, and I think there's something I discovered that night about what remains possible with the piano, like the dimensions of expression that I never really knew existed.

"I'm self-taught, right? By self-taught I mean I've apprenticed with people, I've listened to a lot of music. I've been at the piano since I was four. I don't have many excuses at this point. So it wasn't until 2010 that I realized there were these other dimensions of the piano that one could kind of put yourself in contact with, and dialogue with, and express yourself through. It's like I just discovered this whole new, five-dimensional universe that no one told me about. In the last eight, nine years, I've been trying to catch up." He laughed. "But I feel good about some of the solo pieces that I've put on some of the recent albums, like that version of 'Blood Count' that's on *Break Stuff*, and the first track on *Mutations*.[43] I feel good about those. Like, those are sort of dealing with what I'm talking about in a way."

"I like the solo album, too, for what that's worth," I told him.[44]

"That's the one that I mentioned that Eric Reed singled out," he replied. "So it's not like it's a bunch of bullshit on there. I realize that there's much deeper to go, but there always is."

The Iyer albums for ACT with the greatest impact, however, were the two he did with his principal working group, his trio with Crump and Gilmore. *Historicity* (2009) earned Iyer his first Grammy nomination, for "Best Jazz Instrumental Album, Individual or Group." More importantly, it established the trio's free-flowing interplay and its adeptness at conjuring creative covers of both familiar popular music (Stevie Wonder, M.I.A., Bernstein/Sondheim) and works by composer heroes (Andrew Hill, Julius Hemphill). Iyer's albums prior to *Historicity* had featured his own compositions almost exclusively, the lone exceptions being Iyer playing John Lennon's "Imagine" solo to close out the 2005 album *Reimagining* and two more on 2008's *Tragicomic*, a solo version of the standard "I'm All Smiles" and a trio exploration of Bud Powell's "Comin' Up."

The shift from quartet to trio also seemed to give the music room to breathe, creating space that called to mind the same sort of "sound of listening" that had impressed Iyer when he first discovered Thelonious Monk. The trio built on all these things on *Accelerando* (2012), whose focus on movement and dance was underscored by the set-closing "The Village of the Virgins," excerpted from the suite Duke Ellington composed for Alvin Ailey's ballet "The River."[45] Once again, the trio performed a mix of originals and unique spins on existing pieces, among the latter works by Herbie Nichols and Henry Threadgill alongside pop tunes by Flying Lotus and Rod Temperton as well as a trio version of "Human Nature."

Accelerando did not capture another Grammy nomination, but it did land Iyer on the covers of both *JazzTimes* and *DownBeat* magazines. In the case of *Down-Beat*, he was being celebrated for having won five categories in the magazine's sixtieth annual critics poll: Jazz Artist, Jazz Album, Jazz Group, Piano, and Rising Star Composer.

Iyer's work had received favorable notices from the beginning: his first album after settling in New York, *Panoptic Modes*, was among a half-dozen *New Yorker*'s Steve Futterman selected as best albums of 2001, listed with Moran's *Black Stars*. Critic Gary Giddins featured him with Moran and Iverson after catching the three of them during a week of solo piano performances at the Jazz Standard in 2002 (Matthew Shipp and Fred Hersch were among the other pianists featured), singling out Iyer's "stirring triptych of Ellington's 'Le Sucrier Velours,' Monk's 'Epistrophy,' and a Cecil-like barrage engineered around Hendrix's 'Hey Joe' for special praise.[46]

But the quintuple win in *DownBeat* marked the beginning of a new level of visibility for Iyer.[47] That same summer he took over for Dave Douglas as artistic director of the Banff International Workshop for Jazz and Creative Music, and earlier that year he was awarded both a Doris Duke Artist Award and a Greenfield Prize as a composer. In October 2013, he received his MacArthur Foundation fellowship (joining past recipients Zenón, Moran, and George Lewis), and in January 2014 began his professorship at Harvard. He moved from one German record label to another, releasing his first recording for ECM, *Mutations*, in 2014, quickly followed by the film *Radhe Radhe: Rites of Holi* (2014), the trio album *Break Stuff* (2015), *A Cosmic Rhythm with Each Stroke* (2016), and the sextet album *Far from Over* (2017). The centerpiece of *Mutations* was a ten-part composition for string quartet and piano that Iyer had written nearly a decade earlier, and its release coincided with a number of new compositions by Iyer in a classical vein. Meanwhile, Iyer somehow found time to record on occasional sideman gigs, with artists such as Dave Douglas, Arturo O'Farrill, Ralph Peterson, and Trio 3—the latter a cooperative unit comprising the elder masters Oliver Lake, Reggie Workman, and Andrew Cyrille.[48]

All this busyness and success did not sit well with everyone. The commissions and grant money that began flowing Iyer's way around 2012 must have been a particular sore point for Iyer's detractors. Shortly after his MacArthur fellowship was announced in September 2013 the naysaying went public on social media, where the sniping at rivals perceived to be overrated and/or getting too much attention that used to take place in the jazz publications is now more likely to surface. Guitarist Kurt Rosenwinkel, another influential musician of the same generation as Iyer (they were born almost exactly one year apart), posted the following on Facebook: "Well I guess I will be the one who says it: Vijay Iyer is not a great pianist. sorry, Vijay, nothing personal, but amongst the deluge of praise I must as a voice of the initiated be one who gives a counterbalance. No touch, no tone, no melody, nothing exceptional in any way. sorry, im not hating im just deglorifying. its just not true. sorry."

In an early comment on the lengthy thread that resulted, pianist Mark Shilansky, having seconded Rosenwinkel's low opinion of Iyer's touch, added something that suggested what might really be provoking their complaints: "I wonder if we'd have such a reaction to him if he wasn't so hyped, and THEN winning the MacArthur." Rosenwinkel's follow-up confirmed that the attention Iyer was getting weighed heavily in what was bothering him:

> well i am mostly reacting to the hype, because it is not deserved. I've got nothing against him, i dont know if he worked the system or not, all i know is that everyone is falling all over him and there really is no musical reason i can discern. I think it says alot about the people who write about Jazz, who the critics are, who the people are who go along with all of that, how the jazz industry latches onto someone who comes through the pipeline in a certain way that gets promoted and lauded, etc. Its a shame that there isnt more credibility and integrity vis a vis the music that this happens. Nothing against Vijay, its not his fault and i regret any reflection on him for my statement. He is obviously a determined and respectable musician. But its just way overblown, out of proportion and almost orgiastic from the writers themselves. Its about business mostly.

Others began posting comments pro and con. Iyer's defenders included musicians with whom he had worked, among them Rez Abbasi, Josh Roseman, Marcus Gilmore, and Tyshawn Sorey. Gilmore's opinions were particularly intriguing, in part because, aside from having worked in Iyer's trio for several years, he bridged the worlds of postmodern (he had already worked with Steve Coleman and Christian Scott before joining Iyer while still in high school) and straight-ahead jazz (the legendary bebop drummer Roy Haynes is Gilmore's grandfather). Gilmore dribbled out his series of comments via his cell phone, in response to a pair of Rosenwinkel's assertions: "Vijay Iyer is not even anywhere close to being the greatest jazz pianist or artist right now" and "what has his trio done that isnt what we have already heard from the Bad Plus, Esjorn Svennson [sic],[49] The Bandwagon, or Brad Mehldau?"

Gilmore's comments follow, the ellipses indicating their piecemeal arrival in the thread:

> I've never heard Vijay refer to himself as a jazz artist or jazz composer . . . although he has been highly influenced by the legacy of Thelonious Monk, Cecil Taylor, Muhal Richard Abrams, Andrew Hill, Henry Threadgill, Duke Ellington etc . . . Herbie Nichols, George Lewis, Roscoe Mitchell, Steve Coleman, . . . is there even a greatest jazz artist now? I honestly don't even know what that means . . . I've listened to quite a bit of Brad's albums as well as Bandwagon. I've checked out a couple of the bad plus. I've even listened to some of EST trio. surely there are some similarities. I don't know what you've heard of Vijay's. I will say he has composed some truly unique material. It's easy for me to say because I've played a great deal of his music. . . . I've also played with Jason, Brad, and Ethan. They are all extremely unique.

I recall Iyer having something to say on the thread himself—something remarkably level-headed and civil considering the criticism aimed his way—but have been unable to relocate it.[50] But a month later Iyer began a thread of his own sparked by a line from an academic review of the Robert Glasper album *Black Radio 2*.[51] The thread, begun November 7, 2013, used the line as its subject heading: "a common reaction amongst a sector of traditionalists within the jazz community." One of Iyer's own first comments on his thread read simply: "Same sh*t, different pianist, different month."

"The quote in this status message came from an academic (ethnomusicologist)'s review of Rob's new album," Iyer went on to explain in a subsequent comment, "and I was struck by how accurately the phrase described not just Rob's and my recent experiences but countless experiences in the history of this music. That phrase could be from a review of *A Love Supreme*, or *Bitches Brew*, or *Tomorrow Is the Question!*[52] or just about any classic record that we now hold to be canonical, as well as plenty of crap albums too. But what characterizes all of it is that some group of people wishes to assert that an artist does not belong to this loose, fuzzy, problematic category that gets called jazz. That kind of assertion is what gets people branded as traditionalists, in a music that's actually not even old enough to have any."

When another commenter noted that the jazz community had become more cutthroat and competitive since the 1970s, when he said musicians endorsed one another's applications for grant money and even "C List" musicians could make a good living, Iyer responded: "The obliteration of most NEA funding under [President Ronald] Reagan and [North Carolina Senator Jesse] Helms, the drying up/ starving of the jazz circuit, the consolidation of power in a few major labels, the neoconservative movement (and the invention of a 'tradition' that you were in or out of), the master narrative that ignored half of the music's history, the jazz education industry's irresponsible output of thousands upon thousands of career-seeking musicians glutting the marketplace, Napster, Youtube, Facebook—these are a few things that have happened since the NEA was supporting the jazz community in the 70s."

I hadn't asked Iyer about any of this the first couple of times I interviewed him, having read somewhere that he'd decided he'd said all he was going to say about it. But then in subsequent conversations with musicians about the artists I was featuring in this book, a couple of them, off the record, had questioned his abilities. One said Iyer's music left him cold but noted the many commissions and prizes Iyer kept winning. Another called him "the most overrated jazz musician in history, given the amount of *DownBeat* awards he's won"—a view he suggested upward of 95 percent of his colleagues share. This second critic went so far as to acknowledge

Iyer to be an excellent composer, arranger, and conceptualist. "He's an excellent musician, he's just not an excellent jazz improviser."

And yet there are numerous musicians who disagree. As zealous a guardian of jazz tradition as Wynton Marsalis was said to admire Iyer's work. Gayle King, guest-hosting an episode of the PBS program *Charlie Rose* featuring Iyer in March 2015, began the interview by telling Iyer what Marsalis had told her about him: "He's very smart, I love him, I respect him, he makes great music, and I look forward to playing with him one day," and, "This cat can really play."[53]

Jason Moran praised Iyer in a "Before and After" for *JazzTimes*, that magazine's copycat spin on the Leonard Feather–originated "Blindfold Test" in *DownBeat*, in which musicians attempt to identify the lead instrumentalists on unidentified jazz tracks.[54] Craig Taborn and Kris Davis, like Moran, happily played duo with him at the Harvard symposium honoring Geri Allen. Allen had herself involved Iyer and Moran in the University of Pittsburgh–hosted Mary Lou Williams Cyber Symposium, which featured Iyer, Moran, and Allen performing a three-piano improvisation remotely from Harvard, Columbia, and Pitt in real time using Internet2 technology.

Terri Lyne Carrington and Esperanza Spalding played with Iyer at the Geri Allen memorials at both Newport and Harvard. When Iyer weighed in on a Facebook thread begun by vibraphonist Warren Wolf asking why so many jazz musicians insist on making complicated music aimed primarily at their fellow jazz musicians, Wolf's response was full of praise.[55] Also complimentary was the guitarist Matthew Stevens, who told me, "I can't say enough about [Iyer]. He's great." When I told him about the musicians I'd talked to who thought otherwise, Stevens called it "an occupational hazard" that came with the amount of critical acclaim Iyer had received. "From my perspective as a musician," Stevens said, "it's important not to let that stuff influence you one way or the other."

Then there were the three musician fans of Iyer named Christian. Christian Scott was effusive when asked his opinion of Iyer.[56] Christian Sands, aside from sharing a piano bench with him at Newport, had studied composition with him. And Sands's sometime employer, Christian McBride, admired Iyer's work sufficiently to have booked the three Iyer performances at Newport that year, McBride's first as the festival's artistic director.

I spoke with McBride in 2016, the summer before he succeeded George Wein in that role, seeking his input on the musicians I was featuring in this book. McBride enthusiastically supported Iyer's inclusion. And the Rosenwinkel brouhaha emerged elsewhere in the conversation, from a discussion of the saxophonist Kamasi Washington, whose three-CD *The Epic* had won Washington national acclaim in 2015. McBride rued how success can put a target on a jazz musician's back.

"I just finished a three-part seminar, a three-part series about Cannonball Adderley at the Jazz Museum in Harlem," he told me, "and one of the things that I had said about the jazz community, and I said this in jest, is that the absolute worst thing that could ever happen for a jazz musician is success. The minute you become one of those few musicians that sort of 'crosses over,' quote, unquote, right away your credibility is questioned, almost all the time, by the bulk of your community. Once Kamasi got hot I heard these people buzzing around WBGO, 'Why is this guy so hot all of a sudden? He's just riding on that Kendrick Lamar stuff. That cat, he can't really play.' And I'm sitting there going, 'Wow, I didn't think people still had these kind of arguments in 2016.'

"Now, this one particular person asked me what I thought about Kamasi, and I said, 'Well, I dig Kamasi a lot, we worked together in Gerald Wilson's big band.' And they said, 'He played with Gerald Wilson?' I said, 'Yeah. He's not exactly a newcomer. I worked with Kamasi about ten years ago. He played in Gerald Wilson's big band for a while, and we also did some recordings together with George Duke.' And they went, 'Really?' I said, 'You guys should do some history before you go around saying somebody "doesn't deserve" something.' "

That made me think of Rosenwinkel. I asked McBride if he had heard about the Facebook controversy involving Iyer.

McBride chuckled.

"You know we went to high school together," he reminded me. (I had, in fact, seen McBride and Rosenwinkel play together as high schoolers in my *DownBeat* days, along with their Philadelphia High School for the Creative & Performing Arts classmate Joey DeFrancesco, at a composition for high school and college bands that the magazine was involved in.)

"Something else about Vijay," McBride said, "is that—I've read this somewhere; he might have tweeted it or whatever it was—somebody acknowledged him as one of the hottest up-and-comers in the jazz world, and Vijay said, 'Considering I did my first tour with Steve Coleman in 1996, I'm glad they're still considering me a newcomer.' When he started getting hot, it wasn't like he hadn't already been on the scene for a long time before. I like his diversity. I've heard his trio many times, and they did the Monk tune on *Break Stuff*: I think they did 'Work.' It was swinging. And then he also was part of this project led by the bassist Carlo De Rosa, and Justin Brown played drums. Walter Smith played saxophone, I'm pretty sure. I can't remember who was playing saxophone,[57] but anyway it was sort of like a hardcore fusion thing. Vijay's playing Rhodes and keyboards on there. And I'm thinking, most people who don't like what Vijay does with his trio I'm sure have not heard this. . . . Successful musicians are always having to prove that they can do what's not hot. It's a shame that has to happen, but most everyone I can think of who has had that sort of success can do that. Vijay, Joshua Redman, Jason. Glasper, of course. In the sixties it was somebody like a Cannonball."

Two other people I spoke with disagreed with Iyer's musician critics and offered explanations for what motivated it.

Reid Anderson of the Bad Plus expressed misgivings about certain artists receiving disproportionate amounts of praise while comparable talents are ignored. "I do like his music," he told me during an interview at his Brooklyn apartment in 2017, shortly after Iyer headlined at the Village Vanguard for the first time. "My opinion about Vijay is he's obviously been given a lot of accolades, and arguably too much—for anyone. I think it's not doing the community at large any favors when they pick one person. He's one of the people in the community. He's very talented, he's very smart, but he's not towering above everyone else, frankly. I don't know him, really; I hope he wouldn't be offended by this. I do think he is certainly, undeniably very talented. And he's deserving as much as everyone else is deserving. He's been given a lot more than most other people, and I think that that's a double-edged sword, too. I'm sure it weighs on him as well. I'm sure he's not unaware of that. But I do like his music. I put his records on. I just went and saw him at the Vanguard. My opinion is, he's one among many talented and creative people out there, most of whom deserve more credit and respect."

Anderson, incidentally, noted in passing that the same applies to his own band when I asked his opinion of Jason Moran: "Jason? I love Jason. He's one of those guys, he's gotten a lot of credit as well. He's really remarkable. I think it's really well deserved. Again, like the Vijay thing, as much as I would say he deserves all of the accolades he's gotten—and you could say this about the Bad Plus, too—these trends come along and one person gets all the attention, all the praise, and it's hard to maintain a sense of proportion. But Jason is a really great cat."

Esperanza Spalding was actually responding to something else, but her answer could explain why Iyer's critics belittle Iyer's playing: his approach to making music differs from their own. I'd suggested to Spalding that jazz was antithetical to the nativism being unleashed by the new Trump administration when I spoke with her in the spring of 2017, ahead of a Boston appearance of her trio with Geri Allen and Terri Lyne Carrington. She wasn't buying it. Whereas I was thinking of political differences, and how jazz is international rather than xenophobic, Spalding was thinking of how musicians react to one another's music, and argued that Trump's contempt for ideas and approaches to governing that differ from his own is very similar.

"The tendency is for people to be exclusionary," she explained. " 'What I'm good at, and what I like, is truth, and the rest of it is subpar.' I don't think we've managed to escape that in the music world at all." Spalding made clear that her qualms toward that tendency apply just as much when she's the beneficiary of it. "Some-body I was hanging out with said, 'The fact that this audience didn't like your music is a testament to how American music consumers are anti-intellectual,' " she told me, "and I thought, 'God, that was a giant leap.' "

The off-the-record critics I'd spoken to, like Rosenwinkel, are skilled and inno-vative musicians. But their tastes, like his, tend to run toward European and Latin music when they build on jazz vocabulary, musics that jazz had been embracing since at least the 1950s. Material that came later, Indian music or hip-hop, say, or the experimentalism of the AACM and M-Base, didn't seem to interest them. Spalding's point might very well apply here.

In any case, the preponderance of musicians on the long list above of musicians who approve of Iyer are African American. The two musicians who had expressed doubts about Iyer's prowess as a jazz pianist, like Rosenwinkel, are both Caucasian. I found myself pondering what to make of that. I decided that African American culture would have good reason to be open to improvisation and innovation, given the ugly history of race in this country. That, too, might have had something to do with who admired Iyer's music and who dismissed it.

I decided it was worth asking Iyer about, and gave him a version of my thoughts on African American culture's receptivity toward innovation.

"All of that's fine," he said, "but I don't think that you've heard all of my albums. I can tell you for a fact that none of those people have heard really almost any of my music, including Kurt. At the time, part of what he was blindsided by is that he had never listened to me. So his way of catching up is clicking around on a couple YouTube links, and saying, 'Oh, what's the deal?' Why is it that people think they can speak about me without listening? That's the real question. He even said so, because actually in the time of that stupid little fucking dustup, he and I had a pretty extended private-message exchange. I was like, 'I've made twenty-something albums, so I don't know what you've heard of mine.' He said, 'I haven't heard much, I admit, but I've heard enough.' Because he teaches at whatever school in Berlin or something, he said, 'I can tell within the first few seconds of someone's audition materials whether they can play or not.' I was like, 'I don't know what you're talking about, man.' But the fact that white men will speak publicly about you without listening to you . . ."

I cut in to clarify that these other musicians who criticized him had emphasized that they were speaking off the record.

"Maybe it's off the record, but it's the same phenomenon," Iyer responded. "They haven't taken into account the entirety of what I've done, or who I've played with, who I've apprenticed with. They don't know anything about me. In fact, they'll say things that are counterfactual about me. Including, I remember Doug—what's his name—Wamble, said in one of those Rosenwinkel threads that I'm ignoring a hundred years of black music. What am I supposed to say? Like, this is a fucking bubble: these people are not paying attention to facts, they're just high-fiving each other because they're getting together and bullying a non-black person of color. So that's what it came down to. It's just white male aggression, that's how I read it. It's nothing else.

"Because I know that I've apprenticed with elders, I've played with elders, I've studied the tradition for decades. I've transcribed all of Monk's music, I've transcribed a bunch of Duke Ellington's music. I've recorded Monk's music, Ellington's music, Coltrane's music, Strayhorn's music, Andrew Hill, Bud Powell, Herbie Nichols, Julius Hemphill, Stevie Wonder. I've done all of that, it's on all of my albums. You don't even have to listen; you can look at the titles, you know? I don't understand why people think they can get away with speaking about me without listening, but the real thing is that they couldn't understand why they had never paid attention to me before. And the reason that they hadn't is also racism, like they didn't think that I was relevant. They had their own possessive investment in the music, and they saw me as outside of it. They ignored the fact that I've been here the entire time, and they still do. So I don't have anything more to say to those people or about them, except that they're a bunch of ignorant jackasses. I don't know what else to say.

"I remember Eric Reed, in the aftermath of all that, he went and checked out some stuff and he sent me a message. He said, 'That version of "Black and Tan Fantasy" was funky as hell.' That's Eric Reed, who played with Wynton. I don't need more cosigning, because I already know that I played with Reggie Workman, and I played with Wadada, who grew up in the vicinity of Emmett Till. I played with Steve Coleman for years, and I've played with elders. I've played with Donald Bailey, who played with Carmen McRae and Jimmy Smith—I played with him for years. I've played with all these elders, who maybe are not part of the obvious power structure of mainstream jazz, but to me, I've been on the ground working on this music for a long time. No one would say to me, who had assessed what I've done, that I've ignored the tradition. It doesn't make any sense. It simply isn't a fact, so when people say it, you have to ask why they're saying it. Not whether it applies to me, because it doesn't. In fact, I have more of an understanding of the tradition than a lot of people who go to the music schools, because those music school curricula leave out the last fifty years of the music—of music that's one hundred years old. How can you neglect half of the history of something and call yourself an expert on it? I mean, that doesn't make any sense. You know?

"So I don't know what more to say. You think that covers it? What else can I say? Because I'm literally asking you, because I don't know how else to address it. You're not the first person to pose this to me. This has been an ongoing thing. I mean, that MacArthur business was almost five years ago, but it wasn't the first time, and it wasn't the last time. So I really don't know what to say. I think it's also the people that, like you pointed out, it's mainly coming from white people. It has to do with their problems with regard to the tradition, what is it for them and why can't they come to terms with something that they're not addressing about it? That's the real problem, and that's its own book right there."

I said something about how Dave King, the drummer in the Bad Plus, was another musician I'd seen maligned on Facebook. King, like Iyer, has developed a recognizable approach to his instrument that annoys traditionalists by straying too noticeably from what came before it.

"Look, look," Iyer said, cutting me off. "That's the thing. I don't sound different from what's come before. It's more that the narrative of what's come before is wrong. It's just dead wrong. Because I sound like Geri Allen, and I sound like Andrew Hill, and I sound like Randy Weston, and I sound like McCoy. I mean, at different moments I sound like different [pianists]. But also, each of them have their own ideas, and so I have been inspired to develop and pursue my own ideas in the ways that they did. And it can't all be about how much you sound like Herbie [Hancock]. It really just can't. That's not enough. And that's what really it seems to boil down to: your Herbie-ness. Because when people talk about authentic jazz playing, they're basically talking about what Herbie sounded like in the early '60s. And there's a lot of other stuff that's happened, before and since, that we have to be able to accommodate. Herbie sounded that way because of a lot of things. I mean, he was influenced by a lot of things, which included Bill Evans and Stravinsky, and that guy who wrote for the, uh, I guess Clare Fischer. A certain harmonic kind of . . ." He let the thought trail off. "But then also he was coming out of a hard bop kind of groove-oriented thing.

"And you know what's funny about what gets said about me, even in this last wave of reviews for my latest album, is that they'll say that it's surprising that I groove. I've recorded 'Mystic Brew,' and 'Galang,' and 'The Star of a Story,' and 'Human Nature,' and quite a bunch of these things, right? It shouldn't be a surprise, unless you have your own hang-up about *what* I am, and you think that I have no business here. So that's what I find happening. It's actually more like what would be called a repetition compulsion. People are repeating the same utterances, even though the facts say otherwise. But the facts are often kind of inconvenient. So, for example, you know Fred Kaplan? He's written the same review about me seven or eight times, which is always that 'In the past Vijay Iyer's music was too structural and too mathematical, but not this time. Somehow he's managed to get something close to a soul.'" Iyer laughed. "He literally says stuff like that, but he's been saying it since like 2005. And he said it again like a month ago. Like, he's still saying it, over and over again."

"I think he also said it about Rudresh's album *Kinsmen*, too," I told Iyer, "if I remember right."

"Yeah, basically the subtext is, 'Well, Indian people should be engineers . . .' "

"Right," I added, laughing, "and accountants and whatever."[58]

". . . and instead here's somebody playing something that I almost empathize with," Iyer continued. "It's kind of like he lapses back into the narrative of 'This person obviously doesn't belong anywhere close to this music.' And by the way, he's a white man saying this, so that has something to do with it. So this is kind of the dynamic. What you're pointing out is the same dynamic, which is that it's not in reference to any effects of any kind; it's actually about themselves. They're talking about themselves, and what you have to analyze is how they're talking about themselves in those moments."

I told Iyer that once, when *Accelerando* had just been released, I had been playing it on my car stereo while driving my younger son to preschool, who at one point suddenly piped up from his carseat, "This song rocks!" The point being that even a small child could recognize the visceral, groove-oriented attraction of Iyer's music.

Iyer chuckled politely at the story. "But they still want to hold something against me," he said of his critics. "It's really weird. At this point, I probably sound like I'm complaining, and I'm not, because I have not suffered in any way because of any of that. Like, I have a lot of music, which is more than a lot of them can say for themselves. A lot of it, like you said, is something about jealousy. But the reason I have a life in music is because I have a community of artists who I feel connected to, and who respect me, and whom I've learned from. We nurture each other. In fact, when that shit happened with Kurt, that week was the premiere of *Open City*, which was the large ensemble project with Teju [Cole], and basically all the musicians that I love, who are very dear to me: Tyshawn, Marcus, and Graham [Haynes], Ambrose [Akinmusire], the young people . . ."

"Elena Pinderhughes?" I asked, naming a superb flutist I'd become aware of a few years earlier through her work with Christian Scott.

"Elena played. Rajna [Swaminathan], Okkyung [Lee], Mat Maneri. You know, it was family. *Josh*—actually, Josh [Roseman] was in it," Iyer replied. "So while all that bullshit was happening, I was spending all day every day with all of them, building this music together, and that was like the antidote to all of it. It sort of neutralized the whole affair for me. 'Cause I'm like, 'Well, here's all the proof I need that those motherfuckers are wrong.' It's right here in the room with me, you know? So I don't need any more than that. I'm not out here suffering because someone like Kirk Knuffke is going on his tirades about me. It doesn't matter."

"I was just reminded that Christian Scott said that you sat in one time with his band and played 'Eye of the Hurricane,' "[59] I told him, "and he said it was the best 'Eye of the Hurricane' he ever did. And I know he plays it pretty much every night, so . . ."

Iyer laughed heartily and said, "That's great that he remembers that."

I told him that the story came up when I had asked Scott what he thought of Iyer's playing not long after hearing another musician call it into question. Scott had passionately defended Iyer, and Wynton Marsalis, too—suggesting that the musicians who talk trash about rivals of that calibre would be humiliated if they ever dared to compete toe-to-toe with them onstage.

"Well, this is the thing," Iyer responded. "All of us have gotten to where we are by making music for people. If this were all just hype and storytelling and bullshit, it wouldn't last. I've been up there making music with and for and among people. That's how this has actually come about. It's not through, *whatever*. It's not even about critics; it's actually about the way it lands with audiences, the way the regular folks respond to the music. That's really how you actually have a life in music. It doesn't come from anywhere else. Because you have to, you know, put your body on the line, and an audience, they're either going to be with it or they're not. It can't just be about a hustle, not for a lifetime. It can't. That just isn't gonna work." He laughed again. "'Cause there's nowhere to hide when you're onstage, is there?

"I mean, I know that I have stuff I have to work on," he continued, "but so does everybody, you know? That's why we're eternal students. That's the way to be in this music—learn from everybody. Billy Hart used to come see me play, because he wanted to hear what we were doing. He wanted to check out what my music was about, and what Rudresh was playing, and what Marcus was playing, and he still hips people to *Reimagining*: 'No, you need to listen to this. This is a way to play drums in complex music—like this, this is the way.' We have this kind of bond, because I've known him for twenty years, and he always shows up and he always embraces what we're doing. I've gotten to play with him a number of times—you know, the same family. And the same with, like, I remember when that business with Kurt happened that Gary Bartz came out, on Facebook, and made this really resonant public pronouncement. He's like, '*Vijay Iyer is one of us. We should be celebrating.*' That's what he said."

Iyer's interest in race and politics extends well beyond defending himself from his own white detractors. He frequently posts links on Facebook pertaining to issues such as immigration, Black Lives Matter, gender, and the election of Donald Trump. His song titles have also sometimes drawn attention to news and politics as well. "Macaca Please," from his 2008 album *Tragicomic*, references the racist term Senator George Allen of Virginia aimed at an opposition campaign member at a campaign stop during what proved his unsuccessful bid for reelection against Democrat Jim Webb in 2006. Iyer's contribution to his collaboration with Trio 3 included his three-part "Suite for Trayvon (and Thousands More)." And the title track on *Far from Over* began life at the Chicago Jazz Festival in 2008 as a celebration of Barack Obama's hoped-for victory, evolving two presidential election cycles later into a protest of Donald Trump.[60]

Months before *Far from Over* was released, Iyer had protested Trump's election more directly onstage. He and Mahanthappa were among the musicians taking part in a New York concert billed as Musicians Against Fascism on the eve of Trump's January 2017 inauguration, and Iyer's SFJAZZ Center five-night residency the following month included a series of images and words ("RESIST" and a struck-through "WHITE SUPREMACY" among them), by the visual artist Chiraag Bhakta, displayed above the stage.

The most direct expression of political activism in Iyer's recorded music, however, has come in his three collaborations with Mike Ladd. The two met in the late 1990s as part of a double bill at Boston's House of Blues, where Iyer was performing with the San Francisco-based hip-hop band Midnight Voices.[61]

"I just remember that what he was doing was not like anything that I'd heard anybody do," Iyer recalled of that first encounter with Ladd. "It was somewhere in the zone of Gil Scott-Heron, but it had this different sense of space. I guess something more *cool*, for lack of a better word, in the sense that you used earlier, which is one of composure in the face of obvious injustice and oppression, and to turn that stance into an art in its own right. And his texts: it wasn't rapping bars; it was more like these poems would kind of unfold in the space of music, and the music itself had all this mysterious texture in it. It was like somewhere between Alice Coltrane and, like, the Meters. It had a sort of futurism in it, and it also had a richness and texture. He was a big fan of Charles Stepney, the producer, so he would sample a lot of beats that Charles Stepney produced, so it had this spaciousness in it. You could hear this, like, imaginary room. That's what I remember about the beat. He had this guy working with him who played these tape loops, a bunch of little cassette tapes, and then run them through effects. Mike himself had this—he still has it—this dented analog set from the '70s called the EMS Synthi. So sonically it was this other world. And then what he was dealing with as a lyricist was also spanning eons, and it was very urbane, witty, sly, and had this wisdom. I was really amazed by it, just intoxicated and knocked out.

"Then when I moved to New York I started seeing him around more. He was living in the Bronx at the time, and he played downtown. He was part of this spoken-word movement that also included Saul Williams and the artist formerly known as

Mos Def, Yasiin Bey, and Suheir Hammad. So he was connected to that world, and he was also connected to, at the time it was called underground hip-hop, and that included El-P, who's now in the group Run the Jewels, had a band back then called Company Flow. The whole Def Jux label. So there was this group called Cannibal Ox. There was another group called Antipop Consortium.

"It was a very rich and innovative moment for hip-hop from my perspective. I was in my late twenties, and it seemed like something new was happening. Hip-hop had been a part of my life since I was a kid, so I think I knew something about it, and I'd been in these hip-hop bands and worked with a lot of emcees. So then to hear what felt like this rich new take on it all—there was something just really imaginative and radical about it that I found myself attracted to."

Iyer's first co-led project with Ladd came about via a commission from the Asia Society. "I thought that rather than do something that was directly about Asia or Asian-ness, per se, to think about other, looser identity formations. And in particular how you might imagine community around a certain common experience of being brown in the West. I found myself at odds with these more ethnocentric identity formations. I'm Indian, my parents are from India. India's a place of rampant, unimaginable inequality and oppression, so if I say that I'm Indian American, I'm basically aligning myself politically with two nation-states that are both profoundly problematic. So, to me, that has to be kept in check. And I noticed, especially among people in these various diasporas, that they sort of lapse into this sort of nationalism in a way that I found dangerous. I sensed something about it that wasn't committed to equality; it was actually about creating a different *inequality*.

"Historically you have these immigrant populations coming in," he explained, "and the way you become American is by internalizing anti-blackness, and I didn't want to be part of that. Because here I was building a life around my relationship to black music. It's not that I wasn't proud of my heritage, but more that I wanted to have critical engagement with it more than an unconsidered embrace of it."

The album that resulted from the Asia Society commission, *In What Language?* (2003), looked at a variety of sometimes harrowing experiences of brown people in airport terminals in the aftermath of 9/11 and the US invasion of Iraq. A second album, *Still Life with Commentator*, followed in 2007, its focus on media saturation and information overload evidenced in track titles such as "Jon Stewart on Crossfire" (with its catchy refrain "Please stop, you're hurting America / Please stop, you're hurting it bad"), "Fox 'n' Friends" (thirty-some seconds of rapid-fire whitebread gibberish), and "Mount Rather (Commentator Landscape #3: Dan Rather)"—landscapes 1 and 2 having been devoted to Aaron Brown and Shepard Smith.

It was their third collaboration that introduced me to Iyer and Ladd working as a duo, when I was assigned to review it for *JazzTimes* in 2013.[62] *Holding It Down:*

The Veterans' Dream Project explored the emotional toll taken on post-9/11 military veterans of color, based on Ladd's interviews with servicemen and women about their "PTSD nightmares and stress dreams." Two veterans—Maurice Decaul, who served a year in Iraq as a marine, and Lynn Hill, who piloted drones over Iraq and Afghanistan from an air force base in Las Vegas—contributed words and vocals to the project, which also included Pamela Z and Guillermo E. Brown on vocals, Liberty Ellman on guitar, Okkyung Lee on cello, and Kassa Overall on drums.

When I asked Iyer if he and Ladd had another project in the works, he noted that Ladd had been looking at African Americans in law enforcement and had, with funding from the Pew Foundation, interviewed a couple of dozen police officers, prison guards, and others working in law enforcement in Philadelphia. They had already tested some of the material from the new project as a module inserted into the middle of a summer 2017 performance of *Holding It Down*.

"As usual, we're dealing with some pretty harrowing stuff," Iyer told me. "But the sweep of his analysis, as a kind of amateur historian, is pretty impressive in its global reach, in terms of its political analysis—in particular thinking about the institution of the police as it historically connected to the slave patrols of the 1800s. And actually he got some of his interviewees to say that. It's not like he had to coax them, but there's something being revealed there. I don't know if it's ever been said so candidly. It's going to be an important work. It's called *Blood Black and Blue*."

Race is not the only social issue Iyer involves himself in. Gender as it relates to the often-misogynistic world of jazz and creative music is another cause important to him. It was a sardonic Facebook post of Iyer's concerning the total absence of women among the many interviews that Ethan Iverson had conducted for his *Do the Math* blog through the years that alerted me that Iverson and Robert Glasper were about to catch flack for a recent such interview. Iyer was later the only male panelist for a discussion of "Jazz and Gender" moderated by Terri Lyne Carrington at the 2018 Winter Jazzfest in New York. Several of the points Iyer made at the event, where his fellow panelists included Angela Davis and Esperanza Spalding, concerned his previous summer overseeing the workshops at Banff.

Iyer boasted that 47 percent of that year's workshop students had been women, an unprecedented high for the Banff jazz workshops, and told of steps he had taken as director to help achieve that number. He spoke of the importance of having female instructors on the Banff faculty, for both male and female students. One story he told brought an audible gasp from the JazzFest audience: "Professor Tia Fuller was on our faculty, and there was a saxophonist—who all of us know, she's a fantastic young saxophone player—and I have to say that the week that Tia was on faculty, this young woman's tone maybe doubled in size. I said, 'What happened?' She said, 'The way Tia put her hand on my belly to show me where to breathe, I've never trusted anyone to do that before.' So that's the kind of intervention that can happen at the level of the body, that maybe we take for granted."

He described Billy Hart talking about the impact performing as a teenager with Shirley Horn's band had had on him, Horn having helped him refine crucial basics like how to swing and how to accompany. "We just started crying," Iyer recalled. "It was such a poignant and authentic moment of human relation that we tend to leave out of the equation."

Iyer talked, too, of having hijacked a Matthew Stevens workshop in order to trick male students into attending a Banff workshop on jazz and gender. "Tia led this revolutionary discussion that also involved Okkyung Lee and Jen Shyu and Imani Uzuri, and myself, Tyshawn Sorey, Rich Brown, and Matt Stevens," Iyer told the audience. "The way we got men to show up, by the way, is that we advertised it as something else. This is where I get to apply the term *gentle ambush*. Sometimes you need to kind of attack folks with something they didn't know they needed. Anyway, a transformation happened that day because there were enough women present in the room that certain things could be said that had never been said before in a space like that about how many people are carrying trauma, and how much healing we all have to do, and how we can support each other through that process."

Iyer has also helped institute change at Harvard. His approach to involving women in the study of jazz there, he said at Winter Jazzfest, had led to some students pushing back with scathing course evaluations for the just-finished fall term. In 2015, Iyer helped get the Grammy-nominated Cuban saxophonist and composer Yosvany Terry hired to lead the Harvard jazz bands after the retirement of Tom Everett, who had founded them some four decades years earlier. The next year, he was instrumental in getting Esperanza Spalding to join the music faculty as a half-time Professor of Practice.

Iyer also played a role in reshaping the undergraduate curriculum for Harvard's music concentration, a change that went into effect in fall 2017. I asked him to explain the change and his involvement in it during our phone conversation. He began by saying that his input involved serving on a committee that had spent a year discussing the curriculum, getting input from visitors from other institutions.

"It became pretty apparent that just across the board that music departments were having to change with the times," he said, "and there've been various strategies that people have implemented to do that. But part of what we were facing at Harvard was that what it meant to be a music major was a very narrow thing, but what music has come to mean, for everybody in the campus community, students and otherwise, is something much broader. And also the fact was that even the recent interests of my colleagues who are career scholars, none of that really was embraced as part of the old music major. There was a very specific track that you had to be on that didn't really take into account contemporary scholarship or contemporary perspectives on the music, or on any music—I mean even Western music. . . . What this meant was that most of the courses that counted toward the concentration were not taught by senior faculty, but instead by a kind of rotating pool of lecturers and precepts, as they're called, and people who have a more transient relationship to the university. . . .

"I think we were looking at all of this and thinking, 'Well, we have leading scholars in the field, we're starting to get leading artists in the field, and why does none of what we know count toward what we would call a music concentration?' It doesn't make any sense. So it was kind of like, after a certain very traditionalist way of thinking about things that was very Eurocentric and very narrow, like I said, in its perspective on what music is—instead of that, we went for a model where there are a lot of different ways to pass through the music department and experience a music concentration.

"There are a lot of different paths to do that now, *including* the old path. The old path still exists. It's not like that's been thrown out in the street or something like that. It's still valued as one possible way to do it, but there are other ways now that involve, for example, more classes that involve performance, or more classes that involve studying aspects of non-Western musics, or maybe you can do a kind of pre-ethnomusicology track, or maybe you can study *American* music on its own, from a historical standpoint. So there are a lot of different ways to do that now. That's all.

"And I suppose I had something to do with it, because I was in the room for a lot of these conversations, where I was participating in these things. My presence has not even so much caused as maybe more indicated that there is a concern about diversity. Because actually Harvard is very diverse, in the sense that it has very aggressive financial aid for students, which means that a good third of the undergraduates are not paying any tuition, and another third are paying basically half or something like that. So you have a very class-diverse student body. You also have a lot of new immigrants, a lot of people from outside the West, including quite a few children of African immigrants, and you have a lot of people of African descent in the US who come from lineage within the US, which means that they're descended from legacies of enslavement. The student body is not like what it was even ten years ago, and it's also more diverse than most of the other Ivies, because their financial aid, like I said, is quite aggressive. It's definitely more diverse than a place like NYU, which is an expensive private school in an urban center. The proportion of represented minorities is disproportionately low there. But at Harvard it's actually higher than at a lot of the other Ivies, so we have a diversity that has a diverse set of relationships to musics of the world, and if we can't address that, then we have to make a case for our own continued relevance. So that's basically how it's been.

"It's not like I was the one who spearheaded the idea, but it's more I was able to be in the room to say, 'Hey, look.' I remember there was a conversation before that year, in a senior faculty meeting where there had been this outside assessment of the music department. And they had pointed out the lack of diversity among music concentrators, and the then-chair of the department asked us if we had any suggestions for how to address this. I was the one who broke the silence, because nobody knew what to say, and also at the time I was the only senior faculty of color, so I just pointed out, 'Well, students don't see themselves reflected in the curriculum, then why should they come here? Why should they decide to be a music major if what they think of as music, you can't even locate it anywhere in the spectrum of what we have to offer?'

"I think that was part of the sea change. That was one small part of it. I think my ongoing presence has [meant] I'm able to remind people of what's obvious, and I'm maybe able to say it because I came in like, 'I don't know what you guys have been smoking, but here's what's apparent to me.' I walked in four years ago: 'Well, I know what I know, and I can see these mismatches.' I also remember when I first came in, I didn't have any illusions about starting a big new program or something like that. I really just wanted to figure out where the students were at, you know? And I also figured that I might attract some students who might otherwise not have any relationship to the music department. And that's what happened. Students came to me who had never taken a music course before, but not because they weren't musicians, but rather because they didn't see anything of interest to them in the department. So there was suddenly more diversity in my classes than in a lot of other courses in the curriculum, and it became obvious that we were not serving these students somehow. So I was able to just point that out, and shine a light on it."

I noted that Iyer had told an audience at SFJAZZ Center that he'd been turned off by the music curriculum at Yale as an undergraduate there, and told him it reminded me of having interviewed the pianist Steve Kuhn for the *Globe* in 2004. Kuhn had said he had emphasized other liberal arts courses as much as possible while studying music theory at Harvard in the 1950s, in large part because of the disdain in which jazz was held by the Harvard music faculty at the time.

"Well, I think there's another side to it," Iyer replied. "I can speak to my experience, but I also can say that quite a few of the students I've encountered have related to this. For example, I have a few students who are children of African immigrants. Their parents didn't send them to Harvard to study music. No one would: very few people except those who have significant privilege and security, know that their children will be OK no matter what. Most people wouldn't make that a priority for their children. A lot of these immigrant families are struggling to build a foundation for themselves and their families, especially non-Western immigrants who feel a sense of precarity just being in the world, or being American, being *considered* American. This is something I can remember from my own childhood, although it's probably worse now than it was then. So to my parents, the prospect of becoming an artist didn't make any sense. It's not that it wasn't valid; it's more that we had no understanding of how to do that. That was something I had to discover much later. I didn't even make that choice until I was twenty-three, well after I graduated from college at twenty. So I'd already been several years down another path before making that realization for myself, and making that choice, and it was a hard one. So I guess I can relate to a lot of these students. A lot of my students are not music concentrators, but that's not because they're not serious about music. It's more because they're American, and they don't necessarily think that it's a smart move to try to be an artist in America. And it isn't."

He laughed.

"They're right, basically. So often they come around to it over the course of their undergraduate years—to realize that, yeah, it's not an obvious path, and it's not necessarily savvy career-wise, but sometimes they realize that it's something that needs to happen, and they feel called into it. They feel like they have to be part of it. I mean, that's what happened to me. I couldn't deny that that's who I was. And those are the people who should be doing it, you know? Not people who just somehow by default became a music major or something like that. So I give people space to kind of figure that out."

When the school year wraps up, though, and when he's not teaching at Banff, Iyer is free to devote his full attention to pursuing *his* calling. In mid-May 2018, he led his sextet for a six-night run at the Village Vanguard, where bookings have become more receptive in recent years to music that isn't straight-ahead jazz. (Iyer had made his belated first appearance as a headliner there the previous May; his mentor Steve Coleman only beat him by a year and a half, having first led a group of his own at the Vanguard in November 2015.) Other dates were lined up in the United States for May and June, including another in New York at (Le) Poisson Rouge with his trio and guest saxophonist Matana Roberts, with a European tour to follow in July.

But before departing Cambridge for the summer, Iyer let off some end-of-semester steam by performing four sets over two nights a few blocks from Harvard Square. With him at the Regattabar were Nick Dunston on bass and Tyshawn Sorey on drums, his regular trio mates Stephan Crump and Marcus Gilmore busy elsewhere with performances of their own.[63] At his first set Friday, Iyer told the audience that he has been playing with Sorey, a fellow professor (at Wesleyan University) and MacArthur grant recipient, for seventeen years and that "future professor" and virtuoso Dunston had played his first gig with the two of them the night before.

The music they made together was both free and full of groove, the trio moving fluidly from one piece to the next. A memorable stretch occurred toward the set's end, when the group's interpretation of Thelonious Monk's "Work" slid into "Human Nature," with piano chords providing the first hint that the transition was underway before the familiar melody was unveiled. Dunston did some bowing on "Human Nature," and I recall Sorey jolting me back to the music from some note-taking with a sharp crack from his drums.

Playing for a full house in a jazz club with two peers seemed therapeutic for Iyer, who looked relaxed greeting well-wishers between sets. One of these was Mike Ladd, a Cambridge native, who had watched the first set with his mother—whom I recognized from Iyer having pointed her out during similar post-show mingling at his *Blind Spot* performance with Teju Cole three months earlier. Iyer didn't appear to be in any hurry to get back onstage. But for all his other activities—teaching, composing, writing, etc.—making live music is what he lives for.

Please visit the open access version of Make It New *to see a video resource for Chapter Two:* https://doi.org/10.3998/mpub.11469938.comp.2

CHAPTER THREE

RUDRESH MAHANTHAPPA

In the January 6, 2002, issue of the *New Yorker*, listings editor Steve Futterman offered his six picks for the best jazz albums of 2001. Topping the list was Jason Moran's *Black Stars* (2001), on which Moran and the Bandwagon were joined by the elder master Sam Rivers on saxophone and flute. The third album cited was Vijay Iyer's *Panoptic Modes*. Futterman's short write-up read: "Iyer is an extravagantly gifted new-jazz pianist and a quick-witted composer, but his greatest strength is his skill as a bandleader. On this captivating quartet recording, he establishes a lock-tight rapport with his energetic rhythm section and a cognitive interaction with the alto saxophonist Rudresh Mahanthappa, another talent to keep a steady eye on."[64]

Fifteen years later, Mahanthappa's Indo-Pak Coalition, his stellar trio with guitarist Rez Abbasi and drummer and tabla player Dan Weiss, unveiled music earmarked for their second album, with electronics and Weiss's drum kit added to the instrumentation on *Apti* (2008), their much-praised debut. The set took place January 8, 2017, at New York's Webster Hall, part of the annual globalFEST celebration of world music, which overlapped that weekend with the city's annual Winter Jazzfest. Mahanthappa, hired to direct Princeton's jazz program, had begun teaching there a few months earlier, and that night was a vivid demonstration of his visionary approach to music. The three men burned through a set of new material, compositions underwritten by Mahanthappa's grant from Chamber Music

America's New Jazz Works program. The music was so new that they each had sheet music beside them for reference, and Mahanthappa announced that his partners had gotten their first look at one piece, "Snap," only a couple of days before. If they hadn't quite perfected it, the audience didn't notice.

By that January night, Mahanthappa had already long since moved beyond his early association with Iyer and established himself as a star in his own right. His profile shot up with the release of the albums *Kinsmen* and *Apti* back to back in late 2008. *Kinsmen* made the louder splash. It featured Mahanthappa and the Indian saxophonist Kadri Gopalnath fronting the Dakshina Ensemble, a mix of Indian and American instrumentalists that included Abbasi on guitar and sitar. The album was heralded as a groundbreaking synthesis of jazz with the Carnatic music tradition of South India. Gary Giddins, who had given up his *Village Voice* column some years earlier to concentrate on writing books, was sufficiently impressed to return to journalism momentarily to celebrate it and Mahanthappa in the *New Yorker*. The beginning of his piece trumpeted Mahanthappa having broadened jazz in a new and deeply personal way by successfully integrating it with the music of his family's South Asian roots.

> *Jazz musicians have two fundamental goals: creating music that keeps listeners wondering what's next, and finding a novel context within which to explore old truths. (There are no new truths.) Whenever a musician achieves this synthesis, usually after years of apprenticeship and exploration, a rumble echoes through the jazz world. Such a rumble was heard last fall, when the thirty-seven-year-old saxophonist Rudresh Mahanthappa released an astonishing album, "Kinsmen," on a small New York-based label (Pi), quickly followed by another no less astonishing, "Apti," on a small Minnesota-based label (Innova). The breakthrough had been a long time coming, and, curiously enough, it justifies ethnic assumptions that Mahanthappa had for much of his career been working to escape.*[65]

The story went on to describe misgivings both Mahanthappa and Iyer had regarding earlier attempts to mix Indian music with jazz. Giddins spelled out how *Kinsmen* came to be despite that and described in detail what made Mahanthappa's attempt to mix the two traditions so effective. Significantly, in wrapping up his essay, Giddins wrote, "Mahanthappa has said he didn't anticipate the enthusiasm these albums have triggered and, with a long career before him, hopes that audiences won't expect him to build exclusively on this project."

Mahanthappa needn't have worried. He and others of his generation, including everyone in this book, are free to explore other genres of American and world music without being pigeonholed for it. They can all double back to undiluted jazz when so inclined. Mahanthappa's next two albums arrived in 2010, and neither emphasized the music of India. The one he made with fellow alto saxophonist Bunky Green, titled *Apex*, landed the two of them on the cover of the February 2011 issue of *DownBeat* and featured Jason Moran on piano and a couple of tracks with Jack DeJohnette on drums. Those albums seemed to establish a pattern for Mahanthappa, who would jump back and forth from project to project, emphasizing or deemphasizing his jazz, Indian, or other musical interests as inspiration guided him.

Mahanthappa zeroed back in on his jazz roots for another key album, *Bird Calls*, his unorthodox 2015 tribute to Charlie "Bird" Parker, which entailed his creating all-new compositions from tiny excerpts of Parker's recorded oeuvre. *Bird Calls* tied for best jazz album in that year's NPR Critics Poll with Maria Schneider's *The Thompson Fields*, ahead of DeJohnette's *Made in Chicago* (on which DeJohnette was joined by AACM legends Roscoe Mitchell, Henry Threadgill, and Muhal Richard Abrams) and Kamasi Washington's attention-grabbing three-CD debut, *The Epic*.

Kinsmen's success did not prove limiting or obscure Mahanthappa's jazz bona fides. What it signaled instead was his drifting apart from Iyer professionally. The two men had routinely played on each other's albums since Steve Coleman introduced them in 1995, with Mahanthappa on five of Iyer's, Iyer on three of Mahanthappa's, and their 2006 duo album *Raw Materials*.

"Musically it was great," said Mahanthappa, "but from a business point of view that totally screwed me. I became tied to Vijay in this way that I had no autonomy. No one really cared about my own projects. When I was going to try to get a gig, it was, 'Oh, you were just here with Vijay.' And now it comes out of a veiled sort of racism, too. I think Mark Turner used to play in Delfeayo [Marsalis]'s band. Can you imagine if Mark Turner went to play and they said, 'You were just here with Delfeayo?' That would not have happened. So it was really about lumping these two brown guys together."

The music they each wanted to make was less in sync by then as well, Mahanthappa noted. Iyer wanted to make fuller use of his trio with Stephen Crump and Marcus Gilmore, and left Mahanthappa off some tracks of his 2008 quartet album *Tragicomic*. Mahanthappa, meanwhile, had projects in mind that involved guitar.

"I wanted an instrument that was able to bend notes, for lack of a better word, [and] that stuff just doesn't work on piano," he explained. "So our interests kind of diverged. I really think that the piano trio is a very special thing. The piano trio is like a singular organism that can do all these amazing things, and I feel like the minute you throw a horn player in there you've ruined it."

The two men do occasionally still play together. Iyer brought Mahanthappa to the Ojai Music Festival in the summer of 2017, and earlier that year the two of them had performed as a duo at a New York concert protesting the election of Donald Trump. They also both joined Rez Abbasi on his album *Unfiltered Universe* (2017), the third album featuring Abbasi's Invocation quintet (whose other members are Dan Weiss on drums and tabla and Johannes Weidenmueller on bass). But such collaborations are now rare, and it has been years since the two of them and their wives have gotten together for dinner the way they once did regularly, before Mahanthappa and his wife relocated to suburban New Jersey.

So they do their separate things, and Mahanthappa's latest was his long-awaited Indo-Pak Coalition follow-up. *Agrima* (2017) had been set aside to put out *Bird Calls*, because dividing time between the two became unmanageable for Mahanthappa and because Abbasi and Weiss were then preoccupied with projects of their own. His partners' busyness remained the case when Mahanthappa doubled back to what became *Agrima*, but by then his Chamber Music America grant deadline was approaching. The trio recorded their new album a few months after their globalFEST performance, and it was another triumph.

Agrima's South Asian influence remains unmistakable, but its rootedness in jazz and fusion had been ramped up with the addition of the drums and electronics. It is full of memorable melodies, some of them taken at warp speed. Mahanthappa and Abbasi casually swap back and forth the rapid lead line on "Snap," for instance, and comp for each other once it is handed off. And the slower, more balladic opening to "Can-Did" evolves into something fast and fusion-inspired, Weiss shifting from tabla to a drum solo in the process.

The album's arrival in late October landed Mahanthappa on another *Down-Beat* cover, the November 2017 issue, getting this one all to himself. Because the album was self-released, the first time Mahanthappa had sidestepped working with a record label, it also meant that he was overseeing marketing it, something observers are likely to see more of with the ongoing decimation of the recording industry in this era of online music streaming. Mahanthappa pumped sales on social media, offering fans a pre-release download of *Agrima* for $2.50 and the chance to win a pair of Indo-Pak shot glasses. Other items for sale on his website included Indo-Pak socks, a $5 *Agrima* download gift card, and a $40 limited edition deluxe vinyl double LP version of the album. The downloads meant collecting email addresses for self-marketing future albums and performances, a trick Mahanthappa told *DownBeat* he was borrowing from indie rock and hip-hop.

That the music itself was superb was its best selling point. It offered further evidence that Mahanthappa and his Indo-Pak partners, like Iyer, were melding South Asian influences with jazz and other American music with a fluency that their predecessors of the 1960s and 1970s had been striving for.

I first encountered Mahanthappa in November 2011, a few weeks after the release of *Samdhi*, when he brought the band from that album to the Regattabar. I went to the performance to size him up for this book, and I was impressed. What I saw struck me as a wild new brand of fusion. My own interest in jazz had been sparked nearly four decades earlier when a high school friend's elder brother gave my friend and me a lift somewhere and had the Mahavishnu Orchestra blaring on the car stereo. I was soon piling up albums from other pioneering fusion bands led by Miles Davis or recent sidemen of his: Weather Report, the Headhunters, Return to Forever. When guitarist John McLaughlin dissolved the original Mahavishnu Orchestra lineup and began recording acoustic albums with Indian virtuosi of Carnatic and Hindustani classical music in the acoustic band Shakti, I bought and loved those albums as well.

Soon enough, tracing my high school heroes' earlier, pre-fusion albums acquainted me with jazz history. Those early fusion bands broke up, and those that succeeded them failed to hold my interest. With a few exceptions, later fusion bands usually struck me as facile—tired no matter how slickly and energetically their music was played. Something substantial went missing when fusion became its own genre, dominated by musicians who hadn't first established themselves playing acoustic jazz, as stars like Davis, Wayne Shorter, Joe Zawinul, Herbie Hancock, and Chick Corea had all done.

That wasn't a problem with Mahanthappa's group. His music that night was weighty and fresh, with jazz, rock, electronic, and Carnatic influences combining to form something visionary, exciting, and new. I didn't realize it at the time, but the album had been recorded three years earlier, the result of Mahanthappa using a 2008 Guggenheim fellowship to fund a deep dive into Carnatic music via study with Kadri Gopalnath, the Indian saxophonist from *Kinsmen*, and the great mridangam player Jayachandra Rao. (A two-headed drum, the mridangam is the principal percussion instrument in the classical music of South India.)

Mahanthappa had made use of Carnatic influences in his earlier work, most obviously on *Kinsmen*, but his sense of how the music worked prior to his Guggenheim had been self-taught and instinctive. "Almost like you meet the guy who plays beautifully by ear, and you ask him what the notes of a D7 chord are and he can't tell you," he explained. "That's where I was with Indian music. I knew what all these things sounded like, and could tap them out sometimes, but I didn't know what they were called or why they happened the way they happened. So that was one aspect of it. The other aspect was really getting inside how [melodic] ornamentation works. Just very specifically how do some of these work and why? What are the rules? Why can you not play this note unless you play this note before, for example, and getting inside of that."

Mahanthappa spent a month each with Golpalnath and Rao in intensive study. "But the idea was always to take all this information and go write music for the jazz-rock fusion band I'd been wanting to have since I was in junior high," he said. "Here's all this really great knowledge, but I'm going to take it and write for a band that's electric bass, electric guitar, a really loud drummer, and a South Indian percussionist, and I'm also going to do this electronic stuff. So it was kind of crazy, but I think it worked. Unfortunately, that album just kind of flew under the radar in a weird way. It actually sat in the can for a long time before ACT picked it up."

It sounded great that night at the Regattabar, with fellow Steve Coleman acolyte David Gilmore on electric guitar, Rich Brown on electric bass, and Damion Reid on drums. I approached Mahanthappa at the table where he was selling CDs after the set and invited him to be in the book. I caught the band again the following summer at the Newport Jazz Festival, with Rudy Royston filling in on drums, by which time the intervening months spent touring the music had made the playing even stronger. But our first interview for the book didn't occur for another two years.

That interview was set up at the 2014 Newport Jazz Festival, where one afternoon my wife and I joined Rudresh and his wife, Pooja, as they sat on a blanket with their toddler son watching Amir ElSaffar's quintet perform. ElSaffar, a trumpeter from the Chicago suburb Oak Park, has explored his Iraqi roots in his music (taking up the Iraqi string instrument *santur* in the process), and Mahanthappa had performed on ElSaffar's 2007 debut as a leader, *Two Rivers*. ElSaffar studied classical music at DePaul University, where Mahanthappa taught for a couple of years after earning his master's degree in composition there.

Rudresh told me that the band he'd led earlier that day would be recording *Bird Calls* in the coming week, for release in early 2015. I proposed an interview that would do double duty: introduce the new album to *DownBeat* readers and get the two of us started on the book.

So it was that I drove to Montclair, New Jersey, that October for our first interview session. It took place in a practice space he rented in a church a short walk from his home, where he had spent many late nights composing the music on *Bird Calls*.

I arrived armed with some biographical data. Mahanthappa was born in Trieste, Italy, while his father was on sabbatical from his job as a University of Colorado physics professor. His father had joined the UC faculty in 1965, Mahanthappa later told me, ahead of the implementation of the 1965 Immigration and Nationality Act that liberalized immigration policies toward non-Europeans: "In the whole scheme of South Asian immigrants, he's very early."

Mahanthappa and his brothers grew up in Boulder, all three of them playing music. His elder brother played clarinet, his younger brother played flute and saxophone, but neither made a career of it. Mahanthappa found his way to jazz on his own, nudged somewhat by his elder brother telling him that the kids in the jazz band seemed to have more fun than those playing classical. His was not a case of having parents whose collection of jazz albums could help guide him.

"Well, at some point that predates my birth, they obviously were into music," Mahanthappa told me. "They had a subscription to the symphony and stuff like that. But in my time, in my childhood, there were all of these records that they *used* to listen to that they never put on. The only stuff they put on were Hindu spiritual songs, and that wasn't so common. Maybe my mom would put something on on a little cassette recorder while she was doing something else. There were these albums around I used to listen to, classical stuff. But that didn't really connect for me, actually. I was more into playing saxophone. I mean, what are you going to do? If you like playing saxophone, I guess you could aspire to be the saxophonist in Supertramp, but really you're probably going to gravitate toward jazz. So it's more about the instrument leading to the genre, as opposed to vice versa, I think."

He had a teacher from fourth grade through college, Mark Harris, who introduced him to a wide range of music (and much later led him to Matt Mitchell, the pianist on *Bird Calls*, who had subbed in an art-prog-rock band Harris had been in). By his middle teens, Mahanthappa was playing regularly in local bands, "trying to play as fast as Michael Brecker" and "writing really cheesy smooth-jazz tunes" to play with a little funk band he led. His early heroes included Grover Washington Jr., David Sanborn, the Yellowjackets, and the Brecker Brothers. Charlie Parker came along a bit later, and had a more profound and lasting influence.

"That was music that really made me want to practice and be a good saxophonist," Mahanthappa recalled, referring to those earlier influences. "A lot of that music was like what I was hearing on the radio: it was funky, it had a backbeat, it was familiar in that way. But the first time I heard Charlie Parker, that was when I said, '*Hmm*, this might be fun to do for the rest of my life.'"

To that end, Mahanthappa began college at North Texas State University, which boasted one of the country's oldest and most highly regarded jazz programs. It proved a bad fit. "North Texas State then was like joining the military," Mahanthappa said. "Not enough emphasis on distinctive personalities. Thinking outside the box was unwelcome. It was more, 'This is how you play jazz.'" The college's emphasis on big bands didn't appeal to him, and small combos were off-limits until junior year.

Mahanthappa stuck it out two years, then transferred to the Berklee College of Music in Boston. He had clear goals in doing so: "I wanted to study with Joe Viola. I wanted to study with George Garzone. I wanted to study with Hal Crook. I wanted to write music."

He did all that and more, including surviving a miserable 1991 summer job playing on a cruise line, a gig he bolted from after six weeks. He returned home depressed, but his spirits were revived when he sat in on a couple of tunes at a Boulder hotel jazz set and made a lasting connection via a fiery duo passage on a Charlie Parker tune. "We played 'Cherokee,' and at one point everyone dropped out, and it was just me and the drummer." The drummer was Rudy Royston, whom years later Mahanthappa hired to play on *Bird Calls*. "That was such a positive shot in the arm for me," Mahanthappa told me. "I always tell Rudy—I joke about it—but I always say that he saved my life."

When it came time to graduate, Mahanthappa was reluctant to move to New York as many of his classmates were doing. A friend from North Texas State had gone on to DePaul University in Chicago and suggested Mahanthappa join him there at the school's new graduate program in jazz studies. Mahanthappa liked the idea. He figured he could get some experience as a working musician while pursuing a master's degree in composition in a city less frenetic than New York. One day in a Berklee ensemble class, talk turned to the seniors' post-graduation plans. Most said they were moving to New York. When Mahanthappa said he was considering DePaul, the professor told him that the program director at DePaul had been best man at his wedding and offered to make a phone call for him. "So that was the weirdest coincidence, and it all went very quickly," he said. "I went there to visit and hung out a couple of weeks with my friend just to check out the scene, and then I ended up there in the fall."

Mahanthappa spent four years in Chicago, earning his master's degree over the first two and then staying on two more years to work gigs and teach, both private lessons and classes at DePaul and Elmhurst College. He recorded his first album, *Yatra*, while still in grad school, the result of a trip to India in fall 1993.

"I saw some music, both Carnatic and Hindustani music, on that trip that really was life-changing," he told me. "A lot of stuff just kind of made sense to me. So when I got back to Chicago I wrote all the music that became the *Yatra* album." The album, first released in 1996 on a small label affiliated with Columbia College Chicago, re-released by Liberty Ellman's Red Giant label in 2000, and long since unavailable, emphasized his jazz background with blues and rhythm changes and a tune whose title—"Which Coleman?"—referenced two major influences, fellow alto saxophonists Ornette Coleman and Steve Coleman. "Very 'jazz' jazz," Mahanthappa acknowledged, "but for me, so much of the spirit of Indian music is in that album that no one else will ever hear."

Mahanthappa got to know the great Chicago saxophonist Von Freeman while living there, but despite his admiration for members such as Ernest Dawkins and Khalil El'Zabar, didn't manage to connect with the local, original branch of the

Association for the Advancement of Creative Musicians. The issue was geographical: he lived near DePaul, on the city's North Side, and he didn't have a car; the AACM and other important African American jazz incubators were on the South Side.

"Even getting down to Von Freeman's session, like at the New Apartment Lounge, that was hellacious to do on mass transportation," he recalled. "You had to get off at 95th Street and take a bus and then walk through a pretty rough neighborhood. Fortunately, Von started leading a jam session in Wicker Park, and that's how I got to know him. I would go there every week. I think I made it to Fred Anderson's club, the Velvet Lounge, twice in four years. Which is really kind of regrettable and despicable in a way, but I was doing what I needed to do and what I could do at the time. I was only twenty-two."

We were there that day primarily to talk about *Bird Calls*, which Mahanthappa said he considered a departure from his previous handful of projects, one he hoped would give listeners a better understanding of where he comes from musically. "Yes, I'm Indian American," he said, "and I've spoken about that to death in lots of interviews. But my roots as a jazz saxophonist are coming from Charlie Parker. And that's really been a constant through pretty much everything I've done."

The seeds for the project were planted when the promoter and journalist Willard Jenkins invited Mahanthappa and two other alto players to each present new music on what Charlie Parker means to them for a concert series at the Tribeca Performing Arts Center. Mahanthappa had already wanted to take a break from the high volume of his guitar-oriented fusion projects *Samdhi* and *Gamak* (2013)—the latter, featuring David Fiuczynski of Screaming Headless Torsos on guitar, mixed jazz, progressive rock, heavy metal, country, and various world musics in its exploration of microtonality and instrumental ornamentation[66]—and return to a piano-based acoustic quartet. He wrote a handful of new tunes for the Tribeca performance, played them alongside some of his earlier work, and the Bird material went over so well he decided to build on it.

George Wein, meanwhile, had approached Mahanthappa about a project for the 2014 Newport Jazz Festival and suggested he consider assembling a quintet that included a second horn player. When Mahanthappa told him about his Bird project, Wein asked what he thought of hiring a trumpet player and trying to evoke the frontline of Charlie Parker and Dizzy Gillespie.

Given the nature of the music he was writing, Mahanthappa knew doing so would require a special sort of trumpet player. His band would not be playing bebop classics made famous by Parker; to play Mahanthappa's new compositions, his musicians would need to be fluent in the postmodern developments of people like Steve Coleman. "The music is very much now," Mahanthappa explained. "It's odd meters. It's not *as* complicated as other things I've written, but not anybody can just come and play. So just because it's Bird-oriented didn't mean that we should find a great straight-ahead trumpet player."

He chose Adam O'Farrill, son of pianist/composer/bandleader Arturo O'Farrill and grandson of the Cuban composer/arranger Chico O'Farrill. Adam O'Farrill was not quite twenty when *Bird Calls* was recorded, but Mahanthappa suggested that O'Farrill's youth gave him an advantage over many older musicians. "He's of that generation where he's grown up with all of us making this complicated music," Mahanthappa said. "So you have these guys that are in college that can do all of this stuff very intuitively that we had to work very hard to be able to do, because we weren't surrounded by it. It wasn't in the vernacular at all. He had most of the music memorized at the first rehearsal."

Mahanthappa's approach to writing that music had involved late nights spent listening to Parker recordings in his rented church space. He would isolate short segments of those recordings—solos, snippets of melody, etc.—and use them as starting points for new compositions, leaving clues to the source material in the new songs' titles: "Both Hands" from "Dexterity," "Maybe Later" from "Now's the Time," "On the DL" from "Donna Lee," and so forth. Working from that variety of fragments ensured there would be variety among the new tunes, even as everything was rooted in Parker's music. The method might sound nerdy or excessively scientific, but the results were anything but. The tune "Chillin'," his spin on "Relaxin' at Camarillo," has a particularly infectious lead line traded back and forth between O'Farrill and Mahanthappa.

"That aspect's always been very important to me in most of the work that I've done," Mahanthappa told me. "I mean I've done some very heady things, too. But generally, I'm not trying to make music for musicians, music to be analyzed. It's music to listen to. And it feels incomplete to me if it doesn't have that spirit to it— that anyone can connect with it. You can tap your foot with it."

The talk of his compositional approach on *Bird Calls* led us into a discussion of the difficulties of finding a unique voice in a time in which the world is awash in musicians graduating from the many academic jazz programs. I noted that his sound remained unmistakably recognizable on the new album, adding something about how he and fellow alto saxophonist Miguel Zenón, while sounding nothing alike, had each managed to forge their own sound on the instrument despite coming up through the same educational system that their peers had.

"Well," Mahanthappa replied, warming to the topic, "one of the big issues—and I think this has been changing, too—there hasn't been enough emphasis on developing your own sound, developing your own personality."

He recalled complaining to the saxophonist and educator David Liebman about the sameness of the New York music scene a few months after he had relocated there at Liebman's urging. Mahanthappa had come to town wanting to write and play new music. What he found was a lot of musicians playing their instruments at a high level, but doing so without making music that struck him as fresh or particularly worthwhile.

"That's not an easy thing," he emphasized. "I'm totally empathetic with some-one who's not up to the task, for sure. And it's not unique to this music. There's a lot of rock that sounds the same, there's a lot of visual art that looks the same. There are a lot of people in the sciences that keep doing the same thing instead of trying to stretch the boundaries of their discipline. It's the world over. But what Liebman said specifically was that 'There are more jazz musicians than there had ever been, but the number of people who are actually going to do something new still remains the same.' And he didn't refer to it as a percentage. He said the *number* is going to be the same."

I wondered if Mahanthappa thought their ties to specific world musics gave musicians like Zenón and him a leg up toward developing something new. I was thinking both of American musicians exploring the music of their heritage— Mahanthappa, Iyer, and Abbasi tapping into South Asian music to varying degrees; Zenón's forays into folk and pop music from his native Puerto Rico; ElSaffar's injec-tion of Iraqi inspiration into jazz—and of international musicians bringing their native musics to jazz—Lionel Loueke from Benin, Ibrahim Maalouf from Lebanon, Tigran Hamasyan from Armenia, and recent waves of musicians arriving from Israel and Cuba.

"I've never really thought about it that way," he replied. "For me, it's more about speaking to what I'll call the 'New American Experience.' I mean, what does it mean to be American now? It's a big multicultural ball, and again, it's not unique to jazz. A lot of really interesting things in music and art in general are mining some sort of global perspective. But anyone can find that, I think."

"Coltrane, John McLaughlin, people like that have dipped into Indian music," I noted.

"Yeah, for sure," he agreed. "Absolutely. And to varying degrees for lots of dif-ferent reasons, too. I think the interesting thing to me is, when I think about the way I've dealt with Indian music, I don't think I've ever 100 percent thought about it as these building blocks for music. It was a way for me to dive into my culture in a meaningful way. Initially, for many years, it was almost a therapeutic way for trying to define what it means to be Indian American, and trying to reconcile what seemed like disparate parts of my cultural fabric. Where I didn't have to say that I'm Indian, and didn't have to say that I'm American—I could say that I was both and live that experience, live that idea. And so the music was a way to do that. It's just kind of a happy coincidence that people happen to like it, in a way."

I suggested that courage must also be involved in discovering one's own unique voice. That it must be easier for musicians to stick to the tried and true—the music established by their predecessors. Mahanthappa agreed.

"When I went to North Texas," he said, "all the alto players were trying to sound like Cannonball [Adderley], with very few exceptions. That was what you were supposed to do. I wasn't interested in that. And then, I think all the tenor players either wanted to sound like Trane or Brecker. Again, there were exceptions. And there was a time when there were literally hundreds of tenor players that sounded like Michael Brecker. And then there was a time that came later, where there were hundreds of tenor players that wanted to sound like Joe Lovano. Now there are a bunch of tenor players that want to play like Mark Turner or Chris Potter."

That approach never appealed to Mahanthappa, whose first saxophone teacher, in a way a middle schooler could understand, had stressed the importance of musicians finding their own unique voice and not copying. To facilitate this, he made a point of exposing his young charge to a wide array of creative music.

"He would always talk about music as a larger continuum," Mahanthappa recalled. "He might bring Ornette and Sidney Bechet and Stravinsky, and say, 'Listen to these this week.' I didn't know genre from anything. I didn't care. It was all music. It wasn't until I actually went to North Texas that I first heard about hard bop and straight-ahead as opposed to avant-garde. I was like, 'What are these terms?' Because I thought of Ornette and Bird as being, 'Oh, those guys are probably best friends.' It was all kind of the same to me. Maybe Albert Ayler didn't hang out with Coleman Hawkins, but it was conceivable to me."

Mahanthappa's goal going forward became to *understand* Charlie Parker and John Coltrane, and Bartók and Stravinsky. But he wasn't interested in mimicking their playing or writing.

"There might be some people that are really happy to sound like Charlie Parker," he said, "and if that's what makes them happy, then that's what they should do. But it won't necessarily make a huge impact. But does the goal have to be to make an impact? There are all sorts of philosophical questions there."

Economics must be involved as well, I noted.

"Well, and then that gets into the courage aspect, too," he said. "If you're going to stick your neck out, you might have to look forward to no one ever calling you as a sub." He talked about having lost wedding gigs in Chicago for refusing to play his solos like a pop saxophonist, and having realized that if he insisted on playing music his own way, he probably wouldn't have much commercial work. "I had to figure out another way," he said. "So I taught lots of private lessons for many years. And I really enjoyed that, too, even teaching little kids. There's a great joy in that."

I asked if he aspired to join a college or conservatory music faculty.

"Yeah, maybe," he answered. "If something came along. There were a couple of jobs I was asked to apply for over the past couple of years, and for varying reasons I either didn't get them or I turned them down. But I'm always on the lookout for something that just seems appropriate.

"And this goes along with the sideman thing, too," he went on. "I always felt that I want to be called because somebody wants *me*, not because they want an alto player. So again, it's like the high road. Well, Danilo [Pérez] called me to do some stuff, [Jack] DeJohnette called me to do some stuff—and both of those situations were amazing. Joanne Brackeen called me to do something. But Miguel [Zenón] gets called to do lots of stuff, and I think he can fit into more scenarios than me. He obviously has a really original voice, but somehow people can hear it better in what they're doing. Like, 'Oh, I can see Miguel playing on this,' whereas maybe they're not like, 'Oh, I can see Rudresh playing on this.' "

One clear-cut difference between Zenón and Mahanthappa, the two most celebrated alto saxophonists of their generation, is timbre. Zenón's playing leans light and birdlike; Mahanthappa's is just as fleet but denser, darker, edgier. "It sounds like sawing trees," my then-preschooler son called out from his car seat one morning years ago, expressing admiration for a track from *Samdhi*. Invigorating to listen to, that is, but harder to imagine on the side projects Zenón has worked on with people like Guillermo Klein, Fred Hersch, and Jeff Ballard.

"So I get called for very little sideman stuff," said Mahanthappa, "and that's just something I've had to come to terms with. Because there are a lot of people I'd love to play with who probably won't call. I would love to play with McLaughlin. I would love to play with Chick Corea. I would love to play with Hilton Ruiz. There are tons of people. This is a conversation I had with my manager, too: it's like maybe we just need to let people know I want to do this. I've also come to understand that there's a possibility of there being something about the way I've presented myself for years that makes people think I don't want to work as a sideman."

Despite his concerns, Mahanthappa picked up another sideman credit later that year, flying to Cuba to perform as a featured soloist on Arturo O'Farrill and the Afro Latin Jazz Orchestra's *Cuba: The Conversation Continues* (2015). They recorded it in December, a couple of days after President Barack Obama announced his intention to normalize diplomatic relations with Cuba. Mahanthappa reprised his featured soloist role with the orchestra at the 2015 Newport Jazz Festival, performing O'Farrill's sweeping composition "The Afro Latin Jazz Suite"—a tribute to his father Chico O'Farrill's "Afro Cuban Jazz Suite" featuring Charlie Parker—a few weeks ahead of the album's release. O'Farrill, father of Mahanthappa's *Bird Calls* trumpeter Adam O'Farrill, introduced his guest to the Newport crowd with a story about first hearing Mahanthappa's alto sax while driving through Michigan and being so overwhelmed that he had to pull his car to the side of the road to listen. O'Farrill said that right then he began composing the suite with Mahanthappa in mind as its lead soloist.

But Mahanthappa's sideman work has otherwise been infrequent, even after he decided to relocate to New York in 1997 to enhance his prospects for it. "One of the very clear 'It's time to move to New York' moments all came down to one thing," he told me. "It was like, 'Well, I want to play with Jack [DeJohnette] and Dave Holland. That's never going to happen if I stay in Chicago.' So it was very simple. It was like, 'Well, I guess I have to move then.' "

It took a while, but in 2010 he was indeed touring with the Jack DeJohnette Group, recording a live album available exclusively via DeJohnette's website, and making the connection with fellow band member David Fiuczynski that would lead to Mahanthappa's album *Gamak*. 2010 also saw the release of Danilo Pérez's album *Providencia*, the Panamanian pianist having hired Mahanthappa to indulge his own interest in experimenting with global jazz and because he recognized musical ties linking Panama with India. "Panama has a very big community, a connection with India, because of the canal," Pérez explained. "Panamanian rhythms have this kind of internal feeling, very similar times, to the circling of the rhythms [in Indian music]. You can hear that internally, so I heard that connection also—because we have the Spaniard influence, which is also connected to North India and to the gypsies."

In his early years in New York, Mahanthappa's primary sideman connection was with Vijay Iyer, who reciprocated by performing on Mahanthappa's first three recordings to follow *Yatra*.

All three of those early Mahanthappa albums were done with an acoustic quartet, with François Moutin on bass and Elliot Humberto Kavee or Dan Weiss on drums. *Black Water* was a suite "dedicated to all of those who have had the courage to create their own culture and identity upon arriving in this strange new land," commissioned by the American Composer Forum and released in 2002. *Mother Tongue* (2004), commissioned by the New York State Council on the Arts, explored seven languages spoken in India via compositions inspired by transcriptions of the answers native speakers of those languages gave to ill-informed questions such as "Do you speak Indian?" *Codebook* (2006) used cryptography as the organizing principle for new jazz-oriented compositions such as "Play It Again Sam" (for Morse Code inventor Samuel Morse) and "The Decider" (a tongue-in-cheek reference to the then-president).

The albums were praised by critics and established working methods that Mahanthappa continues to employ. His compositions, like Steve Coleman's, made use of complex rhythms and were linked, project by project, to themes often drawn from beyond the realm of music. The projects usually involved funding from arts grants of various types. And the three quartet albums all appeared on Pi Recordings, the boutique avant-garde label run by Seth Rosner and Yulan Wang, whose artists range from established figures Coleman, Roscoe Mitchell, and Henry Threadgill to younger experimentalists such as Tyshawn Sorey, Steve Lehman, and Jen Shyu. Mahanthappa later moved on to the German label ACT, which has a similar avant-garde, world music–friendly aesthetic, but not before recording two additional albums for Pi.

Kinsmen, as noted, was a particular success, inspired years earlier when Mahanthappa's elder brother gave him the Kadri Gopalnath album *Saxophone Indian Style* as a joke gift for graduating from Berklee. The project itself began with a grant from the Rockefeller Society and four concerts in 2005: three at the Asia Society in New York and the fourth at the Painted Bride Art Center in Philadelphia. That set of concerts was so well received that a new round of funding was procured for a second series of seven concerts in late 2007, again sponsored by the Asia Society, along with a couple of days in a recording studio.[67]

The album's reception was overwhelmingly favorable. "It was number one on iTunes jazz for like a month or something," Mahanthappa recalled, adding that at one point Amazon listed a Beatles album, a U2 album, and *Kinsmen* as its top three selling albums at that moment. "I got on *Fresh Air* with Terry Gross," he said. "And then *Kinsmen* was like number two album on the *Village Voice* jazz poll, behind a Sonny Rollins reissue or something. It was very, very crazy."

Critics besides Gary Giddins lined up to praise it as well. Ben Ratliff, having ranked *Kinsmen* the fourth best album of 2008, in an interview soon thereafter listed it among ten great albums to have been released since the 2002 publication of his guide to the hundred most important jazz recordings. Fred Kaplan, writing in *Slate,* also ranked *Kinsmen* the fourth best album of 2008. "Mahanthappa has tried to fuse his homeland's rhythms and modern jazz cadences a few times before," Kaplan asserted, "with engaging but somewhat monotonous results. Here, though, it works."[68]

Stanley Crouch liked the album so much, Mahanthappa told me, that he contacted Mahanthappa to say so and ask if he would be playing in New York soon, then brought Wynton Marsalis with him to see Mahanthappa play an Iyer quartet date at the Jazz Standard. "Wynton was very nice," Mahanthappa recalled. "He was like, 'Man, you're playing your ass off. Sounds great. I'd love to hear you again when I'm in town.' He could have just been blowing smoke up my butt, but he seemed very genuine, like he liked what he heard. He's been a huge fan of Marcus Gilmore," Iyer's drummer and the grandson of the legendary drummer Roy Haynes.

Mahanthappa, for his part, remains surprised by the glowing reception *Kinsmen* received, seeing it as being on the same basic trajectory as the rest of his work. "So *Codebook*," he explained, "there is this use of number theory and cryptography in conceiving the music, but there are a lot of devices in that music that have nothing to do with that and that have more to do with South India and Carnatic music. They're not overt, but they're definitely embedded in the composition. But I don't expect Fred Kaplan or Gary Giddins to be able to be able to pick up on that. I expect someone like Steve Coleman or Vijay to hear it, or a number of other people. But yeah, it's not a Carnatic violin and a mridangam."

Rez Abbasi, featured on both *Kinsmen* and the two Indo-Pak Coalition albums, agreed that the more blatant Indian influence on *Kinsmen* was what people seized on so enthusiastically. "I think what they're hearing is the fact that there are actually Indian musicians on the record," he said. "I mean, a big part of *Kinsmen* is Kadri Gopalnath. And the violinist, [Avasarala] Kanyakumari. Those two flavors, along with the mridangam, which is the Indian percussion instrument, really take Rudresh's music to different levels. In that sense, I agree with those critics. *Black Water* and *Mother Tongue* and all that, you can hear the Indian-ness on those albums as well, but it's not as overt. And that overtness plays a huge role in defining *Kinsmen,* and also in helping people embrace the Indian-ness. I think that's what the critics are speaking to, and not necessarily his inner voice and such."

Despite all that, Mahanthappa suggested, *Kinsmen* may have solidified his jazz roots in some minds by putting him onstage beside actual Indian musicians. "One of the byproducts of *Kinsmen*," he said, was that it "gave me more identity as a real jazz musician. A lot of people projected this sort of Indian-ness onto whatever I played. It didn't matter if I was playing 'Lester Leaps In,' I was always that Indian guy. And to be standing next to a guy who is really playing Carnatic music on the saxophone, and I'm playing this shit that sounds more like Trane, I think that actually demonstrated to people that, 'Oh yeah, this guy's a jazz player.' He actually studied the traditions. He knows this shit. He's not 'the Indian alto player,' which I feel like I was for many years."

"The funny thing is," bassist Moutin had told me when I spoke to him about *Bird Calls* for *DownBeat*, "when I met Rudresh—because he was fluent with odd meters and this kind of language—a lot of people were asking him if his music was connected to Indian music. I remember him saying, 'No, I don't know anything about Indian music. It's jazz.' And it's true; it was jazz. It was coming from Chicago. Having hung out on the Chicago jazz scene for a long time, he had his own ideas, which came also from the whole thing around Steve Coleman. I remember playing a lot of real jazzman standards with him on these gigs, even though he was already writing a lot of original material. But as soon as we started doing recordings, it was really focused on his own thing. And gradually he implemented ideas around which the music would be conceived—like you probably know this one that's conceived around Indian languages, *Mother Tongue*. He also became familiar with Indian music, so of course he started implementing that in his music, too."

Mahanthappa's follow-up and final album for Pi was another important one and the closest of his albums to being straight-ahead jazz. Joining him as co-leader was the veteran alto saxophonist Bunky Green, whose influence on Mahanthappa might be thought of as the saxophone equivalent to Andrew Hill for pianists Jason Moran and Vijay Iyer—a brilliant iconoclast whose relatively low profile made him all the more worth investigating. Green was much admired among musicians familiar with him, having worked with Hill, Charles Mingus, and others early in his career and gone on to record several albums of his own. But like Hill, he never got the recognition he deserved and eventually left the performing scene for an extended period to support himself teaching.

Mahanthappa's introduction to Green came via his Berklee professor Joe Viola. Mahanthappa knew *of* Green, having seen his photo on the cover of a magazine as the then-president of the International Association of Jazz Educators (IAJE), but he hadn't yet heard Green play alto.

"Joe had this closet he kept under lock and key that had a bunch of rare records and funny instruments and stuff," Mahanthappa recalled. "He said, 'Here, take this. You can borrow it for as long you want, but I want it back.' It was this record called *Places We've Never Been*, which was for that Vanguard label out of Chicago in the '70s, '80s. The band was Randy Brecker and Eddie Gomez and Nasheet's dad, Freddie Waits. I don't remember who played piano. And I heard this guy come in on the alto, and I was like, 'Holy fuck, who is this?!' And it was that same thing, where I heard all the tradition. I heard Bird, I heard everything in there, but I heard this very forward-looking perspective. And then I came to know later that he was such a huge influence on Steve Coleman. But at the time, I didn't even know that. Someone else connected the dots for me."

Mahanthappa tracked down an office phone number for Green's teaching job in Florida, where he directed the jazz program at the University of North Florida in Jacksonville, and asked if Green would mind checking out a cassette of what he was working on. "So I sent him the cassette with a nice letter, and then he called a couple of weeks later. He called at like eight in the morning on a Saturday. He was like, 'What are you doing in bed? You should be practicing. . . . Stuff sounds good, man. You just need to keep doing what you're doing.' "

The two met in person a few years later at an IAJE conference, where

Mahanthappa was playing as a featured soloist with the DePaul big band. Green had no recollection of Mahanthappa having sent him that cassette, but Mahanthappa spent the conference reminding him about the coming DePaul performance every time their paths crossed. "So we play," he recalled, "and I was kind of looking to see if Bunky was around, and I didn't see him. And when we were getting off the stage, he was waiting for me with his open arms. He gave me this huge hug. And he said, 'There are only four of us. It's me and you and Steve and Greg [Osby], and somehow we all have to take the alto into the future.' And then we were best friends ever since."

Their collaboration didn't happen for another decade, however, and came about serendipitously when a friend, in the wake of Kinsmen's success, asked Mahanthappa to put together a concert for a series called Made in Chicago. Mahanthappa assembled a group consisting of himself, Green (a Milwaukee native who had lived and taught in Chicago for three decades), Moutin, and a handful of Mahanthappa's favorite musicians from his Chicago days. The concert went so well that Mahanthappa started looking for a way to get Green into a recording studio with him. He mentioned the idea to Jason Moran, who had already backed Green on a previous album, and to Jack DeJohnette, and both men immediately volunteered to be on the project.

"So suddenly," said Mahanthappa, "between Jason and Jack both wanting to play on this album, how is it we're not going to make this album? I went to the Pi guys. I said, 'This is going to be expensive. Jack is expensive, Jason is kind of expensive. Bunky is kind of expensive.' Their first reaction was, 'So we made all this money on Kinsmen and now you're asking us to basically spend all of it on this album?' And I was like, 'Yeah!'"

The resultant album was one of Mahanthappa's best. The company he kept on it—Green, Moran, Moutin on bass, and DeJohnette and Damion Reid dividing the drum duties—scrubbed away any doubt that Mahanthappa is, first and foremost, a jazz musician. It also garnered Green some long overdue recognition. "More than anything," Mahanthappa said, "I think it probably got Bunky out there to a generation who had no idea who he was. It got Bunky on the cover of DownBeat, which I'm not sure would have ever happened any other way."

At one point our discussion turned to my perception that the alto saxophone had in recent years recaptured its prominence in jazz after decades in which the tenor sax seemed the more dominant instrument. Mahanthappa agreed. "I always thought it was just because the tenor, after Bird, and maybe you could say after Cannonball, the tenor was just the lead instrument of innovation." John Coltrane set a standard that people are still trying to catch up to, he said, rattling off the names of several prominent post-Coltrane tenor players who came close.

"So then when does it really come around to alto?" he asked. "Well, Bunky was rather underground. And then you have AACM folks like [Anthony] Braxton and Roscoe [Mitchell], folks like that. I don't want to call them underground, but they exist in a different sphere, I guess, that not enough people know about. But then you have Steve Coleman. I think Steve and M-Base, and I would say primarily Steve and then Osby somehow, they helped all of this happen. They were writing and playing all of this great music at the time where a major label would still take interest. I mean, Greg did all of those records for Blue Note, playing all this crazy, great stuff. And Steve was on RCA Novus, or whatever big labels, playing all of his stuff. And then what also helped—I know that Steve is now a real active sort of educator, these seminar types of formats, but even before he was doing that, he was always interested in reaching local communities. When he was in Europe, if people were interested in his music, he would literally stay up all night and hang out with people and play. And teach them stuff, show them stuff. 'I've been reading this book about Egyptian modes.' Stuff like that."

The influence of Coleman and M-Base, Mahanthappa noted, was not limited to alto players. "He spread a certain gospel in a way that has now filtered down to people like Adam O'Farrill, where what was super rare and even mysterious and virtuosic has become more of a vernacular." Mahanthappa mentioned the great heights that others with M-Base connections had reached. "Cassandra Wilson, you might never guess it, but if you hear the stuff that she did when she was part of M-Base—that stuff is amazing. Gary Thomas is the head of the jazz program at Peabody.[69] You have these people in places of power, so to speak, and they were all just living in Fort Greene trying to figure stuff out like thirty years ago or something like that. I think that's how things go if you don't end up with a shorter life like Trane or Bird. They would have had great positions of leadership in the world of art, and it just didn't happen that way."

Mahanthappa's own leadership appointment began in fall 2016. He was hired as director of jazz at Princeton University, a certificate program for undergraduates majoring in other subjects—somewhat like a minor, as he described it, but less intense than a minor in music would be.

"They were surprised I applied for the job," he told me, "and wanted to make sure I knew that this wasn't a conservatory job." But Mahanthappa recognized that the position came with other advantages, high among them the fact that "I can expose these students to things without the onus of preparing them for a real music career." He also liked the prospect of working in proximity to the university's respected composition and musicology programs. The commute from his home in New Jersey was reasonable, and having a salaried job, he joked, let him "leave a certain sense of desperation behind."

Mahanthappa teaches one course, Advanced Concepts in Jazz Improvisation: Creating Fresh Vocabulary, which he said involves analyzing iconic jazz solos and talking about creating other vocabularies from them, something like he had done with the Charlie Parker source material on *Bird Calls*. In addition, he directs two small ensembles, which rehearse and perform during the school year. As program director, he oversees two vocal ensembles and a creative large ensemble meant "to consider lots of different music, from Count Basie to John Zorn." He also brings top talent to campus for short residencies each year; in his second year running the program, they included the pianists Gerald Clayton and Danilo Pérez, two cutting-edge musicians thoroughly versed in straight-ahead jazz.

Mahanthappa was hired to move the Princeton program into the present. To help achieve that, his own first important hire was Darcy James Argue, three-time Grammy Award nominee for best large ensemble album and the most celebrated composer-arranger under fifty for large jazz ensembles. NPR's Patrick Jarenwat-tananon accurately summed up Argue's accomplishments in a teaser to a rebroadcast of his Secret Society ensemble's performance at the 2012 Newport Jazz Festival: "The composer Darcy James Argue has steadily been rescuing the big band from the dustbin of anachronism."

Argue has described his eighteen-piece Darcy James Argue's Secret Society as a "steampunk big band," his vehicle for exploring what music might have evolved into had big bands remained popular and open to mixing jazz with subsequent genres of music. His two most recent extended works, *Brooklyn Babylon* and *Real Enemies,* both began as multimedia collaborations premiered at the Brooklyn Academy of Music. The latter, borrowing its title from Kathryn Olmsted's *Real Enemies: Conspiracy Theories and American Democracy, World War 1 to 9/11* (2009), mixes music with sound clips from Presidents John F. Kennedy, George H. W. Bush, and Bill Clinton and actor James Urbaniak reading from Richard Hofstadter's classic 1964 essay "The Paranoid Style in American Politics."

The music that Princeton's creative large ensemble class performs under Argue's direction also ranges beyond conventional big band jazz, and guest artists have been brought to campus each year to perform it with them. Mahanthappa commissioned a new twenty-minute piece from the innovative composer Billy Childs, performed by the Princeton ensemble in May 2017 along with earlier Childs compositions arranged by Argue. The following fall semester, the NEA Jazz Master Archie Shepp and Amina Claudine Myers were brought to campus to join the ensemble in a December performance of music from Shepp's Grammy-nominated recording *I Hear the Sound*, a 2013 remake of his 1972 protest album *Attica Blues*.

I spoke with Argue during the fall of 2017, as preparations for the Shepp concert were underway. The music, he told me, would be performed by the creative large ensemble augmented by a string quartet, eight vocalists, and a gospel choir. "It's this very ambitious type of project that is going to necessarily involve students who probably don't know who Archie Shepp is," he said. "It is what I hope will be a meaningful experience for them to interface with someone who is a real lion of the jazz avant-garde and who has had such a storied career, who is eighty years old now and makes music that has such an impactful social message. And that's something that has always been part of the history of jazz. Whether it's implicit or explicit, jazz just fundamentally is protest music by virtue of the fact that it's a black American art form." The exploration of jazz as protest music is unusual in college classrooms, Argue noted, or was in his own undergraduate experience studying piano at McGill University. "The sort of cultural place that jazz has in the history of race in America was not a topic that was explored in any particular depth," he said.

Mahanthappa's decision to bring Shepp to campus was timely, given the resurgence of politics and protest in jazz, which seemed to begin trending with the rise of the Black Lives Matter movement and became more noticeable with the election of Donald Trump. The sexism in jazz itself also began being called out and denounced, albeit more on social media than in recordings or performances.

Mahanthappa joined Vijay Iyer, Arturo O'Farrill, and others for a Musicians Against Fascism concert at New York's Symphony Space the week of Trump's inauguration, but generally his weighing in on social issues has been more understated. His early albums *Black Water* and *Mother Tongue*, in calling attention to the South Asian immigrant experience, gently mock American ignorance about India: the song title "Are There Clouds in India?" on *Black Water* and the question "Do You Speak Indian?" that prompted *Mother Tongue*. The song titles "The Decider" and "Breakfastlunchanddinner" on later albums likewise poke fun at American politics. Unlike Iyer and O'Farrill, Mahanthappa avoids politics on social media because of misgivings he has about the format. He noted the usefulness of organizing physical protest via Twitter during the Arab uprising, but was skeptical about celebrities lending their names to causes with little or no practical effect.

"You can be an armchair activist on Twitter and Facebook," he said. "There are a lot of people that post a lot of stuff on Twitter that have never been to a rally, that would never get their hands dirty in the ways that the word *activism* rings for me. So I kind of steer clear of it in that sense. But I also think there's a good bit of music that I make that makes a social statement that's not always overt. Just being a South Asian American of immigrant parents playing jazz is already quite the statement—what this world can be, and how and why—and making sure that my music has integrity and honesty kind of keeps all of that in check."

Mahanthappa is more inclined to address politics in his music than on social media. He noted that others have already done so, with mixed results. "There are definitely these projects that are in reaction to the times," he said. "Some of them are very good and very effective, and some of them are not. Some of them seem to actually be exploiting the fact that this has happened as a way to create music that rises to the top because it has this orientation."

If and when Mahanthappa does address politics more overtly on a project, he wants to make sure it's done right. "It's not that I don't want to jump in, it's that I think there are lot of bad ways to jump in," he explained. "Maybe I don't feel quite mature or smart enough to do that yet. I liken it to the way I was dealing with Indian music. It took a long time to get to a place where I felt like I could put together a project like *Kinsmen*. I could have just been fooling around with playing blues with a tabla player and claimed that it was some sort of crossover collaboration. But I knew that that didn't feel right. I knew that I had to get to a place where I felt like I could put things forth with real integrity, and I haven't really found a way to do that with music and politics yet."

In the meantime, he keeps his politics largely under wraps. He uses social media almost exclusively for marketing his music. The question of how jazz and jazz musicians should go about marketing themselves is something that's been on his mind for years, as he explained to me during our first interview when I asked him whether he shared the misgivings many of his fellow artists have about having their music labeled *jazz*.

"Vijay and I used to have that conversation all of the time," he replied. "If I say *jazz* to someone who doesn't know the music, what do they think about? They think about their grandfather's music, they think about this little trio in the corner while they were eating dinner—you know, lots of things I don't identify with or even want to be associated with. But what is the other option? I could come up with my own term, which I would have to end up describing. Or I could not have my own term, and when they say, 'What kind of music do you play?' I'd say, 'Do you have ten minutes for me to explain it to you?' Or I could just say jazz and hope that they'll be open to something, that maybe I can come up with a sentence that separates it from those things I don't want to have anything to do with.

"That's always a challenge, and it's an interesting thing. Because—aside from when we talk about the Wynton [Marsalis] team or something like that, where we say jazz is alive and well in that sort of way—I think your question actually brings up a lot of interesting things related to how jazz is being marketed, or how we market ourselves as individuals. I think this idea of developing this artist-direct-to-fan sort of relationship is more important. I would rather people come to see me play because they're coming to see *me*, because they like my music, as opposed to identifying it with, 'I'm going to go see some jazz tonight. What's going on?' Somewhere in between those two things is where I'd like to live.

"That's something I've been thinking a lot about over the past five or six years. Because the reality is if you can develop a following—well, how do I say it? I have this with my own musical tastes. I'm not a heavy metal fan, but there are metal bands that I like, and I look for what they're doing next. I'm not a big dance music fan, either, but there are a couple of people that do some really interesting things. I would never say that I like those genres, necessarily, but I like these particular artists. And I think that's the future for my generation of jazz musicians. And the younger ones, too."

In a winner/loser economy—one saturated with proficient conservatory-trained jazz musicians and absent the record label promotional budgets that predated online streaming—even this generation's most celebrated artists are discovering that they must each find ways to attract a fan base of their own, and that those ways are not necessarily limited to their virtuosity or the originality of their music.

Three years on, Mahanthappa had racked up his NPR jazz poll tie for best album of 2015, his Princeton appointment, and another *DownBeat* cover. That December, the new *New York Times* jazz writer Giovanni Russonello ranked *Agrima* twelfth on his list of best albums of 2017, and it would finish in eleventh place in NPR's annual jazz critics poll. But despite his heightened profile and prestige, Mahanthappa had begun experimenting with new methods of marketing himself.

Surprisingly hands-on methods. *Agrima* was his first self-released album, and Mahanthappa made it available exclusively (and very inexpensively) as a direct download from his website or as a $40 deluxe double LP—meaning no record label, no Amazon or Apple, not even Bandcamp coming between Mahanthappa and his audience. His Facebook page touted a chance to win a pair of shot glasses with the purchase of the $2.50 download. Those driven by the Facebook posts to his website discovered there were Indo-Pak Coalition socks available for purchase as well.

As it happened, the album was released the week of my birthday. I decided to celebrate with a set of shot glasses, stylishly square-shaped 2 1/2-ounce models emblazoned with a dark blue Indo-Pak Coalition insignia. Excellent for measuring the rye in a manhattan, it turned out. A few days after placing my order, an email rolled in from Mahanthappa: "I was tickled to see that you ordered the shot glasses. Did they arrive in one piece? I feel like I'm running a post office out of the house!" In my reply, I told him I'd wondered whether he would be mailing out his merchandise himself. "Yeah," he wrote back. "It's a pain but maybe the way forward."

Please visit the open access version of Make It New *to see a video resource for Chapter Three:* https://doi.org/10.3998/mpub.11469938.comp.3

CHAPTER FOUR

THE BAD PLUS

"Tonight we're playing a repertoire of superlative alto saxophone music," Reid Anderson announced three tunes into the Bad Plus's set with special guest Rudresh Mahanthappa at the 2017 Festival International de Jazz de Montréal. Sure enough, the set turned out to be a nearly equal mix of tunes linked to Charlie Parker or Ornette Coleman ("Laird Baird," "An Oscar for Treadwell," and "The Hymn" for Parker; "Una Muy Bonita," "The Sphinx," "Sadness," "Law Years" for Coleman), with Lee Konitz's "Subconscious-Lee" slipped in midway through for good measure.

It was an impressive display of the musicians' rootedness in modern and post-modern jazz, a grounding that their own separate work can sometimes obscure. Mahanthappa's career has emphasized his original compositions, usually focused, album-by-album, on brainy explorations of some specific aspect of his life and heritage.

The Bad Plus was dubbed early on, by critic Gary Giddins, as an "equilat-eral chamber group," combining jazz, pop, and classical influences to create an approach to improvisational music all their own. The covers they are known for are neither jazz nor traditional American songbook standards but rather pop hits from their own lifetimes, made famous by bands such as Blondie, Queen, and Nirvana.

Those covers helped popularize the Bad Plus, but it's a gross misconception to think pop covers are the trio's primary focus. Bassist Anderson, pianist Ethan Iverson, and drummer Dave King are all accomplished composers, and their original pieces constitute most of the group's recorded output by a margin that would be even greater but for their two albums consisting entirely of covers—*For All I Care* (2008, with vocalist Wendy Lewis), which included classical works by twentieth-century composers György Ligeti, Milton Babbitt, and Igor Stravinsky, and *It's Hard* (2016).

What really defined the Bad Plus was the shared leadership of the trio and the tight arrangements the group employs on both covers and originals. These musicians have always improvised, but you'll search in vain for extended solos on their recorded work or if you catch them live. The Bad Plus has always been first and foremost a band, and one that Giddins's word *equilateral* has applied to across the board.

But in joining forces with Mahanthappa in Montreal they took something more closely resembling a straight-ahead "head, solo, solo, head" approach to the tunes, and the audience at Gesú, Centre de créativité, responded enthusiastically. The musicians left no doubt that, whatever artistic directions their work may have taken them in since, all four of them are thoroughly grounded in jazz.

Even so, there were also moments of Anderson's droll humor to remind people this was a Bad Plus gig. As the set was nearing its end, he paused to acknowledge "the commerce aspect of it," announcing that the musicians would be selling CDs afterward. "There's four of us," he said. "If some of you could stick around it'd be good for us psychologically." It being June 30, he added tongue-in-cheek that audience members should keep in mind the national holiday the next day, and the "traditional Canada Day exchanging of CDs."

The musicians did indeed come to the lobby afterward, where they were greeted by a sizable group of fans. Iverson made a point of approaching Mahanthappa and telling him there had been some magical moments onstage. The Bad Plus has added guests before. Kurt Rosenwinkel would perform with them two nights later in Montreal and had done so previously. Bill Frisell had worked with them in the past and would have a week with them that October at the Village Vanguard. Wendy Lewis and Joshua Redman have each recorded an album and toured with them.

The trio's rapport with Mahanthappa might have suggested something similar would follow, but by then it was highly unlikely. A couple of months earlier, the Bad Plus had announced that Iverson would be leaving the group at the end of the calendar year and be replaced on piano by Orrin Evans.

After seventeen years in the Bad Plus, Iverson's attention was becoming increasingly taken up by his numerous other projects: more strictly jazz-oriented collaborations with elder masters such as Billy Hart, Tootie Heath, Louis Hayes, and Ron Carter; assembling a new trio of his own; writing his award-winning blog, *Do the*

Math; beginning work on a book; and, since fall 2016, teaching at New England Conservatory.

Anderson and King had side projects, too, but remained as committed to the Bad Plus as ever. When Iverson told the others he was leaving, it seemed a good opportunity to prove that the band had been a band all along, and not, as some assumed, an Iverson-led trio. Anderson had worked with Evans before, and they decided to press on as the Bad Plus sans Iverson, provided Evans was interested in taking over on piano.

"Well, we're not going to stop because the piano player wants to stop," King told me the next morning over coffee before scurrying off to rehearse for the following night's gig with Rosenwinkel. "We're showing you now that this is not what that is. And also, Reid and I have written most of the original music. Of all of the original music, it seems per record that there are more Reid Anderson tunes. So, in a way, for that particular group it had a very delicate chemistry and has a sound. But the Bad Plus has a sound when people guest with us as well that is [also] our sound, you know? And it has more to do with the way you think about the music than the tunes. So Orrin, we had him in mind as we asked him, and he said 'Yeah,' so we knew immediately that he was the right person."

By the time we spoke together the new trio had rehearsed together a few times, and the plan called for the revised lineup to record an album in September, release it in January, and hit the road together that same month. The original trio was seen so much as a band, however, that some doubted whether the Bad Plus could survive a substitution and remain recognizably the Bad Plus. I asked King how he thought Evans's arrival would alter the group's sound.

"It's going to be better," he shot back. "He's a little bit of an outsider, an outside art guy. He has good energy, but the music is intact. His interpretation of the music is the way the Bad Plus sounds now, is what we're going to be doing with our new record. But also, our older catalog, which he's been learning, we sound like those three people playing the songs. He's not trying to sound like Ethan. And what's emerged is—you'll have to judge for yourself—it's stronger, and it's still weird. It's still idiosyncratic, and that's what's important to me."

The founding members knew one another well before they became the Bad Plus. Reid Anderson and Dave King went to middle school together in Golden Valley, Minnesota, a suburb on the northern boundary of Minneapolis. The pianist Craig Taborn was there as well, the three of them meeting one another around age twelve.

Minneapolis was becoming a vibrant music town then. Mainstream jazz and other genres were booked at the Dakota, which opened in St. Paul while the three of them were in high school (and has since relocated to Minneapolis). The Walker Art Center presented more experimental music of the sort associated with the AACM and John Zorn. Hip-hop, hardcore, and punk were all prevalent, including homegrown talent such as the Replacements and Hüsker Dü (whose bassist, Greg Norton, years later joined King, Taborn, and guitarist Eric Fratzke to record the 2007 album *The Gang Font feat. Interloper*). These were also, of course, the years in which local hero Prince was establishing himself as a major star, via his mega-selling albums *1999* and *Purple Rain*.[70]

Anderson, King, and Taborn soaked up all of it, establishing the aesthetic paths each would pursue as adults.

"We saw everybody," recalled King when we spoke in Montreal. "Absolutely. [Henry Threadgill's] Very Very Circus . . . So we would have the straight-ahead clubs, go see McCoy Tyner. Keith Jarrett played a few times in the Twin Cities when we were growing up. We went to everything. Branford Marsalis, Sonny Rollins, everybody. And then The Walker had, you know, Sonny Sharrock, Odeon Pope, Bill Laswell, John Zorn, Bill Frisell. It was like, 'Man!' But to us it was just all part of the same stream. We were fifteen years old.

"We were attracted to the raw element of things like Ornette Coleman Prime Time. And the irrational spaces of Sun Ra. There's the combination. I mean, Craig Taborn's into, you know, Kraftwerk *and* Art Ensemble of Chicago. I don't think he sees any difference. He's into Webern. It's the same thing with me and Reid. Even though we're the last of the LP generation. We didn't get raised on clips of things on YouTube. We're from the era, the '70s and '80s—rock radio and the birth of hip-hop—and what that did to us. It's, like, *modern music*."

They were playing music themselves by then. King studied piano from ages five to fourteen, switching his focus to drums in fifth grade to join the school band. (King hasn't abandoned piano; he composes on it, and his 2010 solo album *Indelicate* consists entirely of him on overdubbed piano, drums, and electronics.) King used paper route money to buy a drum pad and sticks. "My parents were not encouraging the drums," he recalled. "My dad was like, 'You should play the trumpet or . . .' I said, No, I wanted to play drums. And as soon as I started playing drums I made a deep connection to it right away. I played in all the school bands, and in seventh grade I bought a little shitty drum set."

Anderson played electric bass early on, the two of them jamming together on jazz, rock, and whatever else struck their fancy.

"He switched to upright when he was seventeen or whatever, and immediately he was very happy," King recalled of Anderson. "In a way, he's incredibly prodigious. I remember his ascension on the upright was so fast. By the time we were in that zone, senior high school, he was in it to win it. Jimmy Garrison, Charlie Haden lexicon."

After graduating high school, Anderson studied upright bass at the University of Wisconsin–Eau Claire, less than two hours from Minneapolis. While there, he met Iverson.

"I went to Eau Claire for one year, and Geoff Keezer's father [taught] percussion there," Anderson told me when we spoke in his Brooklyn apartment, a few weeks after news of Iverson's impending departure. "He knew Ethan, a local, very talented pianist. We were put together because Ethan needed to make a demo tape for something, and we immediately hit it off." In a time and place where straightahead was the dominant form of jazz, Anderson and Iverson were outliers. "It was a very narrow-minded approach to music," explained Anderson, "and we were both interested in Ornette Coleman and the Keith Jarrett American quartet and that kind of thing, in addition to that stuff. So when we first met, we bonded over, like, Charlie Haden. We were just of like minds. We started a real strong relationship and playing a lot from the get-go."

Iverson was still in high school at the time, a half hour away in Menomonie, Wisconsin, on the highway between Eau Claire and Minneapolis.

"You're right to say it's a 'boondock-y' place," Iverson told me one afternoon the year before, at his Brooklyn apartment not far from Anderson's. "Except that now I appreciate Menomonie for being a really gentle and artsy town for a state that's less progressive than Minnesota, for example. Reid and Dave always make fun of me for being from Wisconsin, and truthfully they have every right. Minnesota is a much cooler state. Menomonie was 13,000 people and kind of a hip college town. There was not any jazz, exactly, but my band teacher, who was named Jim Borgaro, was an ex jazz player. He still played jazz, but he was a high school band teacher then. He played some jazz and some pretty good alto."

Iverson wrote music for a children's theater program and played jazz at a local restaurant on weekends. "Friday solo, Saturday with the Jim Borgaro Quartet," he recalled. "I look back on that and think it was amazing I had all that opportunity. At the time, I couldn't wait to get to New York, but I talk to my peers over the years and realize I had a lot of opportunity in Menomonie that I wouldn't have had in most other places."

What Iverson didn't have growing up was any interest whatsoever in rock. A 2004 *DownBeat* cover story on the Bad Plus said Iverson spent his adolescence "geeking out on a farm," studying music obsessively—jazz and classical music, that is (as with Moran and Iyer, Thelonious Monk was and remains a particular inspiration)—and that he was "prone to making statements like, 'I would sooner enter a marathon than listen to Crosby, Stills & Nash or the Doobie Brothers.'"

That didn't stop him from accompanying Anderson on trips back to Golden

Valley, where the two of them and King first began playing together in the late 1980s, usually in the basement of Anderson's childhood home.

Those early rehearsals for all that would follow were short-lived, however. Anderson, on the recommendation of his bass instructor, transferred to the Curtis Institute of Music in Philadelphia, lured by the prospect of relocating to the East Coast—closer to the jazz scene in New York. Anderson studied classical bass at the conservatory, but before leaving town also began playing with some of the local jazz talent, including another talented high school pianist, Orrin Evans.

College became Iverson's excuse for moving to the East Coast as well, in his case directly to New York. "I went to NYU, the jazz department, for two years," he explained. "College is still a good way to convince your parents to send you off to the big city. If you have a place to study, they'll be more willing to let you do that."

A decade or so earlier it hadn't been all that unusual for young musicians to enter a music program for a year or two, be discovered by Art Blakey or another jazz elder, and drop out of school to turn pro. Such was not the case for Iverson.

"I didn't start gigging like a great player like Branford [Marsalis]," he clarified. "I just wasn't at that level. But I realized my tuition was adding up. I was already underwater with student loans after only two years. I thought, How could I get another two years underwater? And Jim McNeely was my piano teacher. He was great, but I always thought the stories about jazz life was what was most important, and I realized I didn't need to spend the tuition money to get the jazz stories. So I dropped out. I worked mostly as a dance class pianist and as a tango pianist. In the '90s, those were the two money gigs I had to stay afloat financially.

"Of course, life was a lot cheaper then," Iverson added. "I don't know how kids do it anymore, moving to New York. It's hard for professionals to live here: established professionals can't figure out how to make ends meet. I had a room for $300 a month. Even then I missed my rent sometimes and had to figure out how to pay it. That sort of stuff. You could get a dozen day-old bagels for a dollar—you could eat for a few days on the dollar's worth of bagels. Now I don't know. I don't think $300 toward rent and a dollar for a week's worth of food goes very far anymore."

Iverson did study privately with Fred Hersch (whose place he would later take on the NEC faculty) and for years afterward with Sophia Rosoff and John Bloomfield. "I started teaching Ethan Iverson when he was twenty-one, or twenty," recalled Hersch, "and he said, 'I'm in no hurry. I want to get this right. If I have some success by the time I'm thirty, I'll be happy.' The week of his thirtieth birthday Bad Plus opened at the Village Vanguard. So he's somebody who wanted to do it correctly and take the time, not just be in a rush to win a contest or have a quote 'career.' "

Dave King eschewed college and conservatory altogether. "I'm free-range," he said during our coffee shop conversation. "I guess, technically, I'm a little more self-taught than the average person. I had private lessons for a bit: a couple differ-ent teachers, but nothing really lengthy or heavy. But when you say 'self-taught' it makes you feel like you're in a bubble or whatever. I learned from the records that I had. I checked out books and was doing some things. But also, I had enough alone time to be able to develop a language that I just felt was personal, which I think is important. And somewhat lacking in some aspects of academia now—there's *too much* instruction."

"I don't like the term *self-taught*," King had told me earlier in Boston, when the Bad Plus was in town for a couple of nights at Scullers. "Just because I didn't go to music school doesn't mean I was alone in a barn with a drum set or whatever. I studied all the great masters very closely. I saw this Mike Tyson documentary where they said he used to sit there and watch all the old fighters and just abso-lutely analyze. That's what I was like. I really, really obsessed over the details."

What resulted was a style that melded rock and jazz influences. The *New York Times*'s Ben Ratliff described King's drumming as "a wild, funky mixture of John Bonham and Jack DeJohnette." Britt Robson, writing in Minneapolis's hometown *City Pages*, called it "two parts Keith Moon to one part Art Blakey."

But those descriptions came later, in the early days of the Bad Plus. Before that, King gave both New York and Los Angeles brief trials and returned to Minneapo-lis, where he drummed in alt rock and other bands until forming the eclectic jazz trio Happy Apple with saxophonist Michael Lewis and electric bassist Erik Fratzke in 1996. "That's the band that kind of inspired the guys in the Bad Plus to form a band," King told me. "The band is still active, even though we haven't had a record in many years. We're on the Sunnyside label. We released many records, and we still play. We played Chicago for years. We used to play Fred Anderson's Velvet Lounge."

Anderson and Iverson, meanwhile, were in New York edging their way into the local jazz scene. Smalls Jazz Club was a hub for much exciting new work from musicians of their age cohort.

"I was hanging out there a lot," Anderson acknowledged. "I was always a little bit on the outside. I occasionally would play at Smalls, but not too often. But yeah, I moved here in '94, '95, and just kind of fell in with certain people who had moved here at the time. Mark Turner, Kurt Rosenwinkel, and I knew Orrin from Philly already. Nasheet Waits and Sam Newsome. Just like you do: you try to meet as many people as possible and form relationships and see who you like playing with. Bill McHenry, of course—we have a long, really good relationship. But I've always been kind of an outsider. I was never really part of the scene."

He and Iverson each began putting out albums in the late 1990s, mostly on the Barcelona-based Fresh Sounds New Talent label, taking turns as each oth-er's sideman (Iverson had managed one in 1993 as well, titled *School Work*, which featured Dewey Redman—Joshua's father and Ornette Coleman's *Science Fiction* sideman—on tenor saxophone). Anderson's *The Vastness of Space* (2000), with Ben Monder on guitar rather than Iverson on piano, was heralded by critics for his compositions, two of which later migrated to the Bad Plus repertoire. Iverson's *The Minor Passions* (1999), with Anderson on bass and veteran Billy Hart on drums, made Ben Ratliff's "Another 100: More Albums You Should Own, or at Least Know About" list of also-rans in his *The New York Times Essential Library* book *Jazz: A Critic's Guide to the 100 Most Important Recordings.*

"Ethan's always been into some interesting stuff," Mahanthappa once told me of those early, pre-Bad Plus years. "I remember seeing him do a solo piano thing where he was playing standards, and before he played each tune, he would recite the lyrics in this very deadpan sort of way. And then he would sit down and play all this shit, and the whole thing was almost a performance piece. I was like, 'Who is this guy?' That was years ago."

Iverson, by then, had graduated from his early dance-class gigs to becoming musical director for Mark Morris Dance Group. Morris, of course, is one of America's preeminent choreographers, "arguably the most successful and influential choreographer alive," opined the *New York Times* in 2004, "[a]nd indisputably the most musical."[71] Working with Morris proved crucial to Iverson when he, Anderson, and King decided to form the Bad Plus. The Minnesotans' love of pop tunes coexisted with their love of postmodern jazz, but Iverson's taste in music had skewed more exclusively cerebral. Morris's work reminded him that art and entertainment could coexist and thrive together. That something could be abstract and also connect with people.

"That's totally dead on, and I think probably what it is is high and low," Iverson told me. "I am sort of a brainy guy. I said earlier I'm not physically gifted. At the end of the day, what I do when I'm left to my own devices is I like to look at classical twentieth-century music scores, and I have this sort of intellectual lifestyle. That's just who I am. When I was twenty, I was fascinated by twelve-tone music. That's the poster boy for intellectual music: twelve-tone music. I really checked it out. I wrote some pieces, I'd play a lot of it.

"But anyway, the point I'm trying to get to is that Morris showed me that it could be smart as fuck but also funny and engaging and just entertaining. And I think actually that's hardly just Morris. All American art. We have that sort of ability to be super smart yet also be entertaining. That's, of course, jazz. Any jazz. I said earlier that I thought Steve Coleman's system's a little intellectual. It's sort of like twelve-tone music, which is a little intellectual. I'm not saying you shouldn't do it. You should do it, in fact. I support it. I'll write a grant for it—do it. At the same time, just entertaining is good, too.

"I think a lot of the best American stuff has both. Any of that classic jazz—Duke Ellington, Monk, Coltrane—whatever the best stuff is. It can be intellectually analyzed for days, of course. You can take all the same tools you take to Beethoven. It's totally smart stuff. It's also grooving and fun. Like film noir: you can get all the expressionist, thick, abstract stuff in the world; at the same time, you've got the sentimental love story and some guns. This is some classic American art, high and low at the same time.

"Anyway, so Mark Morris: very intellectual patterns in the dance; at the same time, something very lighthearted about it. The pleasure centers get activated as well as the brainy centers. So that was a big influence on me, and probably I couldn't have played in the Bad Plus if I hadn't worked with Mark Morris. I think I would really be more like—I wouldn't compare myself qualitatively—more shall I say in the strictly Paul Bley, Andrew Hill, very idiosyncratic, only-for-the-connoisseur kind of musician. With the Bad Plus I ended up all of a sudden on all the covers of all the jazz magazines, in a way that Bley or Hill never did. That's something I owe Mark Morris. That's what I like, too. I've grown into wanting music that really communicates and activates the pleasure centers as well as being intellectually impregnable.

"I'm not against experimental music. I think there's a real need for it. But I was lucky enough to sort of end up in my right place, which is a certain amount of that and a certain amount of everything else, too."

Iverson's right place, for seventeen years anyway, was principally with Anderson and King in the Bad Plus. King sketched out for me how the three came to become a band. The others would come see his band Happy Apple when it came to New York to perform, and both liked the idea of it being a committed ensemble with a name. Anderson and Iverson were already playing in each other's groups by then, and they agreed to reunite with King in Minnesota for a trio gig, which took place at the St. Paul club Artists' Quarter in May 2000. Anderson and King had recorded some reconstructed rock songs together in Los Angeles some years earlier, and suggested they try the same thing as a trio.

"Ethan's like, 'OK,'" recalled King, "and that's when we started the conversation about, 'What can we do?' Ethan didn't know *anybody* at this point. He hadn't heard of the really big [rock] bands, and that started to become an interesting idea." Iverson, unlike his partners, would be coming to the cover material cold, with no emotional attachment to the songs, treating them purely as music to be altered as the three of them saw fit. They wound up playing originals from each of them and Nirvana's "Smells Like Teen Spirit," the latter because it remained such a formative song for rock fans of their generation. "Ethan," said King, "hadn't even heard *that*."

They loved the results at those first shows and spent the next five months planning how to build on them. "We were so excited about how we sounded together that we leapt right into it," said King, who thought up the band name and got them booked as the Bad Plus for two more shows in St. Paul that December, this time at the Dakota. On that same trip, taking advantage of the existing relationships Anderson and Iverson had with Fresh Sounds/New Talent, the Bad Plus entered Creation Audio in Minneapolis and recorded their eponymous debut album.

The album was released the following August, with a record release performance slated for the New York club Roulette on September 13. But the 9/11 terrorist attack caused that show to be rescheduled for December. That wound up working in the band's favor.

The Bad Plus got a triple dose of good publicity from *New York Times* critic Ben Ratliff that month that helped speed them on their way to being signed by a major record label. A December 2 profile of Iverson, titled "Building a Jazz Career by Working Outside Jazz," told of how the pianist was juggling his work as Mark Morris's music director with seven performances over the next couple of weeks, among them the three with the Bad Plus at Roulette. Ratliff then gave those Bad Plus shows a glowing review ("A New Trio Gives an Artful Mauling to Old Pop Radio Hits"), published December 20, that emphasized the group's serious musicianship and unique, tightly focused arrangements, concluding "When a band starts life at this level, there's great hope ahead."[72] Three days later, Ratliff ranked their Fresh Sound debut fifth on his list of ten best albums of 2001.

Iverson, meanwhile, had met the legendary A&R man Yves Beauvais at one of his solo concerts and invited him to check out the Bad Plus at Roulette. Beauvais, who had recently joined Columbia Records after a distinguished career at Atlantic (the 1993 Ornette Coleman box set *Beauty Is a Rare Thing* was one of his more notable achievements there), was unimpressed by what he saw that first night at Roulette. The drumming was too loud, he thought. But the high praise from Ratliff helped persuade Beauvais to keep the band on his radar.

The Bad Plus spent early 2002 playing shows to build on the early momentum—some they set up themselves in New York and Minnesota; one at Columbus, Ohio's Wexner Center for the Arts, whose director of performing arts, Chuck Helm, booked after catching one of those first shows at Roulette; festivals in Europe that Fresh Sound had helped arrange. The group also got a night at the Village Vanguard at the end of June as part of that summer's JVC Jazz Festival. Ratliff wrote another favorable review ("A Genial Trio Plays Stylistic Cat and Mouse"), singling out King's drumming for special praise. The house was packed that night, and Beauvais was back in the audience. This time he loved what he saw, and signed the band to a contract that led to four albums. Club owner Lorraine Gordon was won over that night, too. "We thought she would hate it, of course," recalled King, "and she ended up giving us a week. She booked us for February 2003, which ended up being our release shows for Columbia."

On a whim, King asked if Beauvais could contact renowned recording engineer Tchad Blake—whose many previous clients included stars like Tom Waits, Elvis Costello, and Los Lobos—and see if he would be willing to work on their jazz album. To King's surprise, the next thing he knew the Bad Plus was headed to England and Peter Gabriel's Real World Studios for a couple of days in fall 2002 to record their Columbia debut, *These Are the Vistas*. "Totally live records, by the way," said King, of that and the two more with Blake that followed. "That first record has zero edits, zero overdubs. The takes are complete. The second record, there's like one edit—we even talk about where we did an edit. The third record is again, mostly first takes on all these records."

It was *These Are the Vistas* that made the Bad Plus, if not *famous* famous, at least *jazz* famous. Fred Kaplan profiled the band and the new album for the Sunday arts section of the *Times*, previewing the Village Vanguard shows. Gary Giddins caught a sold-out show there and assessed the Bad Plus and their new album for the *Village Voice*.

Giddins joked early in his review that a cynic might assume that the Bad Plus covers "cloying pop tunes" covers to make their originals sound better by comparison ("whiskey to wipe away the taste of grenadine"). "On the other hand," he added, "since the Bad Plus's few covers are chosen less for melodic or harmonic grounding than for hooks—those repeated morsels or sweetened riffs that nag the memory like nursery rhymes or '50s commercials—they serve the same useful function as standards, orienting and flattering the audience. This falls under the rubric of admirable commercial savvy, and undoubtedly contributes to the increasing enthusiasm for a group that has the disarming appearance of an adventurous jazz piano trio. In truth, it's an equilateral chamber group that merges jazz, pop, and the conservatory in a heady and original way, assessable and seriously playful."[73]

I got my own first look at the Bad Plus in January 2004, reviewing a set at the Regattabar as part of what proved a successful bid to establish myself as the *Boston Globe*'s weekly Jazz Notes columnist.

"Simply put," I wrote, "pianist Ethan Iverson, bassist Reid Anderson, and drummer David King have been exciting listeners everywhere by bringing rock 'n' roll attitude and a sense of humor to avant-garde jazz. They've been billed, tongue in cheek, as 'the loudest piano trio ever,' and they are best known for covering Top 40 rock by Blondie ('Heart of Glass') and Nirvana ('Smells Like Teen Spirit) on *These Are the Vistas*. But their jazz chops are abundant, they interact as tightly and telepathically as any top-drawer trio, and their peculiar approach to fusing jazz and rock is entirely acoustic."

I made clear that the Bad Plus shouldn't be anointed anything as grandiose as the future of jazz, but that their approach to the jazz trio was fresh and engaging. The friend who saw the set with me, a guy receptive to jazz but no aficionado, thought the group's new approach to jazz trio enhanced the music's relevance. What particularly impressed me that night, though, was the sight of a line snaking its way from the club door to the stage after the set was over, young fans waiting to say hello to the band members, get CDs signed, and what have you. It remains the only time I've seen a line that long of enthusiastic fans in many visits to the Regattabar.

"Columbia didn't think it was going to be this knockout thing," King said of the new album and the fans the surrounding buzz generated. "They were just prepared for it to do OK, but as soon as it started getting great reviews, they started to put some promotional dollars into it. So we really caught the tail end of the major label system. The Bad Plus were one of the last [jazz] groups to really benefit from a major label."

Big crowds and major label attention didn't sit well with everyone and neither did the pop covers. By the time the Bad Plus released its follow-up album, *Give*, a backlash was underway. The Bad Plus was then generating so much buzz, positive and negative, that it appeared on spring 2004 covers of the rival jazz magazines *DownBeat* and *JazzTimes*.

The *JazzTimes* coverage beat *DownBeat*'s by a month, arriving in April, and comprised a three-part package. The main story was a straightforward profile based on Tad Hendrickson's interview with the band. An even-handed assessment by John Murph offered praise, concluding that the band was neither "jazz saviors" nor "jive-ass suckas," but raised the possibility that race was contributing to their success. "From the perspective of a black person," wrote Murph, "witnessing the Bad Plus being so lovingly embraced by jazz establishment and mainstream press, so early in their career, leaves a slightly bitter taste. Meanwhile, equally daring and inventive black artists such as Steve Coleman, Jason Moran, Greg Osby and Orrin Evans have had to toil for far more years to receive such praise."[74]

The choice of those four in particular, of course, had taken on added meaning as Evans was about to join the Bad Plus. Moran, like Evans, is a contemporary of the three original Bad Plus members—all five men born in the early 1970s—and Moran already had five albums out on Blue Note when the article appeared, and would soon surge back ahead of the Bad Plus in recognition. Anderson, Iverson, and King had done their share of toiling in obscurity before the Bad Plus got them attention. That they beat Coleman and Osby (born in 1956 and 1960, respectively) onto magazine covers better illustrated Murph's sense of injustice.

The third part of the *JazzTimes* package was a memorable takedown of the band by veteran music writer Bill Milkowski, best known for his biography of Jaco Pastorius. Milkowski opened his essay by announcing that, contra the rave reviews the band had received from the *New Yorker*, *New York Times*, *Esquire*, *Rolling Stone*, and others, he came "not to praise the Bad Plus but to bury them."[75] He especially loathed the covers, the band's volume, the classical influences that he thought obscured the jazz ("loud but ultimately more beholden to Beethoven than bebop, more Rachmaninov than 'Rockin' in Rhythm' "), and, most of all, King's "ham-fisted" drumming.

The Bad Plus weren't the first among their peers to interpret contemporary pop songs. Brad Mehldau put Nick Drake's "River Man" and Radiohead's "Exit Music (For a Film)" on his 1998 album *Songs: The Art of the Trio Volume Three*, and has recorded more Radiohead, the Jimi Hendrix hit "Hey Joe," and others since then. Jason Moran put the Björk tune "Joga" on his 2000 album *Facing Left*, having already recorded her "All Neon Like" with Greg Osby for Osby's album *Inner Circle*, and did a version of "Planet Rock" on his 2002 solo album *Modernistic*. But the Bad Plus started doing so right from their first album, and the original versions of the songs they covered often skewed less arty than the others' choices.

The covers helped make fans of people unaccustomed to jazz and other instrumental music, and entice them to enjoy the Bad Plus originals. Detractors considered that pandering. Not surprisingly, the band members reject that view. Anderson and King had been talking of covering pop tunes for years, and doing so not to lure listeners but to suit their own tastes.

"It's something that we would have liked to hear ourselves," Anderson told me. "Dave and I used to sit around when we were in high school, I remember very clearly, at my parents' house. Because we were interested in jazz, we were going out to see jazz in Minneapolis. Some local groups, some really great musicians. We would just say, 'Wouldn't it be great if we had a band and we went out and we were playing the Police, but it was a jazz group.' So this idea was really in the air, and in our minds, since a long time ago, since the '80s. In fact, Dave and I made a recording in 1992, where we played Led Zeppelin's 'The Ocean,' and a crazy version of 'Better Get it in Your Soul,' Mingus, and, uh, what else did we do? I think we did another. We did 'Spanish Castle Magic,' Jimi Hendrix. So this was something that was on our minds. When the Bad Plus started it was just in there somehow as, 'Let's try this.'

"I always say about the cover tunes, they really gave us more freedom because we're playing 'Smells Like Teen Spirit' or 'Heart of Glass' and in a way we can get away with anything," Anderson added. "It gave us the freedom to go in unexpected directions, but also we always gave it up to the song. We would always let the hook be the hook on some level, embrace the pop sensibility of it. But we could be playing the most out free jazz in the middle of it, and it would make sense, too. It was fun for us. It was what we were naturally inclined to do anyway. But from the audience perspective, it's like, 'Oh wow, they're playing "Heart of Glass." ' And you bring the hook back and do it in a dramatic manner. There's something very satisfying about it."

Not every Bad Plus cover incorporated free jazz. " 'Smells Like Teen Spirit' is basically just a modal jazz tune the way we play it," he noted. "I really would beg to differ with somebody who draws a distinction, musically speaking, between that and something from *A Love Supreme*, in terms of the structure. Take away the John Coltrane and Nirvana part of it, it's a modal jazz tune, and we're just playing. It's very much going to be jazz. If you know 'Smells Like Teen Spirit,' you haven't even imagined that some jazz group would do such a thing. And I know that Dave and I as kids—we didn't know Ethan then—it would have blown our minds. We craved something like that."

That last point is key. Yes, the covers have attracted fans to the Bad Plus. But the fact that the band is playing them is more for their own satisfaction than to entice or mollify listeners. I told Dave King a few weeks later in Montreal about Robert Glasper telling me that he had once asked Herbie Hancock why the bootleg recordings of the classic Miles Davis quintet had so many standards on them rather than the great new pieces Hancock and Wayne Shorter were then writing for the band. Hancock's answer was that Miles made of point of offering his audiences music they were familiar with.

"For us, we never thought about it," King countered. "We were just like, 'This is music we like.' Well, we could play 'All the Things You Are' for the nine-trillionth time, or we could play 'Heart of Glass.' The calculation is the attention to aesthetic and detail that we have. How people are going to receive it has never been part of it. We wouldn't have lasted this long if we were making decisions based on some sort of audience reaction. Oftentimes we've challenged the reception of what we are. When I read the program here, it's wrong."

He meant the official program handed out at the Montreal festival, whose blurb on the Bad Plus emphasized the group's pop covers (and also implied, erroneously, that *Western* classical music—as opposed to the classical, Carnatic music of India— was part of the mix of what Mahanthappa is known for): "The Minneapolis trio, idolized for their many audacious covers, pushes on through the invitation series, welcoming a saxophonist with a revolutionary artistic view, the dazzling Rudresh Mahanthappa, with his array of projects fusing Indian music, classical and jazz."

"You think you're going to show up and hear a bunch of David Bowie songs all night?" King huffed. "It's just ridiculous. It has never been that, and it never will be. We just made a record of all interpretations"—it had been nearly ten years since they'd last covered a pop tune on an album, he noted—"and [during subsequent touring] we played one a night, maybe. Maybe two. . . . When we make decisions it's not based on imitation. It's based on, 'This is what we want to hear.' That's an important thing to know: in that band—Ethan, everyone—that's the ethos from the get-go."

"It's not as simple as an eight-by-ten glossy or a pull quote about Nirvana or whatever," King had told me in Boston. "When we came out, if all you saw was this big push from Columbia and this big trio that has rock influences you might have already made up your mind about something that in a way compartmentalized us unfairly. I don't mean everyone has to be treated fairly. I understand it. But I think the Bad Plus in time has shown it's always been a much more complicated relationship with references, with where we're coming from. 'One guy's a jazz guy.' We were all raised improvisers playing straight-ahead jazz. In fact, the guy who's 'the classical guy,' the pianist, is not—the *bass player* has a degree from the Curtis Institute.

"So again, this idea that it's easy to understand what we're up to . . . When Stanley Crouch saw us, one of the things that he said was, 'When you guys swing, it's so swinging.' He said, 'I thought this was supposed to be some rock thing.' And he was really talking to me. He ended up calling me on the phone a bunch of times. He said that he came into the show being told that we suck and that we can't play. He came back three times."

"The fact is we are part of a community," said Anderson, when I later brought up King's Crouch story. "We didn't just come out of nowhere. I was playing at the Vanguard long before the Bad Plus. Stanley would come down and I knew him. We had a very nice relationship. I remember going down to the Vanguard and sitting next to him. This was when the Bad Plus was getting a lot of attention all of a sudden. He was asking me what I was doing, and I said, 'Oh, I'm just playing with my band,' and he said, 'What band is that?' And I said, 'The Bad Plus.' He was clearly shocked, because he viewed me in one way and he actually respected my playing, and he of course had this impression that the Bad Plus was a bunch of meatheads that didn't know anything about music and just suddenly tapped into something. They hit pay dirt, you know? And to his credit, Stanley Crouch would show up and actually check out music. And he liked the Bad Plus."

"There was never a hard line of only people who were into rock or adventurous or whatever, or the straight-ahead jazz critics didn't like us," King told me. "[Gary] Giddins was a big supporter early on. It's more like taking the time to absorb that it's really a modern jazz group. It uses a lot of texts to improvise, which include that neoclassical movement. We're all huge fans of those Wynton records of the '80s. People would be shocked to know that those were my bibles. I know every note of that record. I know every note of *J Mood*."

I told him that others in this book shared his admiration for Marsalis, whose early recordings—*J Mood* and *Black Codes (From the Underground)*, especially—they consider his most adventurous.

"Absolutely," said King, "and it's *group music*. That's not like straight-ahead jazz. That's a concept, a full concept using odd time signatures. A lot of those guys came out the '70s fusion background. Jeff 'Tain' Watts didn't come out of a straight-ahead jazz background. Not at all. He's the first to say it. When Branford was trying to get him in the band, he said, 'You better shed this and this and this,' because [Watts] wasn't coming from there."

"So the idea that there's this purity out there, behind some story you can tell of some puritanical approach to the music is ridiculous," King declared. "And all of our heroes were critically maligned. So when that started to happen to us, we were excited. We were like, 'If we were just pleasing everybody we would think maybe we aren't doing it.' [Ornette] Coleman wasn't doing that. Thelonious Monk wasn't doing that. Those are our heroes. Keith Jarrett's American quartet. Those are all just absolutely idiosyncratic gangsters. Those weren't hirable side guys.

"Our longevity has hopefully shown our commitment to group music, the idea that there is no leader, and also the expansion of the piano trio language. We felt like one of the things we contributed to the most, with all humility, was [redefining] what a piano trio is, both dynamically and democratically. So we would use wild dynamics, like you said. It's whispering. People show up and think they're going to hear this loud band, and it's ridiculous."

The previous night, in fact, their set had been remarkably subdued compared to those I had seen before. I had said so to my wife, who was seeing them for the first time. The next day I told King I remembered him rising up from his drum stool at that first show I'd seen in 2004.

"And bashing," he interjected.

"Beating the hell out of the drums," I added, echoing the thought.

"Absolutely," he agreed, "and that's the idea. Not to sound pretentious, but it was more of an art project. The Bad Plus is really this collective of conceptual guys. We're all leaders outside the project. There's not like this one passive guy that can just play. You can't be able to just play if you're in the Bad Plus. It's got to have ideas. Some of those things, they're really legitimate ideas of using noise elements, using really outsized dynamics on purpose. These are not just like, 'I don't have any control, so I guess I can just do this.' We would *laugh* at that idea. 'We're using triadic harmony, not the Bill Evans harmony, so we don't understand harmony.' Ethan Iverson and Reid, they're harmonic *geniuses* of their generation. We would just howl at some of the reviews. How uninformed."

I noted that Milkowski had taken particular issue with King's drumming, calling it "ham-fisted" twice in the same article.

"Yeah," King replied, "within the review, I remember he'd almost say like, 'These guys are obviously clever' or something. And, of course, he hated it and needed to be the guy to take it down, but the fact is, he probably thought we were going to be done here [i.e., release a few albums and disappear]. And sixteen records! It's like, '*Bill, sorry* . . .'

"And the support we got. I mean, I got an e-mail from Bill Frisell after that. Frisell, who has been a huge supporter since day one. He came out right away. He goes, 'These guys are the real deal, check these guys out.'"

"Well," I put in, "he's one of those guys who's not constrained by what jazz had been."

"That's exactly correct" King agreed. "We're children of the Frisell-ian kind of concept, where you're not just sort of this downtown '80s musician. You've been inspired by everything from contemporary to classical to blues to golden-age jazz—*the Bad Plus* is truly inspired by. So [Frisell] came out right away saying, 'Now you're in line with all your heroes.' He said, 'The tallest weed always gets cut.'"

The Milkowski takedown did knock King off balance momentarily, he admitted. But only momentarily. Milkowski dismissed the Bad Plus for not sounding more like the better-known jazz piano trios of the past, but that had never been the band's intention.

"You can't help but go, 'Wow, he's talking about us like we're Mussolini,'" King said. "At the same time, it's pretty harsh, but you get over that first moment you're being told you're completely worthless on your instrument, in a major jazz magazine, to understanding and knowing, '*No, you're not.*' We know what we're doing. And we knew what we were doing using the engineering we were using in those records to make things sound humongous. That record *Give* sounds huge. It just sounds like, 'Well, you want to put on a record and get a bold statement, or do you want to hear a completely perfectly round, warm piano trio playing in the background of your cocktail party?' That was our idea: If the door's going to open, we're going to come through with a fucking missile. We're not going to just come through like, 'We hope you like us.'

"And that's the way we've always conducted our work. We're not going to deny that we are a part of our generation, even though we have incredible respect for all streams of jazz. Every member of the Bad Plus can talk very eloquently all night long about a lot of aspects of the music. But really, what we're interested in is never denying that where we come from is a quilt, it is a mélange of influences. And if we just push some way in the name of purity for jazz, it's ridiculous. There's minimalist composers we're into, there's great electronic music, and instead of getting a DJ and a keyboard player we use influence within the composition, and we use this traditional lineup of acoustic instruments, and we think that's really interesting. I think it's interesting to sound like Sonic Youth all of a sudden."

"And then *Science Fiction* at other times," I said, "or *The Rite of Spring*."

"Yeah, *The Rite of Spring*. I think it's an interesting idea to allow things, to use them with a high aesthetic. Like you said, when we did the *Rite*, we didn't do it like a jazz tune. We didn't take a section and blow on it. We play *The Rite of Spring*. We're a part of that world at that point. It's not improvised. There's no improvisation in that."

"And you did it with dancers," I said, having seen the Bad Plus accompany the Mark Morris Dance Company performing the ballet the year before at the Brooklyn Academy of Music. The trio played the music from the orchestra pit, and the collaboration with the dancers came off without a hitch.

"We wrote a drum score," King emphasized. "That is a drum score. I'm not just sitting up there jamming away with *The Rite of Spring*. It's a completely detailed situation.

"We try to honor every aspect of every situation we're in. Not like a tourist, you know? Maybe that's the reason why some of the people in the rock community thought we *were* interesting and good, because it didn't sound like some jazzed-up version of something. We were trying to meet the music on its own terms. It wasn't just like 'Put some jazz harmony on a Blondie tune and now it's jazz!' Or 'Smells Like Teen Spirit,' throw a bunch of two-fives on it, and some Bill Evans harmony and swing it or whatever. It's much more like, 'Let's try it and figure out a language within this music of this day.' And a music that you can't deny is a potent commodity for a generation. So what do jazz musicians do if they're playing pop music? Do we just put some jazz harmony on it and all of a sudden it's sophisticated? That was never enough for us. And that's the ethos of the band, continues to this day with this new record."

Criticism of the Bad Plus may have faded through the years, but it didn't disappear. I stumbled onto a fascinating Facebook thread in the spring of 2014 whose host's caustic view of the band's pop covers and King's drumming rivaled Milkowski's. That seemed, for the most part, the consensus among others chiming in their opinions. A couple of contributors I recognized as being, like the host, skilled musicians lacking the renown of the band they were denouncing. But at one point the acclaimed composer/arranger/bandleader Darcy James Argue jumped in exclaiming, "Tough room!" He and the host were soon engaged in a thoughtful discussion of the Bad Plus's merits or lack thereof. Argue's contribution included defenses of both the group's pop covers and King.

"I'm actually totally with you on your general point about most jazz covers of recent rock tunes coming across like twee instrumental soft rock," he wrote. "I absolutely agree that so much of that is clueless and tone-deaf and embarrassing to anyone who knows even a little bit about rock music. I just don't agree that the Bad Plus are an example of this! They are actually one of the few jazz groups to put some thought into the cultural context for those kinds of covers."

As for Argue's take on King's drumming: "And say what you will about Dave King (who has gotten a totally mystifying amount of hate on this thread), he is one of the few jazz drummers who is actually a legit rock player, someone who's been active on the Minneapolis punk/indie scene for years, has a band with Hüsker Dü's Greg Norton, etc. The idea that he somehow doesn't groove seems absurd to me, but I guess some people also said Paul Motian didn't swing, so . . ."

Guillermo Klein is another celebrated composer/arranger/bandleader quick to stand up for the Bad Plus. Klein left his native Argentina to study at Berklee, became an important presence at Smalls in the early 1990s after graduating and moving to New York, and is now best known for the lyricism of the music he writes for his group Los Guachos. Klein dismissed the Bad Plus critics I'd been reading as "idiots."

"I would say of the controversial aspect, that doesn't affect art whatsoever," he told me. "If you are 'the Bad Plus,' just the name itself is a little controversial—this little inside thing to stir you up. 'We are the Bad Plus.' That's kind of the nature of that band, just to show what's possible. Who plays the *Sacre du Printemps* in a trio, to that level? Nobody. So you can say you don't like it or whatever, but certainly you have to take your hat off. And the way they cover pop tunes, some of them are incredible, man. I remember hearing them many times. But one gig, at the Bimhuis, in Amsterdam, they were playing with Wendy Lewis, and they were singing some Pink Floyd tunes. That was incredible. I really, really was transported by the band.

"Anybody that talks shit about them, they should go out and listen to them live. And then they should also think about all the stuff they've done with music. They're doing another thing that is noticeable, which is a crossover from classical music to pop music. Not even jazz. You are mixing those two together in a masterful way. Maybe you don't like it. I could see that the detractors of them, maybe you don't like the cynicism that sometimes emerges from the music. That's an aesthetic issue."

"I know the three of them as individuals," Klein continued. "And I think Reid Anderson, the lyricism is incredible. He's a master composer. Ethan is an amazing pianist, and he's doing a lot for the jazz community, actually: He's writing for his blog. He's a very informed and eager guy. And Dave King is another force of nature. Coming from the rock, he was maybe like Emerson, Lake & Palmer—what would they do in this time? I would think they come from that view, but with much more jazz tradition. I'm so glad they became one of your book's choices. I totally agree."

I mentioned that line of young fans I'd seen at the Regattabar the first time I saw the Bad Plus, and suggested that their enticing a younger audience to jazz was a good thing. That prompted Klein, a Berklee graduate, to point out that what the Bad Plus brought to the music that was new—the pop covers, in particular—wasn't something they picked up in classrooms.

"When you talk about Boston," he said, "the problem with jazz musicians is that they think jazz belongs to a university, where you learn [to play it] more and more. And that's not true. Jazz is a way of life, man. Like it or not. These guys are basically surviving in the jazz community doing that type of thing, and 'We Are the Champions' is a standard. Any tune that leaves room for improvisation, any tune that leaves room for revision of the tune, that could become a jazz tune. . . . It's not about some type of rhythm or form; it's about what you can do to the music to make it alive every time you play. I think that's what jazz is becoming more and more.

"And, of course, the blues," he added. "That's the hardest topic of the moment, which I respect very much. Once there is no blues, it's hard to feel any sort of jazz. But that's another big topic."[76]

It's not hard to marshal support for the Bad Plus from other top musicians. Billy Hart, for example. The master drummer leads a quartet that has Iverson on piano, but he's an admirer of King's drumming as well. When I first met with King, in fact, I brought along a copy of Hart's response to a "Before and After" feature from *Jazz-Times*, a knockoff of the ongoing Blindfold Test column in *DownBeat*, originated by Leonard Feather in the 1940s. Musicians are played unidentified tracks by several artists and asked to guess who is playing on them and to assess the quality of the music. Hart was played "Autumn Serenade" from King's album *I've Been Ringing You* (2012). Hart was stumped, guessing that the drummer's knowledge of the New Orleans dirge and Afro-Caribbean drums suggested it must be someone Hart's age.

Hart was surprised when interviewer Willard Jenkins told him he'd been listening to King. "He really wants to play from the standpoint of a John Bonham, not even a Steve Gadd, more of a—for want of a better word—a rock perspective," he told Jenkins. "But he wants to play contemporary acoustic music and he's pretty convincing when you hear him live. That was heavy that he actually could play that New Orleans dirge like that; I couldn't think of a young guy that could play that slow."[77]

King was delighted by Hart's reaction, which he was hearing for the first time, and said he was looking forward to showing it to Iverson. And Hart offered even greater praise for King and the band when I phoned him at home, interrupting an afternoon nap during a weeklong run at Birdland with David Liebman and Joe Lovano's Saxophone Summit in June 2017.

"He's a great musician," Hart said of King. "Last time I saw him was with Craig Taborn. Brilliant, man. Have you heard that record?"

"Craig's album, right?" I replied. "*Daylight Ghosts*. Yeah, I have. Those guys, you know, they grew up in the same suburb of Minneapolis."

"See, that's a whole scene," said Hart. "Ethan grew up up that way, too. A bunch of these cats. What is it, the bass player in the Bad Plus?"

"Reid Anderson."

"There's a bunch of people up there. Not only that, I had a bunch of students that are from up there, and they all have brilliant minds. All these cats are not only into prog rock, but they were into Ornette Coleman, this weird combination. And that's what they sound like, to me."

"And that's cool with you, right?" I asked.

"Of course it is," he answered. "It's a natural occurrence." Hart had ventured beyond straight-ahead jazz himself as a member of Herbie Hancock's Mwandishi band in the early 1970s, adopting the African name, Jabali, that Iverson still sometimes uses for him.

"What gets a little weird," Hart added, "is the marketing and selling of it. And maybe that's logical, too. It just doesn't seem to include me in it. It doesn't, you know? In other words, makes me feel like, not only do I have to spend all my time studying music, but I have to study business also. But anyway, we keep feeding it [jazz] with young energy. But that's been going on, you know, since Louis Armstrong. So that's what I think about it, the young cats. And the few I know are very exciting to me. Marcus Gilmore—*Jesus Christ*, you know? Tyshawn Sorey, you know? They both been over my house."

"Those cats all play beautiful, man," Lovano answered when I asked if he was familiar with the Bad Plus. "I've played with them a couple times, playing some of Paul Motian's music. Those cats are from Minneapolis. When they were in high school [Motian's trio with Lovano and Bill Frisell] played out there, at the Walker Arts Center. They were at our gig. They've all talked about how that night inspired them, and made them realize that they could develop in their own music and have a way of getting out there and playing their music after they heard the trio, with the way we were playing together."

Lovano had no objection to the Bad Plus covering pop tunes.

"They're playing music that they know, that they grew up with," he explained. "Yet they're revamping them and playing with their own feeling, and also being inspired by Ornette and Dewey Redman and Old and New Dreams, and the trio with Paul, and Keith Jarrett's music with Dewey. I mean, they're coming from a serious place as far as their influences. The times I've had a chance to play with them we've played some of my music and things that they were doing. One time at the Stanford Jazz Workshop we collaborated and did some stuff, and it was beautiful. Great energy and really powerful, and yet intimate at the same time."

A younger cat of my acquaintance, Christian Scott, also spoke well of the Bad Plus. "Oh yeah," he told me. "I used to see them all the time on the festival circuit. Those motherfuckers could get down."

When I mentioned the Bad Plus's detractors, Scott was dismissive of them. "It's always the same stuff," he said. "Guys are looking around saying, 'Why do these promoters call these guys? Why are these guys working so much?' But the work in this music is not just practicing the [instrument]. That's like 20 percent of the work. It's a business, man. . . . The point is, What do you need to do to cross into that space? Not being mad at the musician for playing music. Get your stuff together. My whole thing is, and I say this all the time: 'If you mind your own business, you'll be super busy.'"

Anderson and Iverson, of course, have also heard the criticism. Anderson ignores it. "There's much less of it these days," he noted. "The fact is, we're still here, and we're still making creative and personal music. I'll put it up against anyone's music, honestly. You're not going to say the Bad Plus doesn't know what they're doing if you know anything about music. If you can comprehend what we're doing, you're not going to think, 'That's nothing.' I have no problem with somebody not liking us: it's absolutely their right, and that's totally fine. I'm opinionated myself, and there's some things I really don't like. But I think early on it was a bit weird, like the whole Milkowski thing—it was kind of legendary, like, 'Oh my gosh, was it necessary to attack us on that level?'"

I asked him if, when fellow musicians did the attacking, he thought jealousy had something to do with it.

"It was partly that," he answered. "We got a lot of attention. Even though we had been laboring in obscurity for a long time—I mean, we were in our thirties when the Bad Plus took off. We weren't like so many musicians that got plucked out of universities, and all of a sudden they've got careers. We were at the stage in our lives where we thought we weren't going to *have* a career. So yeah, part of it is, like, 'Who are these guys?' All of a sudden these three white guys are getting all this attention, and this is a problem. I also honestly think that if you just hear the description of the Bad Plus, and have some superficial knowledge—like you've heard a couple bars of 'Iron Man' or something like that—yeah, I would hate that band, too."

Iverson doesn't fret about the Bad Plus being controversial any more than the others do. "My reaction from the beginning has been what an honor to be part of something that's controversial," he told me. "I mean, all my heroes are controversial. A lot of my very favorite music, movies, books remains at least a little controversial even though the creators are long dead. That's the power position. Sometimes you see someone get nominated as the 'it' person in any field, and everyone sort of has to go along. But inevitably that person has less power at some point, because they didn't have to fight all the way from a more pure place. Man, so many people are *such* idiots. If I wanted to have all the idiots like me all the time, the sacrifices I would have to make, you know? It's just an honor to be controversial."

Because the pop covers are maybe the most controversial and/or misunderstood thing about the Bad Plus, I wanted Iverson's take on them. Some had suggested that the covers were done tongue-in-cheek, but the band members always insisted that wasn't so.

"Well, Reid and Dave love that stuff so much," Iverson explained. "I'm a person who's sort of in a different space. For me it's a little bit more like raw material, and 'How can you summon a complex emotion?' 'Tongue-in-cheek' sounds like an SNL skit, or something like that. Never that kind of poking fun at a song. Because I've got news for anyone who thinks that pop songs aren't valid music. *You* write one. See how easy it is to come up with a great pop hook. I mean, inevitably any song I have to learn for the Bad Plus, I'm *singing* it in my head all week. *Why?* It's a gener-ated ear worm of a very pure and beautiful type. It's incredibly hard to do that. It's no *easier* to come up with a great piece of pop music than a great piece of abstract modernist jazz. In fact, it may be *harder* in some way to come up with a really memorable tune than to come up with what most of us play in modern jazz today.

"So in that sense it's definitely not tongue-in-cheek, poking fun at it. Is it a complex emotion? Sure. I think that when Thelonious Monk plays 'Just a Gig-olo' there's incredible irony in it. Irony of a very sophisticated kind. When Duke Ellington plays 'Summertime,' I think there's real complex emotion. Same thing with John Coltrane and 'My Favorite Things,' which is really the perfect example, not technically but in terms of you take a song and really create a band identity around the sort of pop song. Some of those pop songs the Bad Plus played early in our career helped really forge our sound, in the way 'My Favorite Things' helped forge the sound of the John Coltrane quartet.

"And if anyone wants to say jazz guys shouldn't play pop songs, that's the most absurd argument ever. Because they always have. And we probably should have been playing them more than less since 1969. The state of jazz would be healthier now than if we hadn't given up on that."

I mentioned the line of young fans I'd seen at that first Bad Plus performance

I attended, prompting Iverson to express sympathy toward devotees of serious music who are put off by the Bad Plus's pop covers. "It's really hard to make or love music that is unappreciated by the masses," he observed. "People who put down the Bad Plus, I get it. You're into your really hardcore music. I understand why us playing 'Iron Man' bothers you. I never had any problem with it really. The Bad Plus shouldn't be for everybody.

"You never know what works or what doesn't," he went on. "I remember Gunther Schuller came to a gig at the Regattabar, and we played our usual set, which at time had a piece by Milton Babbitt, a faithful [arrangement]. Here we are playing a note-perfect piece by Babbitt at the Regattabar, and everyone claps loudly afterwards. And I go to talk to Gunther. He was actually so nice about the gig, because I think he also was really tired of what he perceived to be post-Coltrane modal jazz blow-athons, and that's not what we do. Which a lot of jazz wasn't, by the way, but in his mind, it had really been taken over by that Coltrane model. He was delighted by our songs and everything, and he was so nice. But I asked him about the Babbitt and a shadow fell on his face. I could tell that it really bothered him. I don't think we had enough of Babbitt's original dynamics, and had a feeling it wasn't a good idea in his mind either. It just goes to show—that was a good moment for me—you never know how stuff is gonna land. A person who understands that music best was bummed about the Babbitt; the audience loved it. What are you gonna do? I firmly believe it was the right thing to play the Babbitt, to heck with Gunther's very highfalutin' opinion. But that's a legit opinion I respect."

"That music can also cause a visceral reaction in lay people," I said, meaning experimental music that falls outside the familiar parameters of straight-ahead jazz. "The music I like the most has both of those things somehow." I cited Ornette Coleman and Henry Threadgill as examples of composers whose work engages both the minds and the guts of listeners.

"I do think some of the hardest jazz to understand is straight-ahead jazz," Iverson said, zeroing in on the idea of people reacting viscerally to music. "It's swinging and everything, of course, but I think you really need to know something to appreciate it. Something about how it works. Not that you have to be a musician, but I think your average fan in the '50s, when they were listening in the glory days, really understood something about how it worked. When free jazz broke open the older generation didn't like it, but a lot of young people did like it. It remains something that actually communicates, because of the sheer intensity of the music. Especially in a live setting. But I think there's a whole group of people that like rock and free jazz because of how it communicates directly, but don't think much of a Sonny Rollins trio record. It just doesn't scan. There's not enough that they can figure out there. You sort of have to know something about what's going on.

"Same thing when you're listening to a Bach fugue. You can listen to Bach, but if you don't appreciate that the theme enters and the voices come in in a certain way, you're not gonna get as much out of it. There's lots of people in our culture that don't know what a fugue is. There's people in our culture that can't appreciate a classic Sonny Rollins trio. I almost think there's more people who can appreciate free jazz—or rock for sure, obviously. Free jazz is actually closer to having some kind of accessibility in some kind of way. You can understand the theatrical, artistic intent behind it. Some people might think that Sonny Rollins trio is just background music, that nothing's happening."

"The fact is," said Anderson, "we have a seventeen-year body of work. We have a lot of stuff. Our own compositions alone is a pretty big world, and there's a lot of committed music in there—and a lot of, dare I say, really sophisticated music. Not to mention doing something like *The Rite of Spring* or our takes on covers, from Aphex Twin to Ornette Coleman to whatever. I'm quite comfortable presenting that evidence. And I do believe a lot of people have come around, when people have actually listened to more than part of one song. If you do go in there, I doubt you're going to go out the other end saying, 'Yeah, these guys are a joke.' "

"The Bad Plus's longevity will depend on how long it can thrive amid group textures," Gary Giddins wrote in his early assessment of the trio in the *Village Voice*. As it turned out, the original members stayed together for seventeen years and were still thriving together musically when Iverson decided to move on.

A couple of decades is a long time to maintain interest in a project, even one refreshed as frequently as the Bad Plus did theirs: avoiding the pop covers that made them famous for five albums, then doubling back to an album entirely of such covers for their final one with Iverson; their introduction of electronic instruments on 2012's *Made Possible*; deep dives into major works by Stravinsky and Ornette Coleman (and smaller ones into those two, other classical composers, and Paul Motian); and the collaborations with Wendy Lewis, Joshua Redman, and others.

Iverson's focus shifted elsewhere, and not just in the type of music he wanted to perform. He'd begun teaching at New England Conservatory (NEC). He was writing more and more, and not just for his award-winning blog. He had begun work on a book, and in August 2017 made his first contribution to the *New Yorker*'s culture blog, a piece titled "Duke Ellington, Bill Evans, and One Night in New York City."[78]

I've seen Iverson teach a master class at NEC that emphasized early jazz piano of the stride era and another that consisted of a trio rehearsal with fellow NEC professor Billy Hart and NEC alumnus Ben Street for their trio performance the next day at Boston's BeanTown Jazz Festival, the three of them fielding questions from students on breaks and afterward. But I also got a good sense of what an excellent teacher he would make from talking to him that day in his apartment. Iverson is as good an interview as he is an interviewer.

We spoke some of his reluctance to record a solo piano album ("I've thought about it a lot but I'm not quite ready. I'm working on it.") and the physical aspects involved in playing piano ("Playing uptempo bebop changes, that's an athletic event. . . . It's a physical beatdown on your body to do it. At some point you just play slower tempos, you take it easy, then you're really in the cycle of giving up your capital.") before working around to his piano influences. He'd told Ben Ratliff about how he, like others of his generation, had been wary of the usual models that the pianists ahead of them had been drawn to. I mentioned an LP I remembered from my high school days that featured a couple of tracks apiece from McCoy Tyner, Chick Corea, Herbie Hancock, and Keith Jarrett.

"I'd add Bill Evans," he said. "The base line when I moved to New York, really feels like, was Herbie Hancock. People really want to sound like Herbie, and he's very influenced both by McCoy Tyner and by Bill Evans. And then Chick Corea is sort of Herbie with a little more angularity and Latin. The purest of those guys is really McCoy. And McCoy is very influential, but I actually think he's more seen through the prism, shall we say, of Chick Corea or Herbie Hancock, more than pure McCoy. And then Bill Evans is everywhere if you're not really dealing with modality, you know?

"That's changed remarkably. I was hardly the only person that felt that stuff was tapped out. I think if you made a list of whatever you think the hot players are of my generation . . ."

"Jason and Vijay," I offered.

"For sure," Iverson agreed. "Craig Taborn. None of us have that Herbie Hancock base the way I felt was in the air at the time. Herbie Hancock, he's so great, but it's one version of the music. It's Herbie's version.

"You know, an influence on all these people of my generation who's very import- ant is Geri Allen—at least these albums of the '80s—who had real command of form and composition, and she was also really surreal and had something very different, but you could play it with a straight-ahead rhythm section or play it with a free jazz group or whatever. Whatever the context was, she had a solution that really was fabulous. She really was sort of like the mother of us all, really, I think on some kind of level."

"Can you speak to other huge influences?" I asked.

"That's the only one I can think of, if you talk about Vijay or Jason and Craig Taborn and me, for example, which I'm not sure I belong in that company, but fine—if that's the company, then I think that's the only one that's that obvious."

I asked about other instrumentalists and composers, noting that Iyer and Miguel Zenón had both cited Steve Coleman's enormous influence on post-Coltrane jazz.

"I don't approve of Steve Coleman's overwhelming influence," Iverson replied. "He's a genius, but I don't like how it's so dogmatic.

"In general, any of the people that foster the cults have their way of doing things, but it's not really the way the *masters* did it, although they themselves are masters. Classic example, and I think the first cult, was [Lennie] Tristano, who's great. And *he* was incredible. But then you've got all these people spouting this lingo and having the system that was Tristano's system that produced pretty ineffectual music. Barry Harris is a cult, OK? Barry's great, but then you got all these bebop nazis wandering the earth that, they're not relevant or particularly striking musically. Kenny Werner has this thing about effortless mastery. Dave Liebman and Richie Beirach have this thing, this real sort of organized way of talking about the music, with polychords and a certain kind of angularity—Coltrane meets modern classical or something. Steve Coleman has his very elaborate systems, from African music and from the refraction of the pentatonic scale in mathematical ways. All these guys are great musicians, but none of the really great jazz players I know think about it that way. All the great jazz players I know study music, internalize it, and then it sort of comes out in some form of natural and personal fashion. That's the really heavier space, in my opinion.

"The thing about Steve's music is that of course his music is very powerful. But there's some way it really, uh, builds walls around things. And at some point, it's become, with the new generation, the post–Steve Coleman guys, it really feels like playing jazz standards isn't the way you should learn the music. When you've got eighty years of the best players learning how to play jazz by learning to play jazz standards, I don't understand how you come along and say, 'No, well that really wasn't it; this intellectual way you're processing the music is it.' The other thing about Coleman is he writes a part for everybody. In my opinion, all the great rhythm sections have been free—they play what they want. Everyone's a composer in the band. Everyone internalizes what the music is they like, and then they play that music that they like on the bandstand. It's a very European model, Steve's music. Now he might say it's very African, because also he doesn't use sheet music and stuff. And he's a genius, and that music is very successful. But I really think it's a model that works for him, and now it's become *too* influential."

Our conversation moved from Coleman to jazz's relation to social issues and politics. I told Iverson I recalled seeing a jazz critic, in the documentary *Icons Among Us* (2009), suggest that the social conditions that had caused African Americans to invent jazz and keep modifying jazz through its heyday were disappearing, undermining the impact of subsequent developments in jazz. I also told him that Jason

Moran named Fred Hersch, Mary Halvorson, and Iverson as among those with whom he had frank discussions on race, misogyny, and other matters.

"Sometimes I do think jazz was a twentieth-century music," Iverson responded. "That your book is invalid. Because, actually, what it was was a sociological experiment. It is really about race. Jazz really does come down to race. Now, as a white guy growing up in Wisconsin in 1973, I am not the arbiter here. I write about it a lot on my blog, but I hope no one thinks that I come across as the arbiter more than a guy who asks questions.

"I do think at the end of the day that jazz we love was really about the American experiment working out its slave history. Absolutely. At the same time, as much as it's a sociological product, that didn't mean . . . it's too bad, in a way, in our politically more advanced space, I think that it can be hard to accept how connected it all was, in terms of the white people and the black people.

"I think the end of jazz happened when finally black people had some political power and could have record companies—and do Motown and soul and R&B and hip-hop. Why the hell are you gonna support all those white jazz magazines and white record companies and all that shit if your people are finally getting respect and paid by your people, right? So that essentially probably ended jazz, because the geniuses from the black musical community, there was no longer any reason for them to submit to George Wein and Alfred Lion. There was no reason for them to pick up a *DownBeat* and find out Dave Brubeck won number one jazz pianist anymore. That's just the way it works. Now, I happen to be—so much of the music I love the most is by white jazz musicians. Paul Bley. Gary Peacock. Paul Motian, who talked up his Armenian thing in a certain kind of way but at the end of the day is just a honky. C'mon, what are we really saying here? [Lee] Konitz makes sure people know that he's Jewish. Fair enough, we've all got a fraction of suffering in our background. All humans do. Probably any art, you gotta have some stuff in your background that gives you the grit that makes the pearl. Of course. That's the way it works.

"At the same time, whether it was a black musician or a white musician, the music that ended up being jazz, in my opinion, was seldom a very overt political statement. You listen to Miles Davis and Red Garland and John Coltrane playing 'If I Were a Bell'—essentially the best jazz you can have, it's the highest level—it's very hard for me to read it as a political thing. They were great musicians making music, you know? Who knows where it ends? People say it like they can hear the deafness in Beethoven's late music. OK, maybe. Maybe not, though. He was just a great composer making some crazy music. You can get into the sentimental side of it. You can get into the sentimental side of black nationalism, in terms of Albert Ayler or whatever. Fine, you want to do that? I can't say you're wrong. But what makes

Albert Ayler so great is not making a political statement. It's because the music is so fucking awesome. And that I sort of really believe. Most artists, no matter who they are—what sex they are, who they like to fuck, any of that stuff—every artist is mostly motivated by ego and avarice. That's the end game, really. For anybody. It all goes into the mix, but I think at the end of the day, when I put on Ornette Coleman, *Science Fiction*, there's something political there in some vague way. But really, it's simply beautiful."

Of course, it wasn't just a desire to contemplate jazz history that lured Iverson away from the Bad Plus. He also became increasingly preoccupied with performing a purer form of jazz with some of its living legends. I caught him at the Regattabar in early 2017 leading a brilliant trio set with Ben Street and drum eminence Victor Lewis. A few weeks earlier, a friend had emailed out of the blue to praise Iverson's album with Ron Carter and Nasheet Waits, *The Purity of the Turf* (2016). "You know my feelings about Ethan Iverson," my friend wrote, "but the version of 'Darn That Dream' he does on the new one is fantastic." I had thought his skepticism was aimed at the Bad Plus as a whole, not Iverson, and said so. "Iverson always strikes me as mathy masquerading as muscular," my correspondent wrote back. "But that take is great and dark."

Iverson's longest-standing relationship with a jazz master is with Billy Hart, dating back at least to that 1999 Iverson album *The Minor Passions*. Iverson has since toured and recorded three albums with the Billy Hart Quartet, a group that was initially assembled by Iverson for a date he co-led with the tenor saxophonist Mark Turner.

"So what happened was," Iverson explained, "I played with Billy with another group, and I was so blown away. I always loved his playing, but he was the first time I played with one of the great jazz drummers. There's no great jazz without any great drummers. It's just gotta have a great drummer. And all of the people on any of those albums from the '50s, '60s that we love, the drummer is always anointed. Billy's one of those guys. He was the one that I got to know first, and there's also something very youthful about Billy. He always wants to check out the newest thing. That's not true of Louis Hayes, for example. Louis Hayes and I never crossed paths, and they never will.

"I forced some other situations, but Billy Hart was really the guy who wants to hear what a young perspective would be. I was so blown away I just started pursuing him and trying to hire him because he seemed available, which he is available still to a remarkable degree to young musicians. You've gotta pay him, but that's about it, he'll show up to play music. At one of those gigs Mark Turner came to the gig, and we talked about how much he liked it and how much he loved Billy. And Mark, I had played with Mark's quartet, Mark and I sort of knew each other a bit,

I always thought he was great. And I played with Ben [Street] a fair amount. With Reid and Ben, I thought they were the two best bass players, and I thought Mark was the best horn player, of my generation. And then Dave sort of covers all the modern stuff ever. He's the best, probably—I'm not gonna say he's the best, there's a lot of great drummers out there—but whatever, in the terms of the modern language, I'm so covered with Dave. But the counterweight would be playing with a real master drummer like Billy.

"So that quartet, I put that quartet together as an almost instantaneous reaction to having some success with the Bad Plus. These are the bass player and the tenor player I wanted. I don't want to lose contact with it. I don't want to cut the umbilical cord to these guys because of the Bad Plus. And there's no sense in having a young drummer if I've got Dave King over there. But like a master Afro-American tradition guy who's also willing to play with us. We did a week at the Vanguard as the Ethan Iverson/Mark Turner quartet, and at the end Billy said, 'I'm really comfortable with this, come play a gig for me at Montclair next week,' and we learned Billy's music for it. And it *immediately* took it to another level. It was like, *bing*. He was the elder, he was on the microphone, we were playing his tunes. And everyone felt it. So I was like, 'Billy, do you want this band? We'll do this band if you want this band.' He said, OK. And so that's how it went."

The quartet begat another sideman situation for Iverson and Street with another master drummer, Tootie Heath, whom Hart knew well as a fellow native of Washington, DC.

"I called Billy for a little trio gig," Iverson recalled, "and he couldn't do it, and he said, 'Why don't you call Tootie?' I said that Tootie wouldn't play with me, and he said give him a call, give it a shot, and Tootie showed up. See, with Tootie I think there was some luck, because Tootie had never been a leader, and essentially he's always had leaders telling him what to do. And he shows up to play with me and Ben, and Ben and I essentially know every song, and we know whatever he would want to play. We would just encourage him to do whatever he wanted. I think that was like this real moment of freedom for him. Like, wow. I remember him telling other people that 'These guys, they'll let me do anything'—sort of disbelief. He's a straight-ahead master, and he's been around guys who only wanted a very certain thing. Tootie has other interests, there's something a little avant-garde about Tootie himself. That was really a marvelous relationship with Tootie. To play with either of those guys and Paul Motian—there was really something remarkably similar.

"To really play with an old master jazz drummer, it's really something different. And it's sort of an argument that jazz is a twentieth-century music, because they're going. And when they're all gone, I don't know. We'll just be left with this modern, meta jazz. Which is great—I play it—but it's not what it was."

"Dave and I have been best friends since junior high school," Anderson had told me that afternoon in his apartment. "Not much has changed, you know? In like, thirty years or whatever. Back then we were just walking around Golden Valley looking for stuff to do, and these days we'll be in, you know, Germany, looking for something to do."

With Iverson's announced departure, the old friends would soon begin touring and recording with Orrin Evans. Neither was ready to end the Bad Plus, though both of them, like Iverson, had projects outside the core group. King maintained a variety of bands alongside the Bad Plus, most notably Happy Apple and Dave King Trucking Company, and involved himself in other projects with edgy, talented musicians such as John Zorn, Tim Berne, Chris Cheek, and his other old friend from Golden Valley days, Craig Taborn.

Anderson also had other interests, but they didn't involve his main instrument. "I'm not that interested in playing bass with other people," he told me. "In fact, not really at all." Instead, he'd begun exploring electronic music in a serious way. There were bits of it with the Bad Plus, on the album *Made Possible* (2012) and on the band's live performances of music from the Ornette Coleman album *Science Fiction*. He had toured a couple of times in a band led by Jeff Ballard, with Lionel Loueke on guitar both times and Tigran Hamasyan and Kevin Hays each making a tour on piano. The month we spoke, he was headed to Minneapolis to back the progressive tap dancer Kaleena Miller and her troupe with the electronic music accompaniment he'd composed for *Shift*, a forty-five-minute piece Miller had choreographed. "We'll see what happens," Anderson said of his explorations with electronics. "It's my interest, and it's what I have some kind of crazy vision for at some point."

For King and Anderson, though, the Bad Plus remained their primary artistic focus, which they thought less and less the case for Iverson. That caused friction, especially given that Iverson, as the pianist, was frequently assumed to be the band's leader. One reason Anderson began handling the band's emcee duties early on had been to dispel that notion.

"Reid and I are in this band because this is *the band*, this is our main project," King explained. "And what it started to feel more like is that Ethan is parlaying his exposure from the Bad Plus to help the things he wanted to do, which was controlling him. It's never boiled over into a fight or anything like that. It was much more just a spot of tension. . . . And then Ethan just straight-up quit. There was no talking to Ethan about leaving. He just said, 'I think it's time for me to move on.' And we considered our next move over a month, and we decided it's not time for us to let go of this life's work that ultimately we have cared for very deeply. We've really curated this thing as our baby."

When we spoke in Montreal, King had said that, of the three of them, Iverson was the member the Bad Plus could survive without. The next time we talked, he made a point of clarifying that he hadn't meant to diminish Iverson's involvement in the band. "I really regret if you walked away from that thinking that Reid and I are sitting here going, 'Well, Ethan is expendable,'" he told me. His point had been that Iverson's departure provided the chance for Anderson and him to prove the Bad Plus really was and will remain a collaborative working *band*, not a conventional pianist-led piano trio.

"The truth is that Ethan isn't—and would admit to this in two seconds, and has in print—he hasn't been an equal artistic member of the Bad Plus's overall style, of our photo shoots, of our song choices, of our entire original book, everything," King said. "Of the three of us, he has written the least amount of music, and he has never really been in the mix of this sort of concept of reworking things, although he has gone along with it and enjoyed the challenge of deconstructing things, which is what he loves to do. He wouldn't do it unless he wanted to be there, but over the years he wanted to be there less and less. And we felt like his agenda of parlaying it into the fame of his blog, working with all these older masters that he's wanted to do, it just started to become, like, 'What's up, Ethan?' . . . Meanwhile, he's the pianist and half the time getting credit for being the architect of the Bad Plus because he's the pianist. You can imagine what that would feel like after a while."

This was especially grating on Anderson, according to King. "One is perceived as the architect of something," he said. "Meanwhile, Reid is the bass player. So you have this sort of bass player-ism—bass players feel forgotten about a lot of the time—and then you've got Reid, who is brilliant, one of the greatest composers of his generation, who has written the lion's share of the original music of the Bad Plus . . ."

"I counted 'em up," I cut in, having previously tallied the number of compositions by each of them that have made it onto Bad Plus albums. "He's done twenty-nine, and you and Ethan each have nineteen." Two of Anderson's twenty-nine made it onto a second Bad Plus album, in fact, raising his total to thirty-one to the others' nineteen.

"So there you go," King replied. "How often do you see an article where it looks like the pianist is the leader, and meanwhile Reid is wanting the attitude to be like, 'Hey, this is a group and this is a group mentality.' Because if one of us feels left out, others have to stand up to that. And I think there was this overall perception that Ethan wasn't throwing down enough on that front."

The concept of a band being greater than its individual parts is paramount to both Anderson and King. "When you have bands with identities you can be fans of them," King told me. "People like that: committed ensembles. That only can

happen if those people are there. Well, that creates enthusiastic music apprecia-
tors, and that helps everybody."

"Honestly, I think that's what everybody wants," said Anderson. "Everybody
wants to be in a band. There's a different energy when you're up on stage and
you're playing your music, versus when you're the hired sideman and you're playing
somebody else's music. It's just different. You can have good music the other way,
but . . ."

Because of that, the Bad Plus had never performed with anyone subbing for one
of the founding members. A handful of times there have been duo performances—
when Anderson and Iverson did so because King missed a flight or when Anderson
missed a week with arm trouble and Iverson and King pressed on without him.

"What we're offering is like, 'Hey, this is specifically what we do,'" said Anderson.
"It has a sound, and it has a committed energy, and a consistent energy, and it's
something you can be a fan of. Like, I'm a fan of the Police, right? So if Sting shows
up with two other guys, it's not the Police."

As it happened, I'd interviewed Henry Threadgill the day before. Threadgill
had been heaping praise on his own group Zooid for its members' unusual sense
of commitment to the band, and criticizing the typical run of musicians today
for their lack of such commitment to their bandmates. "Musicians would be in
trouble if I go to teach, because nobody would be down there in the trenches with
'em," he'd said at one point, later adding, "The young musicians don't know how
to behave."

"There's a logistical and economic reality to the jazz world that makes that very
hard to do," said Anderson, "but at the same time, one of the things I think of when
you're talking about Henry Threadgill and that level of commitment is like, yeah,
knowing the music, showing up, a level of personal responsibility of like, OK, people are going to come to see us. Some of them have never heard us before. We have
this opportunity to reach an audience. Why not show up and be prepared instead
of, like, sort of knowing the music, everybody's got their music stands, we're kind
of reading it on the bandstand."

Threadgill, I added, had been especially critical of musicians who abandon a
performance commitment to accept a conflicting one paying a few bucks more.

"Well, that's true too," Anderson said. "I would totally agree with that. That's
why we've stuck it out for this long. And when Orrin comes into the band, it's going
to be the same mentality. Hopefully we'll have another seventeen-plus years with
Orrin, you know? It's the commitment to having a sound, knowing this music,
embodying this music and this thing. And something that can evolve, but also just
has a core that's always there. And I think that this is something that I personally
want in music that I'm a fan of. That's why people love the John Coltrane Quartet.

What are we talking about? It's Elvin Jones, Jimmy Garrison, McCoy Tyner, and John Coltrane. It's a band sound."

I asked Anderson if he was nervous about the Bad Plus retaining its fans with the change in pianists.

"I think some people are going to be skeptical, some people are going to be excited, some people are going to be curious," he answered. "We don't really have any control over that. I do know that it's going to be fantastic with Orrin, and I believe we're going to win a lot of new fans. One thing about being a band this long, you have a body of work. People actually know our music. That music is still going to be there. And it's not going to sound worse, I'll tell you that much. I think that's an important part of the equation."

I introduced myself to Orrin Evans about a month later at the Newport Jazz Festival, where, as noted by Giovanni Russonello in his *New York Times* review of the festival, Evans was making his ridiculously overdue Newport debut in a career of more than two decades and twenty-six albums. Evans played a set in trumpeter Sean Jones's quartet that afternoon, but he was particularly impressive playing solo at the festival's Storyville stage earlier that same day. He had an active left hand, à la Moran and Iverson, which he used to play walking bass lines more than typical stride, and his right hand often took on a bluesy lyricism that seemed influenced by Keith Jarrett as he worked through a set of originals ("For Miles," "Captain Black") and covers (the standard "I Want to Be Happy," David Bowie's "Kooks"). He ended the set by accompanying himself singing the Trudy Pitts piece "Blessed One the Eternal Truth."

"For solo playing and trio, yes," Evans said, confirming the Jarrett influence when we talked by phone the following week. "It's funny, man. That's only my third, fourth solo piano concert ever in my entire career. It's something I kind of, I run from it on purpose. Everyone else has told me I need to do it, and then when this situation popped up I'm like, 'Ahh, alright.' "

We spoke as his son drove him to a recording session with Tarbaby, the trio Evans co-leads with bassist Eric Revis and drummer Nasheet Waits, superb musicians best known for their work in the Branford Marsalis Quartet and Jason Moran's Bandwagon, respectively. I asked if he had been surprised when Anderson and King asked him to replace Iverson in the Bad Plus.

"Totally," he said. "I've admired their band and admired everything about them, all three of them. It's still daunting and a little, I don't want to say 'overwhelming' but a little intimidating, for lack of a better word. I have made a career, twenty years, out of trying to be the best Orrin Evans. Although Tarbaby is a collective, and I've got other projects, it's always been about me promoting myself and me doing it, and it's never been signed to a major, major label or any of that kind of stuff. But for twenty years I've enjoyed a group [the Bad Plus] that has kind of put their stamp in the history books of jazz already. I'm excited about the possibilities. I'm excited about being included in their journey. But also, there's a lot of feelings. Feelings of fear, you know? Because you're coming into something where everybody else is already."

Evans has known the three of them for years, and recorded a couple of albums with Anderson, Waits, and others in the years when the Bad Plus was being launched. He met Anderson when the bassist was at the Curtis Institute. Evans was then in high school at Girard Academic Music Program, a magnet-school rival to the Philadelphia High School for Creative & Performing Arts, whose many illustrious alumni include Christian McBride—who as Newport's new artistic director ended the career-long omission of Evans from the festival—Kurt Rosenwinkel, Joey DeFrancesco, and Amir "Questlove" Thompson of the Roots and *The Tonight Show* fame.

Anderson and Evans first connected when Evans hired Anderson to sub for his usual bassist at a family birthday party, giving Anderson a lift to the gig in his 1979 Monte Carlo. Evans had an album that he liked blasting in the car when he picked up Anderson, and asked the conservatory student, two years his senior, what he thought of the music. Anderson told him he thought it sucked.

"I'm blessed to have friends like Reid, Eric Revis, Nasheet Waits," Evans told me, "and I say those people because when they're around me, they challenge me. They never say, 'That's cool!' Although, I tend to do that with them sometimes. I'd rather not tell you I don't like you. That's a whole other conversation. But with them, they'll quickly say, 'Why you listening to that!?' And I have to quickly explain myself. And sometimes, once I explain it, they're like, 'Cool.' But they will make you work to know how to support and represent what you like. And I've always appreciated that about them."

Curious, I asked what the music Anderson objected to had been, assuming it must have been some sort of pop that Anderson considered not up to snuff. Evans swore me to secrecy and named an album by a highly regarded jazz pianist.

"I'll be damned," I told him. "That's really putting your nose up in the air about something, to say that sucks."

Evans laughed. "See what I got to deal with?"

I told Evans that King had told me a few weeks earlier that Evans had already rehearsed with Anderson and King, and that the band sounded better with Evans in it.

"My goal as a piano player is for it to sound different," Evans replied, "but at the same time respect the tradition that Ethan has set. And the other hard thing about it is, I guess the best way to put it is, most people are full of shit. That's the reality of it. Most people say what you think the other person wants you to say. I kind of just said that myself. I said being around [Anderson, Revis, Waits], they challenge me. For me, I'll just be like, 'Oh, you like that. Cool.' Ninety percent of the time I probably liked what they put on. But still, in that situation, I'm going to be like, 'Whatever, it doesn't matter.'

"But what I'm walking into, in this situation, I have to believe that they're being honest. And that's a new thing, because in jazz we [typically] get, 'Oh man, you sounded great. Oh man, you sounded good, it was really enjoyable.' So I guess the most difficult thing is figuring out what it is that everyone likes about each other's playing, and what everyone doesn't like about everyone's playing. What is it that Reid does that gets on Dave's nerves? Maybe I can play differently when that happens.

"I'm on my way to the studio right now to do a record with Tarbaby, two of my brothers. There's different things we love about each other's playing, and there's probably little things that we do that we don't like. So if someone had to come into Tarbaby, they'd have to figure out the dynamics of the band. That's what I'm hoping to do with this situation. Without direct information, like, 'Hey man, don't ever voice your chord like that, I couldn't stand that!' But trying to hear musically what we all need to happen on the bandstand."

Anderson had praised Evans's combination of post-bop piano chops and outside sensibility when we spoke. "He has this avant-garde sensibility to him too," he said. "Part of what courses through the veins of the Bad Plus is [that] you have to have a foot in something a little weirder." Evans, Anderson said, was "a bit of a weirdo. I think that's one of the job requirements."

Evans had no objection to that characterization when I repeated it to him.

"Everybody that I'm close with and associated with, it is the land of misfit toys where we all meet up," he said. "Not because what we're doing over here is so different; it's because what we're doing over here is all of it. I don't mean that to sound egotistical or braggadocious, but there is an extremely healthy respect for the tradition of this music. And the tradition of music in general. Everybody thinks it's the publicity to have a quote, unquote 'pop tune' on the record, and the reality is maybe they just like that tune because they respect music. So you'll hear that. The people that live in the land of the misfit toys will go from Jelly Roll Morton all the way up to whatever is present now that people find relevant—whether that's Childish Gambino or something very similar. It's basically just a respect for music. The people that live in that land of misfit toys are kind of overwhelmed by the respect that we have for music, for true music. Whether it's out, in, bebop, post-bop, whatever terms you want to use. So when you get overwhelmed with all of those other things, you're like, 'Oh, I just want to play.' You end up in that land of misfit toys, you know what I mean?"

I told Evans I'd been listening to one of his albums the night before, a trio disc with Christian McBride and Karriem Riggins titled *The Evolution of Oneself* (2015), when his cover of the country tune "Wildwood Flower" came on. My wife had asked, 'Who's this, is this Orrin Evans?' When I confirmed it was, she said, 'He'll fit right in.'

"That's one of the [examples] I was about to mention," he said.

I asked if he'd be expected to suggest songs for Bad Plus cover treatment, and whether he'd already thought of any good prospects.

"I've got a few things in mind," he answered. "That's really intimidating, I can't even lie. Because not only are you coming to the band, you're coming to the band with your whole self. Sometimes you can join a band and hide out in their music. Which was also scary to me, because I'm like, 'I got to find me, while I'm hiding in their music.' Now you have to make sure they like the way you play *and* the tunes that you bring to the table. That's a lot. *A lot*. Not a lot as *oooh*. A lot as far as, *I got to get ready*."

Evans was already friends with the founding Bad Plus members when the group first formed, so I asked him if he'd been surprised by the quick success the band achieved.

"I wasn't surprised," he said. "Nothing surprises me anymore, as far as what people will like and what people will be into. They deserve it. They deserved it at that point, and they had a mission. They really had a mission. 'This is what we're going to do, and this is how we're going to do it.' Everything they received, they deserved. They stayed a band for seventeen years and still are [a band]. But if anything, I don't know if 'surprised' is the correct word, but I'm always *intrigued* by everything that happens on the scene. And I love success when anyone's getting it. I'm always intrigued by it. How'd this happen? Whether it's the Bad Plus, whether it's any other artist, *new* artist, that's on the scene. And the thing is not what you get that first day. It's what you do with it. What they've done with it is amazing."

Evans, in contrast, had labored in comparative obscurity. Tarbaby, his Captain Black Big Band, and his numerous other projects had earned him respect among the jazz cognoscenti, but his career made a good case for a point Anderson had raised about certain musicians getting outsize praise while comparable talents get ignored. When we talked, Evan brought up the absurdity of continually being ranked in the "Rising Star" category (formerly "Talents Deserving Greater Recognition") in *DownBeat*'s annual critics polls this far into his career. He had just been ranked third in the new one.

But Evans was philosophical about it. "Everything happens for a reason at the time it's supposed to happen," he said. "Sometimes it doesn't happen for people the way they think it's supposed to happen, but the reality is, 'Man plans, and God laughs.' " He rattled off the names of several musicians who arrived in New York at the same time he did: Jason Moran, Eric Harland, Karriem Riggins, Ali Jackson.

"We all jumped ourselves in New York the same year," he said, "and all our careers have taken a different path. And there's probably one day that we could all go back and say, 'This is the day that we did this.' I remember I was playing at a club in New York with my wife, and my wife was pregnant with my son who is now in a car and is going to drive me back from my studio session. This was almost twenty years ago. And this guy walks in off the street. My band was [drummer] Ari Hoenig, this bass player Darryl Hall, who now lives in Paris, and that's it. We were playing trio, my wife was singing, and this alto player comes in and is like, 'I just moved to town and am looking for opportunities to play.' . . . He sits in and plays, and twenty years later—that was Rudresh."[79]

Not long after talking with Evans, I spoke again with King. Toward the end of our conversation, we ran into some kind of phone trouble and kept getting disconnected. I'd just read King, as I had Evans, that bit in the John Murph article about Osby, Moran, Coleman, and Evans being black musicians who hadn't yet achieved the sudden renown of the three white Midwesterners comprising the Bad Plus. I also noted Murph's sensible judgment that the Bad Plus were neither jazz saviors nor frauds.

By this time King and I were frustrated enough to give up on our phones, but he texted back something as level-headed and accurate as Murph's early assessment of the band had been: "I was simply trying to say that we never called ourselves saviors of anything, and I've never considered ourselves anything other than voices from our generation."

Please visit the open access version of Make It New *to see a video resource for Chapter Four:* https://doi.org/10.3998/mpub.11469938.comp.4

CHAPTER FIVE

MIGUEL ZENÓN

At the Hacienda Sabanera concert venue in Cidra, Puerto Rico, Miguel Zenón, a wiry man a few months shy of forty, with a shaved head and wearing a Pittsburgh Pirates Clemente[80] T-shirt, warmly greeted the all-star sidemen he had assembled for the afternoon's performance. It was August 21, 2016, and the three musicians had ridden here from their San Juan hotel together on a rented white bus. During that ride, guitarist Julian Lage and bassist Scott Colley looked over the Sonny Rollins charts they would be covering—music that Lage noted everyone learns in music school, then moves on and forgets what a "bad ass" composer Rollins is. Drummer Clarence Penn, sitting a few rows ahead of them, described having nearly been hired by Rollins years earlier, only to have the gig fall through when a second rehearsal persuaded Rollins that Penn's playing style didn't mesh well with that of his longtime bassist, Bob Cranshaw.

The venue was remote enough that the bus driver had needed to pull over a couple of times for directions, which jibed nicely with the point of the concert: Zenón was awarded a MacArthur Foundation fellowship in 2008 and used a portion of his grant money to introduce jazz to remote communities across his native Puerto Rico—a practice he has continued with help from other donors after his MacArthur money ran out. Each performance in his Caravana Cultural series is built around the music of a single jazz great (John Coltrane, Miles Davis, Duke Ellington, Joe Henderson, and Charles Mingus are some who preceded Rollins), with Zenón giving a short, pre-concert talk on how jazz works and outlining some career highlights of the featured legend.[81] A handful of local music students typically sit in with the pros for the concert finale.

Zenón recruits a different crew of sidemen, generally top talents he doesn't regularly work with, for each event. Colley, for example, recalls having been on tour in Europe with Zenón in Antonio Sánchez's band when Zenón got the call from the MacArthur Foundation, but they haven't worked together much since. Penn had worked with Zenón only once before, when he hired the alto saxophonist to play on Penn's birthday at the Manhattan club Jazz at Kitano the previous March; not long afterward, Zenón invited Penn to join him for his next Caravana Cultural event. Lage and Zenón had likewise worked together just once, when Lage sat in with the SFJAZZ Collective, but Colley and Lage have been colleagues for years, both in Gary Burton's quartet and in Lage's own trio. (Penn was familiar with both of them as well, having worked in various bands with Colley and recording with Lage on Burton's 2004 album *Generations* when the guitarist was not quite sixteen.)

In Cidra, the one-off quartet had a brief rehearsal, then sat down at a table beside the stage for a lunch of takeout chicken, rice, and *papas rellenas* (potato croquettes stuffed with ground beef). Audience members began trickling in, including a handful of young fans who chatted up Lage about his new trio album *Arclight*, which had been released that March. Soon, most of the three hundred or so plastic chairs lined up facing the stage were filled with concert goers, and Zenón launched his lecture.

Zenón, speaking in Spanish, began by noting that jazz, like various types of Puerto Rican music, involves improvisation, but that the musical language is different. He described Sonny Rollins as having come from Harlem, the "epicenter of African American life," and moved on to a career overview that emphasized a selection of Rollins's best-known collaborators and recordings. Zenón delivered his talk holding his alto saxophone in his right hand and his iPhone in his left, using the latter to check his notes and cue up music samples, among them parts of "Valse Hot," "Tenor Madness," "I'm an Old Cowhand," and the Caribbean-accented "Jungoso. " He ended with a recent recording of "Sonnymoon for Two," with Rollins joined by Roy Haynes, Christian McBride, and Ornette Coleman at a concert celebrating Rollins's eightieth birthday.

As he wrapped up, Zenón offered to take questions from the audience. A young man went first, asking if Zenón had ideas regarding the current state of jazz and where it may be headed.

"I think the most significant thing jazz has currently is its ability to incorporate elements that come from outside jazz," Zenón replied, without hesitation. "Conventional jazz is American, but it has opened up an ability to be very inclusive, incorporating elements of Latin American music, African music, classical music, popular music. In this case jazz, instead of staying sealed up within itself, has opened itself up to incorporate elements from other places. And I think this is the most significant thing, because jazz is not only bringing in music from other places but also musicians from other places—Latin Americans, Africans—who are attracting this inclusive character that jazz currently has, which I think is the most important element right now."

Zenón himself is a prime example of these developments. His Caravana Cultural concerts introduce straight-ahead jazz to Puerto Ricans, but his career has been built largely on the reverse: introducing a wide range of Puerto Rican music and culture to jazz. This was most overtly done on four projects: *Jíbaro* (2005), *Esta Plena* (2009), *Alma Adentro* (2011), and *Identities Are Changeable* (2014).

Jíbaro, Zenón's third album as a leader, celebrated *La Música Jíbara*—the pure-bred folk music of Puerto Rico's rural interior, whose spirit he captured in pieces he composed for his quartet. *Esta Plena,* Zenón's Guggenheim-underwritten tribute to the hand-drum-propelled indigenous music of the modern island's urban melting pot, arrived four years later. *Plena,* he points out in the disc's liner notes, "was not only influenced by bomba and jíbaro music, established genres of Puerto Rican folk culture, but also by music coming from the Dominican Republic, Haiti, Cuba, and other Caribbean islands." Supplementing Zenón and his stellar longtime quartet on the album is a fiery *plena* group led by master *panderetero* and vocalist Hector "Tito" Matos. *Esta Plena* earned Zenón his first two Grammy nominations, for Best Latin Jazz Album and Best Improvised Jazz Solo.

His next album, *Alma Adentro: The Puerto Rican Songbook,* switched things up. Zenón had written all the music on *Jíbaro* and *Esta Plena*, including the lyrics that appear on half of the latter's ten tracks. *Alma Adentro* consists entirely of his instrumental arrangements of Puerto Rican pop standards, two apiece by each of five historic composers. Zenon's quartet is supplemented with woodwinds orchestrated and conducted by the outstanding Argentine composer and bandleader Guillermo Klein. The album earned Zenón another Grammy nomination, this time for Best Large Jazz Ensemble.

All five *Alma Adentro* composers, like so many natives of Puerto Rico, spent some of their lives living in New York City. That Zenón himself had settled in the Washington Heights neighborhood of Manhattan, married, and recently become a father helped inspire his next major project, *Identities Are Changeable*. A multimedia work commissioned by Montclair State University's Peak Performances performing arts series, the project examined evolving Nuyorican identity through English-language interviews Zenón conducted with New Yorkers of Puerto Rican descent, among them jazz bassist Luques Curtis, New York University Latino studies professor Juan Flores (author of *The Diaspora Strikes Back*), actress Sonia Manzano (Maria on *Sesame Street*), and his sister Patricia.

Zenón composed a six-part song cycle, framed by the overture/outro theme "¿De Dónde Vienes?" (Where are you from?), that used complex interlocking rhythms to convey the complexities of dual identity raised by the interviews in relation to six themes—such as race ("Same Fight" couples the similar challenges faced by Puerto Ricans and African Americans), language, and culture. The music is performed by his quartet plus a twelve-piece horn section, with excerpts from the interviews woven into the music. The full-fledged production—also performed at San Francisco's SFJAZZ Center and at Carnegie Hall, and with a student horn section at Boston's New England Conservatory[82]—includes a video component by David Dempewolf, recommended to Zenón by Jason Moran, whose *In My Mind* tribute to Thelonious Monk's 1959 big band performance at Town Hall also featured a video by Dempewolf.

The album version of *Identities Are Changeable* included the audio sans video and earned Zenón another Grammy nomination for Best Latin Jazz Album. A live big-band version was performed without the interviews a few months before the album's release at the 2014 Newport Jazz Festival and aired soon thereafter on NPR's *Jazz Night in America*.[83] The music had also been field-tested early on by the quartet in clubs including the Village Vanguard.

I caught one of those Vanguard sets in late spring 2013, having spoken with Zenón earlier that day in one of three lengthy interviews he granted me in restaurants near his home. At the first of those interviews the year before, his newest album had involved him shifting his attention from Puerto Rico and his quartet to the Julio Cortázar novel *Rayuela*, in a project Zenón co-led with the French pianist and composer Laurent Coq. But he had recently premiered *Identities Are Changeable* in Montclair and said he was looking forward to recording it. I asked if he planned to continue mining his Puerto Rican heritage for musical inspiration.

"The way I see it," he replied, "is that for a while I was trying to find a way to learn more about myself through Puerto Rican music and just try to understand what being Puerto Rican meant to me. I found a way to do that though exploring a lot of those traditions and a lot of folklore and trying to filter that through what we do as a band or what we do when I write music and conceptualize things. I've been doing it for a while, done a couple projects, and I can't really say I'm going to do this forever, but there's definitely a lot more for me to explore."

When I suggested that his doing so gave his music a distinctively strong voice, he agreed. "I think something that's undeniable about folklore in general is that it's so connected to our core as human beings. I can play you some Puerto Rican music, or something in our music that comes out of folklore, and you might not be familiar with it, but you still recognize something in there that sounds more rooted than just chords and notes and stuff. Something that came out of human nature, out of people. I think that's the greatest thing about it, to explore this thing. It's almost like a universal thing, and I feel that it grounds me better—the more I know it, the more I explore it. It makes me more connected to the real source of music and inspiration. Because, like you said, a lot of us went to college and to school, and we learned the language and the rules and blah blah blah. But all of us started playing music because it called us. There was a call for us. It wasn't because of the notes and the fancy rhythms and all that; it was this call to express ourselves. And a lot of us are trying to get back to that—that initial attraction, just a pure attraction, like childhood."

Zenón's call to music came in childhood. He grew up the eldest child in a working-class family in San Juan's Santurce barrio, in the Residencial Luis Lloréns Torres housing project. ("Here you would call it a project," he clarified. "In Puerto Rico, it's organized differently, but it's the same thing.") It was there that he got his initial music instruction, starting at age ten, from Ernesto Vigoreaux, an elderly man who traveled to Lloréns Torres daily to work with the kids there. That led to his enrolling at Escuela Libre de Música, the performing arts middle school and high school he attended between ages twelve and seventeen.

That Zenón wound up playing alto saxophone there was accidental.

"What I actually wanted to play was the piano," he told me. "But the first day of school, where you have to enroll in the classes, I was a little late for some reason with my mom—and when we got there, everyone had the same idea, of course. Everybody wanted to play piano. So I had to pick something else, and I think there was someone in my family or something that had a saxophone lying around. So I just picked the sax. But I think I was a lot more interested in music in general than in a specific instrument."

School days were split between classical music instruction and the usual run of non-music subjects. Zenón excelled at both.

"I was always good with academics," he recalled. "I would say for the first three or four years, I never really considered music as a choice of life—it was just a hobby for me, like playing basketball or all this other stuff I did. I was seriously interested in the natural sciences, and I was really into math, physics, stuff like that. But then I discovered jazz, through friends: Charlie Parker here, Miles Davis there. And I started seeing, not the concept of improvisation—like I said before, improvisation's kind of what's all around—but the idea of improvisation tied to a language that was so integrated and so developed as it was in jazz.

"Plus, that tied to a specific dexterity that was connected to the instrument. When I heard Charlie Parker play for the first time, I couldn't believe it was improvised, because he was playing so clean, so fast, with such great technique and sound. Which is what I was being taught in school: the proper technique and being able to play fast. So that kind of pulled me toward wanting to know more about what that was all about, listening to more records, getting more and more into it."

But it was jazz improvisation itself more than technique that hooked him. Zenón became so enthralled that he declined a scholarship to the island's best engineering college, the Recinto Universitario de Mayagüez, in favor of studying jazz on the US mainland. ("I sort of changed my mind last-minute," Zenón admitted. "My family wasn't too happy about that.")

"As a saxophone player I was really impressed with Charlie Parker," he recalled, "but the idea of improvisation was what was really the catalyst for me. That drew me in, because when you actually realize that that's what they're doing, it's mind-blowing. From that the interest grew, and I made up my mind I wanted to follow that path and eventually made it to Berklee."

It took Zenón a year and a half to get to Boston, time he needed to raise funds via scholarships, financial aid, and assorted paid gigs on the island. He arrived for spring semester 1996 and spent the next two and a half years earning his degree under the tutelage of stellar professors such as Bill Pierce and Hal Crook.

He also honed his music skills off campus. He played Latin-oriented world music in the popular local group Mango Blue, his Israeli Berklee classmate Anat Cohen beside him in the front line on tenor sax. ("So I'm standing by Miguel and it feels great the way he plays. How do I get that?" remembers Cohen of their time together and how it helped shape her feel for Afro-Cuban rhythms. "Miguel was a big influence for me.") He toured with Boston's progressive Either/Orchestra, some of whose other notable alumni through the years include John Medeski, Matt Wilson, and Jaleel Shaw.

But Zenón's most important off-campus connection during his Boston years was with pianist Danilo Pérez, then teaching at New England Conservatory (he now oversees Berklee's Global Jazz Institute). Pérez, a native of Panama, had gone from playing in Dizzy Gillespie's United Nations Orchestra to recording his own albums, the first two of which included his Gillespie orchestra mate David Sánchez, who had preceded Zenón by several years as a saxophone student at Escuela Libre de Música. A third Pérez album, his Thelonious Monk tribute *Panamonk*, would be released toward the end of Zenón's first semester at Berklee.

Pérez and Sánchez were already both key inspirations to Zenón, two recent successes at coming to the United States and mastering modern jazz while retaining their Latin roots. Jazz has always had Latin connections. Its self-proclaimed inventor, Jelly Roll Morton, spoke of early jazz's syncopated rhythms as his music's "Spanish tinge." The Puerto Rican trombonist Juan Tizol co-wrote the Duke Ellington classics "Caravan" and "Perdido." Dizzy Gillespie hired the conga player Chano Pozo in the late 1940s and launched Afro-Cuban jazz. Stan Getz had the 1964 bossa nova hit "The Girl from Ipanema," and Sonny Rollins successfully explored both bossa nova and calypso. Latin Jazz as its own category came to include those things, mambo, salsa, and more.

What set the music of Pérez and Sánchez apart when they joined Gillespie was that jazz was already their primary focus. So much so, Pérez once told me, that he needed to be reminded of his origins by another Gillespie alumnus, the Cuban clarinetist and saxophonist Paquito D'Rivera. "He was actually the first one to hit me in the head saying, 'You're Latino and you sound just like a jazz player. You got to go back to your roots,'" Pérez recalled, laughing. "It's funny, because I really just wanted to play swing, and my life was going that way. But something kept pulling me the other way, too."

Not long after D'Rivera's admonition, Pérez released his second recording as a leader, *The Journey* (1993). A concept album whose theme is built around the introduction of slavery to Latin America, *The Journey* was a big influence on Zenón. Pérez recalls Zenón describing it to him in great detail during one of the younger man's many visits to play and discuss music together at Pérez's home, visits that began after Zenón, despite being a self-described "shy guy," bounded onstage after a Pérez performance in Boston to introduce himself. Pérez had already been alerted to keep an eye open for Zenón by the Puerto Rico–based music writer Carlos Iramain.

"I remember the thing about the concert," Pérez confirmed, "but I also remember clearly him coming [to my] home and saying, 'I'm Miguel.' We actually played a little bit. He showed me a couple things, and I said, 'Show me what you've been doing.' I remember giving him an assignment immediately. I said, 'This is all good, but you need to check out Johnny Hodges.' So I had him working in my home for hours, transcribing Johnny Hodges and playing. I don't remember the song I gave him, but my house was like a little cultural center where a lot of musicians came through."

Pérez does remember Zenón being hardworking, disciplined, studious, persistent—an impression the young man made on him very quickly. Pérez boasts of having singled out Zenón as someone people would be hearing from soon in a joint interview he did with David Sánchez for the November 1996 issue of *DownBeat*. When interviewer Eugene Holley asked about jazz musicians of Latin origins from their own generation who had influenced them, Sánchez rattled off "John Benitez, Richie Flores, Eddie Simon, some younger guys," at which point Pérez chipped in, "We met a saxophonist at Berklee named Miguel Zeno [*sic*]."[84]

Zenón graduated Berklee a couple of years later, in spring 1998, and, like many of his classmates, relocated to New York. But he didn't just move there looking for gigs. He was also pursuing a master's degree in jazz performance from the Manhattan School of Music.

"I just went there because I wanted to learn more about jazz," he recalled in one of our conversations. "I had never had a formal jazz education. Everything I knew before Berklee about jazz, I had learned on my own from CDs, reading a few books here and there. And then when I finished that, some people said, 'You should try going to New York, see how it goes.' But I didn't want to just come here and just kind of *ehhh*. So I decided, 'Maybe if I do a masters, I can have an excuse to be in New York: I'm *doing* something. And while I'm doing that, I'll go to jam sessions and I'll meet people.' Basically, that's exactly what happened. I was there, but I was always playing, and I was meeting people. It was a good transition just to get into a scene here—meet a lot of people through school, and meet a lot of people through just being in New York and going to jam sessions and going to spots here and there."

Chief among those spots was Smalls Jazz Club, which in the late 1990s was where a new generation of jazz artists was honing its craft late at night in front of audiences paying a $10 cover. Joshua Redman, Brad Mehldau, and Kurt Rosenwinkel were among the many influential rising stars to have performed there in those years, as did Norah Jones before her 2002 album *Come Away with Me* made her famous. The Argentine pianist/composer/band leader Guillermo Klein lived nearby and had a weekly gig at Smalls, as did Israeli bassist/composer Omer Avital and Jason Lindner, who besides leading his own bands now plays piano and keyboards in the quartets of Anat Cohen and Donny McCaslin. Zenón would eventually perform and record with both Klein and Lindner. He would also get together with many of the people he was seeing there to pick their brains.

"One of the things that was great about New York for me was that I realized this actually could happen," Zenón said. "I moved here, and I remember going to gigs at Smalls or wherever, and I was just new in town. I would go up to Mark Turner or Seamus Blake or the guys that I liked. Greg Osby or whoever. And I'd just be like, 'Hey man, my name is so and so.' You know, some kid. But I was really blown away by how open they were to sharing. It's like, 'Man, maybe we can get together sometime and just talk about music.' And I got together with all of those people at some point. Just play together, talk about music, what are we checking out, play a session, listen to music. That had a big impact on me. Not only was I able to get a lot from those conversations with more experienced players, and players who I admired greatly—but also, I kind of said, 'Man, it's actually OK to share and feel part of this community.'"

This, he noted, was in contrast to his undergraduate days in Boston, where the students would overhear bits of one another playing in neighboring practice rooms but mostly stayed focused on their own individual development. In New York he found a greater opportunity to woodshed and talk music and other matters with fellow musicians.

"There were a lot of specific things, musical things, of course," Zenón remembered. " 'Check out this record. This is what I got from this and that.' But I think, in general, it was more intangible kinds of things. Just talking with them about how they thought about music, talking to them about certain experiences they had playing with so and so, or on the road. For me, a lot of it, too, was just realizing that they were regular guys. They like basketball, they like food, they're cracking jokes. It was more about, 'OK, so these guys whose records you listen to, you're transcribing, now you're talking to them about boxing or something.' That kind of thing was a big part of it, too."

Two such New York connections proved especially important for Zenón. The first person he looked up upon moving there was David Sánchez. Pérez had already introduced the two of them, and had recommended that Sánchez consider hiring Zenón for his band. "David had talked to me about making some changes in the group, and I said, 'Man, you got to listen to this saxophonist,' " said Pérez. "That was a sort of like his first apprenticeship."

"I met David through Danilo while I was in Boston," Zenón said. "He was kind of the same way Danilo was in Boston. I'd go over to his house, and we'd play and listen to music all day. He brought me to his shows, met a lot of people through him, eventually started playing in his band. Another mentor figure. And I would say those two guys, they were really the guys that I looked up to. They were the people whose road I wanted to follow."

"I'll tell you exactly what happened," Sánchez later told me. Zenón was studying with Pérez at the time, and Pérez asked Sánchez to listen to Zenón play and give him some sax-specific pointers. "He played for me," said Sánchez. "I'm almost sure it was at Danilo's place, and if it wasn't, definitely Danilo was there. So he played and we talked a little bit about the instrument and the sound."

Sánchez was in town to perform with his band at Scullers, and asked Zenón if he would like to sit in with them on a tune or two.

"Back in the day I was playing originals most of the time," Sánchez recalled. "But he said, 'I know some of the stuff.' Then it turned out that he pretty much knew the whole recording, and interestingly enough, on that recording—that recording I made with Danilo, it's called *Street Scenes*—I wrote something for two saxophones." That track, titled "The Elements," had Sánchez's tenor trading lines with guest star Kenny Garrett's alto.

"It was alto and tenor, so [Zenón] knew the parts. I was very impressed with not only his talent, but he seemed like a very dedicated person, right away. We also discovered that he played with some of the bands that I played with in Puerto Rico. And he was interested in the folklore! I'd never met anyone that was interested in the folklore, and he's that much into jazz at the same time. That's basically where I come from. I came from Afro-Puerto Rican rhythms from the start, from my first recording. So I told him, 'When you finish [Berklee], if you are coming to New York, make sure you call me.'"

Zenón, of course, was eager to do so. And he made the most of the opportunity.

"He came to Brooklyn and we started actually working on pieces together," said Sánchez. "These are things that I'm actually working on. The next week he would come and play the stuff incredibly. Better than me! And I thought, 'This guy's quick!' Not only that, he wrote a piece based on the sounds I was working on."

Zenón joined what became Sánchez's sextet, and that tune, "El Ogro," appeared on the album *Melaza* ("Molasses," 2000). He stayed with Sánchez for two more high-profile albums, *Travesía* (2001) and *Coral* (2004), contributing two compositions to *Travesía*. But the association paid other dividends as well. Zenón recruited his fellow Sánchez band sidemen Hans Glawischnig and Antonio Sánchez for what became his own quartet, joined by pianist Luis Perdomo. That group played its first gig together at an East Village dive on September 4, 2000, according to an old calendar that Perdomo dug up (Zenón believes that another David Sánchez associate, Adam Cruz, played drums that first night), and the quartet stayed together until Antonio Sánchez's schedule became crowded leading his own band and touring with Pat Metheny. Henry Cole, a fellow Puerto Rican whom Zenón had gotten to know through mutual friends, took over on drums in 2005, and that version of the quartet remains intact.

It was also through David Sánchez that Zenón met Branford Marsalis, who co-produced *Melaza* for Sánchez in the A&R job he then held with Columbia Records. When Marsalis later left to form Marsalis Records, he signed Zenón to a recording contract that led to his next five albums, ending with *Alma Adentro*.

Marsalis told me that what attracted him to Zenón was the younger man's intelligence. "His *musical* intelligence," Marsalis clarified. "A lot of the music that I hear now, there's a lot of intelligence, but it's more like mathematical intelligence, not musical intelligence. He has the mathematical intelligence as well—you can hear it in a lot of the music that he writes, in the structure. But when it comes to the simple things that our hearts are learning, he can do all of those things with ease. He can play a ballad and not have to play it in double time. He can play 'Great Is Thy Faithfulness' with a certain amount of passion in his sound. The fact that his band stayed, so that the music challenges them. He's the real deal."

Right at their first meeting Marsalis zeroed in on another important influence on Zenón, a contemporary who, as Marsalis had before him, once spent some time touring with the rock star Sting.

"Yeah, he was playing with David," Marsalis recalled of Zenón, "and I noticed that he had done something which was really difficult. He'd been checking out Steve Coleman's music a lot. I could hear it in his playing. Steve's playing is very, very intelligent, scientific, and clinical. And he was able to take that information and still make it sound like Miguel. I think a lot of people trying to play like Steve would have a difficult time doing that. Because it's so specific. And I just walked up to him and said, 'You been checkin' out Coleman, huh?' And he kinda grinned. He says, 'Yeah, man.' I said, 'That's tough shit.' But it sounded like him when he did it, and I'm like, 'All right.' "

Zenón's connection to Steve Coleman was indeed crucial, and went beyond merely listening to his music. It began around the time he was forming his quartet.

"I've played with him a little bit," Zenón said, "and I've hung with him a lot. He's one of those guys, he's really into just getting together and just talking and playing. I remember—I haven't done it in awhile—but I remember just spending all day with him. Just talking and playing, and listening to music, and playing some more, and talking. We'd look at some books. He's into that. A lot of people see him as this sort of guru figure that's leading the way."

"I think Steve is probably the most influential jazz musician of the last twenty years," Zenón elaborated. "Seventy-five percent of the guys that you talk to now are going to bring up his name. And I think it's because he encompassed very early on—I mean, he's been doing this for *thirty-five years*—and he very early on was able to put together this balance between something that's very intellectual and something that's very earthy and has to do with groove. That got to a lot of people with time, especially now with this music becoming so global and so exposed to so many pieces of information coming from everywhere. People are reaching outside of music to find things to bring to music. Like the thing that David Gilmore did [the live album *Numerology*, on which the guitarist was backed by Zenón, Perdomo, Christian McBride, and others], for example, and a lot of other stuff. Some of the stuff that people are doing with art and literature. But Steve's been doing this for years."

Inspired by Coleman, Zenón has been doing a good deal of that sort of thing himself, whether tapping into Puerto Rican folk music on *Jíbaro* and *Esta Plena* or exploring life beyond music on *Identities Are Changeable*.

Coleman, Zenón noted, "was very influential in the sense that when you heard his music, there was obviously something there that wasn't necessarily coming out of music. So it made it interesting. It was a study of natural sciences or a specific kind of religious thing or spiritual thing, or music coming from another place in the world. I think that was the thing that for me, and a lot of people from our generation, that kind of opened the door. It's not that he was the first one that did it, but he was very clear about what he was doing. He was treating it almost like a research project, like a scholar in a way. And that was the thing that a lot of people in my generation grasped on. And, like you said, he's a guy that's so well rooted in tradition as well—not only jazz, but funk, James Brown, and all that stuff, too. So his music, even though it can be very intellectual, it can be very fun to listen to because he grooves, and he has something for you to grab on. So he had a very nice balance, and it represented a lot of things a lot of us were trying to find."

That rootedness in tradition is critical for taking music to new places, in Zenón's view, which explains why he believes that the narrower, neoclassical approach to jazz tradition espoused by Wynton Marsalis and others also had a lasting, salutary effect on his generation.

"I wouldn't necessarily totally detach the stuff that's happening now from the stuff you were talking about in the '80s, with Wynton and the new traditionalist kind of vibe," he explained. "I think that also opened the door to a lot of stuff that's happening now. I feel that trying to create something different just for the sake of it, to me, is a lot less interesting, and it doesn't last as long as something that's well rooted. It's coming from a place where you start somewhere, and that makes you blossom into a personality. It happened with Charlie Parker, Coltrane, Steve Coleman, a lot of these great musicians. They started imitating their idols, and that brought them to discover themselves. I think that specific thing is a lot purer than just saying 'I'm going to do something different' as a sort of revolutionary act. It's purer when it comes out of a source.

"I even feel that the generation before me—like the Brad Mehldaus, the Mark Turners, the Kurt Rosenwinkels, Brian Blade, Christian McBride, those guys—they had, at least for my taste, an even better balance of these two worlds. They were really the best. They said, 'OK, so we've got all this stuff down. We can swing, we can play the blues, we can play changes, all this stuff.' Whereas now, I think we're kind of springboarding off what they did. But those guys, they were the first guys who had feet in both worlds and could do both things real well. Still when I hear those guys that's what speaks to me the most. When I hear Brad or Kurt, they're really dealing with tradition, but at the same time, you hear their personality. They're still swinging, they're still connected to that. But at the same time, you still hear modernity and all this stuff that you connect with. Same thing when I hear Steve and Greg Osby, guys from that generation. It happens to me a lot more with that generation than the current generation."

Zenón is doing what he can to help see it happen in the coming generation. He has taught music at numerous clinics around the world, and beginning in fall 2009—a couple of weeks after the release of *Esta Plena* and fresh from receiving his MacArthur award the year before—he became a permanent faculty member at New England Conservatory. That gig, like Moran's and Iverson's, entails his traveling to Boston seven times a semester to work with NEC students.

Zenón's teaching came up during one of our early chats in Washington Heights.

"I don't have preconceived things for me to tell them—aside from basic things," he told me. "Especially with saxophone players: I find at that age, most of the stuff they need to work on is really basic things. Because part of the problem I encounter with students that age, at the college level—who are good—is that they want to be part of the present. You know, they want to sound like the guys they admire, the guys they hear on the record, the guys they go see at the club. They want to be able to do that, so that's what they practice, and that's what they write, and that's what they listen to. But they have a lot of holes, in terms of their formation—not only stylistically, but also in their instrument, too. So a lot of the stuff I do is basically finding these holes that they have and working out specific ways for them to fill them up. Because that's kind of the way I learn, too."

I told him his remark about the young players being overly focused on the present reminded me of something Robert Glasper had told me about not wanting to sound like musicians from the 1950s and '60s, because music should reflect his own life and times.

"Yeah, I agree with that," Zenón replied. "It's not that I want to play like Charlie Parker or Johnny Hodges, or whoever. I'm not going to play like them because I'm not them. But I do feel that there's a certain lineage in the tradition that has taken us up to the point of where we are now. It doesn't matter what music you play—it could be jazz or hip-hop or funk or whatever—it just didn't happen out of nowhere. It developed into something. And for me, at least, I feel that the more I know that lineage, the better I'm going to be as a musician, and the more rooted I'm going to be as a musical personality. The more I'm going to be able to express myself in an honest way, if I know, 'This is what happened before me, and this is what's been done.' I kind of take it from there."

Zenón contrasted the younger generation's obsession with making an immediate mark on the present with his own student days at Berklee in the mid-1990s.

"I'm not really that much older than them," he said, "but I remember when I was coming up I wouldn't even think about writing my own music. My whole thing was, 'OK, I've gotta check out these solos.' And all my friends were like that. The whole thing was 'learn tunes,' and maybe it's a generational thing, but I think maybe that had something to do with the changing of the guard and it being a lot more crowded."

To succeed professionally, the well-trained musicians being churned out by the country's many jazz programs eventually need to develop distinctive voices. But Zenón tries to keep his students from getting ahead of themselves. Their musical personalities will emerge most fully and naturally, he believes, with a thorough mastery of both history and technique.

"The problem is not necessarily that the students lack personality," Zenón explained. "It's just that I feel that they're missing a lot of basic knowledge, a lot of basic stuff. And, you know, it's common. It's normal. It happened to me, too. It's happened to everyone. And I feel like, for me, what did it was realizing in time that I needed to fill up these deficiencies that I had. Once I did that, I felt more comfortable, I felt more relaxed, and I felt I could get to a personal thing in a more organic way. But then again, it's different for everyone."

I got a taste of how Zenón helps students overcome their deficiencies one sunny September afternoon at NEC, observing him conduct hour-long private sessions with three students. These included Alex Quinn, a trumpeter from South Portland, Maine, and Kenny Cha, a guitarist from South Korea. But the lesson that stuck with me most was with an alto saxophonist from suburban Chicago named Jonah Philion, and not just because he and Zenón play the same instrument.

Philion, in his third year of a five-year dual degree program that would earn him a bachelor of arts from Harvard College (where he was majoring in physics and math) and a master of music from NEC, arrived a bit winded from having bicycled over from Cambridge. He was wearing a T-shirt touting a youth program overseen by the Maywood Tennis Association, where he had worked as a volunteer after playing the sport at nearby Oak Park and River Forest High School. I found out later that he had also taken Vijay Iyer's creative music seminar at Harvard.

What stuck out about the lesson was how willing this young overachiever was to devote the first twenty-plus minutes of his hour with Zenón to working on something that appeared, on the surface, to be quite rudimentary. Zenón had been having him practice working on equalizing the air stream he was utilizing at different volumes and registers. Far from objecting, Philion arrived at the lesson praising what the exercises Zenón had given him had already accomplished.

"I'm already feeling myself get a lot stronger," he reported. "It's one of those things you can feel an improvement immediately. It's already getting stronger so fast. It's also a realization of how much I have to grow in that regard, right?"

"That's very cool," Zenón replied. "You want to start with those exercises and then we do this?"

Philion made several series of whole notes, moving slowly up and down a scale, eventually adding some overtones to the drill, Zenón offering advice after each attempt.

"When you attack the note first, try not to waste so much air. Just try to get it to come out right away without overblowing. Start with nothing. Relax the embouchure so the reed can vibrate."

"Let's try it now. I want you to hold it for four beats. When you get the overtone, try to hold it for the duration, so that you can get the note focused. Get it clean. Control it."

They tried a slow ballad next, "Misty," Zenón comping lightly but credibly on piano. But Zenón was still listening to correct Philion's air stream.

"That's good," he said as they finished. "That's getting a lot stronger. As you keep working on this, the key is focusing now. Focus on the air stream. Never shifts. Loud, soft, whatever it is—it's always the same. Even that last note you played, keep the air flowing through it."

"It sounds weak, right?" asked Philion.

"It just sounds inconsistent," Zenón clarified. "You play in the middle one way and the high register another way. It sounds inconsistent. So this is a good exercise. Do your exercises. Blow notes, overtones, octaves. Then you play a melody. When you play melody, pay attention to all those things. How those exercises brought you to a sense of self-awareness about your sound."

The final half of the session was the fun part, a chance to run through the transcription Philion had been assigned of Cannonball Adderley's solo on "Love for Sale," from the Miles Davis album '58 Sessions, one of Zenón's favorite Adderley solos.

Zenón comped again as Philion played it the first time through.

"That's nice," he said as they finished. "For now, concentrate on your phrasing and feel."

Zenón grabbed his own horn and demonstrated, as Philion looked on smiling at the ease with which Zenón did so.

"Let's hear it for a second," Zenón said, as he prepared to cue up the recording Philion was working from for a close listen. "You know those little inflections and swirls, those turns and all that stuff? That's really the key to the solo. And also the way he feels the eighth note."

As they went through the recording, Zenón paused it here and there to analyze snippets of Adderley's phrasing in close detail.

"See how it pulls back on the B flat?" he observed at one point, singing the lick to demonstrate. "That's a Charlie Parker trick. Charlie Parker used to do it here."

Zenón demonstrated again using his horn, and they moved on to the next fine point Zenón wanted to call attention to.

"Keep working on this, exaggerating a little more on the phrasing," he instructed, after having Philion play the solo through a final time. "The idea with this stuff, we have to bring it as close as possible to become them. Everything they're doing we're trying to emulate, capture—sound, articulation, attack, if they laid back—the whole thing. So for next time a little more of this. Try and see if you can memorize it next time."

As Philion's session wrapped up, he and Zenón discussed whom Philion might be able to get to play with him for Zenón the next day. Being at Harvard made that a little tricker for Philion than other NEC students, but Zenón assured him that he could get by with another musician or two, possibly plucked from the sign-up sheet outside the relevant classroom door.

Playing with other musicians is essential to Zenón. "As much as I like playing with my band," he once told me, "I wouldn't feel complete if I didn't play with anybody else."

"I would say I've kind of reached a certain point where I don't have to take every gig," he clarified, "so I just take the gigs that I want to take. But I feel that if I just played with my band and didn't play with anybody else, I don't think I'd be able to deal financially the same way. I actually need to play with other people in order to keep it going. And I like it too, which is cool. But it has to be a balance for me, at least at this point in my life. Like I said before—maybe it's me, the kind of person I am, but I would sort of consider my musical career a failure if I didn't play with other people, if I just played with my band and I just organized everything around me being a leader. Because to me, that's not what it is. You want to be part of something greater."

As we walked toward his hotel after the final lesson that afternoon at NEC, I asked about a performance he had coming up in Chicago in a couple of weeks. He told me that he would be premiering his commissioned work for saxophone and string quartet, "Yo Soy La Tradición" (I am tradition), with the Spektral Quartet, the brilliant ensemble-in-residence at the University of Chicago. Zenón's modest description of the event that day made it seem a relatively small thing. But Howard Reich, longtime jazz critic of the *Chicago Tribune*, had effusive praise for both the piece and the performance:

> Commissioned for the occasion by the Hyde Park Jazz Festival, the piece elegantly blurs distinctions among jazz, classical and folkloric music. Substantive yet accessible, rhythmically intense but often melodically soaring, "Yo Soy La Tradicion" shows Zenon—as in previous work—finding inspiration in the musical, cultural and religious rituals of his native Puerto Rico. Yet this is no kitschy appropriation of familiar dance forms. Instead,

Zenon has crafted a vast work in which meter, tempo, texture and instrumental tech-
nique are in constant flux. Certain passages bristle with complex interactions between
Zenon and the Spektral Quartet. Others prove disarmingly direct by virtue of their poetic
melodies or buoyant rhythms or extended passages of hand claps for all the musicians.
Zenon has built forward motion into the string writing so deftly that you never really
miss the rhythm-section accompaniment that typically drives small-ensemble jazz. It's
a major work that ought to be recorded, and Zenon should enter it for the Pulitzer Prize
music competition.[85]

"Yo Soy La Tradición" was actually Zenón's second collaboration with the Spektral Quartet. The first had come when the French accordionist Julien Labro emailed
Zenón during a run at Chicago's Jazz Showcase to say Labro and the quartet were
recording an arrangement of Zenón's "El Club de la Serpiente" and wondering if he
would like to sit in. He did so, and the piece appears as a track on the 2014 album
From This Point Forward. "I went in and the whole thing was super fun," recalled
Zenón. "When I approached was by Kate [Dumbleton] from Hyde Park a bit later
[about the commission], I thought it might be nice to involve a Chicago-based
ensemble and reached out to Spektral."

Zenón had recorded the original version of "El Club de la Serpiente" with
another Frenchman, the pianist and composer Laurent Coq, as the climactic final
track of their 2011 collaborative album, *Rayuela*. Inspired by the renowned novel of
that title by Julio Cortázar (*Hopscotch* in its English translation), *Rayuela* resulted
from Zenón's love of the book, he and Coq having long discussed finding a project
to work together on, and Zenón having finished his five-album commitment to
Marsalis Music.

The first time I met with Zenón, *Rayuela* was recently out on Sunnyside Records
and another album, *Oye!!! Live in Puerto Rico* (made with the Rhythm Collective, a
group of Puerto Rican percussionists with whom he had toured western Africa for
the US State Department several years earlier), was a year away on his own soon-
to-launch label, Miel (Miel is a mashup of the first names of Miguel and his wife,
Elga). He was also well into his *Identities Are Changeable* project, having premiered
it in Montclair and its Carnegie Hall performance scheduled for that fall.

Rayuela was a particularly intriguing project, for both its connection to literature and its unusual instrumentation. Cortázar already had links to jazz through
his short stories "El perseguidor" ("The Pursuer"), with its protagonist modeled
on Charlie Parker, and "Las babas del diablo," which inspired the Michelangelo
Antonioni film *Blow-Up* (1966) and its music score by Herbie Hancock. *Rayuela*
was Cortázar's experimental masterpiece, a deeply philosophical novel set in
Paris and Buenos Aires that famously offered its readers an alternative method

of hopscotching from chapter to chapter rather than reading them in numerical order.

"Cortázar is just so creative," Zenón enthused when we spoke that afternoon. "It's almost like he's trying to find new ways to write to keep himself on his toes while he writes. I just thought he was really refreshing, and I still do when I read it now. I always find new things."

The novel has jazz associations as well. The "Club de la Serpiente" that inspired Zenón's composition is a group of Paris-based characters that gathers to discuss the arts, philosophy, and other intellectual matters while spinning jazz albums. And the artistic liberties Cortázar employs in organizing the book have their own connections to the music.

"There are definitely similarities," agreed Zenón when I suggested as much. "Some of that character definitely attracted me to it. Just the freedom to experiment and to try things and give you different roads to one place or to different places."

It had been Zenón's notion to focus the Coq collaboration on the novel. "We were trying to come up with an idea, and I suggested this might be a way to go just because of all the connections in the book already, with France and Latin America, something that's really present in a lot of characters in the book," he said. "That's the whole plot. And you know how jazz is so present in the book, and how Cortázar is such a big fan of jazz and music in general. Laurent didn't know the book, so he read it, and we started to come up with ideas about what we could do with the songs and what he wanted to do with it and what I wanted to do with it—and we came up with an instrumentation that we thought could make this a project and not just something that was more abstract. This was actually like a band that functioned specifically for this project."

Zenón and Coq brought some of their own playfulness to the album. The track sequence doesn't correspond to either reading sequence offered by Cortázar, and the two composers flipped expectations of which of them wrote pieces based on what scenes: Zenón wrote the five set in Paris, and Coq wrote those set in Buenos Aires.

"We did that on purpose," Zenón confirmed. "We just thought it would be too obvious if he did the Paris and I did the Latin America, so we switched it around. And what was interesting is that even though I've been to Paris many times, because of work and stuff, and he has never been to Buenos Aires—Laurent doesn't know the city at all, so he was writing this music based on the ideas he was getting from the book itself—it brought it to a different level. It was interesting how he sort of perceived the city and the ambience from the city just by reading a book and looking at pictures and stuff like that. It was interesting just to hear him talk about it."

As for that unusual instrumentation, Zenón and Coq rounded out their quartet with two of Zenón's former Manhattan School of Music classmates: Dan Weiss on drums and tabla and Dana Leong on trombone and cello. "It gave us a lot of space to work, and a lot of configurations we could deal with—make it more chamber, something more of a jazz configuration, different things."

Zenón knew both men well from having attended the Manhattan School with them. Weiss had recently taken up tabla in those years, and his mastery of the instrument is used to careful effect on *Rayuela*.

"Dana was a little younger than we were," Zenón recalled, "and when I met him he was a trombone player. We played in ensembles and combos together in school, and he was so talented. And eventually I found out through someone else he also played cello, and was like, 'Really?' We never talked about it. He never mentioned it. It was actually his first instrument. And the way he came to it actually was, he was playing around and Henry Threadgill, the saxophonist, composer, was looking for a cellist and somebody else said, 'I think Dana plays cello.' Now that's kind of his main instrument."

"I think Dan has read it," Zenón said. "I don't know about Dana. I don't think any of them were as deep into the book as I was. I think part of it, too, was the book was inspiring the compositions themselves, but the plan—we're just playing, basically. Compositions and the idea of the project were inspired by the book. But when we play, we play."

Rayuela was a one-time collaboration. Another Zenón collaboration has been going since 2004. According to David Sánchez, Joshua Redman dropped by a London club to check out Sánchez's sextet. "I remember him saying, 'Who's the alto player that you're playing with?' And I said, 'Oh, you don't know him. It's a guy, Miguel Zenón, from Puerto Rico.' A month after that, I heard that [Zenón] got the call to be in the SFJAZZ Collective."

That group's home base is now the SFJAZZ Center, a West Coast answer to Jazz at Lincoln Center that opened in 2013. The collective is an evolving eight-piece all-star ensemble whose members each year celebrate a top composer with fresh arrangements of the composer's works and tribute pieces of their own. Redman was the group's artistic director initially, and Zenón is the only original member remaining. These days Sánchez works beside Zenón in the frontline, having succeeded Redman, Joe Lovano, and Mark Turner as the collective's tenor saxophonist in 2013. The group is very much a collective, with its members divvying up the composing, arranging, and stage announcements equally. But judging by a March 2017 performance in Rockport, Massachusetts, the others appear to defer to Zenón as the senior partner among equals. The collective's thirteenth album, focused on Miles Davis, was released that same month.

Zenón has also been among the high-profile artists-in-residence hosted by the SFJAZZ Center over the years. Jason Moran was another artist-in-residence the year Zenón served, as were Bill Frisell, Regina Carter, and John Santos. Vijay Iyer and Esperanza Spalding, also profiled in this book, have since received the honor, for which the recipient spends several nights showcasing a range of his or her work.

In Zenón's case, his series began with an opening night alto sax/piano duo set with Danilo Pérez, who had just arrived on a flight from South Africa but gave a strong performance nonetheless. Tito Matos and his five-piece Viento de Agua played a first set on night two, then after an intermission Matos and two of the *plenaros* joined Zenón's quartet for four tunes from *Esta Plena*. Brazilian vocalist Luciana Souza joined Zenón's quartet for night three, which featured her singing a mix of her compositions ("Filhos de Ghandi," or "Children of Ghandi"), his ("Sangre de mi Sangre," a celebration of Zenón's wife and young daughter), and covers. The residency ended on night four with Pedrito Martinez sitting in with the quartet on congas and voice.

I was fortunate to be there for all of it, and to my mind the highlight among many was Zenón and Martinez coming out for a duo performance of Juan Tizol's "Caravan" as an encore. As I wrote in an account of the week for *JazzTimes*, "Zenón kept referring to and taking liberties with the familiar melody, gently lyrical one moment and taking things out a bit the next, and he did what amounted to comping on his alto when Martinez took the lead on congas. The encore didn't last long, but nothing could have sent the audience home happier."[86]

Zenón continues to accept occasional sideman work. He's on *Authority Melts from Me*, Bobby Avey's 2014 suite for jazz quintet inspired by Haiti's 1804 slave revolt and its more recent political tribulations. Two other notable recent projects saw him working beside the guitarist Lionel Loueke in bands led by pianist Kenny Werner and drummer Jeff Ballard. Ballard, best known for his longtime association with Brad Mehldau, had been leading Zenón and Loueke on trio gigs in New York before they recorded *Time's Tales*, his debut album as a leader, which also came out in 2014 and led to the trio performing elsewhere. I caught them in Boston at Scullers, where they added a surprising and thoroughly engaging cover of the Frank Sinatra hit "A Very Good Year" to the repertoire from the album.

Ballard also plays with Zenón in Guillermo Klein's Los Guachos ensemble, Zenón's most involved and long-standing sideman role by far. Zenón had become familiar with the group from their weekly performances at Smalls before he played with Klein for the first time in the late 1990s, subbing on a trio date. Fernando Huergo, a friend of Zenón's from Berklee who, like the vocalist Luciana Souza, commuted between Boston and New York for many of those weekly gigs with Los Guachos, made the introduction.

"We were playing trio with sax and bass," Klein told me, "and then one day the sax player couldn't make it. Fernando said, 'Why don't you call this guy?' So I called Miguel, and he came to play this restaurant gig. What really captured my attention is he played some of the tunes without reading them. And those were my tunes, they weren't standards. I asked him, 'How did you do that?' And he said, 'Well, I heard them at Smalls.' This was in, like, '97, '98."

Not long afterward Zenón subbed on alto for one of Los Guachos' three tenor saxes. "He sounded so good I asked him to stay,'" Klein recalled. "So instead of three saxophones, they became four saxophones. And I would make new parts. I would tell Miguel to double some parts. I just wanted him to be in the music because he made the band sound better. That's the magic he has: wherever he goes, he makes the band sound better."

"He mastered the instrument from an early age," Klein added. "I barely saw him practicing the instrument, actually, but I heard him playing very long notes and focusing on the sound. That aspect makes the band tune better as well. Everybody in my band has a great sound. I experience that playing with other people, like the chords wouldn't sound that good. I know, for example, that every note Miguel plays he knows what it means in the chord."

Russ Gershon, the leader of Either/Orchestra, has told of Zenón's unusual focus and maturity as a young man, and of how he himself would sometimes look to Zenón for cues onstage. Zenón serves a similar function as a sort of adjunct leader in Los Guachos, according to Klein.

"I recently wrote this suite for *Los Guachos V*, our latest record," he explained. "One of the pieces is a twelve-tone piece, and he had the lead of the piece, kind of a feature. It's very challenging to hear it while we play. I thought the only one who could really play that was Miguel. It's very interesting how he organizes the band to his playing. I've seen Chris Cheek following Miguel. Chris Cheek is one of the most talented musicians on Earth, and when we play he follows Miguel for time and cues. He has *presence*."

That presence in Los Guachos extends beyond alto saxophone to flute and vocals. I remember being surprised to see him singing on one tune when I caught the band at the Village Vanguard. "Everybody sings," he told me, laughing, when I asked him about it afterward. "But not everybody does it in public, I guess. I've been singing since I was a kid. I'm not Plácido Domingo or whatever, but I can hold a pitch, I think."

"I think he has a beautiful voice," was Klein's take. "Sounds like an angel, you know? After the gigs, I would hear him singing the tunes, just humming the tunes or humming his parts or singing. One day, on one tune, I said, 'Man, it would be nice if you could sing this as an alto, because I can't reach it.' That may have been the tune you heard him singing. I want to do more of that, an alto [voice].

"In the band he plays flute as well," Klein added. "That's a really great thing. Here is this lion, like in the jungle, and he plays saxophone and all the animals follow and so on. Give him the flute, where he barely practices, you know? We do it so it puts him in a different place. It's a great sensation, too. It's a very different timbre. I'm glad he allows me to experiment with that. This is the only life we have, and we have to experiment. He's totally open for that."

Zenón and Klein have become close friends and collaborators. Aside from Los Guachos, Zenón backed Klein and pianist Aaron Goldberg on their co-led album *Bienestan* (2011). And Klein tells of Zenón having recruited him to write the woodwind arrangements for *Alma Adentro* while the two shot pool during a Zenón stopover in Barcelona, during a period in which Klein held a teaching appointment in San Sebastián, Spain. Zenón was looking for something similar to what Klein had written on commission for the MIT Woodwind Ensemble and their Los Guachos bandmate Bill McHenry. Klein's job on the Zenón project was to add orchestration without altering the melodies and harmonies Zenón was providing him.

"I remember one tune, there was a chord that sounded really bad," recalled Klein. "I tried to make that chord work, and I couldn't find it." Rather than simply fix it himself, he phoned Zenón and discovered that the chord had been copied wrong; the chord Zenón had intended fit perfectly. "That tells you how much clarity he has in what he wants," Klein explained. "I would totally highlight that part of his persona. He's very clear, he knows what he wants. He has a work ethic that is remarkable."

Zenón has similar praise for Klein, and has even gone so far as to write a composition for him. Klein, who left his teaching job in Spain and settled in New York's Hudson Valley, got his first inkling of Zenón's tip of the hat to him at a show near his new home.

"He was playing at the Falcon, which is a club in upstate New York close to my house," Klein recalled. "I think he opened the set with that tune, and I started recognizing some chords that I play—some chords and some devices that I use and some lines. They were intertwined in a way, and I was like, 'Man, this is so cool.' I didn't think that was related to me. I was kind of feeling that the language was there. There was a sort of language in common. And then the rhythm came, and when they started playing this clave that I used on many tunes, I was, 'Oh man, he's giving me a nod here. He's waving hello, that kind of thing.' When the tune ended, he said, 'l just wanted to play this tune that is dedicated to my friend who is here in the audience. The name of the tune is "Cantor." '

"When he said 'Cantor,' l felt so honored, man. Such a big emotion. Because 'cantor' means 'singer,' and that's the deepest thing a musician can name you: a singer. You can sing with the voice and you can sing with piano and you can sing with the orchestra. It's just a beautiful statement. It says a lot about our mutual understanding. You can have all techniques and all the weapons and everything, but if it doesn't sing then there's something missing. Even the rhythm has to sing, you know? That was quite a beautiful gift from him."

"Cantor" came out on Zenón's quartet album *Típico* in February 2017. That album's theme was more self-referential than the handful that immediately preceded it. There were a couple of tunes that arose from teaching exercises Zenón employs at NEC and an instrumental version of "Sangre de mi Sangre," Zenón's tribute to his wife and daughter. But the album was primarily a celebration of Zenón's long-standing quartet.

The title track referenced the Latin roots of three of the four band members. The outlier, Austrian bassist Hans Glawischnig, is featured on "Sangre de mi Sangre," plucking counterpoint to its lullaby-like melody and then building a contemplative solo from it that becomes the track's centerpiece. Zenón's fellow Puerto Rican Henry Cole is featured on "Las Ramas" (The roots, a nod to Cole's own 2012 album *Roots Before Branches*), which Zenón wrote around a complex rhythmic pattern Cole often employs on drums. Venezuelan pianist Luis Perdomo is spotlighted on "Entre Las Raices" (Amongst the roots), whose melody Zenón derived from a Perdomo solo on the pianist's album *Awareness* and set up to demonstrate his mastery of the jazz styles that inspired him coming up in Caracas, bebop and free jazz, as exemplified by Bud Powell and Cecil Taylor.

That the quartet has remained intact since Cole joined the others in 2005 has been a blessing, allowing them to achieve an unmistakable group sound. Zenón credits the example of Branford Marsalis for holding a working group together: Marsalis has made minimal adjustments to his quartet—one apiece on piano, bass, and drums—since forming its original version in the mid-1990s.

"It's definitely an idea that's coming back," said Zenón. "Really having a group of people that you play with all the time and develop a sound as a group that makes the music better. [Branford]'s definitely one of those guys that ingrained the idea of a working band and the possibility of that being realistic. I've been lucky, too, that I've found guys that are into it."

When I mentioned this to Cole, and rattled off the other artists in this book who had managed to keep a group together for more than a decade (this was a couple of months before the announcement that Ethan Iverson would be leaving the Bad Plus), he countered that my examples were rare exceptions to industry realities. His point suggested it could be that I was drawn to the artists chosen for this book partly because their long-standing bands made them stand out rather than there being some new trend afoot for preserving bands.

"You're picking the right people in terms of that," Cole said, "but that's not common. Everyone will tell you how hard it is to keep a band—any band—together. Not even for guys like Michel Camilo, Joe Lovano, or [John] Scofield. They change all the time. The promoters don't want to hear the same band, so in order to find work, they need to say, 'OK, come up with some kind of concept project.' "

In any case, *this* quartet has endured, and it played an invigorating set at Boston's Villa Victoria Center for the Arts on *Típico*'s release date, which coincided with Cole's birthday. There was a celebratory vibe to the event. José Massó, host of the popular local radio show *¡Con Salsa!*, was there and told me a story about having seen Zenón play the same venue with David Sánchez's sextet early in Zenón's career. When Massó told Sánchez how strong his playing was that night, Sánchez responded that he had no choice: he was looking over his shoulder at the young alto player charging up behind him. (Sánchez laughed and confirmed the story for me a few weeks later.)

The quartet moved on to a six-night run at the Village Vanguard the next week, followed by a short US tour that concluded in late March at the Puerto Rico Heineken Jazz Fest in San Juan. From there, Zenón spent April touring with the SFJAZZ Collective in support of its Miles Davis project, with a stop at the New Orleans Jazz & Heritage Festival in early May. That Memorial Day weekend, he would join a new Guillermo Klein sextet for performances at New York's Cornelia Street Cafe and at the Falcon, the same Hudson Valley venue where his quartet had introduced Klein to "Cantor." Four months later, he was in a Chicago studio recording *Yo Soy La Tradición* with the Spektral Quartet, with an all-star benefit concert he was overseeing for Puerto Rico and the victims of Hurricane Maria planned for Berkeley, California, shortly thereafter.

Zenón would like people to see a through line in all of this, and in those deep dives he takes into jazz tradition on his Caravana Cultural excursions as well. At that Sonny Rollins event in Cidra, he and the sidemen he'd assembled whipped through a handful of Rollins classics with artistry and aplomb. Then four local high schoolers joined them onstage to jam on "Tenor Madness." Cidra's mayor, Javier Carrasquillo, offered an official thank you and handed Zenón some flowers, after which the student musicians and several of their classmates gathered around Zenón for their families to take photographs.

"It's really about being honest with yourself and saying, 'This is what I am,' and trying to represent yourself," Zenón once told me of what he would like his art, in all its variety, to accomplish. "Hopefully after a while you'll be able to connect all the dots together in a logical way so that people will be able to see you through the music."

Please visit the open access version of Make It New *to see a video resource for Chapter Five:* https://doi.org/10.3998/mpub.11469938.comp.5

CHAPTER SIX

ANAT COHEN

In December 2012, the *New York Times* business columnist Joe Nocera, indulging a taste for live Brazilian music, went to Jazz at Lincoln Center to watch percussionist Duduka Da Fonseca lead a quintet at Dizzy's Club Coca-Cola. Nocera was so transported by band member Anat Cohen's work on tenor saxophone and clarinet that night that he wrote about it for the front page of the paper's Sunday arts section several months later. Titled "Jazz's Skinny Stepchild," Nocera's piece celebrated Cohen's success in reuniting the clarinet with modern jazz.

"As good as her saxophone playing was," he wrote, "Ms. Cohen on the clarinet was a revelation. Using the clarinet's upper register, she could evoke infectious joy. In the lower register, her playing could conjure a deep, soulful melancholy. On up-tempo numbers, her improvisations weren't just bebop fast; they had a clarity and deep intelligence that is really quite rare. She made it look effortless, even as she was playing the most technically difficult of all the reed instruments. She only played a handful of songs on the clarinet that night, but every time she did, she took my breath away."[87]

Nocera went on to reveal that he had played clarinet in grade school himself, then set the instrument aside as uncool when he became interested in jazz in high school, switching to saxophone and flute. The clarinet, he explained, had fallen into disuse in jazz with the rise of bebop in the 1940s. Even Cohen had changed her focus to tenor sax in high school, when a teacher told her that clarinet didn't fit well with modern jazz and she discovered John Coltrane.

The piece described how she had worked her way back to the instrument, and ended touting a duo set Cohen had coming up that week with pianist Fred Hersch. "If you drop by," Nocera concluded, "you'll get to hear something that is rarer than it ought to be: the beautiful sound of a clarinet, in the hands of a master, playing great jazz as if the instrument never went away."

I had my own eureka moment involving Cohen about a year before Nocera's. I'd seen her perform once before a few years earlier, as lead tenor in the saxophone section of the Diva Jazz Orchestra, the excellent all-women big band led by drummer Sherrie Maricle. But performing in a large group kept the focus off Cohen, and half of that night's set featured guest vocalist Marlena Shaw. I don't recall Cohen playing clarinet at all that night, though I had heard her playing it on one track of the orchestra's then-current album, *TNT: A Tommy Newsome Tribute*.

But in November 2011, the week after my introduction to Rudresh Mahanthappa's *Samdhi* band, I went to the Boston club Scullers to check out the 3 Cohens, the group she co-leads with her two brothers, saxophonist Yuval and trumpeter Avishai. Anat had been featured on the cover of *JazzTimes* that October (she and her brothers would soon share the January 2012 cover of *DownBeat*). But I wasn't prepared for how much I would enjoy that night's show. The only time I recall having been as impressed watching a jazz sextet had been three decades years earlier in Chicago, when Art Blakey's Jazz Messengers had come to the Jazz Showcase with nineteen-year-old Wynton Marsalis in its front line.

The Cohens themselves were superb, joyfully interacting with their horns via tight unison lines and deftly woven counterpoint. They nudged the bar higher and higher for each other when they soloed, and clearly relished playing with family. "You shaved yesterday, right?" Anat joked at one point, teasingly referencing Avishai's very full beard.

The three members of that night's stellar rhythm section were similarly impressive. The Cohens' fellow Israeli Omer Avital was casually outstanding on bass, driving things along with a deep, rich tone and often smiling and half-dancing as he did so, clearly reveling in the fun of playing with such virtuosic friends. Johnathan Blake, son of the jazz violinist John Blake, had his drum kit set up unconventionally, his cymbals level with his snare and tom toms, but played brilliantly. So did pianist Aaron Goldberg, most flashily on Yuval Cohen's bebop-charged "Freedom" but with deft contributions to all the styles of jazz the band dipped into that night.

They began the set with Avishai's hard bop–oriented "Shufla de Shufla" and stuck primarily to originals by each of the siblings: Yuval's Charles Mingus–inspired "Blues for Dandi's Orange Bull Chasing an Orange Sack," Avishai's balladic "Family," and Anat's lovely bossa nova–flavored "Tifla (Prayer)" among them. But they also reached deep into jazz history for a pair of covers, Duke Ellington's "The

Mooche" and, as their encore, the early jazz standard "Tiger Rag." The abrupt shift from the modern material was unusual, and the off-handed surprise of it—and Anat's switch from tenor to clarinet for the two pieces—made them stand out as highlights in a set overflowing with skilled and exuberant musicianship.

Several years later in a conversation with Goldberg, I brought up what happened that night and how musicians like Anat, with her clarinet and the siblings' fondness for early jazz, were refreshing jazz by reintroducing it to abandoned aspects of its early history. In Jason Moran's case, for example, by injecting postmodern jazz with doses of stride piano. Goldberg credited Wynton Marsalis with blurring the distinction between old music—the jazz predating the rise of bebop in the 1940s— and new music.[88]

"We were used to hearing it on these old scratchy records, so we think of it as old music," Goldberg said, meaning music identified with Louis Armstrong, Duke Ellington, and their big band–era contemporaries. "But it was revolutionary at the time, and it still sounds super revolutionary if played well. It sounds modern—it *was* modern, and it's timelessly modern in a way that Stravinsky sounds timelessly modern, Bach sounds timelessly modern. Great music continues to sound super fresh forever."

Thanks to Marsalis and Marcus Roberts, Goldberg said, his own and subsequent generations of jazz musicians, "guys like Jonathan Batiste, Aaron Diehl, Christian Sands . . . or even somebody like Ambrose Akinmusire, who is not viewed as a classicist at all, a hyper-modernist," have stopped assuming modern jazz begins with bebop. "And I hear it," he added. "My peers can be totally modern in their approach to ragtime music, or totally modern in their approach to stride piano. If we can play a bebop tune that was written in 1947, why can't we play a Dixieland tune that was written in 1927?"

Or, for that matter, why can't they play *choro*, the clarinet-friendly music of Brazil that predates Dixieland and shares its emphasis on melody, syncopation, and counterpoint? Or record a live album of swing-era classics at the Village Vanguard to honor Benny Goodman's centennial, backed by an all-star trio of jazz modernists? Anat Cohen has done both. In fact, she released two albums with Brazilian collaborators in 2017 that were nominated for Grammy Awards. *Outra Coisa*, a duet album with Marcello Gonçalves of the seven-string guitarist's arrangements of orchestral music by Moacir Santos, was one of five finalists for Best Latin Jazz Album, alongside Cohen's onetime college classmate Miguel Zenón's *Típico*. *Rosa Dos Ventos*, her second recording with Trio Brasileiro, comprised *choro*-based originals by each of the band members, whose inclusion of samba, flamenco, and Hindustani influences earned it a spot on the year's Best World Music Album shortlist. (The winners that year were *Jazz Tango*, by Pablo Ziegler Trio, for Best Latin Jazz

Album, and Ladysmith Black Mambazo's *Shaka Zulu Revisited: 30th Anniversary Celebration,* for Best World Music Album.)

Cohen might have been a finalist for a third 2017 Grammy nod had her album *Happy Song,* the debut recording of her versatile new Tentet, not been released in October, a week past the deadline for consideration that year. The project was conceived, with her longtime collaborator Oded Lev-Ari (their friendship goes back to high school in Tel Aviv, and they are partners in running the record label Anzic Records), to celebrate the hundredth anniversary of the first jazz recording, the Original Dixieland Jass Band's "Dixie Jass Band One Step" and "Livery Stable Blues." *Happy Song* includes a pair of Benny Goodman–associated tunes, the swinging "Oh, Baby" and the sad song he usually ended sets with, "Goodbye." But the idea was to suggest that the spirit of jazz has evolved to encompass other aspects of Cohen's clarinet virtuosity, with original compositions by Cohen and Lev-Ari and arrangements of pieces from Brazil (Egberto Gismonti's "Loro") and Mali (Neba Solo's "Kenedougou Foly"). Cohen and Lev-Ari even set aside their lifelong disinterest in klezmer music to record "Anat's Doina," and were stunned at how enthusiastically audiences embraced it.

Little on *Happy Song* precisely fits *jazz* as usually defined by Wynton Marsalis, but that doesn't make Cohen and her music unwelcome at Jazz at Lincoln Center. In January 2018, she took a break from touring the album to spend three nights there as one of four featured clarinetists performing "Benny Goodman: King of Swing" with the Jazz at Lincoln Center Orchestra. A few years earlier, she and her Choro Adventoroso bandmates Vitor Gonçalves, Cesar Garabini, and Sergio Krakowski performed a set at the same location, later aired on NPR's *Jazz Night in America.*[89]

To Cohen, jazz is as much an approach to performing music as it is a specific genre. As she put it the first time we sat down for an interview, the day following a 2015 Boston performance by her quartet: "When I describe my music, I say, 'Listen, it's open. It's world music. It's improvised. Sometimes it's unclear [what its genre is], sometimes it's a little bit on the pop side—but it's all under the umbrella of jazz.' "

Cohen's interest in jazz began at the conservatory she and her brothers attended in Tel Aviv–Jaffa, where she began studying classical clarinet at age twelve. Her first experience playing jazz came a year or two later.

"Once you could play a little bit you joined this band," she explained. "Suddenly I'm sitting there, and I have no idea about improvisation. I play classical music, and I come and start playing the music of New Orleans and all the transcribed arrangements of the Original Dixieland Jass Band and other arrangements. And I'm loving it, because I get to breathe written solos. I don't need to know how to improvise, and I can just focus on the way the music feels. How you're constantly playing with the other musicians. Everybody is intertwining their lines, and everybody is getting up for solos. It was so much fun. I loved it so much. And that was my introduction to jazz."

At sixteen, Cohen began playing saxophone. "The same conductor, he ran a big band rehearsal every Friday, and he told me, 'Hey, why don't you pick up a tenor saxophone and come play second tenor in the big band.' " She assembled a tenor from a storage room of old instruments and a boxful mouthpieces and reeds, and thus began her initiation into more modern jazz.

"My brothers are the same," she added. "Same route: our introduction to jazz—talking about the '80s at this point, maybe the beginning of the '90s—was through playing with the big bands and the music of New Orleans. So this is part of our nostalgic time of being young—of having our friends for life from the same conservatory, of us bonding over music, of us playing in the same bands. So I think this is beyond what we talked about regarding the history of jazz, but everyone has got their own personal story. The music of New Orleans means a lot to us. Pops is one of our favorites ever—forever."

We'd been talking about how the 3 Cohens make a point of reaching back to older jazz classics in their performances. "You've got all that subsequent vocabulary of jazz at your disposal," I noted, "so when you go back and play those older pieces it's like you're making them new again." I'd seen that music go over especially well with audiences, but few modernists besides Cohen and her brothers show any interest in playing it. A notable exception is the Canadian vocalist/trumpeter Bria Skonberg, who specializes in *hot jazz*—another term for traditional New Orleans jazz or Dixieland—and with whom Cohen would share a stage in Central Park, at the New York Hot Jazz Fest, the week Cohen and I spoke again the next summer.

"The reason why people don't do it as much," Cohen responded, "is that it's really hard to find an organic way to go backward and stay current at the same time. How to play something that is old without changing the way you play, without changing the sound of the band. How to find a way to still be yourself and to still keep the sound. To go from playing Flying Lotus[90] to playing Louis Armstrong to saying, 'OK, it's all part of who we are. We are complex people. We're not just one thing.' "

That the three Cohens retain a fondness for jazz that predates bebop is a product of their home life as well as what they encountered at school. Their father, who worked in real estate, was a knowledgeable fan of classical music whose record collection also included classic jazz that he had brought with him to Israel from a decade he spent living in the United States. Their mother played piano and accordion and taught music at a kindergarten/grade school. Cohen and her brothers would improvise with one another from their separate rooms while they were practicing, and the three of them wore out a copy of a favorite record of theirs, the 1956 collaboration of Ella Fitzgerald and Louis Armstrong *Ella and Louis,* by playing it so often.

Born in 1973, 1975, and 1978, respectively, Yuval, Anat, and Avishai followed similar paths to becoming professional jazz musicians. Their formal musical training in Israel took place at the Tel Aviv School for the Arts and the Thelma Yellin High School for the Arts in addition to the Jaffa Music Conservatory. Yuval and Anat followed that with service in military bands[91] and then scholarships to the Berklee College of Music in Boston. Avishai went directly to Berklee at eighteen, then moved to New York after taking third place in the 1997 Thelonious Monk Jazz Trumpet Competition.

Jazz instruction as an adjunct to classical training was on the rise in Israel as the Cohens were growing up in the 1980s, with the return home of musicians who had gone abroad to study jazz in the United States. Later, two American saxophonists with Israeli wives moved to Israel and further enhanced interest in jazz there. Walter Blanding Jr. spent four years teaching in high schools and running his own private school in Tel Aviv in the late 1990s before returning to the United States, where he became a prominent member of the Jazz at Lincoln Center Orchestra. Arnie Lawrence,[92] who with bassist Reggie Workman had founded the jazz and contemporary music program at Manhattan's New School University in 1986, made extended visits to Israel on sabbatical and summer breaks. In 1997, he moved permanently to Jerusalem and founded the International Center for Creative Music, where he accepted both Jewish and Arab students, attempting to use jazz education to bridge the divide between Israelis and Palestinians. He also opened a small club called Arnie's Jazz Underground that he operated until his death in 2005.

Lawrence played an especially key role in the rise of Israeli jazz through the combination of his work at the New School and in Jerusalem. Three key Israeli musicians—bassists Omer Avital and Avishai Cohen (same name as Anat's brother but no relation) and trombonist Avi Lebovich—arrived in New York in late 1991 to begin studying jazz that winter at the New School.

Avital quickly fell in with New School classmates such as pianist Brad Mehldau, guitarist Peter Bernstein, and drummer Ali Jackson Jr. in helping forge the artistic ambience at Smalls Jazz Club, where young musicians steeped in jazz history experimented with ways to expand on it. Avital built a reputation as an excellent bassist, bandleader, and composer there before returning to Israel between 2001 and 2005, where he studied the musical traditions of the region and his Moroccan and Yemeni roots. Since then, both his own music and that of the collaborative quartet Third World Love he formed with Anat's brother Avishai, pianist Yonathan

Avishai*, and drummer Daniel Freedman during his stay in Israel, has often featured an exciting, danceable combination of hard bop and those sephardic influences. "I sometimes call him the Middle Eastern Art Blakey," Oded Lev-Ari told me.

The bassist Avishai Cohen was hired by Chick Corea in 1996, and gained international renown recording and touring in Corea's Origin sextet before focusing on his own mix of jazz and world music leading his own groups. Lebovich performed with various groups in New York and London before returning to Israel and launching the Israeli Jazz Orchestra. They and their close contemporaries pianist Anat Fort[93] and guitarist and oudist Amos Hoffman[94] established a sort of American beachhead for Israeli jazz musicians. The wave that soon followed—Anat Cohen and her brothers, saxophonist Eli Degibri, guitarists Yotam Silverstein and Gilad Hekselman, and others—further demonstrated the possibilities for Israeli musicians making careers for themselves playing jazz. A 2011 article on Anat Cohen and New York's Israeli jazz scene in the online magazine *Tablet* reported that, in the previous few years, Israeli musicians made up about 9 percent of the students studying jazz and contemporary music at the New School.[95] When I saw Avital perform at New York's 2017 Winter Jazzfest, all four sidemen in his quintet were young Israelis.

"You had three great jazz educators in Israel at the same time, in the '90s, starting to teach jazz,"[96] explained Aaron Goldberg, who arrived at the New School the same year as Avital and spent a year studying there before returning to his hometown of Boston and earning a degree at Harvard. "A whole generation of young Israeli guys got exposed to high-level jazz education in high school, and that's why ten years later you have every year ten, fifteen, twenty, thirty, forty new young highly competent Israeli musicians in New York."

Anat Cohen's connection to Arnie Lawrence was struck up during her time in the Israeli Air Force band. Later, on Wednesday nights, the siblings would sometimes drive together from Tel Aviv to Jerusalem for Lawrence's weekly *harif* (Hebrew for spicy) sessions, where whoever showed up would comprise that night's band. "It could be ten saxophones and a kazoo player," she told me. But her first encounter with Lawrence occurred when Yuval took her to see him perform in Jaffa.

"I remember Yuval went to sit in," Anat recalled. "I never really liked to sit in, but Yuval liked to sit in with Arnie. I was just there listening, and then Arnie told him something and Yuval came and handed me his alto saxophone. I looked at Arnie, and Arnie kind of nodded for me to come and play. At that point I'd never ever touched an alto saxophone in my life. I was playing tenor, but I did not play alto. But there was something really positive and wonderful about Arnie."

---

*Yonathan Avishai's first name was spelled Yonatan on those Third World Love albums, but was modified to read Yonathan on his website and on later albums.

She and Lawrence played a blues together, and Anat later asked Yuval what Lawrence had told him. " 'Give your sister the horn.' That's it. It became the beginning of a real friendship."

Lawrence also became Cohen's most important mentor. What he taught her went beyond the scales, chords, and other technical aspects of music she had studied in school. It had more to do with communication.

"He would talk to me about the conversations we have in music," she recalled, "and I was like, 'Conversations? What does he mean? What is this conversation?' So I started to pay attention. He was talking about the beauty of the music. 'You have to look for the beauty.' I was like, 'What is it with all these terms?' It sounded so abstract. And today I can understand what he meant, and I wish I could tell him that I understand."

Lawrence also urged her to look inside herself to find and emphasize her individuality in her approach to music, and not to compare herself to her brothers. "That was an invaluable conversation," she told me. "To my future, to who I am as a person, and to who I am as a musician."

Her encounters with Lawrence helped fuel her decision to follow Yuval to Boston and Berklee. There she encountered other mentors on the college faculty. Tenor saxophonists George Garzone and Billy Pierce are thanked by name in the notes to her first album. Phil Wilson persuaded her to develop her special voice on clarinet, an instrument she had mostly abandoned on joining her high school big band. Hal Crook gave her what she calls another of her life lessons. "We got to the end of the semester, and I did my final exam. Hal came to me and said, 'According to what you played, you could get an A, but I'm going to give you a B+.' I'm like, 'What? But why?' He said, 'Because you have a talent, and if you really worked hard, you could have done so much more.' I was like, 'Hmm.' To be honest, I didn't work extremely hard. I did what I needed to do to pass. He made me realize that when you're not trying to be the best you can, it doesn't really pass."

She also learned from her peers and off campus. She lived in nearby Brookline in what she refers to as a "little kibbutz," sharing an apartment, sequentially, with her elder and younger brother. In the apartment next door lived the Israeli saxophonist Eli Degibri, who toured with Herbie Hancock after graduating from Berklee and has since returned to Israel to teach, and Oded Lev-Ari, who was studying arranging and composing with Bob Brookmeyer at New England Conservatory. Anat and Lev-Ari, in their high school years in Tel Aviv, had once pooled their money to buy and share a copy of the Sonny Rollins album *The Bridge*, his first recording following his famous period spent practicing his saxophone on the Williamsburg Bridge. They now live on opposite sides of that very bridge, Cohen in the now trendy Williamsburg neighborhood of Brooklyn and Lev-Ari in Manhattan's East Village, near where Rollins lived during his bridge sabbatical.

Because her English was imperfect upon arrival, Cohen gravitated toward other international students at Berklee, which sparked her love of music from Brazil and elsewhere in Latin America. She credits playing Afro-Cuban and other world music in a two-sax horn section with Berklee classmate Miguel Zenón in the popular local band Mango Blue with sharpening her feel for playing Latin rhythms, and she was introduced to Brazilian music by bassist Leonardo Cioglia, who later played beside her in the Duduka Da Fonseca quintet.

Those sorts of gigs in Boston helped sustain Cohen even after she graduated Berklee and moved to New York a year later. "It took months and months and months before I started to gig in New York," she told me. "I did play with the Diva Jazz Orchestra, but even then the gigs were not in New York—it would be gigs taking a plane somewhere. So my New York scene was playing some bar gigs and playing for the bucket, basically. I played some gigs with Leonardo Cioglia. He moved to New York a little before me and always had some weekly gig somewhere, and he would call me to come play."

Cohen went regularly to Smalls in those years, but it took years before she began playing with her generation of jazz experimentalists there.

"My dream would be to get into that scene," she said. "I'm not a big jam-sessions fan, but I would hang out there all the time. I used to play this Brazilian gig every Monday at Café Wha, and on the breaks I would run from Café Wha to Smalls to hear Jason Lindner's band. That was months after I moved to New York. It was a great band and a great gig, but it was the same time as Jason's big band, and I remember when Jason finally called me to sub in the band, I quit the band in Café Wha. It was a few years later we're talking about. I probably did some gigs already at Smalls by then, but Jason called me to sub in his band and it was my dream. I was like, 'I'm out of here, I'm going to play jazz in New York.' "

That it took Cohen years to crack the modern jazz scene at Smalls is not something she blames on sexism. But she doesn't necessarily exclude it as a possibility. The first time we spoke I asked her about being a woman jazz musician and whether sexism had affected her career early on. This was a couple of years before Robert Glasper dropped his term *musical clitoris* in a 2017 *Do the Math* interview with Ethan Iverson and the emergence of the #MeToo movement later that year had cast spotlights on misogyny in jazz.

"Yes and no," Cohen had answered. "That's the moment when being a person from Israel really comes to my advantage, because when people react that way I have no problem to just tell them what I think. But I think it's an evolving issue, because, as you say, it's in all layers of society and it's in all professions. It's really very personal. Some people, they grow up in a more chauvinistic environment. Some people, they grow up in a chauvinistic environment and they learn how to be politically correct. In a way, it's like you never really know.

"It's like you go to South Africa and you say apartheid is over, right? But yeah, there's on the surface the way people behave and then there is what they don't say but how they act, and some looks. It comes in little subtleties. So those things you encounter here and there with individuals, you kind of realize it's just men-women relationship. They've got to feel good about themselves. They've got to feel powerful. It's fine. I have no problem, and I don't really think about it much. If I get upset, I just walk away or I just say something."

Things were more difficult for Cohen when she was less known. She brought up an instance in Israel where a musician had phoned her brother Yuval to play a gig. Yuval couldn't take the job, but he told the caller that his sister played saxophone and was available. The offer was politely declined.

"I don't know if it's because somebody says 'it's my sister' or it's because it's a girl," Anat noted. "People are sharp and cunning. Sometimes you hear comments. Some professions are a little bit more manly than others. I have rough encounters here and there with sound guys. I mean, it happens less now because my name is on the marquee—so whatever, there's no more marquees anymore—but people know, 'OK, she's headlining . . . my job is on the line here.' I would play, and then the sound guy was like, 'Well, you got to play into the microphone, honey.' Some comments like that. They really would never say it to some other guy. So I just turn around, I take a deep breath, I talk to my band, and I'm like [deep breath], 'OK.' I try not to create more friction than needs to be."

Cohen's business and sometime artistic partner, Oded Lev-Ari, has witnessed various manifestations of misogyny in the jazz world from a male perspective. Misogynistic and homophobic comments have come up in green room conversations with other musicians. He also mentioned that an interviewer had recently suggested that it must have seemed remarkable to Lev-Ari that Cohen had focused for years on playing saxophone, "because saxophone is such a masculine instrument." What instead struck him as remarkable was the notion that musical instruments have a gender.

"I had to say, I didn't grow up with this view," Lev-Ari recalled. "There were a lot of female saxophone players around me, and I just didn't have the same association. So there's a lot of this, like, stating it as a fact. It's just kind of baffling."

Lev-Ari brought up his wife, Amy Cervini, a vocalist with a handful of impressive albums on Anzic, both on her own and in a collaborative group with two other singers.

"She has this vocal trio called Duchess, and I'm their musical director," he said. "I've been on the road with them, too. I don't necessarily say I'm Amy's husband. I'm just around and people don't know, and the kind of attitudes that I experience, towards them, taught me a lot about how, in general, the world views and treats women, but also, in particular, in jazz. Amy's an accomplished musician. She has a classical piano degree, she's played saxophone. She's a musician and a bandleader, and sometimes people don't get that. Some people will call solos onstage when she's there, and she has to kind of say, 'No, no, no. I run the show, and I will say who plays the next song.' Which is something that no one would ever do with a male bandleader. *I've* never encountered it. I can't imagine if there's a male band-leader, and one of the sidemen says . . . it's clear that you don't do that. Anat is in a completely different place now, obviously."

The creation of Anzic Records in 2005 played a pivotal role in getting Cohen to that different place. At the time, musicians releasing albums on their own labels was still a novel idea, and one that usually involved said musicians having already rising to prominence recording for established labels. Generally, too, their labels focused exclusively on their own work.[97] Dave Holland, for example, launched his Dare2 Records in 2005, ending his long association with ECM, and has focused the label on his own projects ever since. Miguel Zenón followed his five-record deal with Marsalis Music by creating Miel Records, where his own work has appeared since 2013. Jason Moran left his long association with Blue Note to form Yes Records with his wife, Alicia Hall Moran, and their albums began appearing on the label in 2016—four of his and two of hers as of January 2018, with another of his in the pipeline for release later that year.

A handful of prominent jazz names took a broader approach. Branford Marsalis moved on from an A&R job with Columbia Records to start Marsalis Music in 2002, and signed Miguel Zenón and several others to record deals to supplement his own output. Dave Douglas, after a brief run on RCA and numerous albums on smaller labels, launched Greenleaf Music in 2005 with three albums of his own and the debut recording of the collaborative group Kneebody; Greenleaf has since released albums by Donny McCaslin, Linda Oh, Rudy Royston, and others in addition to Douglas's own. Greg Osby followed his departure from Blue Note Records by creating Inner Circle Music in 2008, which has since grown to include more than forty artists besides himself.

All this was in response to the upheaval in the record industry at the turn of the millennium. The introduction of compact discs and digital technology in the 1980s and 1990s made file sharing possible, which led to widespread music piracy. The peer-to-peer file sharing company Napster greatly exacerbated such piracy from its launch in 1999 and until it was shut down three years later due to copyright issues. Apple's launch of its iPod in 2001 and the iPhone six years later both made storing pirated music more convenient, and iTunes further decreased record sales by making it possible for music buyers to purchase individual tracks rather than entire albums. Online streaming services made it legal to listen to music without owning it, via subscription services such as Pandora (2005), Spotify (2008), and others soon to follow: Tidal (2014), Apple Music (2015), and two options available from Amazon Music, Prime Music (2014) and Music Unlimited (2016).

Meanwhile, the major record labels that had capitalized on mainstream jazz's resurgence in the 1980s and early 1990s began abandoning the field, among them Columbia, Verve, RCA, and Warner Bros. The vogue for young lions playing neo-classical jazz had faded, as fads do, a process hastened by some of the lesser "young lions" never measuring up to the designation. Some excellent smaller labels were born in the United States in the late 1990s and early 2000s that helped take up the slack: Maxjazz (1998), Mack Avenue (1999), Pi (2001), Motéma (2003). ArtistShare introduced the concept of fan-funded record projects by established artists in 2001, with composer/arranger/bandleader Maria Schneider and guitar great Jim Hall among the first to place projects there. Blue Note Records got back in the business of putting out new music in the late 1980s, with Joe Lovano, John Scofield, and Greg Osby among its early signees and Wynton Marsalis and Terence Blanchard coming over from Columbia in 2003.

But the emphasis at these new outlets leaned toward signing established talents. For many of Cohen's contemporaries—her brother Avishai, Jason Lindner, Omer Avital, Miguel Zenón, Brad Mehldau, Kurt Rosenwinkel, Robert Glasper, Ambrose Akinmusire, Ethan Iverson, Reid Anderson, the Bad Plus—getting one's early records released meant connecting with Fresh Sounds, a Barcelona-based label that in the early 1990s had begun adding new music to its existing line of jazz reissues.

Cohen opted to take a different route and put out her debut album herself.

"It was 2004, actually, when I recorded my first album, *Place & Time*," she told me one sunny June day in 2016, describing how Anzic Records came to be. We were seated on the balcony of the Williamsburg apartment of Daniel Freedman and his wife, where Cohen was staying temporarily after several months of non-stop traveling. "At that time, there was a wave of a lot of the New York cats, the people I was hanging out with, putting out albums on Fresh Sound, for example. I remember the deal was like, you basically—like most record labels—'You give us the master and we'll put it out, and you'll buy your record from us for $7 or whatever, X amount of money.'"

That approach had its merits: getting a new artist on an actual label, with whatever curatorial quality-control that implies, and letting the label take responsibility for distribution. But the label then controlled the master. That could be disastrous, as Cohen's friend Omer Avital had discovered a few years earlier when he was signed to a deal by Impulse!, recorded what was meant to be his debut recording as a leader, and then saw the album go unreleased when Verve Music Group acquired Impulse! and changed the label's focus to reissues only.[98] That was a worst-case scenario, but there were other reasons Cohen was leery about tying her fate to an existing record label, particularly at a time when technology was making it possible for artists to create their own imprints and release their music themselves. All the more so when cash-strapped major labels lacked the marketing budgets that might justify surrendering control of one's art.

"I gathered the money, and I made my recording," Cohen explained. "I have the master and spent *a lot of money* on it, a lot of agony—because the first album is probably the hardest. It's like before the first child, which I haven't had yet. I was like, 'I made all this effort, I've done everything on my own. I wrote music, I got the musicians, I paid the studio, I mixed it, I mastered it. Do I just now give it to someone else and not know what happened with the album? Not know how many were printed, not know if it was ever sent to any journalists, not know if anybody listened to it. What happens from the moment I recorded it?'

"Frankly," she continued, "it's very easy and cheap today to make a record if you're not paying the musicians, if they're all friends and you say we're just going to go for a few hours to the studio and document what I do. That's really easy. The name of the game is really how to get consumer attention. Now it's getting harder, because there's overflow because recording became so easy and so cheap. But at that time, in 2005, I was like, 'You know what, I don't want to give the master to anybody.' I invented the name Anzic Records—Anzic means 'Anat and music.' I basically hired a publicist, and I said, 'OK, I got a bar code.' That was the beginning of Anzic Records."

Anzic became a full-fledged label soon afterward, when Cohen, working with the philanthropist and businessman Colin Negrych, formally established Anzic Records, LLC, and assembled a group of six albums, including two of Cohen's own, for release in 2007. Negrych supplied the capital and was the label's initial owner, running it as one of his philanthropic endeavors. Oded Lev-Ari was hired as general manager. Lev-Ari later told me that *Place & Time* (2005), despite respectful reviews and high praise from Nat Hentoff in his liner notes ("Anat Cohen has the quality of all lasting jazz musicians. She has presence."), had not proved as impactful as hoped.

"You need a little catalog to get distribution," Cohen explained, "because people don't just take one CD. We said, 'OK, let's gather our friends,' which at the time it was the gang. It was Jason Lindner; it was Avishai, my brother; it was [saxophonist] Joel Frahm. It was the people who were hanging out and playing together."

The idea, she said, was to have the artists involved in every aspect of the process. Most importantly, there would be transparency concerning money issues. The musicians would go into projects with a realistic understanding of how overspending on the making of an album could undermine their ability to recoup their investment. They would get accurate accounting of how much money their recordings were earning through sales and streaming, and they would be expected to make themselves available to help the label promote their work.

"A jazz record label, you're not making money," Cohen acknowledged. "So at some point we realize, 'OK, Anzic Records is a tool for us—the family, the core people—to put the albums we want to put out. We have the facility, we're established, we have the distribution, we have the mechanism.' It's working. If I want to put out an album tomorrow, I say, Great, here is an album. It exists. And it can exist. But to tell you that we are going out and doing A&R and finding markets, it's not that kind of label because that's not sustainable. But I'm very, very proud of that fact that all my albums are on Anzic Records. I own, and all the artists actually own their masters. I own all my albums, and I have control over everything I recorded. Wherever I've gotten to so far, I've done with my own record label, which is kind of incredible."

"Now everybody's putting albums out on their own," she continued. "And there's always the question, because you say, 'I recorded a track. Do people really listen to full albums? Do I need to put out a full album?' People listen to one song on iTunes, they listen on Spotify, they put on Soundcloud—everything for free, just so people can just hear it. We've come to the point of saying, OK, where is the business part, and where is it just people want to have a creative outlet? Great, you can put all the music for free. So what makes it a business, really? So at this point—"

"It's a marketing tool," I offered.

"Yeah," she agreed. "It just becomes expensive business cards. At some point I'm realizing, the new Macintosh, they don't even have a slot for CDs. Physical CDs, they're going to disappear. It costs a few thousand dollars to print CDs, so if you're not printing CDs, do you need to make a full album? You can just make a track. What's the cost? We're living in times that the record industry is changing so fast, and we're talking about just in the last ten or fifteen years."

This wasn't the first time Cohen had made mention of how technology was affecting jazz. In our initial conversation, she suggested that short attention spans contributed to the relative lack of interest in the genre, which requires close, open-minded listening to be appreciated. "It's becoming harder and harder," she said, "because after five minutes if you don't check your phone, if you don't look at your messages, if you don't see what happens in the world, everybody starts to get anxiety. Maybe shows should become fifteen-minute segments."

She brought up Portuguese *fado* houses—restaurants where patrons drink wine and eat, interrupted periodically by brief, intense performances of singers and musicians—to buttress her point. "It's so emotional. They perform for fifteen minutes, and then they leave. You just sit there. You feel the experience, and then after fifteen minutes or whatever, a half-hour, they come back. So you get to experience the music, but you're not trapped. I guess I'm just thinking about it now. When people grow up hooked up to Facebook and social media, it's very hard to expect them to sit down for an hour or an hour and fifteen minutes. Undivided attention, it's impossible."

Other technological advances have proved helpful. The crowdfunding services now widely used by musicians hoping to finance their recordings didn't exist when Anzic began—Kickstarter, the best-known of them, launched in 2009. Some later Anzic projects have made use of those services since Cohen and Lev-Ari bought the label from Negrych in 2009 and made it more of a commercial enterprise. (Albeit not a very profitable one: "I joke with people sometimes," Lev-Ari told me. "I say, 'We've been breaking even since 2009.'")

In 2007, CDs were still very much a thing, however, and the two of Cohen's included in Anzic's initial batch of releases, *Poetica* and *Noir* (both released that April 3), began what turned into a career-transforming year for her. *Noir* assembled a large ensemble, the Anzic Orchestra (whose shifting cast of eighteen members included three cellists, her brothers, Ted Nash, Ali Jackson, and Antonio Sánchez), and superb arrangements by Lev-Ari to undergird Cohen's solos on clarinet and saxophones.

Poetica was more intimate, and the first Cohen album on which she played only clarinet. It featured her quartet with Lindner on piano, Avital on bass, and Freedman on drums, augmented on four tracks by a string quartet playing arrangements by Avital. But the album did wonders for establishing the uniqueness of Cohen's voice. Beyond its focus on her clarinet, her tune selections set a mood that set her apart from mainstream jazz. Several of the pieces, including two Cohen originals and one by Avital, were of Israeli origin, even if one of Cohen's celebrated a restaurant she had made repeat visits to during a stay in Caracas, Venezuela. But the group's cover of John Coltrane's "Lonnie's Lament" fit the album's mood as well, as did the French song "La Chanson des Vieux Amants" and the Brazilian ballad "Quando Eu Me Saudade." The emphasis was on melody and emotion, the latter usually including varying doses of what the Portuguese call *saudade*—an untranslatable mix of longing, melancholy, and nostalgia that sometimes works its way into Cohen's own compositions. The music was international and not at all fixated on genre.

"I've never been a purist," she told me in one of our conversations. "I've always wanted to learn about music that excites me, that makes me emotional. A lot of it is old music, because I'm a sucker for melodies. I've never been like, 'OK, it has to be this style, and if I play this rhythm then it's not really jazz, and I shouldn't play it.' I try to go with what feels good to me and not by what will feel good for other people."

These two albums, aided by a marketing campaign overseen by the veteran publicist Don Lucoff, made a handful of the right people feel good: those who book important jazz venues. In early May, Cohen's two groups were performed back-to-back nights at New York's Jazz Standard, the quartet show earning a favorable review from Ben Ratliff in the *New York Times*.[99] Later that week, the quartet performed at the Kennedy Center's annual Mary Lou Williams Women in Jazz Festival in Washington, DC.[100] Cohen would return to the same festival two years later with the Anzic Orchestra.

In July, Cohen became both the first Israeli musician and the first woman horn player to headline at the Village Vanguard, with the Anzic Orchestra substituting for the Vanguard Orchestra's regular Monday night set and Cohen's quartet featured the rest of the week. "The way I remember it happening," Lev-Ari told me, "someone put on *Poetica*—maybe Jed [Eisenman, the Vanguard's longtime general manager] put on *Poetica* at the club—and Lorraine [Gordon, the club's owner] heard it and said, '*That's* the kind of music I want at my club.' " The next month, Cohen led her quartet in her first appearance at the Newport Jazz Festival.

On the heels of all that, Cohen was voted "Up and Coming Artist" of 2007 by the Jazz Journalists Association and won the first in her long string of Clarinetist of the Year honors from the same organization, twelve and counting through 2018.

"Those two albums really opened the doors for her," said Lev-Ari. "*Noir* got a hot box review from *DownBeat* that year. Don Lucoff, from DL Media, started doing the press for both albums, and he was really instrumental in getting a lot of this attention going. It was very unusual for an artist to release two albums simultaneously—pretty ambitious albums, too: a large ensemble and a string-quartet album. They were both excellent, and Anat had gathered enough attention by then that people knew her name."

I asked him why Anzic had decided to release both albums at once. "I think the reason was, Why not?" he answered. "They're both great albums. Everyone thinks we shouldn't do it, so probably we should. The [conventional] thought was, 'Oh no, the booking agent needs one thing to concentrate on for six to nine months. That's what they need to sell, and then you should release the other one.' And I remember we kind of went against it. We said, 'No. We don't want to wait. Let's do it now.' "

Anzic Records has had a hand in jump-starting other careers as well, and played a key role in building the wave of Israeli jazz musicians described earlier. The 3 Cohens albums have all appeared there, including the group's 2004 debut, *One*, which migrated to Anzic after beginning life as a self-released project in Israel. Anat's brothers each released strong projects of their own on the label, among them three of Avishai's with his all-star trio Triveni, featuring Avital on bass and Nasheet Waits on drums. (Avishai has since begun recording for ECM Records.) The collaborative quartet Third World Love—Avishai Cohen, Avital, Daniel Freedman, and Israeli pianist Yonathan Avishai—put out two of their five recordings on Anzic, and Oded Lev-Ari released his own debut album, *Threading*, in 2015.

Beyond the Israelis, Anzic has brought out titles by each of the other three members of Anat's quartet: Jason Lindner, known to the pop world for performing on David Bowie's final album as a member of Donny McCaslin's quartet; Daniel Freedman, whose globe-hopping aesthetic sense is captured in his 2012 album title *Bamako By Bus*, made with a core band of Lindner, Avishai Cohen, Lionel Loueke, and Meshell Ndegeocello supplemented by guests such as Omer Avital, Mark Turner, and Pedrito Martinez; and Joe Martin, who succeeded Avital as the quartet's bassist after *Poetica*. Anzic has also released albums by an assortment of other groups Anat has worked with, and by a handful of other talented friends and peers, among them Lev-Ari's vocalist wife, Amy Cervini.[101]

"If you do it yourself," Lev-Ari told me, discussing the pros and cons of running one's own label, "you need to learn the mechanics of it. A record label, they would make it seem like it was a completely mysterious, dark art—making albums and releasing them and selling them. And it's not. There's certain things that you can't do if you're a small player like us. You can't force people's hands: 'We won't give you this album unless you do this.' You can't play those games. But there's a lot you can do, including talking directly to press and to radio and to fans. Which also creates long-lasting value for you, because these are the people who you are selling the CDs to. If you don't do it for an intermediary, for a label, with their agendas, you're doing it directly."

"There are negatives," he conceded. "There are no gatekeepers. Anyone can record a CD, which on one hand is great. On the other hand, there are some advantages to having some kind of curation as to what reaches the marketplace. We're living in a world where that just doesn't happen."

But it did happen at Anzic Records, where a de facto collective of Cohen's friends and collaborators established a standard for quality that set Anzic recordings apart from the deluge of self-released albums that began flooding critics' mailboxes in the 2000s. Other young artists have begun launching labels that take a similar tack. The Curtis Brothers, pianist Zaccai and bassist Luques, run Truth Revolution Recording Collective. Fabian Almazan's Biophilia label adds an environmentally conscious twist, releasing origami-shaped album covers that contain liner notes but no CD—the packaging contains a download code instead, the idea being to avoid despoiling nature with needless plastic (and to spare the label the expense of having CDs manufactured).

Cohen, of course, has continued releasing her more jazz-oriented albums through Anzic. *Notes from the Village* (2008) featured her quartet playing a winning mix of originals and covers of John Coltrane ("After the Rain"), Ernesto Lecuona ("Siboney"), Sam Cooke ("A Change Is Gonna Come"), and Fats Waller ("Jitterbug Waltz"). *Clarinetwork: Live at the Village Vanguard* (2010) was her first live recording, a result of Lorraine Gordon asking her to put together a program honoring Benny Goodman's centennial. The disc was recorded on July 5, 2009, with Cohen backed by Benny Green, Peter Washington, and Lewis Nash on seven standards associated with Goodman, and it is phenomenal—respectful modernists having a ball digging hard into classic, pre-bebop jazz. The music swings like mad while never seeming stuck in the past, and the disc remains formidable documentation of Cohen as a bona fide jazz musician.

Two subsequent albums with her working quartet were also strong. *Claroscuro* (2012) added Paquito D'Rivera on clarinet, Wycliffe Gordon on trombone, and Gilmar Gomes on percussion on select tracks. Lindner's "Anat's Dance," the interweaving clarinets on Artie Shaw's "Nightmare," and a "La Vie En Rose" featuring Gordon's Louis Armstrong–inspired singing are among the notable moments in a wide-ranging program.

Luminosa (2015) skewed more toward world music and was even better. Cohen's Choro Adventeroso ensemble substituted for the quartet on two tracks, and Gomes and guitarists Romero Lubambo and Gilad Hekselman supplemented the quartet on others. There were quartet covers of Flying Lotus, Milton Nascimento, and the team of Edu Lobo and Chico Buarque ("Beatriz," a slow ballad featuring Cohen's bass clarinet and Lubambo's guitar) as well as four impressive pieces of Cohen's own. "The Wein Machine," dedicated to Newport Jazz Festival founder George Wein (who in his later years began riding from stage to stage at Newport in a golf cart so designated), was the closest to straight-ahead jazz of anything on the recording, with a walking bass line and identifiably "jazz" melody surfacing now and then, and Cohen on tenor sax. "In the Spirit of Baden" was her exhilarating clarinet homage to the Brazilian composer-guitarist Baden Powell. "Happy Song" was a frolicsome clarinet feature, repurposed two years later as the title track on her Tentet album. "Ima" was deceptively slow and simple but suffused with emotion, a prime example of *saudade* inhabiting Cohen's own work.

She and I talked about *saudade* in the summer of 2017, as her album *Happy Song* was nearing release, and of how melody and emotion—joyful, sorrowful, and all varieties of emotion—take precedence in her work over whether something is or isn't jazz.

"I like to search for the whole area of emotion," Cohen explained at one point. "So yes, moments of groove, of happiness, of silliness, of playfulness. And then there's moments of retrospection, moments of introspection, moments of—it can be anything. When my father, for example, was in the hospital, I did a tour in Europe. He was lying in the hospital, and I was playing a song called 'Ima.' Now, 'Ima' means 'Mother.' On this night, I dedicated this song to my father, and I was playing his music, and I was crying. Playing and crying. So the audience does not know that I'm crying, and I'm crying tears, but I can close my eyes, and at the end of the song I can turn around and wipe my tears. The music would just take me there.

"Of course, I wrote the song, so for me it symbolizes what the family symbolizes. But music can really take you to a certain time of your life, a certain place. It's like smell. It reminds you of something, makes people nostalgic. They listen to something they grew up with, and it brings back all the emotion of all the times they had while they listened to this music. It's very personal. [Musicians] can only express what is going on with themselves, and maybe if it's honest, other people might feel something. It might take them somewhere. Obviously not to the same place. You cannot make somebody feel something. You can just evoke something. It will never be the same. It will be empathy."

This emotive quality of good music, Cohen emphasized, applies to all types of music the world over.

"So this word *saudade*, in the music of Brazil, the kind of melodies that people play," she said, "if you think about the music of New Orleans, jazz is the same. There's a slow melody, it's just simple melodies. Well, some are not so simple, but they have intense, expressive melodies. That's what I like. If [musicians] play classical music, that's what I like: the horn player to find a melody that they can relate to and express it in the best way that they can. That's all my goal in life, because I play one note at a time. I'm a melody person. So the words *choro*, *fado*—for that matter you're talking about flamenco music, you're talking about the Jewish cantor. This is all about taking a melody, and it's *how* you play. It's not as much what you play. You can take the simplest melody and just really make it your own, and look for how to express it."

Sometimes, of course, the "how" of how musicians play fails to measure up. Lev-Ari put it well when I spoke with him a few months later. I had just compared my response to my first time seeing the 3 Cohens play the music of New Orleans at a club to the cliched Dixieland ensembles I've occasionally noticed performing outside baseball parks on game days. Lev-Ari knew exactly what was missing from the latter. "It's not about breaking it down with this instrumentation—the clarinet is playing this part and the trombone is playing this part and the trumpet is playing this part," he observed. 'What you want to get is human interaction and the human experience. That's kind of the default, and if it's not there it's a cardboard cutout of what the music is.' "

Lev-Ari was speaking from the West Coast, where he and Cohen's Tentet had just begun to tour in support of *Happy Song*. There are moments in performing the album's repertoire where Lev-Ari comes onstage to conduct, and he told me about one of them that had happened the night before. It occurred as he led the band while Cohen and guitarist Sheryl Bailey soloed on his composition "Trills and Thrills." With musicians of Cohen's caliber, there is no such cardboard-like lack of emotional depth.

"There's a big guitar solo, and it intertwines with a clarinet solo," he said, setting his scene. "I had goose bumps, and I was thinking to myself, 'It's your music. You wrote this tune, it's your friend playing it, you hang out all the time and have been hanging out for years—and you still get this feeling. How great is that?' So I feel it in her music—not necessarily the sadness, also the joy—but I feel it in a lot of the music that I love. It's Brahms.[102] And it's Ockeghem,[103] who's this fifteenth-century monk from Luxembourg. I feel it in all sorts of ways, in all sorts of situations. That's one of the things that I chase as a musician. I want that feeling. I want to feel that, whatever that is."

Happy Song topped off 2017, a year even more productive for Cohen than 2007 had been. That June I'd seen her and Fred Hersch play two of sets together at Mezzrow (their playfully virtuosic "Jitterbug Waltz" was particularly memorable), and they had already recorded a duo performance in California that spring for release early the next year on Anzic. Her pair of Grammy-nominated Brazilian albums were released the same day (April 28), as *Noir* and *Poetica* had been a decade earlier.

But *Happy Song* was special. It celebrated the clarinet on the hundredth anniversary of recorded jazz, and it did so with an eclectic array of music dear to Cohen, performed by a versatile cast of gifted international musicians. Counting Lev-Ari, six of the Tentet's members are from overseas: Cohen, Lev-Ari, and young upright bassist Tal Mashiach (Israel); Vitor Gonçalves, who doubles on piano and accordion (Brazil); cellist Rubin Kodheli (Albania); Nadje Noordhuis, trumpet and flugelhorn (Australia). The five Americans are Sheryl Bailey, guitar; Owen Broder, baritone sax and bass clarinet; Nick Finzer, trombone; James Shipp, vibraphone and percussion; and Anthony Pinciotti, drums.

The album opens with two of Cohen's pieces—"Happy Song," set to a rock rhythm, and the sweetly elegiac "Valsa Para Alice"—and closes with her arrangement of Neba Solo's Malian dance hit "Kenedougou Foly" as an upbeat coda. In between come Lev-Ari's "Trills and Thrills," the Brazilian composer Egberto Gismonti's "Loro" (a tune previously recorded by such jazz artists as Charlie Haden, Chick Corea, John McLaughlin, and Esperanza Spalding), and a couple of songs associated with Benny Goodman: the swing classic "Oh, Baby" and his frequent set-closer, the regret-laden "Goodbye."

Most notably, "Oh, Baby" bleeds directly into Cohen's first recorded exploration of klezmer music, on a piece titled "Anat's Doina." It turns out that some Israeli musicians keep klezmer at arm's length much as generations of American musicians have avoided playing early jazz. Conversely, American jazz musicians such as Hankus Netsky, Don Byron, and David Krakauer have taken up klezmer, much like Cohen and her brothers did New Orleans jazz. The tendency to turn up one's nose at the music of one's grandparents seems to be universal.

Lev-Ari told a story illustrating the point, from when he led an all-star contingent of musicians that included Anat, Madeleine Peyroux, Ron Carter, Mulgrew Miller, Bucky Pizzarelli, Ingrid Jensen, Marcus Strickland, Antonio Sánchez at the 2009 Ouro Preto Jazz Festival. The set celebrated Billie Holiday on the fiftieth anniversary of her passing, and joining the Americans for one number was the Brazilian samba star Mart'nalia.

"She gave a 'God Bless the Child' performance that was riveting," Lev-Ari recalled. "Then a journalist, after the show, came to me and said, 'Why did you pick Mart'nalia? I mean she was great, but we had no idea that she could sing jazz.'" As they continued talking, Lev-Ari realized the journalist was insinuating that samba is inferior to jazz, an opinion that Lev-Ari told him he disagreed with. "So," Lev-Ari told me, "there might be something about things that you grow up with that you kind of take for granted. I can't speak for the American experience."

He could, however, speak to a comparable Israeli experience. "This album includes the first time either one of us is doing anything that has anything to do with klezmer," he told me, referring to *Happy Song*. "We talked about it, and we decided we can't do an album around the clarinet without doing klezmer, especially being from Israel. But just in general, you kind of can't do it. And we had to go beyond the cutout, the cardboard version, and to see what it is in this music that is appealing, and connect to it. So we sat around and listened to stuff with new ears. Not, 'This old music. This is our grandparents' music.' Not that, but rather to connect to it."

Their study led them to "Anat's Doina," a three-part suite in which two pieces of spirited original music by Cohen (titled "A Mayse" and "Foile-Shtick") bracket the mournful traditional klezmer tune "Der Gasn Nigun" ("The Street Tune"), the final two segments arranged by Lev-Ari.

"If we talked two years ago I wouldn't know this," Lev-Ari admitted, "but a *doina* is a classic klezmer form, featuring a virtuoso clarinet player—violin player, a trumpet player, whatever it is—where there's kind of a fantasy sweeping first movement, where it's moving and improvised, out of time; and then there's a slow dance, in the middle; and then there's a fast tune. It's an established form, called a doina, and there are many different doinas. This is 'Anat's Doina.'"

The overwhelmingly enthusiastic reception the piece has received in concert took the two of them by surprise, Lev-Ari told me. "This is one of the tracks that people respond most to. People call it the centerpiece of the album, and we completely did not intend it to be."

Was it jazz? It really doesn't matter, at least not beyond the precincts of the jazz police. The best musicians are less concerned with genre than the two categories of music long ago designated by Duke Ellington: "good music, and the other kind."

Cohen has her own unique take on what constitutes "jazz" and "jazz musicians." The former is a genre filled with possibility, which can be played well or badly; the latter, in her idealized conception of the term, is an honorific that must be earned. "Not everybody who plays jazz is a jazz musician" was how she once described it to me. "Some people only play what's safe, and that's not for me what jazz musicians are. Jazz musicians are the people who can really do anything, can play all the other kinds of music *and* play jazz.

"The word *jazz* might not describe exactly what you're doing," she added. "I confess that there's a conflict here in what I'm saying. I like to think of myself as a jazz musician. Am I fluently conversant in bebop? No. Do I explore intensely the language? No. Did I explore it? Yes. Do I want to learn it? Yes. Am I fluent in it? No. Do I speak Portuguese? Yes. Am I fluent in it? No. But it gave me the basis to say, OK, this is an influence. Jazz-*influenced* music? I don't know."

Please visit the open access version of Make It New to see a video resource for Chapter Six: https://doi.org/10.3998/mpub.11469938.comp.6

CHAPTER SEVEN

ROBERT GLASPER

Hosted by the popular alternative rock band Wilco, the Solid Sound Festival has taken place every other summer since 2013 in North Adams, Massachusetts, on the grounds of the Massachusetts Museum of Contemporary Art (Mass MoCA). The eclectic event mixes music, comedy, visual art, and more on a variety of stages—some outdoors, others inside the museum itself—over the course of a weekend.

Jazz isn't typically prominent in the mix at Solid Sound, but Robert Glasper's bid to engage a bigger, younger audience and make jazz relevant again brought him to the Berkshires for the festival in 2017. So there was the Robert Glasper Experiment setting up Saturday afternoon at Courtyard B, one of the festival's three outdoor stages, where rocker Peter Wolf, best known for his work with the J. Geils Band, had played a set a couple of hours earlier. And there would be another set of experimental jazz on the same stage the next day, when Wilco's lead guitarist, Nels Cline, performed with his Nels Cline Four bandmates Julian Lage, Scott Colley, and Tom Rainey.

Glasper is a bona fide jazz pianist and composer, having recorded a couple of acclaimed acoustic trio albums for Blue Note Records in the early 2000s. But his profile rose dramatically with his 2012 album *Black Radio*, recorded with his electric group, the Robert Glasper Experiment, and a variety of singers and rappers he had come to know while moonlighting as a sideman to Mos Def and other high-wattage hip-hop and neo-soul stars. *Black Radio* won the 2012 Grammy for Best

R&B Album. Its follow-up, *Black Radio 2* (2013), earned Glasper a second Grammy for its updating of Steve Wonder's "Jesus Children of America," which took 2014 honors for Best Traditional R&B Performance.

Glasper didn't abandon jazz. His next album, *Covered (The Robert Glasper Trio Recorded Live at Capitol Studios)* (2015), reunited him with his acoustic trio mates Vicente Archer and Damion Reid for instrumental interpretations of a range of pop hits—songs by active artists such as Radiohead, John Legend, and Kendrick Lamar as well as "Stella by Starlight." The trio also toured: I caught a couple of enjoyable sets at Scullers in December 2015 that included Glasper cracking wise from the piano bench between tunes and slipping quotes from Christmas carols into a couple of his solos ("God Rest You Merry, Gentlemen" popped up momentarily in Prince's "Sign o' the Times").

Other opportunities followed the *Black Radio* albums' success. Glasper worked with Don Cheadle on music for the feature film *Miles Ahead* (2015), and was given access to Columbia's vaults to update the Miles Davis catalog with the album *Everything's Beautiful* (2016), which went top ten on *Billboard*'s R&B/hip-hop, jazz, and contemporary jazz charts, reaching number one on the latter two. He produced several tracks on a companion album for the Netflix documentary *Nina Revisited: A Tribute to Nina Simone* (2015); played keyboards on several tracks of Lamar's 2015 critically lauded, platinum-selling, and multiple Grammy-winning rap album *To Pimp a Butterfly* (he played on Lamar's album and recorded *Covered* on the same day); and contributed to two other celebrated pop albums that same year, Maxwell's *blackSUMMERS'night* and Anderson .Paak's *Malibu*. In October 2016, he backed Common on an NPR Tiny Desk Concert at the White House, along with Bilal, Derrick Hodge, drummer/producer Karriem Riggins, flutist Elena Pinderhughes, and trumpeter Keyon Harrold; Glasper, Common, and Riggins later shared a 2017 Emmy Award for their song "Letter to the Free" from the Ava DuVernay documentary *13th* (2016).

Glasper also doubled back to the Experiment for another album, *ArtScience*, released September 2016, this time dropping the guest-star formula and having the band handle its own vocals. Glasper himself sang lead for the first time on "Thinkin Bout You."

The band was promoting *ArtScience*, more or less, when I saw them in summer 2017 at Solid Sound. The courtyard area was nearly empty between sets as the Experiment did its sound check. As they played some of their vocoder version of John Coltrane's "A Love Supreme," Glasper was wearing the faded blue jeans and loose, sleeveless T-shirt he would perform in. Casey Benjamin, the lone remaining member of the original Experiment lineup, wore a two-toned gray muscle T-shirt, cutoff jeans, and cowboy boots, his ensemble topped off with a floppy hat. Given

Benjamin's flashier attire and prominent spot at the front of the stage, it wasn't all that surprising to overhear one photographer turn to another during sound check and ask, "Which one's Robert Glasper?"

Benjamin has recorded and still occasionally plays saxophone with the vibraphonist and composer Stefon Harris, but with the Experiment he has an array of other duties: vocals, vocoder, synthesizer, and keytar in addition to his saxes. On drums was Justin Tyson, a much-in-demand young talent who would be joining Esperanza Spalding in the studio that fall for her *Exposure* project (Glasper would be with them on one track as well, playing piano as a featured guest). Rounding out the band were turntablist Jahi Sundance, who had performed that role on all three Experiment albums, and Glasper's fellow Houston natives Mike Severson and Burniss Earl Travis, on guitar and bass, respectively. Severson's guitar had been added to the band beginning with *ArtScience*. Travis, a.k.a. Boom Bishop, had succeeded Derrick Hodge on bass when Hodge got his own record deal with Blue Note and became busy writing film scores and touring with neo-soul star Maxwell.

That afternoon's set started out with "Cherish the Day," an early 1990s hit for the pop star Sade that Glasper had covered on his first *Black Radio* album, with Lalah Hathaway doing the vocal. Benjamin did so at Solid Sound, breaking off his singing to grab his alto sax and blow a ferocious extended solo, people in the audience nodding along to the beat; the band then segued into "No One Like You" from *ArtScience*, with Glasper soloing on Fender Rhodes electric piano and synthesizer, and the music morphing back to "Cherish the Day" momentarily before ending a half hour into the set.

Glasper paused to introduce the band and take a cellphone video of the audience now packing the courtyard, and the music resumed. Severson ended his solo on "Find You" (also from *ArtScience*) to uproarious applause, and Tyson's drum solo was the centerpiece of a cover of Kendrick Lamar's "How Much a Dollar Cost." But it was the set closer, the Experiment's take on the Police hit "Roxanne," that fully ramped up the crowd. I took an iPhone video of my own of that exuberant response, which included a pair of young women standing in the front row beside me clapping and howling their delight to the final notes of "Roxanne."

That sort of audience reaction isn't common at jazz performances. Jason Moran's Fats Waller Dance Party later that summer at the Newport Jazz Festival got some people up and dancing, and when the Roots closed out Newport that same Sunday there was an exuberance up near the stage to match what the Experiment had produced at Solid Sound. But generally the atmosphere at jazz events is more staid, even at festivals. And at jazz clubs, there is usually a scarcity of young women fans.

Or so Glasper told me when he dropped by the Solid Sound press room to catch up after his set. He filled me in on separate new projects he had underway with

Herbie Hancock and Common, and explained his take on the controversy arising from a *Do the Math* blog interview he had given to Ethan Iverson earlier in the year, in which he had equated a satisfying rhythmic groove in music to "a musical clitoris" and the two were upbraided for sexism. Both eventually issued apologies for the ill-chosen remarks. Glasper published his mea culpa on Facebook, which elicited scores of appreciative responses, including those from accomplished jazz artists such as Kate McGarry, Ingrid Jensen, Rachel Z, and Tia Fuller.[104]

Something else Glasper told me that afternoon in relation to the controversy tied him to two of his musical heroes, Herbie Hancock and Miles Davis, and their refusal to be pinned to a genre or keep jazz locked in its past. Jazz should reflect its own time, Glasper has often argued, sometimes not so diplomatically, or it risks making itself irrelevant to the wider culture. It is the perceived irrelevance of excessively tradition-bound jazz that he holds largely to blame for the absence of young women in jazz audiences. That and jazz musicians' insistence on showing off their virtuosic technique at the expense of making music that connects with people.

"Herbie told me Miles told him, 'If there are no women at your shows, your music's dead,' " Glasper recounted.

He laughed and repeated himself.

"Herbie told me that: 'Miles told me that if there are no women at your shows, your music's dead.' Honestly, most jazz musicians don't think about women whenever they're playing. They think about dudes. They want to hear guys go, 'Oooh! His chops were amazing!' They don't think about women. I think about women, which is why women are at my shows."

Another reason is Glasper's refusal to stay locked in jazz's past. He has zero interest in his music sounding the way jazz did in the mid-twentieth century, the familiar post-bebop variety that is now considered straight-ahead jazz. And his success in helping jazz capture new audiences was forcing the jazz establishment to take notice.[105]

"I feel like now the jazz world's kind of adapting," he told me that afternoon, "because they need people like me, people like Espy [Esperanza Spalding], people like Christian Scott, and Terrace Martin and Kamasi [Washington]. They need people like us to compete. We're their gateway into a Kendrick Lamar."

The person most responsible for Glasper becoming a musician was a woman. His mother, who performed as Kim Yvette, sang professionally in a range of genres: gospel, R&B, jazz, blues . . . on occasion, even country. Glasper dedicated his first Blue Note album, *Canvas* (2005), "to the loving memory of my mother, Kim Yvette Glasper. You're the reason I play."[106] He also introduced the album's final track with a recording of her singing the blues. "I've always said I wanted to have my mom on one of my CDs," Glasper told me the first time we spoke, for a 2006 profile in the *Boston Globe*. "Whenever I played in Houston, she would come sit in with me. We used to jam at home together and stuff."

Glasper's mother was choir director at their Baptist church, and took him with her to rehearsals and her other gigs when he was as young as two. By eleven, he was on stage playing piano with her at church. Glasper was mostly self-taught on the instrument, picking up pointers from musicians associated with his mother. Early on, he didn't read music.

When *New Yorker* editor David Remnick interviewed him for the *New Yorker Radio Hour* in 2015, Glasper said his formal training had consisted of six months of classical lessons in seventh grade and a year or two of gospel lessons in seventh and eighth grade.[107] Remnick was astonished. He had just watched Glasper play a five-minute solo-piano version of Bilal's "Levels" live in the radio studio.

"Mothers at home are listening to this and crying," Remnick told Glasper. "They have no way to convince their kids to sit there [practicing the piano], like I did for years . . ."

"But I was an only child," Glasper explained, "and all I did was play the piano. Once I started playing, that's what I loved to do."

"And you could play on the keyboard what you were hearing in your head?" Remnick asked.

"I could play what I heard in my head, and I loved to learn songs off the radio."

"I hate you," deadpanned Remnick, to Glasper's amusement. "And theory, too—you could just pick this up like nothing?"

"Yes," Glasper confirmed, "and I got really good at it once I went to the High School for Performing [and Visual] Arts, in Houston."

Glasper had a couple of other interests in high school besides piano. Before arriving at HSPVA for his sophomore year, he spent his freshman year at a local school, dreaming of basketball stardom.[108] When that didn't pan out, he told one interviewer, he "moved that bench over to the piano," transferring to HSPVA at the suggestion of the pianist in his mother's band. By this time he had begun developing a fondness for jazz.

Glasper acquired a Chick Corea tape in ninth grade that made a particularly strong impression, Chick Corea Akoustic Band's *Alive* (1991), and decided he wanted to study music. HSPVA was the only high school in Houston offering a focus on music. "You could do music classes, but the only music you could really take was classical or jazz. I still won't take classical, but I already had a little interest in jazz. So it was like, 'OK, I'll do jazz.' "

Glasper had also played some clarinet in middle school, and admitted to an early fondness for Kenny G in those years when he and I spoke in January 2012 for a *JazzTimes* feature previewing the first *Black Radio* album. Glasper had just mentioned that his song "F.T.B.," from his album *In My Element* (a new version of the tune with lyrics, written and sung by Ledisi, would appear on *Black Radio*, retitled "Gonna Be Alright"), was getting airplay on smooth jazz radio stations. So I asked about his attitude toward smooth jazz. His answer wasn't far removed from how he wants to fuel listeners' interest in his jazz through his own excursions into the pop music he loves.

"We need smooth jazz," Glasper told me. "I'll tell you why: To me, it's a stepping stone for people who don't know anything about jazz to get a better idea of what it is. 'Oh wait, he's playing an Anita Baker song. I know that song. Oh, he's taking the solo now. Now he's playing the melody again.' It gives them a little bit better grasp on how a jazz song goes. You can't just take up an average person and put on some Trane and expect them to be like . . ."

I brought up the obvious exception, Coltrane's "My Favorite Things."

"Right," he conceded, "but even people nowadays know what the hell that is." He then steered the conversation back to where he draws a line concerning smooth jazz.

"I'm just mad at people who promote the smooth jazz and blend it all together and say, 'This is jazz,'" he said. "As long as you put 'smooth jazz' by it, I'm not angry. Why should I be angry? You need that. It's a bridge, to me. I'm not one of them people walking around hating it. Like, I used to own Kenny G albums. I used to listen to it. He's probably one of the reasons why I'm playing jazz. I have that *Silhouette* album, and I used to wear that joint out in like seventh grade. I played clarinet in seventh grade, so I used to mimic Kenny G, play out the side of my mouth on the clarinet, and the band director used to get mad at me."

"The girls liked it," I ventured.

"The girls liked it, yeah! So it's really a stepping stone for people to understand a jazz formula. And it's something they can identify with more than 'Resolution.'[109] Especially people of this generation. The older generation understands jazz and what it's about, because that was the hip-hop during their day. That was the big new music."

Glasper offered a metaphor for the role he sees for smooth jazz in relation to the real thing: a black fish he said was useful for keeping fish tanks clean, so that people could better see its more visually appealing tank mates.

"It's not a beautiful fish," he said, "but it's there to clean the tank, so it has a purpose. Smooth jazz is like that. I don't own any anymore, but I think it's needed. It has a big audience. The average smooth jazz person probably has a bigger audience than the average jazz person. What's the reason for that? It's probably not because they are better on their instrument. It's probably because they are playing songs that people know. It's probably something as simple as that, and [that] they know how to play simpler. So at some point, make a song or two that's kind of simple, and people will hear it and maybe like it and maybe come to your show. And when they get to your show, then you can prove, 'Hey, I'm really good on my instrument.'"

"Here's the grown-up stuff," I suggested.

"Here's the grown-up [stuff], yeah!" he agreed. "But by then they are already a fan. They have those two songs, so now they're hooked. Too late."

He laughed.

"I forget what you call that fish,"[110] Glasper added. "It just latches onto the glass and it eats up all the fungus off the glass. It keeps the tank clean. I've never used that analogy before. It's not beautiful to me, but you want it there. You need it."

It was authentic jazz that Glasper studied at HSPVA, as had the recently graduated Jason Moran before him. The story goes that Glasper semi-bluffed his way into the program as part of his audition when program director Robert "Doc" Morgan asked him to name his favorite jazz pianist. Glasper was nervous, so had trouble answering, but eventually blurted out "Oscar Peterson!" Years later, he confessed to Morgan that he then had yet to listen to Peterson; he had plucked the name from a huge poster touting Peterson and the Montreaux Jazz Festival that he spotted across the audition room.

The HSPVA jazz program has helped launch many notable careers in recent years. Two of Glasper's bandmates at Solid Sound, for instance. Mike Severson had played with Moran on the high school recording that Glasper heard and later cited as evidence that Moran had passed through McCoy Tyner and Kenny Kirkland phases en route to finding his own voice. Burniss Earl Travis, Glasper told me, graduated in 2008, having been the recipient of a scholarship established by Moran.

But there are bigger names, too. The school has been particularly strong at producing outstanding drummers, among them Eric Harland, Kendrick Scott, Jamire Williams, and Chris "Daddy" Dave. (Chris Dave, whom Glasper has called "the Tony Williams of my generation," played on Glasper's *Double Booked* and both *Black Radio* albums, and his numerous other credits include work backing major pop talents such as D'Angelo, Maxwell, Adele, and John Legend.) Tenor saxophonist Walter Smith III, guitarist Mike Moreno, and pianist James Francies are three other instrumentalists from HSPVA who went on to success on New York's jazz scene. And then there is the best known onetime HSPVA student of them all, Glasper's classmate Beyoncé Knowles, with whom his younger cousin LeToya Luckett performed in the original Destiny's Child lineup.

Glasper mastered jazz piano, its lineage, and music theory sufficiently at HSPVA to earn offers of full scholarships from both Berklee and the New School, choosing the latter in order to move directly to New York. A good call, as Glasper crossed paths with important influences immediately upon his arrival in the fall of 1997.

"My very first day at New School I met Kenny Kirkland on the street," Glasper told me at Solid Sound. "He was going into the Citibank, I was going to school—on 13th and 5th, there used to be a Citibank. He parked his Lexus right there. I was crossing the street. He got out of his Lexus, and I walked up to him, and he talked to me like five minutes. He gave me his card. I was like, 'You give lessons?' He was like, 'I'm busy with Sting and *The Tonight Show*, but give me a shout.' That sold me on New York. The first day of school I meet my hero? My son, his middle name is Kirkland: Riley Kirkland Glasper."

Soon after moving to town, Glasper also phoned Jason Moran, who invited him to his home in Harlem, where Moran introduced Glasper to the classic Duke Ellington recording *Money Jungle*. "We had fried chicken," Glasper recalled, "and we listened to *Money Jungle* and we painted."

"Painted?" I asked.

"He had two canvases," Glasper replied.

"Do you paint?"

"No," said Glasper. "He was like, 'Do you want to paint?' I was like, 'Sure.' So we painted and he put on *Money Jungle*, and we listened to *Money Jungle,* and we ate fried chicken."

Glasper's most influential encounter in those early days in New York was with a New School classmate, vocalist Bilal Oliver, a graduate of Philadelphia's High School for the Creative and Performing Arts.[III] The two became fast friends and professional collaborators.

"We hung out all the time," recalled Glasper. "We started writing songs in my dorm room, and he got signed to Interscope Records our sophomore year. And then he dropped out, and we started going on tour."

Much of Glasper's education during his New School years was extracurricular. He tested out of most of the basic coursework—theory, ear training, etc. "So all I did was ensemble classes," he said, "like John Coltrane ensemble, Herbie Hancock ensemble, Miles Davis ensemble. I did every ensemble like five times."

And he gigged relentlessly. Glasper's Bilal connection helped him cross paths with the elite of the neo-soul and socially conscious rap movements then in ascendance in New York, at a time when the Roots were introducing the idea of rapping to live music rather than to recorded music samples. Glasper forged lasting ties then that led to his *Black Radio* projects and beyond.

"I used to give Common piano lessons when he lived in Brooklyn," Glasper recalled in another of our conversations. "Pretty much all of this started because of the neo-soul movement back in, like, '99, '98. That's when I first moved to New

York, in '97, so I was around for that whole movement. I was going to all the jam sessions. That's when everybody was kind of coming up and gathering at these jam sessions, so it was easy for me to play with Tina Jenkins Crawley, Common, Mos Def, Q-Tip, Erykah Badu. I've done stuff with Kanye West—he's actually jumped onstage with me a few times. At the Blue Note Jazz Club once. It was hilarious."

Glasper was out and about on the jazz scene in his New School days as well. It was not unheard of for him to grab breakfast somewhere after spending the night hanging out at Smalls Jazz Club and head directly to class. He began touring with some top jazz musicians, too—Roy Hargrove, Christian McBride, Russell Malone—and the willingness of some of his professors to let him do that helped him graduate.

Glasper's first jazz recording as a sideman came about accidentally while he was in Los Angeles touring with Russell Malone. He and drummer Damion Reid dropped by bassist Robert Hurst's home studio for a jam session; they did so again the next time Glasper was in town, and this time Hurst recorded it—and called Glasper a few months later to say he was releasing it, titled *Unrehurst* (2002). A follow-up live album with Hurst, *Unrehurst Volume 2*, and with Experiment drummer Chris Dave replacing Reid, was recorded in 2007 at the New York jazz club Smoke and released in 2010.

By then, Glasper had already released two trio albums of his own. The first, *Mood*, was done for the Fresh Sound label, like so many debuts of the late 1990s and the following decade, and released in 2002, with Hurst and Reid on bass and drums. It showcased the pianist's jazz skills in a range of contexts, from the opening cover of Herbie Hancock's "Maiden Voyage" (with Bilal adding ethereal vocal effects, the arrangement arising organically from Glasper exploring a Radiohead tune) to the phenomenal extended cover of "Blue Skies" to Glasper originals such as the modernist title track (Mike Moreno and John Ellis supplementing the trio on guitar and tenor sax, respectively), the waltz "In Passing," and the hard bop burner "L.N.K. Blues" (John Ellis and Marcus Strickland both joining the trio on tenor). There was also the two-minute "Interlude," which offered a taste of the laid-back groove and billowing chords that would come to characterize his work with later projects.

It was an auspicious debut, though it being on a small label meant it didn't attract a lot of attention. But it caught the attention of the right people. He was signed to Blue Note for his second trio album, *Canvas*, for which Vicente Archer took over as the group's bassist.

I first encountered Glasper a few days before *Canvas* was recorded, when his trio performed at the Regattabar in May 2005. Blue Note publicist Cem Kurosman had taken the unusual step of traveling to Cambridge for the show, which we watched together from a back table. That set persuaded me to interview Glasper before his next Regattabar appearance the following January, about three months after *Canvas*'s release.

The new recording was less concerned with demonstrating instrumental prowess than *Mood* had been, and more focused on Glasper establishing his unique voice. Herbie Hancock's "Riot" was the lone cover, the result, Glasper told me, of Vicente Archer suggesting it the afternoon of that previous Regattabar show and the trio working out an arrangement of it at sound check. (The influential tenor saxophonist Mark Turner was added on the album version, and Glasper switched to a Fender Rhodes for it.)

"It wasn't something I meditated on," Glasper explained. " 'Gotta do Herbie'— nothing like that. The same thing with the first record. I love Herbie, but I'm not one of them cats that rushes home to put on a Herbie record. I mean, he's definitely an influence, but yeah, same thing with the 'Maiden Voyage.' I was playing a Radiohead tune, 'Everything in Its Right Place'—that's what that is, a mixture of 'Everything in Its Right Place' and 'Maiden Voyage,' on the first record. I was just playing that other tune, and I heard 'Maiden Voyage' on it. 'OK, cool.' He's one of my favorite composers, though. He's a killer composer."

Canvas highlighted Glasper originals, emphasizing more his approach to groove and harmony, and the spaces between notes, than how fast he could play. Making music took precedence over displaying technical mastery, which isn't generally the case with young jazz musicians. Glasper, then twenty-seven, showed an unusual maturity in discussing that approach as well.

"You don't always have to be athletic," he told me. "I know I have chops. I know I can play with some of the best of them. Not that I'm the fastest or anything like that, but I mean I can hold my own when I really need to. But everything has its correct place. Sometimes your chops can overtake the music, or people are so into that, you know—you already proved you have chops, now do something musical. They forget what the whole purpose of the music is. Like people now my age aren't even thinking about an emotional approach to the music. Music is supposed to control emotions, if you're doing it the right way. There's a place for athleticism, there's a place for music—so try to find a balance."

The emotion was particularly strong on the final track of *Canvas*, "I Remember," a tribute to Glasper's mother, whose murder had occurred just over a year before the album was recorded. It opens with an excerpt of a live recording of her belting out a raucous blues. His mother's voice fades into a piano meditation from Glasper, with Bilal adding otherworldly wordless vocals partway through, somehow suggesting Glasper's mother being added to a heavenly choir. I asked Glasper about how the piece had come together.

"I had the middle part of it," he said, "the part with no vocals, just the piano part—I wrote that right after everything happened, and then took a break from it. Then once I busted this record, I wrote the end part where I have Bilal come in, vocally.

"Bilal's my best buddy and my favorite singer at the same time," he continued, "and my mom was my favorite singer and my mom, which is like my best buddy. So it kind of started off with my mom and ended with Bilal paying homage to my mom. 'Cause he loved my mom, too. It just kind of flowed together. I didn't even tell Bilal what to sing. I just put the track on, and he came in and listened to it, like one minute, and went in and did what he felt. 'Cause he had his own thing, you know, because his grandmother had just passed two months prior to that. He sang at my ma's funeral. So he had shit to get out, too. I just let him do what he wanted to do on it. And that was how it happened."[112]

We also talked about how critics and publicists had begun playing up the hip-hop influences in his music. Glasper considered whatever hip-hop influences worked their way into *Canvas* to be "minute," insisting that what he and his trio were playing on the album and in concert was jazz.

Glasper blamed the misconception on his having spent so much time backing elite rappers and singers when he wasn't playing jazz—"with Mos Def, with Q-Tip, with Bilal, with the Roots, whatever. But this is a jazz record. It's pretty much strictly a jazz record. I have like a hip-hop interlude on there, randomly after 'Chant'—there's like an interlude that's not even listed. It goes on for like thirty seconds. It's just like a beat playing with a chord. But the album is a jazz album. So for some reason it just grew from 'Robert plays with hip-hop guys' to 'Robert made a hip-hop jazz album.'

"Basically, all the guys in my trio listen to hip-hop," he said. "We all check it out. When we lock into the groove, we groove really hard. So I guess in some kind of way you can kind of tie that into that, which is cool. But it's not a hip-hop-meets-jazz record. . . . So many people have written like, 'Yes, and it's hip-hop jazz style.' *No.* 'It fuses jazz and hip-hop and soul music.' *No.* I just do those kind of gigs on the side. Like McCoy [Tyner] played with Phyllis Hyman,[113] but that ain't called a fuckin' 'R&B jazz record.' "

I asked about the relationship between jazz and hip-hop and whether he thought it had been growing stronger, and Glasper answered with a capsule history. "It's kind of getting more [strong] as far as the live-band aspect of it goes," he said, "but people have been sampling jazz stuff for years. Most of the old hip-hop, from the beginning of hip-hop days, just sampled old jazz records and put a hip-hop beat to it. Bill Evans and Ron Carter are the most sampled cats. People would just take a piece of something they played on a jazz record and put it in a machine, called an MPC,[114] and loop it for like four bars, and then put a hard hip-hop beat to it and rap over it. Now people are skipping the whole sample part and just hiring bands.

"It's funny," he added, "because jazz and hip-hop can go hand in hand, really. More so when it's the jazz into the hip-hop, though. But when you have jazz players that can do both—they can play hip-hop, they can play jazz—it comes off a lot better. Sometimes you have jazz people [who] want to incorporate hip-hop in their music, and it's not the thing to do."

Glasper wasn't ruling out bringing hip-hop more prominently into his own music eventually. "I've been tempted to do some hip-hop stuff," he acknowledged, "and some other kind of stuff, too. But you know, I kind of try to wait, and when I do it, do it in a good fashion. Because so many people that do it, it's wack—you know, just for the sake of doing it, like, 'Ha, I'm doing something different in jazz.' So I'm just waiting. I'll wait till it really comes to me."

It took Glasper another six years to fully tap into his pop side on a recording, and when he did so on *Black Radio* the emphasis was on R&B more than hip-hop. But the next two jazz albums he released before then kept moving incrementally in that direction. *In My Element* (2007) had a cover of the great Sam Rivers piece "Beatrice" and an original ballad written for Glasper's favorite current pianist, "One for 'Grew (For Mulgrew Miller)." But it also updated the "Maiden Voyage/ Everything in Its Right Place" mashup from *Mood*, this time without the vocal, and included a jazz-trio-explores-beats homage to the late hip-hop producer J Dilla ("J Dillalude"), introduced by a voicemail message from Q-Tip suggesting the idea.

There was also a nod to Glasper's gospel background ("Y'Outta Praise Him"), which moves from a meditative piano intro to celebratory energy when the trio kicks in; likewise, a second tribute to Glasper's mother shifts from contemplation to a quiet exuberance as it begins to accompany spoken excerpts from Reverend Joe Ratliff's eulogy. "Who else but Kim could bring the gospel to jazz, cowboys, everybody?" Ratliff says at one point. "It becomes eclectic by design."

Glasper's next album ramped up his own eclecticism. *Double Booked* (2009) was split between his acoustic jazz piano trio (Chris Dave taking over for Damion Reid on drums) and his new electric band, the Robert Glasper Experiment. By then Glasper had begun performing regularly with both, a fact illustrated on the album with a joke: dueling voicemails from Terence Blanchard and Ahmir "Questlove" Thompson of the Roots expressing concern that they'd each booked one of Glasper's bands at different venues for the same night. ("We want the Experiment to come do their thing," Questlove tells him. "All of y'all: I want Chris 'Daddy' Dave, I want Derrick [Hodge], Casey [Benjamin], and you. I want you to do all that oraculous, spaced-out past-geometry, near-calculus stuff you all be doin'."[115]

The original music on both halves of the recording is worth paying attention to. On the trio portion Glasper flaunts his chops for a stretch of "No Worries," then lays back and lets the infectious vibe of the refrain hold much of the interest on "Yes I'm Country (And That's OK)." Glasper's piano and Benjamin's saxophone are showcased on the Experiment's "Festival," and Bilal joins the group to sing his original "All Matter." But the contrast between the bands is best documented by the two covers: Glasper giving Thelonious Monk's "Think of One" a pyrotechnic reworking replete with a bit of stride piano with the trio, and Benjamin's vocoder and the Experiment transforming Herbie Hancock's "Butterfly" into something all their own a couple of tracks later.

The Hancock cover suggested Glasper had more pop-oriented plans in mind for the new group, as Hancock himself had done with his popular funk band Headhunters in the early 1970s and with his landmark hip-hop hit "Rock-It" in 1983. And sure enough, when the Experiment played the Regattabar in October 2011, Glasper spent a few minutes regaling the audience about the album the group had in the works with Mos Def, Erykah Badu, and Lalah Hathaway. I thought the project sounded like something worth writing about. *JazzTimes* magazine agreed, and the following January I traveled to Blue Note's Manhattan offices to interview Glasper about it.

Glasper was seated playing a Yahama grand piano, his back to me, as I was led into the room where the interview took place. As I later described the scene in *JazzTimes*: "Glasper is wearing blue jeans, a gray hoodie and a dark knit hat, and is entranced mid-tune. As he grooves his way through a progression of pillowy chords, the melody to 'On Green Dolphin Street' pokes out just often enough to be recognizable. He senses he's being watched, and the spell is broken. 'Oh!' he says, startled. He rises from the piano bench, laughing. 'Wassup?'"[116]

He laughed again when we took our seats and I read him back his quote from our earlier interview about waiting for the right time to explore hip-hop and other genres, to avoid the risk of being "wack."

"Jazz is my first love," he explained, "and I just really wanted to solidify myself as a jazz pianist and get some records out, stay with that, and then move on to something else, because the media and everybody, they're quick to peg you as something: 'Oh, the hip-hop guy.' They couldn't wait to do that to me. But now I have a body of work. That was very important to me to do that—especially being a young black pianist. People are so fast to peg me as something other than a jazz pianist."

"Yeah, I'm a jazz pianist, it's what I do," he emphasized. "But I also like other things, like everyone else. I like chicken *and* I like beef. It's not that big of a deal. The point of this record was to bring music to the mainstream people to hear: something they can identify with, and that I identify with. I identify with jazz. I identify with gospel. I identify with soul. I identify with neo-soul. I identify with pop, R&B, rock, pop rock, hard rock—all that. It's all a part of me. So I don't want my music to be just a secret for jazz people."

Glasper made the case that jazz ought to be the most innovative music. "To me, that's the definition of jazz," he said. "It's the reflection of the society at the time. You should be able to put on a jazz record and listen to it and be like, 'Yeah, that was '65.' So you're telling me now, it's 2012, you should be able to put on the record and be like, 'Um, that's '60-something?' Why should I reminisce about a time I wasn't there for? We wouldn't even have the '60s, we wouldn't even be able to listen to *A Love Supreme*, if people of that age group were reminiscing about older times."

Jazz was once the popular music of its day, he reminded me. "We're going along with the tradition. I'm not changing the tradition or anything. I'm just making jazz cool again." Glasper mentioned Miles Davis hanging out with Richard Pryor not so long ago, and the Supremes showing up at Tony Williams concerts. "We had swag back then," he said. "Now we're just known as nerds that no one cares about or something. We're like this little jazz society. 'Give them a password to get in.'

"I'm just trying to make the music hip again, but not by selling out," he insisted. "I'm not saying, 'Let me do hip-hop now, or let me do R&B, because I think that's going to sell records.' I didn't pick up the phone and call random people trying to do a hit record. This is family to me. It's just who I am. Like Herbie had another side. That's who he was. It's like, 'Hey, I did "Maiden Voyage"; I did "One Finger Snap." I did all that, so now I feel like doing this.' This is where the times are going, so you don't want to get left behind."[117]

Jazz, Glasper suggested, in its eagerness to preserve its past threatens both its present and its future. "Every other music appreciates its past but is very vibrant about their future and their now," he said. "Country music, pop, R&B. Nobody's saying, 'Yeah, Chris Brown is cool but you gotta check out Marvin Gaye if you really wanna know.' That's some jazz shit. 'Yeah, Jason Moran's cool but you gotta check out Wynton Kelly.' I always say, 'They kill the alive to praise the dead.' And that's going to kill the music. That's why jazz is not very relevant music anymore. Trane moved on. *Love Supreme* wasn't the beginning of jazz. That was '64. He moved on from 'Night in Tunisia.' "

Glasper had things to say about jazz's failure to market itself properly as well. "A jazz record costs more than an R&B record," he noted at one point. "I used to go to Virgin Records and look. My record is $18.99, and Beyoncé's record is $11.99. Hmmm. You really want to turn these kids onto jazz? No young person is going to go into the store and be like, 'OK, let me take my chance on this person I don't know and spend $20.' No, they're going to buy Beyoncé, and then they're going to have some change left over and go get something to eat."

Of course, we also talked about the music on the new album, including specific songs. How its title track, sung by Mos Def (now calling himself Yasiin Bey), had a name derived from an old joke that planes should be made from the same material as the black boxes that survive crashes. How early on Glasper had pictured Erykah Badu singing a jazz tune to open the album, which turned out to be the Afro-Cuban standard "Afro Blue." When I asked how covers of songs by white rockers David Bowie and Nirvana—Bilal singing vocals on the former, "Hermione," which also included Glasper's most fleshed-out piano solo on the album; Casey Benjamin running the lyrics to "Smells Like Teen Spirit" through his vocoder—came to be on a record called *Black Radio*, Glasper laughed and reminded me that "rock is a black music." And he didn't just mean seminal figures like Sister Rosetta Tharpe, Chuck Berry, and Little Richard. Glasper told me of Mulgrew Miller having told him that Elvis Presley had derived much of his early style from hanging out in Memphis with Calvin Newborn, the guitarist brother of pianist Phineas Newborn Jr.

Black Radio was released the next month and won its R&B Grammy the following February. By the next time Glasper and I spoke, as *Covered* was being released in 2015, he had earned his second Grammy, for *Black Radio 2*. I asked if he had been surprised by that first Grammy.

"Very surprised," he told me. "In today's climate, the industry itself just doesn't care about instrumental music. I went back through the years and looked at people who have won it. It's all like John Legend and Alicia Keys and Erykah Badu, D'Angelo won it for *Voodoo*. Chaka Khan won it. These are prominent *singers*. R&B stars. *Stars*, you know. Here I am this piano player who probably just played a blues last night at some club. Now I'm onstage accepting a Grammy, beating out R. Kelly."

Glasper was returning to his jazz trio on *Covered*, but he made no apology to jazz purists for having indulged his fondness for R&B and hip-hop on his pair of *Black Radio* albums. Or retaining the right to do so again in the future. "A lot of people through the years have been, 'Oh, you've abandoned jazz. You're a traitor.' Or, 'You're selling out,' " he said. "And no, actually R&B music probably has more of an impact on my life than jazz does. I grew up on R&B music. That's what was playing in my household, mostly. My first songs I learned on the piano were R&B songs. I didn't get into jazz really until I was in high school. So I'm really going back to my roots by playing R&B."

But all that came later. The weekend of my 2012 interview with Glasper I saw a double bill featuring Geri Allen solo and Jason Moran and the Bandwagon at the Tribeca Y. I ran into Moran as he mingled with the audience before his set and asked if he'd heard Glasper's as-yet-unreleased album, and he said he had and liked it. I later emailed him seeking more detail for the *JazzTimes* piece. Here's what Moran wrote back:

> *I remember hearing Double Booked and being struck listening to "Butterfly." Immediately afterward I called Robert and congratulated him on accomplishing something that had NEVER been done in the music. He made a true original statement while covering someone else's composition, and that is quite an achievement. Like Monk playing Ellington, we have Glasper playing Hancock. So once Robert started telling me of the plans he had for Black Radio, I immediately thought that this was going to be the BIG statement. This would be the statement I heard glimpses of in his early recordings. He was ready, and here it is. He has produced a recording that snapshots the current state of who he is as an artist. He snapshots his community, his sound, his family and the creative state of black music. These elements have been evolving for a while. And he is occupying a space in the music that genuinely nods to all forms, and sacrifices nothing in the gene splicing. It's marvelous to hear, and I know his mother is proud.*

Glasper's piano hero Mulgrew Miller was more lukewarm in his enthusiasm for the new record. "I understand that their reality is a little different from mine. They're in a different age group, and they came along at a different time. So they're just dealing with their reality," Miller explained. "It's not what I prefer to hear Robert do as a piano player, but I respect it. I respect what he's trying to do, and I certainly respect him and his talent." Glasper, it turned out, was delighted by Miller's reaction, quoting it back to me in a subsequent conversation unaware that I'd been the journalist Miller had told it to.

The Miller quote reaffirmed something the Experiment's bassist, Derrick Hodge, had told me earlier: "Mulgrew Miller, Terence Blanchard, Terell Stafford—all those guys were very supportive of whatever I wanted to pursue or play. They'd say, 'Respect the history, respect the tradition, learn as much as you can. But be you. What you do with that information, that's uniquely yours.' "

Blue Note president Don Was told me that on his first day on the job Glasper brought in an unmixed version of *Black Radio*. Was said it had reminded him of a handful of revelatory records before it—Pharoah Sanders's *The Creator Has a Master Plan*, Stevie Wonder's *Music of My Mind*, his first exposure to Jimi Hendrix—in being "familiar puzzle pieces put together in a shockingly new and seamless way that was captivating and mesmerizing."

Was made the case that Glasper's new project, as radically different as it sounded, was nonetheless in line with albums from Blue Note's glory days of a half-century earlier.

"If you go to the birth of the Jazz Messengers," he pointed out, "Art Blakey wanted to change the beat around, man. He wanted to throw a backbeat in there now and then. And Horace Silver wanted to play gospel licks, and he'd throw Southern stuff on top of it. It was a radical departure. Doesn't sound like it now when you listen to it, but I think that was always the case. I asked Herbie. As soon as I got the gig, I called Herbie Hancock up, and he said, 'Remember, those records that you love from that period, these were young, avant-garde guys. And they were pushing the boundaries.' . . . I think Robert has come up with one way of embodying the traditional Blue Note aesthetic [while] making it something thoroughly new."

Was rejected the idea that by working with singers and taking his music in more of a pop direction Glasper was selling out. "Selling out implies compromising your art for the sake of making a buck, and I don't think Robert's compromising anything," he argued. "Listen to the track with Meshell Ndegeocello. Listen to the piano on that. It's what he does when you go to see him with his trio, an acoustic trio. His playing hasn't changed. He's simply surrounded himself with some different textures. Which is what Miles Davis did. Miles didn't change his playing that much. He just put himself in new territory all the time and played his way out of it. I think Robert's in the tradition of jazz, to be honest. Being sedentary is selling out."

I was particularly keen to talk to Ndegeocello herself about Glasper and *Black Radio*. Unlike the other big-name singers and rappers who contributed to it, Ndegeocello was also an accomplished instrumentalist, whose 2003 album *Dance of the Infidels* had seen her performing with a revolving cast of jazz all-stars including Jack DeJohnette, Don Byron, and Kenny Garrett. Like Glasper, she refused to be confined by genre. I told her as much when I got her on the phone, and asked her opinion of Glasper coupling his jazz sensibility with the more pop-oriented music on *Black Radio*.

"I don't really like the word *jazz*," she answered. "I don't know what it means anymore, and I have all the historical information that I've been given. So I just come from a time where most people want to feel good, experience some sort of interaction with the music, whether they can have it with their body and dancing, or if they want to use their thought and see where the instrumentalist can go and what kind of audible pictures they can paint. Improvisational music isn't entertainment for most people; it's usually just trying to peer into what the instrumentalist can express. How well do they express themselves—through the technique, harmonically, melodically, all that. But I think the music also came from brothels, so"—she laughed—"you kind of want the beat to be hot, too. You want to be able to interact with it physically, without your mind.

"Robert comes from that—the church and having the experience of the dance music. All those things within you. You realized there's only about twelve notes, unless you go to some of the Eastern countries. You're just trying to create an experience that the band as a collective enjoys, that the singer feels they can express themselves with, and I think that is black music. That's the only genre I'd say is all-encompassing. There is no one thing, and you're just trying to find your place within it. The genres help you create a generalization so that you can market things. And I'm really hoping people listen to Robert's album and realize it's just a really nice collection done in an interesting way, with a guy who I think is incredible with self-expression and harmony.

"This is the most improvisational record I've been on in a while," she added. "I also like Robert. He's very witty, he's very smart, and then there's an incredible aesthetic. He just references so much."

At one point on *Black Radio*, as had become customary on Glasper albums, the music cuts away for some recorded dialogue. In this case, Glasper and his band are discussing the sorry state of music on the radio and jazz's lack of popularity. The implication is that he wanted their new album to help rectify both problems. Ndegeocello had a similarly dim view of the current state of pop music, but Glasper's new album left her hopeful.

"The radio's dead," she asserted. "If you want to get on the radio, you definitely are dancing with an unusual dance partner, and I wish you well. I think there's a few people who have that market locked down." She mentioned that she was then reading the book *Life: The Movie*, by Neal Gabler, in which the author discusses how Americans have preferred entertainment to high art throughout the nation's history. "So I think we're living in a society where, yeah, some people just want to go and listen to straight dance-beat pop songs," Ndegeocello said. "I think you just have to work a little harder to get people to work a little harder with their listening. But I feel positive about it, because there are people like Robert and Bilal and Mos Def who are pushing boundaries, and not being trapped in some political thing as well. They just want to play music."

Glasper's desire to make jazz more contemporary is bound up with his wanting to make it more popular. Even when he doubled back to his original acoustic trio to record the 2015 release *Covered (The Robert Glasper Trio Recorded Live at Capitol Studios)*, Glasper zeroed in on creating jazz covers of pop music people of his own generation would recognize—tunes by Joni Mitchell, Radiohead, John Legend, Kendrick Lamar, and others. "Originally I wanted to call my album *iPod Shuffle*," he joked when I interviewed him as the album was about to be released. He also kept those covers laid back and groove-oriented, limiting his more ostentatious displays of piano technique to the lone cover from times past ("Stella by Starlight"[118]) and a track he titled "In Case You Forgot" (i.e., a friendly reminder of his virtuosity, aimed at younger pianists who were borrowing the easier-to-imitate aspects of his style).

In that sense, Glasper is old school—someone already so busy performing, recording, and producing that he doesn't have time for (or need) the sort of steady teaching gig that so many other top musicians use to supplement their incomes.[119] He would no doubt like to keep it that way and build on it. In fact, Glasper made a point of telling me, "At the end of the day, this is a business. A lot of musicians fall by the wayside. They play what they hear and do what they want, and they don't put any thought to strategy." In the case of *Covered*, that meant focusing on songs familiar to current audiences, even as Glasper gave in to his desire to return to jazz and his acoustic trio for the project. "It's an incentive to people who don't really listen to jazz to peep this record," he said. "So I could make everybody happy, including myself."

Glasper told me that Miles Davis had been similarly conscious of his audiences, a fact he became aware of while working on the score for *Miles Ahead*. The film gave Glasper the chance to get to know Herbie Hancock, who shows up performing in an all-star band with Glasper, Wayne Shorter, Esperanza Spalding, Gary Clark Jr., and Antonio Sánchez as the credits roll. "I asked him, 'How come on all these bootlegs I have of the Miles Davis Quintet, I never hear y'all play "Pinocchio" or "Nefertiti" or "Fall" or any of these dope songs? I always hear you play "'Round Midnight" and "Autumn Leaves" and the blues,' " Glasper recalled. "And he was like, 'Well, when we were making records back then, no one knew our songs—Miles wanted to play the songs that people knew.' So Miles was always aware of his audience. And that made him great: being a great musician, but also being aware. For some reason, people think being aware of your audience is corny."

Hence the importance to Glasper of that Miles Davis quote about how "if there are no women at your shows, your music's dead." Glasper is proud of his music not having that problem. And he admires other jazz groups for appealing to women. In fact, it was Glasper complimenting Ethan Iverson about the Bad Plus's ability to draw attractive young women to their performances in that notorious *Do the Math* interview that led to the controversy that jazz journalist and author Michelle Mercer, in a post for NPR's culture blog, dubbed "the Saga of Musical Clitoris."

The offending interview happened as Glasper was about to disembark from the 2017 Blue Note at Sea jazz cruise in order to attend that year's Grammy Awards. Mercer summed up the problematic portion of his encounter with Iverson in a couple of paragraphs:

Midway through his interview, the charismatic Glasper decided to build some rapport with Iverson in a manner familiar to straight men the world over: by talking about how much the ladies love them. After asserting his own unusually authentic conversance in R&B, hip-hop and jazz, Glasper brought on the flattery: "I've had people tell me about your music. Like women you would think never listen to jazz: Young, fine, Euro chicks ask me, 'I heard this band, the Bad Plus, do you know them?' "

"I guess that's one of the reasons to play, really," replied Iverson. Yes, Iverson knew what Glasper was talking about. Glasper went on. "I've seen what that does to the audience, playing that groove. I love making the audience feel that way. Getting back to women: women love that. They don't love a whole lot of soloing. When you hit that one groove and stay there, it's like musical clitoris. You're there, you stay on that groove, and the women's eyes close and they start to sway, going into a trance."[120]

I'd read the interview soon after Iverson's newsletter announced it had been published. The "musical clitoris" line jumped out as being clumsy, and the hyperbolic description about women going into an orgasmic trance when mesmerized by a groove was also over the top. Both remarks could obviously be read as sexist, and I wondered what flak Glasper might catch for them. I got my answer when I chanced upon a Facebook post from Vijay Iyer shortly thereafter. Mercer would soon include a barbed and witty reference to Iyer's similarly acerbic post in her NPR piece.

"Inevitably, Iverson's defensive position attracted some scrutiny," she wrote. "The jazz pianist Vijay Iyer, a MacArthur 'genius' grant winner and Harvard professor, did some math on Iverson's blog and posted the results on Facebook: ' "I'm a liberal and I'm feminist," said a man who published interviews with forty-two men and zero women.' "

"Glasper's comments came as a shock to exactly zero people who've spent any time in the jazz world," Mercer noted elsewhere in her piece, offering testimony as to why she and so many others found the interview so deeply offensive. "I've heard variations on the 'women can't really follow jazz' theme ever since I first started hitting jazz clubs and loving extremely long solos. To be a female jazz fan and critic is to live with a frustrating irreconcilability: I have an intellectual passion for creative, complex music and, sometimes, the musicians who make that music doubt my ability to appreciate its creativity and complexity."

The *Do the Math* interview and Mercer's response to it both appeared in March 2017. The ensuing reaction to them proved the first in a series of public discussions to follow over the next year and beyond on the sexist attitudes that confront women who want to perform or write about jazz. The talented young vibraphonist Sasha Berliner, then still a student at the New School, posted "An Open Letter to Ethan Iverson (And the Rest of Jazz Patriarchy)" on her website on September 21.[121] The Harvey Weinstein scandal that launched the #MeToo movement broke in early October, and on October 20 the Newark jazz radio station WBGO posted Lauren Sevran's essay "Sexism in Jazz, From the Conservatory to the Club: One Saxophonist Shares Her Story,"[122] which described the same sort of demeaning remarks from music professors and unwanted sexual advances from male musicians that Berliner had detailed in her piece. In November, the *Boston Globe* published two stories by reporter Kay Lazar concerning the Berklee College of Music having quietly dismissed eleven male professors for alleged sexual misbehavior toward female students. The Berklee firings, Berliner's post, and the Glasper interview were all mentioned in Giovanni Russonello's *New York Times* December piece "For Women in Jazz, a Year of Reckoning and Recognition," which also focused on a number of notable achievements by women through the year, among them the *Exposure* project that Esperanza Spalding recorded live on Facebook that fall (which, ironically, Glasper showed up to appear on as a guest artist on one track).[123]

Over a few days in New York in mid-January 2018, there were three panel discussions on sexism in jazz. Mercer led two of them, one on "Gender and Jazz" at Jazz Congress at Lincoln Center, the other a Jazz Journalists Association–hosted discussion of "Women in Jazz Journalism" at the Jazz Gallery. Terri Lyne Carrington (one of Mercer's Jazz Congress panelists) oversaw a panel comprising Vijay Iyer, journalist and musicologist Lara Pellegrinelli (who also served on Mercer's JJA panel), trumpeter Arnetta Johnson, Angela Davis, and Esperanza Spalding at Winter Jazzfest, titled "Jazz and Gender: Challenging Inequality and Forging a New Legacy." Jazzfest producer Brice Rosenbloom grabbed a microphone at that discussion's conclusion and promised to strive for parity for women when booking the next year's festival.

Glasper's impolitic remark had, inadvertently, helped put all this on the table. Jazz people had begun talking openly about the mistreatment of women who attempted to have careers playing jazz or writing about it, and suddenly appeared determined to correct that injustice.

Most of this hadn't yet occurred when I encountered Glasper at Solid Sound that June, though, and I wanted to know more about his take on the blowback to his talk with Iverson. I hadn't had the same reaction to it that Mercer had, no doubt partly owing to the same sort of male blindness to the sexism women routinely endure that got Glasper and Iverson in trouble. But also because Glasper and I had covered the same ground a few years earlier, when I interviewed him about *Black Radio*. He had made the same troublesome point then about women appreciating space in music—that is, the absence of the flurries of notes, esoteric rhythms, and harmonic busyness that many people find off-putting about much modern jazz—but without the sexist language.

"Space is so important to me," he had said. "Space is important to most people. Chops are only important to people who play an instrument."

"Or people who wish they could," I added.

"Or people who wish they could," he agreed. "But that's a very small percentage of the world, you know? And even people who have chops can appreciate space. So at the end of the day, if you play with some space, you're gonna draw the people who have chops, and you're gonna draw people who don't like chops, don't give a damn, don't even know what chops are." He laughed. "You're playing for, you know, college kids. You're playing in front of people, including musicians, who don't buy records, first of all. So why are you devoting your life and your music to impressing the guys?"

"It's funny you say that," I said. "It seems to me it's a guys' thing." I told him about having first been attracted to jazz via the Mahavishnu Orchestra and other chops-heavy fusion bands of the 1970s. "But you didn't see girls that cared about that. It's the boys . . ."[124]

"It's the boys!" Glasper cut in. "Girls like space. Women like sexiness. They don't care how fast you play. If it comes out that you play fast, cool. I can play fast, but that's not my main priority. You know, there's a time for it. But that's so many [jazz musicians'] priority that it takes away from the music. People [i.e., non-musicians] love space, they love melody, they love simple things. They love things that are complex but sound simple, like some Stevie [Wonder] shit. All his shit is complex as hell when you actually check it out. He's a master at that, you know: having something complex underground, but the tip of the iceberg is very accessible to the average person.

"And that's my thing: I want to be accessible to the average person *and* to the jazz cat. So that's why most of my songs are based off of melody. If I can't sing it, I'm probably not going to even write it down or make it a song. I'm just trying to reach the person who does not listen to jazz. That's the best thing. People come to my show and they're like, 'This is our first jazz show. We don't listen to jazz. Me and my wife don't own any jazz CDs, but we love your music.'"

I was mindful of how quickly "*girls* like space" had morphed into "*people* love space" in what Glasper had told me in that 2012 interview, so never took it to mean Glasper was singling out women as being incapable of understanding jazz. He was saying that most people of *both* sexes love melody and space, perhaps even crediting women who aren't musicians for being less susceptible to pointless chops-worship than are non-musician men. In fact, though the sexism of "musical clitoris" and the sentence that followed it would obscure the point, what Mercer quoted in the two sentences leading up to them in the *Do the Math* interview said essentially the same thing: "I've seen what that does to *the audience*, playing that groove. I love making *the audience* feel that way."

I brought up that earlier interview when I spoke with Glasper at Solid Sound, and how we had talked about a subset of men obsessed with music that flaunts chops, but that women and most men in general tend to prefer space.

"It's fucking true," he said. "But the musician women are the ones that have a problem with it. And I'm not playing for the musician women, that's the thing."

"It's beyond that, too," I said, "because this quote goes on to say: '*People* love space, they love melody, they love simple things, they love things that are complex but that sound simple, like some Stevie [Wonder] shit.' "

"Exactly!" Glasper enthused. "And my thing is, everybody loves Stevie. Stevie's the base. You can't go wrong with that. And I look at the crowd. It's a real, actual thing. The jazz crowd does not look like a Chris Brown crowd. You don't see hot, model-looking chicks at a jazz show. That's what I was getting at. You can't say that, but it's a real thing. I've been to probably 90 percent of the jazz clubs in the world. That's an actual fact for anybody that travels: when you walk in there, you know you're not going to see a pile of hot chicks. That's all I was saying. Because you don't expect those chicks to listen to jazz. You just don't. It's like me walking into a place where there was all old people. I'm not going to think that they listen to Lil Wayne, even though they might be so open musically that they do. But just the perception, because it's not in their age range.

"And most jazz, nowadays, everybody thinks it's old. It's the age range. That's why [young] people stay away from it, not that they can't understand the music. But they stay away from it because of what they are fed about what jazz is—and they're like, 'Nah, I'm good.' And I'm like, '*No*, there is good jazz. Listen to me, listen to Christian Scott. Listen to Esperanza Spalding, listen to Kamasi [Washington], Terrace Martin.' I could go on and on and on. But that's a small group of people in the mix, and we're not being played on every jazz radio station. So if somebody's, like, 'Let me check out some jazz, turn on some jazz radio station,' they're going to get Charlie Parker, some dude like that. Because people are paying for those people to stay on the air—'our patrons'—and that's what *they* want to hear.

"So that's where I was coming from. It wasn't that women can't understand [jazz]. But I said something about a musical clitoris . . ."

"That's the big thing," I said, stating the obvious.

"I use that with my guys," Glasper explained. "It's a metaphor. When you hit something and you stay there because it feels good, musically—to me, that's right along with a clitoris. I'm just giving people insight into the psyche of an artist when he's making music for sex. Because, guess what, there is music for sex. You know? Jazz was the first one. We played in burlesque clubs. We were *jazz* musicians."

I mentioned that Ahmad Jamal had once told me that it was the association of early jazz with brothels that caused Jamal to reject the word *jazz*; Jamal's preferred term was *American classical music*.

"When you say the word *sex*," Glasper replied, "in the jazz world they're all like, 'Oh my God! How dare you start talking about sex! Jazz musicians don't play for sex. They don't play for women.'"

Glasper's point seemed to be that so much serious current jazz has distanced itself so far from sex and romance altogether that jazz is no longer sexy, and therefore no longer popular.

He could be right. The days of couples dancing to Duke Ellington and Benny Goodman, or Louis Armstrong and Ella Fitzgerald getting together to record a version of "Makin Whoopee," are long gone. The romantic side of Fats Waller might have disappeared from view, too, if Jason Moran hadn't modernized some of Waller's best tunes for a dance party.[125]

"There's so many women [who agree] with me, too," Glasper added, getting back to the scarcity of young women at jazz performances. "They're all like, 'They're all so fucking sensitive, are you kidding me? I knew exactly what you were talking about, and it's true.' And those are the women who travel the world, they know what it's like. 'Everything you said is 100 percent true.'"

I mentioned Iyer's Facebook post alluding to the absence of women in the bank of *Do the Math* interviews.[126] Glasper replied that he had had more than thirty women appear on his albums. Those women were all rappers and singers, he acknowledged, explaining that that was because his two core bands had kept their personnel virtually unchanged on the recordings. "It's not like I have a bunch of different musicians all the time," he said. "That's set. But there's over thirty women on my albums. My mom was my biggest musical influence. I talk about that in every interview—you know that about me. So how can you say, 'Oh, he's a sexist'? My track record doesn't say anything about me being a sexist, ever, except now these two sentences. Just ignore twenty years. All they did was read that—'clitoris'—and they just saw that."

Glasper pointed out that he had immediately shifted to another metaphor in the *Do the Math* interview itself, this one emphasizing his music's use of space. "It's in the interview," he said. "Right after I say something about the musical clitoris and all that stuff, I said, 'To be non-sexual, it's like I supply a house. You can move your own furniture into it. I'll leave enough space to be the soundtrack to your thoughts.' That's what I was getting at. Most jazz musicians clutter up all the fucking space."

As for the other issue raised by Mercer in her NPR takedown—that Glasper and Iverson had been "talking about how much the ladies love them"—the charge doesn't fully hold up to scrutiny. Iverson's "I guess that's one of the reasons to play, really" is too innocuous to be damning. Glasper's rejoinder to it—"Yeah, it's awesome, something is there in your music that gives them entrance to jazz, otherwise they'd never cross paths with it"—makes clear that it is the group's music he is crediting with enticing women to Bad Plus concerts, not that the women were lusting after Iverson and his bandmates.

In any case, it's hardly a secret that a common motivation for some people to play music is to enhance their sex appeal. And it isn't only men who make use of music this way. One night I was contemplating this possibility, and the other means that women employ to attract men, in connection to Iverson's remark and Mercer's reaction to it. By coincidence, later that same night I decided to give a listen to a year-old interview that I had bookmarked. Esperanza Spalding was the guest for an episode of the podcast *Talk Easy with Sam Fragoso*, which features "long-form conversations with the people shaping our culture today: filmmakers, musicians, comedians, activists, authors, actors."

About a half hour into that interview, Spalding began describing how, around age twelve, she became more serious about music and began climbing through the ranks of the Chamber Music Society of Oregon, from second violin to first violin to concertmaster. "I started playing in smaller ensembles within that institution or organization," she recalled. "So I'd play in quartets and quintets, and I'd start to write for quartets and quintets. If I had a crush on a boy, I'd write something for the instrument that he played. And if I wanted to be friends with that girl, I'd write a cello part, or whatever."[127]

"That is kind of beautiful and, like, scheming," Fragoso told her, amused.

"Oh yeah, for sure," Spalding agreed. "But so many people in this world would probably not do that art that they do if they weren't trying to get some booty out of it. I don't think there's anything wrong with that. It kind of doesn't matter what gets you there, it's what you do with it. That's like a primal human experience, like our sexuality and the need for complicity and attraction. So the various ways that we go about achieving it—I mean, I don't think writing a French horn part is any worse than, like, putting a push-up bra on, you know? You're modifying reality. You're adjusting your reality to attract what you want. Or at least get you in a position where you can get close enough to, hopefully, your charm or your self will attract the person that you want."

That same week Mercer and I happened to run into each other at Winter Jazzfest. I mentioned my findings on the Glasper interview that begat the Saga of Musical Clitoris. She laughed appreciatively at Spalding's push-up bra comment, and listened politely to my explanation of why my read of what Glasper said about women liking space in music differed from hers. She said something about having had to turn around her NPR piece on a short deadline. We didn't dwell on the topic long, but the chat was friendly and, for such a short one, agreeably nuanced. Two journalists who had each served on one of Mercer's panels, John Murph and

Shannon Effinger, wandered by and Mercer introduced me to them, and then the four of us headed off to another venue together to attend a performance of the Sun Ra Arkestra.

The *Do the Math* interview did nothing to slow down Glasper in the months to follow. In September, he made that guest appearance on Esperanza Spalding's *Exposure* project, in which she created an album with that title from scratch within a 77-hour time limit, the entire production broadcast live on Facebook.[128] That same month, he, Common, and Karriem Riggins won their Emmy for "Letter to the Free." Then in January, the three of them made their debut performance as August Greene, the collaborative group Glasper had told me about at Solid Sound, at New York's Highline Ballroom. In February, they did a Tiny Desk Concert on NPR[129] with the feminist theme "Foregrounding Women," featuring guest vocalists Brandy, Maimouna Youssef, and Andra Day. The album *August Greene* was released March 9 on Amazon Music, and the group made several more live performances in the weeks to follow, including one at the Kennedy Center.

Meanwhile, Glasper had announced in December that he had formed another collaborative super group with Terrace Martin, Christian Scott, Derrick Hodge, Justin Tyson, and Taylor McFerrin. That group, calling itself R+R=Now, for "Reflect+Respond=Now, made its first appearance at the Roseland Theater in Portland, Oregon, on April 19, a few days after Glasper's fortieth birthday, having already recorded an as-yet-unreleased album. Glasper was quoted in *Billboard* saying that the band tells "our story from our point of view. Everybody's sound is so different, but we all come from the same concrete garden. It's a very honest, fluid sound that rings of hip-hop, EDM, jazz, at times—hell— reggae . . . a bunch of cats that respect each other so much that we always pass the ball." This project, too, like August Greene, was meant to be political, inspired by the Nina Simone quotation "An artist's duty as far as I'm concerned, is to reflect the times."

And Glasper, like his hero Herbie Hancock, retains the option of playing an acoustic jazz when the mood suits him. I caught a memorable night of him and Jason Moran playing a pair of pianos at the Blue Note one summer night in 2016. Aside from playing phenomenal music, some of it with their fellow HSPVA alumnus Eric Harland accompanying them on tambourine and a Heinz ketchup bottle, they cracked wise bantering with each other about an auction Moran had been to recently where a white piano that once belonged to Duke Ellington had been available.

The two men clearly hold each other in high regard.

"At New England Conservatory a lot of the students really listen to Glasper's music," Moran had told me in 2012, when I interviewed him at his apartment the morning after the Whitney Biennial. "So this kind of groove, they're attracted to it because it's similar to what they've been listening to that wasn't really necessarily jazz." He mentioned having been up until 4 a.m. that morning listening to juniors and seniors from his and Glasper's high school alma mater for a scholarship Moran funds. "I could really hear how Glasper's Chris Dave—the effects of these drummers and these pianists from that school—I hear it in how these kids are playing. So they're looking at that, not so much to the eighty years. I always tell students that you've got to go back eighty, a hundred years now to really settle it in. Glasper knows about that."

Glasper knows how important it is for aspiring jazz musicians to acquaint themselves with the entirety of the music's history, that is. But he also knows that the artists who have counted most throughout that history have been those brave enough to add something of their own to it.

"Jason's the epitome," Glasper told me that afternoon at Solid Sound. "He's like one of the best examples of 'half education and half fuck it.' " He laughed. "That's Jason. It takes so much courage to have the artistic freedom that he has."

Glasper had brought up his pet notion of the willingness to risk saying "fuck it" being crucial to keeping music alive and relevant in one of our previous conversations, but he gave me a refresher at Solid Sound.

"There are two words that are the key to innovation, that have been the key to innovation through all these years," he said. "And those words are 'Fuck it,' whether you say it out loud or you just do it. That's what you have to do: You do what's the norm, and then you say, 'Well, I want to put my own thing on it. Fuck it, I want to do this.' Everybody's going to blab, 'You can't do that!' Then *that* becomes awesome, *that* becomes the norm, and then somebody else says, 'That's cool, but I want to put my own thing on it.' "

"That's the circle, you know," Glasper added. "That's what it is, and it keeps going. That's where I stand now. I had the same mindset as all of our great jazz innovators did: 'Cool, but I'm influenced by something else. I want to do something else. I'm adding *my* influences to it.' That's what makes it 2017. That's why the '30s sound like the '30s, the '40s sound like the '40s, the '50s sound like the '50s. Because there are new influences every decade, and somebody's got to say, 'Fuck it.' And it kept [jazz] alive, it kept it moving—like every other genre of music."

Please visit the open access version of Make It New *to see a video resource for Chapter Seven. This resource can be viewed by visiting the chapter in the e-book:* https://doi.org/10.3998/mpub.11469938

CHAPTER EIGHT

ESPERANZA SPALDING

Esperanza Spalding's first semester as a Harvard University professor included an especially busy few days surrounding President's Day weekend 2018. That Saturday night, Spalding and other top musicians had been featured in a concert honoring Geri Allen, the final event in a two-day festival/symposium devoted to Allen.[130]

Now it was Tuesday night, and Spalding, thirty-three, was hosting a master class featuring the multitalented artist Jill Scott. Her guest would critique performances by four Harvard undergraduates with Spalding and an audience looking on, after which Scott and Spalding would discuss improvisation. The event, part of the Kuumba Singers of Harvard College's weeklong Black Arts Festival 2018, had quickly sold out and been moved to a larger venue, the Lowell Lecture Hall, where Scott, Spalding, and Spalding's music department colleague Vijay Iyer took seats front and center to observe the student performances.

Scott's brief biography in the program notes opened by quoting her: "I sing the blues, I sing folk, I sing jazz, classical. I'm a poet, an actress, I know how to make really good cornbread." It goes on to describe how Scott broke into music when, at a poetry event in the late 1990s, Amir "Questlove" Thompson of the band the Roots approached her to ask if she wrote music. She hadn't at that point, but fibbed and said yes, and proceeded to cowrite the Roots' 1999 hit "You Got Me," launching her multifaceted career as a singer-songwriter, actress, model, and poet.

Spalding and Iyer, though both find themselves most commonly categorized as jazz musicians, take similarly broad approaches to music and art.

First up among the students whose music would be assessed was Arlesia McGowan, a junior studying developmental biology, who accompanied herself on piano as she sang an original composition, titled "Unenduring," whose lyrics referenced a ticking clock and, briefly, the unnamed current president.

"What thoughtful lyrics," Scott told her, rising to her feet to begin her critique. "I would challenge you to slow down, because what you're saying is so impactful. Slow it *way* down. Treat your audience like they're the most intelligent people in the world."

Scott had McGowan make a couple of more passes through the song, slowing her down more each time and emphasizing the need for her to inhabit whatever words she sang. "*See* what you're saying," Scott instructed. "You have to see it. *Taste* what you're saying. See the color of what you're saying. If you don't feel it, the audience won't."

Roderick Mullen, a junior studying government, followed with a performance that stitched together two R&B-oriented songs by the singers Maxwell and Sam Smith. Scott requested a second take, suggesting he focus more carefully on where the two songs merge. "If you need to take a moment, that's fine," she told him. "What we look for as vocalists is water to swim in." She also made note of Mullen's attire, a light-colored suit and bowtie. "From now on," she said, after confirming that he had chosen the look with deliberation, "when you wear something you like, I want you to strut."

Eden Girma, a senior in a double degree program offered by Harvard and New England Conservatory, with a concentration in math and astrophysics at the former while simultaneously pursuing a master's degree in jazz performance at the latter, gave the third performance. Like McGowan, she sang an original piece, untitled in her case, and accompanied herself on piano.

Girma, the daughter of Ethiopian immigrants, had taken Iyer's creative music seminar two years earlier, and he looked on with what appeared to be a mix of pride and the same stunned admiration Spalding and Scott displayed when her performance ended.

"There's a lot of, wow—color, texture, thoughts," gushed Scott, when she managed to speak. "But these together. I would *pay* to see you."

Girma, for her part, was similarly overwhelmed by the reaction to her performance. "That was literally the first time I've ever performed original music in front of people," she said.

"I'll tell you this," Scott responded, "you don't need to sing anybody else's songs." When Girma told her she would graduate in May, Scott began describing cities she predicted Girma would soon come to know through her music. "Performing is a dream," Scott told her. "I'm saying this so you know it's coming."

The event's final student performance was by Michael Wingate, a senior studying government and philosophy with thoughts of attending law school. Wingate was dressed more casually than the others, in a polo shirt and light-colored pants, and had the unenviable task of following Girma.

"Listen, I've had to go on after Chaka Khan," Scott reassured him, adding another name or two to a short list of distinguished artists she had followed onstage in her career that concluded with Aretha Franklin. "Don't worry about them [meaning the audience]. This is your song and your voice."

When he sang his version of Moses Sumney's "Plastic," his voice impressed her. "When you started it felt like somebody put a hot water bottle under your sheets," she told him. "Hot sheets. I'm talking Egyptian. Male peacocks show off what you have, sir."

But she found another aspect of the performance in need of work, and eased around to the topic by discussing the song's lyrics. "What does it mean that the plastic breaks?" she asked.

After a bit of this line of questioning, Spalding spoke up. "Maestro," she said, seeking Scott's permission to weigh in, and when she was granted it, Spalding cut straight to the heart of the matter.

"The price of impact in performance is vulnerability," she told Wingate. "It's not acting like you're vulnerable. It's having the courage to be [vulnerable]."

"Do you know what it's like to be broken?" Scott asked him, quoting a lyric from the song he'd just sung.

"Yes, I do," he answered.[131]

"I would offer, expose your palms," said Scott, suggesting a posture that might help Wingate convey the emotion of the song.

"This is the work," Scott said. "It's gut-wrenching." She told of a song of her own that she avoids performing, because doing so causes her to confront such pain. "This is what we do. We share what it is to be human."

Wingate took a slow, meditative walk around the stage area to gear himself up for a final attempt at the song.

A couple of weeks later, I dropped by to observe Spalding teach a session of her Applied Music Activism class. Afterward, I asked her if Wingate had achieved what Scott and she had tried coaxing from him at the workshop. Spalding assured me that on his last pass he indeed had.

The master class was held just four weeks into Spalding's first semester of teaching at Harvard, where the previous summer she had accepted her half-time appointment as Professor of Practice. That fall, she had been focused on her *Exposure* project, the latest in her series of wildly outside-the-box artistic undertakings. For

Exposure, Spalding and a tight coterie of bandmates, guest artists, and sound engineers created an album's worth of music in 77 hours, with the action being broadcast live round the clock on Facebook. A steady stream of viewers signaled their delight via emoticons and commentary, some in the audience debating whether Spalding really meant her announcement that only 7,777 copies of the resultant album would be produced.

That Spalding could count on significant fan interest in the *Exposure* project, like her Harvard appointment, is a testament to all that she had managed to accomplish at such a young age. In recent years, one sometimes hears certain musicians referred to as *jazz famous*—an ironic, almost wistful term acknowledging that, while said artists are well-known to people who follow jazz, the wider culture remains largely oblivious to them. Few musicians have transcended that designation in the years since rock, soul, hip-hop, and other genres began supplanting jazz as America's popular music. A handful among the living have accomplished this: Herbie Hancock, aided by the crossover success of his funk albums with his Headhunters band and his influential hip-hop hit "Rock-It." Wynton Marsalis, for his role in the creation of Jazz at Lincoln Center. Sonny Rollins, whose famous bridge sabbatical helped him become widely recognized, in the first years of the new century, as jazz's greatest living improviser.

Spalding, more than any musician of her generation, has broken through the jazz-famous glass ceiling and joined them. It began with her association with Barack Obama and three high-profile performances during the first year of his presidency. In February, she sang Stevie Wonder's "Overjoyed" at the White House ceremony at which Obama presented Wonder with the 2008 Library of Congress Gershwin Prize for Popular Song.[132] That May, she returned to the White House for "An Evening of Poetry, Music & the Spoken Word"—a.k.a. the White House Poetry Jam—to play an introductory duet with pianist Eric Lewis and later sing Lauryn Hill's "Tell Him," backed only by her own upright bass.[133] (Another Poetry Jam highlight that night was Lin-Manuel Miranda, who performed a song from a concept album he was working on "about the life of someone I think embodies hip-hop, treasury secretary Alexander Hamilton."[134])

In December of that same year, Spalding performed at the ceremony in Oslo, Norway, at which Obama accepted his Nobel Peace Prize. Spalding sang her song "Espera" with her trio following the president's acceptance speech,[135] and performed again the next night, along with other American musicians, in a Nobel Peace Prize concert broadcast live from Oslo on CNN.[136] Later that month, staff writer John Colapinto of the *New Yorker* began reporting a profile of Spalding the would appear in the magazine's March 15, 2010, issue with a trip to California to see her perform with McCoy Tyner at the Oakland club Yoshi's.[137] (*New Yorker* editor David Remnick's Obama biography, *The Bridge*, was published a few weeks later, making one wonder if it was that Obama connection that put Spalding on the magazine's radar.)

The *New Yorker* article noted other mainstream attention that Spalding was getting: being featured in an advertisement for Banana Republic, appearances on *Late Night with David Letterman* and *Jimmy Kimmel Live*, an invitation from Prince to come to Minneapolis to hang out and jam (the invitation was actually extended to Christian Scott, whom Spalding was dating at the time; Scott told me he got Prince's permission to bring her with him). Colapinto also observed Spalding practicing, and composing and recording her third album as a leader, *Chamber Music Society*, the album that really put her in the public eye by helping her win "Best New Artist" at the 53rd annual Grammy Awards, shocking and upsetting fans of her fellow nominee Justin Bieber.

Spalding was the first artist identified as a jazz musician to receive that honor in Grammy history. But the tendency for success to breed contempt from others in the jazz community didn't apply in her case. Spalding kept up her jazz bona fides by continuing to take sidewoman roles alongside her own projects, in bands led by established masters such as Joe Lovano, Tom Harrell, and Jack DeJohnette, and partnered in a collaborative trio with Geri Allen and Terri Lyne Carrington. Herbie Hancock and Wayne Shorter adored her. So did everyone I asked about her for this book.

"When I first met Esperanza she was nineteen," her onetime professor Lovano told me. "She was placed in one of my ensembles at Berklee in 2003 or 2004, and right away she came in and contributed to the music that we play. She didn't just play the bass. She was into creating melodies and creating her part from within the part to play music within the music. She already had an idea of what that was, and seeing her develop through the years, I'm so proud of her."

When I mentioned having seen Spalding back him on bass at a recent Charlie Parker Festival in Tompkins Square Park, Lovano laughed and noted that their collaborations had become rarer with her "vaulting to superstardom."

Fueling that stardom, of course, was Spalding's ability to sing while backing herself on bass. "She developed a real independence to accompany herself on the bass, and vocalize within that," observed Lovano. "A lot of that was learning tunes singing the melody and playing the bass part in her early development as a player— and it snowballed into her amazing technique."

Geri Allen, too, was impressed by Spalding's ability to accompany her own singing on upright bass. "She has very independent ideas happening, which is even more incredible if you think about it," Allen told me in spring 2017, ahead of two nights of performances at Scullers with Spalding and Carrington.[138] "It's like counterpoint between the bass and what she sings. It's not like she's just doubling a line with the bass, which people have done. But to sing a completely different line, and improvise with the bass and with the voice at the same time—it's incredible."

Allen also praised Spalding's artistic choices. "She's a very exciting artist in terms of the kinds of things that we have to look forward to," she said. "I'm really very, very happy to be collaborating with her. When we're on the bandstand together there's a certain kind of freedom there, a nonjudgmental freedom that allows the music to take whatever direction it will take. There's a trust that has been established, and it's just a lot of fun, it really is, to be able to have that kind of freedom."

"Esperanza, you can't put her in any kind of compartment," said Jack DeJohnette. "She's interested in acting, she's playing other instruments. She's interested in theater—Emily D[139] was that, she experimented with that. Anything she tries to go after, she really goes at it with a quality of enthusiasm and dedication that's admirable. She does some major things with her voice: the ability to sing and play bass at the same time, to split her playing. And she's a fantastic improviser."

Danilo Pérez told of meeting Spalding at the Cambridge club Ryles, where she made a point of introducing herself after learning that Pérez was in the audience. "I remember she was really open. She said, 'I'm a big fan. *Motherland* is my record. I wore it out. I love everything on *Motherland*,' and started singing me songs from it. It was so emotional. But I immediately recognized there was a powerful woman there. She's got something to say, I've got to tell you."

Fred Hersch admitted to some initial skepticism. "When Esperanza came on the scene," he told me, "there was a lot of hype about her, and the circumstances by which she arrived on the scene were peculiar. And I thought, 'Well, who is this woman? How did she get on the cover of *DownBeat*?' " His doubts ended the first time they played together. "I realized that she's a really great listener," he said. "She's an awesome jazz singer—facility and feeling and just kind of off-the-hook, hearing everything. She's also a smart, super-intelligent woman. She's always reading something interesting, she's got a lot of very right-on political views, thoughts about music. She's super-smart and also just really fun to hang with."

Spalding is unquestionably whip-smart and enjoyable to talk with. But her fame and busyness have obliged her to make herself less available to journalists—this one, anyway—than the other artists in this book. Her management company was charged with scheduling her interviews, and because she had just begun teaching at Harvard, she asked that ours take place after she had submitted her students' final grades. When I learned that she would be playing two duo sets with Hersch at the Jazz Standard the night of May 13, 2018, the final night of Hersch's annual run of duo and trio concerts there that year, I suggested we do the interview in

New York. Her management offered time between that night's two sets. I asked for something longer and more private, perhaps after that afternoon's sound check.

I was still awaiting my answer when it came time to board an Amtrak train to Penn Station the morning of the 10th. As I scurried toward the train's quiet car, I came face-to-face with none other than Spalding herself. She greeted me affably, and when I asked about the interview, she said she thought it was settled that we were doing it after sound check.

Spalding was traveling with an older woman, who I later learned was her mother. This was no small thing. Spalding has spoken of her mother as one of her greatest heroes, for having persevered and raised two children as a single mother in rough circumstances in Portland, Oregon. The family was often on the verge of homelessness, and the homes they did have were in declining neighborhoods full of drugs and gang violence. They made use of food stamps, Section 8 housing, and other government assistance programs to help them survive. Spalding has said in interviews that her mother was the hardest-working person she knows, holding a succession of low-paying jobs trying to keep her small family afloat.

Spalding was born October 18,[140] 1984. Her mother is of Welsh, Native American, and Hispanic descent, and Spalding grew up bilingual, with both English and Spanish spoken around the house. Her father was African American, and the only other reference to him that I have found, a 2012 *JazzTimes* profile by Giovanni Russonello[141] that rivals the *New Yorker* piece as the definitive magazine portrait of Spalding, reported that he "became ensnared by the penal system" and that Spalding never knew him growing up.

Spalding's mother[142] had set aside a fledgling career as a singer when she became pregnant with Esperanza's elder brother, and Spalding revealed prodigal musical gifts as a child. The *New Yorker* piece described Spalding at age four hearing her mother struggling with a Beethoven piece, then climbing onto the piano bench and playing it by ear herself. Spalding has said that when she was eight, she would watch her mother get guitar lessons and play back the guitar music the teacher had demonstrated on the piano when they returned home. When she was five, she saw Yo-Yo Ma play cello on *Mister Rogers' Neighborhood* and decided that was the instrument she wanted to play. She wound up with a violin instead, and after a couple of formal lessons continued teaching herself how to play it. Her mother enrolled her in a neighborhood music program, where she met her longtime mentor Thara Memory, who set a high bar for her by refusing to praise the songs she had already begun writing. She soon joined the youth program of the Chamber Music Society of Oregon, eventually rising to concertmaster.

Spalding's mother encouraged her children to pursue whatever dreams they had without being discouraged by their financial circumstances. She also taught them to think for themselves, and instilled in her daughter a lifelong interest in the environment and social issues.

"She somehow found the time to kind of train her kids to be critical thinkers," Spalding explained in an extended interview for the American Academy of Achievement.[143] "So we never would just be sitting and just ingesting something from TV or from a magazine. She always would try to open our eyes to a counter commentary, or a counter perspective. I would always remember [that] we learned the word prostitute, and we came home and we used it, and she said, 'No, there are *prostituted women*.' These are women. Yes, that is awful and it's tragic and it's illegal, but she said these are women, these are human beings."[144]

"I have a really one-in-a-million mom," Spalding continued moments later in the same interview, "and I see over and over again how, for better or for worse, her worldview colors the way I do things and the way I receive information, and I'm really grateful."

That habit of keeping her eyes open to "counter commentary" makes Spalding an enjoyably engaging conversationalist. I found myself subjected to it frequently during my most recent interviews with her. I don't think this is because I'm unusually stupid but rather because Spalding likes examining subjects from alternate angles. For example, when I once compared her to Herbie Hancock for the way she moves easily back and forth between jazz and other styles of music, she responded: "I look at it a different way. Herbie is just being himself. People are writing about what he does and are trying to figure out where it fits into one of those boxes. He's just being himself, it all lives inside of him, you know? He's fully integrated. It's like if you're the child of a Japanese mom and a German dad, everyone's trying to figure out, 'Well, that behavior there, that must be your German part.' Or, 'Oh, the way you just said that must be your Japanese part.' And that's really ridiculous. And I actually think it alludes to how fuckin' segregated we are just in our philosophy of who does what, for what reason. Like, every human being is multifaceted. You're not just a journalist, you're also writing a nonfiction book about jazz. So that's cool: You can be a journalist and a writer, and you can be many, many things. If you also have kids, you're also a father. You're also this and that, and they all bleed into the other, and absolutely inform the way that you do everything that you do in your life.

"And the same is true for musicians. I mean, I can't speak on his behalf, obviously, but I doubt Herbie sat there at a piano and worked on a song and was thinking, 'This is a jazz project. This is a hip-hop project. Oh, this totally is me getting back to my electronic roots.' No, he's just being Herbie. And that's enough. It's enough for him to just be Herbie without the identifiers that are convenient. It just means that when he plays, you just have to come open to hear what he's giving as an artist.

"Not to take it too meta, too fast, but that's the challenge of our time. Of dealing with people. Of institutions and organizations and religious institutions and teachers, everything, to have the patience and the courage and the versatility to take people as they come, and not fall back on an association that can help you prepare for how you're going to interact with them, or how you're going to assess them. It's really hard to do. I can barely do it. I can't do it all the time, but I think it's a worthy challenge. And I would like to hope that we can do it more, at least in music, where the stakes are pretty freaking low, you know?"

When I told her at our sit-down at the Jazz Standard about Jason Moran being told by his future wife that figuring out *why* he was making the music he chose to make would put him ahead of his peers, and that that consciousness of purpose seemed to benefit the others in this book, she also pushed back.

"I think some human beings are better at formulating the *why* into a language medium that we understand," she argued. "Like, they can articulate their motives via language. Some people can't. It doesn't mean that they are lacking in, like, any broad-reaching motivation for the music that they make. But I think there's so much that goes into doing a performance, or any mode of expression, and I don't believe that anybody would dedicate that much energy and life and hours and travel time and time away from friends—I don't think anyone would do it if there wasn't a really deep, personal, spiritual, cultural, community-based reason. It's kind of like the danger with deferring to those who can articulate their *why* [is] that maybe we start to think that they have more of a *why* than others. And I don't think that's true. Actually, I think we just process motivation in different ways. All of us do."

I suggested that being able to describe their why might make musicians' work easier to understand for non-musicians.

"Well, then you might be engaging with just the one level, like a verbal level of the story, which is not the whole story," she said. "That could also be myth, like you think you're engaging with something that has to do with music, and that could all be a lie, too. Sometimes people just go off into a mission and then make an excuse later that they think people will be able to buy into. And what would happen if you hadn't been introduced to a theme, or a narrative? You'd have to use your imagination."

"It would reach you in some different way," I offered, seeing her point. "A more personal way."

"I guess so," she responded. "Maybe, maybe not. But, again, putting the emphasis on ability to articulate with language, when we're addressing an art form that isn't necessarily language-based—there's already a translation there."

When I told her that interviewing the creative people in this book had been inspiring (my wife had compared the Moran chapter to a master class in creativity), perhaps dangerously so for someone who doesn't have their skills, her mother's refusal to allow her children to limit their potential peeked through.

"Yes, you do," she countered. "Yes, you do."

"It may not be the way the editors like it," I ventured, following her lead, "but this is how it's going to be."

"That's the practice," she confirmed. "That's the practice."

"We'll see if I survive doing it, but . . ."

"You know, feedback is an editor," she cut in. "Response is an editor, too. It's OK. You absolutely are a creator."

Two more examples were sparked by the *New Yorker* piece about her. I told her how much I'd admired her declaration "Idol worship doesn't help this music in any way," which I was planning to use as an epigraph.

"I don't mean it in the sense of 'forget what those guys did,' " she clarified. "I mean addressing, honoring the legacy, and what happened, and also recognizing that these are *human beings* who have infinite capacity, just like anybody does. Knowing that we have unique, unbounded capacity, too, that we can cultivate if we're not trying to emulate what already worked. Because I do think honoring our elders and our predecessors is critical, but I also think you can't try to *become* them. You have to be your own thing, and know that [emulation]'s not where the source flows—it flows from your life. That [i.e., what came before] can be evidence of what's possible."

When I reminded her that Colapinto had written that a recurring theme in Spalding's early songwriting had been art and imagination as a means of escape, and suggested that *Emily's D+Evolution* explored that idea as well, she responded with yet another rebuttal.

"I think 'escape' is misleading," she told me. "I don't advocate escaping shit. I advocate running into it with your chest bared, and trusting your training and your creative capacity to transform the poison in the medicine. Because I don't think we can escape anything in this world—like we can barely escape planet Earth, how far have humans really gone? I don't think we can escape anything. The only way to change the dynamic—change our relationship to something that is uncomfortable, destructive, or toxic—is to address it. So it's not escaping; it's using creativity to address it. That's real alchemy. Real alchemy is when you take the creative process, and you transform a toxic, life-sucking trauma into a medicinal, energizing, humanity-affirming new product. . . . Not to escape it. It can change the consequences of our relationship to it.

"But I don't believe in escaping shit," she repeated. "I mean, except the abusive husband, or an abusive relationship. But even that, if you just escape the circumstance without addressing how the circumstance was forged from both sides—societal trauma and conditioning on both sides—then what are you really escaping? Like, be acute, but you still have to address the systemic or endemic, you know?"

And then with barely a pause, she turned the tables and rebutted herself for a change, puncturing the philosophizing with a little self-deprecation of her own.

"I mean, I'm thirty-three," she acknowledged, smiling. "This will all probably— I'll change my mind in ten years."

When I first interviewed Spalding at any length, she was twenty, and about to graduate from Berklee. The college was planning to put a three-story-tall likeness of her on the Boylston Street wall of the Berklee Performance Center,[145] and it seemed a good time to introduce her to *Globe* readers. We met at the Starbucks across Massachusetts Avenue from Berklee's main buildings, but the room was too loud to record an interview. She suggested we move to a practice room, which led to the most memorable moment of the interview.

We'd been talking about her bass playing and how she had come to love the bass, having passed through topics such as the types of music she likes to sing (jazz, Brazilian, and R&B), how she got into Brazilian music (she dated someone from Brazil, visited the country for a month, and came back to Boston and studied Portuguese), and her strong preference for learning music from performances rather than from recordings.

Having small hands made playing bass painful initially, she told me. "But I liked the sound, I like the role of the bass in the band," she said. "That's a big thing. I don't want to be a front man, and I don't like having to play solos all the time. Also, I didn't have a practice-type personality. I just like to play when it makes me happy. Sometimes sitting for six hours, it doesn't make me happy, so I don't want to do it. But now, more and more over the last couple of years, I love even holding it now. It's bizarre. It's kind of like this blossoming love. For someone who didn't practice very much, bass just came very naturally to me. I knew how to play the bass. I knew what made sense somehow. And so that was really appealing. And people would say to me, 'You're a great bass player.' Nobody ever said, 'You're a great violin player, you're a great piano player.'

"It's nice for me to have a role where I get to be so mentally there but I don't have to prove anything. And I love that. Because one thing that really turned me away from jazz was like the, 'Yeah, look what I'm doing. It's so killing, it's so fresh. Yeah, it's progressive.' And I don't care enough to actually work on trying to present myself that way. So I love that responsibility—just you have to be the fundamental thing. You have to just show your purpose, only to make the other thing tie together. You're the groove. It's kind of like being the drummer. You have a responsibility, and it's beautiful if you artistically and credibly do that responsibly. But it's like ministers in a church. There's the ones who just tell you the word, and that's their purpose. And then the people who say it poetically, and you're like, 'Aaah.' So that's like the difference between good bass players and bad bass players.

"So yeah, I really love it," she said. "With singing it's kind of cool. I'm starting to be able to do that."

"I've never seen that happen," I said. The idea of a singer accompanying herself on upright bass was hard to picture. It was already unusual seeing a woman playing the instrument, particularly a woman of Spalding's petite build.

"You want to see some?" she asked. "OK."

She picked up her bass and accompanied herself singing a few bars of a standard with a walking bass line, then switched to something Brazilian with more abstract accompaniment.

"I'm just comping for myself, and I'm just singing," she said, setting her bass back down. "That's just what I've been practicing, and I really want to do it. Part of the good thing about being a bass player is you're expected to do, like, walking bass lines, and so when you make an album that's what you do. But there's a lot of things that we don't do as bass players, because they're really hard. So I just would rather take the time to figure out those things."

Spalding didn't remember her practice-room demonstration when I brought it up to her over a decade later at the Hal Crook retirement concert, but when I told Christian McBride about it that summer, it rang a bell for him.

"I think I remember that article!" he told me.

"Really? This was for the *Boston Globe*."

"What year would that have been?"

"It was like, 2004 or 2005 maybe."

"I was on the road with Pat Metheny, our trio, and Antonio Sánchez and Pat had that article, and we were reading it."

"No kidding? I think they called it something like 'Ace of Bass.' "

"Yeah, yeah, yeah, yeah!"

Spalding and I covered other basic ground that didn't make it into that newspaper story. She told me about having been homeschooled between the ages of nine and thirteen or fourteen, which, because her mother had to work so much to support the family, meant that Spalding had mostly taught herself.[146]

"I'm a very independent person—like, *aggressively* independent," she told me. "For me it was great. I only had to do what I like. I like being at home working at my pace. But I liked to do the work." She knew she had a test at the end of the year she would have to pass, so she spent most of her time playing music and writing and singing, then four months before the test would begin studying for it in earnest. "The school system here, it's like they slowly drag you along at this monotonous pace. So for me [homeschooling] was great. But I could see where some parents would be hesitant, because you really have to have initiative and make yourself get it done."

Spalding auditioned for and won a scholarship to Northwest Academy, an arts-oriented high school. But homeschooling had spoiled her, and the monotony of classroom learning again became oppressive. She dropped out at fifteen and passed her GED the next year. Before quitting high school, however, she discovered her new instrument. She had risen to concertmaster in Portland's Chamber Music of Society of Oregon youth program, but by this time she had grown tired of the violin.

"I was so sick of this friggin' instrument," she recalled. "I was like, 'I'm quitting.' I skipped classes and went into the band room, and it was lying in the middle of the room." She said she picked up the bass and attempted a few notes on it. "The music teacher came in and said, 'Oh, you want to play bass?' I was like, 'No way.' He taught me to play a blues line, and that got me that gig with the blues band."

The bass lent itself to improvising in a way that playing violin in an orchestra did not. Also to the prospect of playing live music and being paid for it. Spalding was hooked.

She didn't mention having joined the indie rock band Noise for Pretend, her first taste of singing while playing bass; it was as a member of Noise for Pretend that Spalding recorded her first album, *Happy You Near* (2002). But she did tell me about beginning studies at Portland State University as a sixteen-year-old scholarship student. She had only been playing bass for a year and a half, and her classmates were older and more experienced on their instruments than she was. But she said she probably would have stuck it out had her mentor, the local trumpet standout Thara Memory, not harassed her into applying for a scholarship to Berklee.

Spalding drove to Seattle to audition, won the scholarship, and then organized a benefit concert to earn herself the money to get to Boston. She stayed with a family friend in Canton, Massachusetts. Her first semester at Berklee, she auditioned and was hired to join Patti Austin's backing band on a tour of Italy. The income from that tour allowed her to move to downtown Boston.

"I didn't process going and pursuing a career in music," Spalding told me that day in the Berklee practice room, explaining her initial hesitation to leave Portland. "I've completely turned over." She laughed. "I've gone over to the other side."

I found out later that Pat Metheny had played a crucial role in that transformation. He and Gary Burton, still a Berklee administrator at the time, had overseen a student recording project that Spalding performed on. Afterward, Metheny approached Spalding and asked her what she wanted to do with her life. She had been thinking of giving up music and studying political science, so that she could have a greater impact in the world by contributing to causes she believed in. Metheny told her she possessed what he called a rare "x factor" and that, if she pushed herself, the sky was the limit for what she could achieve via music.

Because she was about to graduate, I asked Spalding what it was like studying with Lovano and what she thought about her experience at Berklee.

"The best thing about coming here was meeting people," she replied. "I met Joe Lovano in class. Plus, it sounds strange, but the thing that got me most motivated to get the momentum going was knowing that the next day I'd have to play for Joe Lovano. I don't want to sound the same way I sounded last week. I want to sound better than I sounded last week. That's the biggest thing. I had this other teacher, Hal Crook.[147] He just scared the shit out of me the first time I took a class with him. He just freaked me out. I was like, 'Whoa, he knows everything.' "

"How'd he scare you?" I asked.

"He's so on it," she said. "He never said much to me, but I heard him saying things to other people. 'Man, I have to get myself together.' So knowing that every Thursday from 4 to 6 I have to play, it gets you in this other kind of mindset."

Spalding also mentioned taking an important ensemble class with Grammy-winning vibraphonist Dave Samuels, who later moved on to teach at New England Conservatory. Her main bass instructor at Berklee was John Lockwood. And lasting connections were being forged with both professors and classmates. Lovano hired her as she was graduating, and she eventually went on to record three albums with his band Us Five. She and Luques Curtis shared the bass duties in their classmate Christian Scott's band. When we spoke, Spalding had just recorded her debut album, *Junjo* (2006), with Berklee teachers Aruán Ortiz and Francisco Mela on piano and drums, respectively, and was about to perform a concert at Roxbury Community College (ticket price $7) with classmate Leo Genovese taking over for Ortiz on piano.[148]

Genovese, who came to Berklee from Argentina, has been Spalding's go-to pianist ever since. He was featured on her albums *Esperanza* (2008), *Chamber Music Society* (2010), and *Radio Music Society* (2012); she appeared on his *Seeds* (2013) and *Argentinosaurus* (the latter a trio album with Jack DeJohnette on drums, released in 2016 by the Paris-based, subscription-only label Newvelle Records). They both supported Berklee professor and tenor saxophonist George Garzone on his *Crescent* (2015), and toured with Lovano and DeJohnette in the all-star Spring Quartet. When Spalding wanted guitar rather than piano and keyboards on her *Emily's D+Evolution* and *Exposure* projects, she hired another Berklee classmate, Toronto native Matthew Stevens, whom she had played with in Scott's band while in and just out of school. (He's the best!" Spalding enthused when I mentioned I had talked to him during our interview at the Jazz Standard. "That's my brother, man.") For Stevens, too, she returned the favor, singing on the track "Our Reunion" from his 2017 album *Preverbal*.

Spalding hit the road with Lovano right after graduating, and joined the Berklee faculty the following fall, a couple of months shy of her twenty-first birthday. Aside from the three recordings she made with Lovano's group Us Five over the next decade, she recorded on others with the pianist and Berklee professor Nando Michelin, the trumpeters Tom Harrell and Christian Scott, and vocalist Bobby McFerrin. She made guest appearances on albums by Stanley Clarke, Mike Stern, Nicholas Payton, Terri Lyne Carrington, and Jack DeJohnette. She also sang on a track from Janelle Monáe's *The Electric Lady* (2013), as did Monáe mentor Prince, with whom Spalding and Christian Scott had spent time rehearsing, beginning in 2007, for what proved an unrealized jazz-oriented project.

She also began leading her own projects. *Junjo* was a trio disc with Mela and another Cuban expatriate, pianist Aruán Ortiz, both of whom were teaching at Berklee when it was recorded. Spalding has said she considers it a collaborative effort, but she contributed the most compositions to it and the album is in her name. It also introduced Spalding singing and playing bass simultaneously, something that Mela had told me Spalding was still developing when I'd profiled her for the newspaper a year earlier.[149] There were jazz pieces by Jimmy Rowles and Chick Corea, another that revealed her fondness for Brazilian music, Egberto Gismonti's "Loro" (a song much beloved by jazz musicians, given the number who have covered it), and one sung in Spanish, co-written by the Argentine lyricist and poet Manuel Castilla and composer Gustavo Leguizamón. This last song, "Cantora de Yala," was the lone one on which Spalding sang lyrics; her vocals elsewhere on the album were wordless, hornlike improvisations and melodies.

Junjo was recorded for the Spanish label Ayva Music. Spalding's second album, *Esperanza*, was with the larger American label Heads Up, and landed her on *Billboard*'s sales charts for the first time. It was more of a showcase for Spalding, who was backed by a core group of Genovese on piano and keyboards, Otis Brown III on drums and background vocals, and Jamey Haddad on percussion, with guests including Donald Harrison, Ambrose Akinmusire, Horacio "El Negro" Hernández, Niño Jostle, Gretchen Parlato, and Theresa Perez.

The album was wide-ranging in styles, opening with a nod to two of Spalding's heroes, the same Milton Nascimento song ("Ponta de Areia") that had opened Wayne Shorter's classic 1974 collaboration with Nascimento, *Native Dancer*. Other covers included "Body and Soul," performed in 5/4 time and in Spanish ("Cuerpo y Alma"), and Baden Powell's "Samba em Preludio," the Vinícius de Moraes lyrics sung, like the Nascimento tune, in Portuguese. Spalding's own compositions included a straight-ahead jazz piece featuring Harrison and Akinmusire ("If That's True"); a tribute to her sometime drummer featuring Akinmusire's trumpet and Spalding's wordless vocals ("Mela"); the song of gathering hope she would later sing at Obama's Nobel ceremony ("Espera"); and a handful of songs about romantic relationships, pro and con, Harrison contributing saxophone to one of the latter ("She Got to You").

Spalding's next two albums were more exploratory, taking her music a bit further in directions beyond jazz that were all her own. And yet they also hearkened back to her history of playing in classical ensembles until taking up the bass in high school, and of the touring she did with Patti Austin and the Ray Charles tribute band that bookended her student days at Berklee.

Chamber Music Society took its title from Spalding having played violin and risen to concertmaster in Portland's Chamber Music Society of Oregon youth program. Spalding's voice and bass were supported by Genovese, Terri Lyne Carrington on drums, and Quintino Cinalli on percussion, the chamber feel of the project enhanced by Entcho Todorov on violin, Lois Martin on viola, and, on two tracks, cellist David Eggar. Milton Nascimento himself sang with Spalding on her piece "Apple Blossom." Other highlights included Spalding putting music to and singing the William Blake poem "Little Fly"; Spalding and Gretchen Parlato singing their arrangement of Antonio Carlos Jobim's "Inútil Paisagem," Spalding's bass and a hint of percussion their sole instrumental accompaniment; a version of "Wild Is the Wind," from the 1957 film of that name (and previously covered by the likes of Nina Simone, Shirley Horn, and David Bowie); and the set-closing "Short and Sweet," a slow, elegant piece featuring exquisite solos by Spalding and Genovese, supported by Carrington's brushes.

It was *Chamber Music Society* that won Spalding her Best New Artist Grammy, beating not just Bieber but also Drake, Florence and the Machine, and Mumford and Sons. Her next album, *Radio Music Society*, earned her two more: Best Jazz Vocal Album and Best Instrumental Arrangement Accompanying Vocalist(s), an award she shared with her early mentor Thara Memory. It was also a finalist for Best Long Form Music Video.

Radio Music Society, as its title suggests, was an attempt to make intelligent, instrumental pop music suitable for radio airplay. Spalding toured the music on it with a jazz big band of peers—Genovese, Daniel Blake, Igmar Thomas, Corey King, and music director/alto saxophonist Tia Fuller among them. They made a stop at Boston's Orpheum Theatre on Earth Day, where Spalding announced that she was releasing a free download of a video made from her version of Wayne Shorter's "Endangered Species," to which Spalding had added lyrics. The album itself featured other big names. Lalah Hathaway joined Spalding on the Shorter tune, and Joe Lovano played sax on Spalding's cover of Stevie Wonder's "I Can't Help It" (written for Michael Jackson's hit album *Off the Wall*). Lionel Loueke played guitar and Algebra Blessett sang with Spalding on "Black Gold," Terri Lyne Carrington played drums on most tracks, and Jack DeJohnette or Billy Hart played on most of those she didn't.

Some of the more memorable originals were "City of Roses," the portrait of Spalding's hometown that earned her and Memory their shared Grammy; the tribute to the mood-lifting powers of radio that opens the album ("Radio Song"); a metaphorical homage to an unnamed mentor ("Cinnamon Tree"); and a big band–fueled rumination on unrequited love ("Hold On Me"). Words of encouragement sung to men ("Crowned & Kissed") and black boys ("Black Gold") bracket the lament "Land of the Free," whose three stanzas sketch the story of Cornelius Dupree's exoneration after thirty years of imprisonment, the song ending with the sound of a cell door being bolted.

Spalding's next two projects, *Emily's D+Evolution* and *Exposure*, were more radical departures from familiar jazz, classical, or pop. I got my first look at the former at a May 2015 performance at Boston's Paradise Rock Club. It seemed like a test run of the fully fleshed out show I would review a couple of years later at the Schubert Theatre,[150] but there was already theatrical staging involved, and Spalding had begun growing into her alter-ego Emily. Some of her tunes reminded me of Joni Mitchell, and the friend I was with said Spalding reminded him of Janelle Monáe. The Monáe comparison made sense, both because Spalding was taking on a persona and because of the *Electric Lady* track Spalding had appeared on with Monáe two years earlier.

When I told Spalding about the comparison three years later, she responded, "Cool. Hey, I am a great admirer of her. I feel so inspired to just go for it. She makes me feel like, 'Yeah, fuck it. If I don't do what I want, then nobody else is going to do it for me.'"

Monáe had come up as we discussed their mentor Prince. Spalding had been telling me about Prince's philanthropy, and of his wide-ranging curiosity. "There's this book called *The Secret Life of Plants* that we were tripping on for a while," she recalled. "Loren Eiseley talks about this roaming[151] eye. [Prince's] curiosity was like this: the roaming eye, 360 scope, 360 exploration—like a lighthouse.

"What is really deep, though, is how in that gut-wrenching void that is left by his absence, I feel like Janelle has totally—she was *already*, in my estimation, the greatest popular artist of our time. And I say that with full knowledge of Beyoncé. Of *our generation*, I should say—of my generation, her generation, our generation. But I feel like with the passing of Prince, it's like she just expanded into the space, and she's occupying the space that we *neeeed* occupied. Her archetype is like non-archetype, and somebody has to occupy that space. . . . She was already at an 11 and now she's like at an 80, you know what I mean? It's really deep how that works. I mean, I think she's so deep, and she's so intimidating, that I think a lot of people can't stand to stay close to the music long enough to receive the fullness of its genius. Because she's scary: she raps, she writes, she dances, she sings, she's beautiful, she's confident, she can act. And it's *her*. It's not like people have put it into her like an act or a persona."

The album *Emily's D+Evolution*, released in March 2016, was excellent. Strong, smart lyrics. Fleet, confident singing, with protean shifts in vocal style from song to song. Superb musicianship from the power trio of Spalding's electric bass, Matt Stevens's guitar, and Karriem Riggins's—or Justin Tyson's—drums.

The fully fleshed out concert version was even more impressive. The song "Ebony and Ivy," inspired by Craig Steven Wilder's history of the exploitation of slave labor by elite American universities,[152] was particularly vivid in performance—Spalding's character going through a mock graduation ceremony as a sort of centerpiece to the action unfolding.

The whole thing was a departure from what people think of as jazz, the presence of a storyline pushing it beyond even the theatrical aspects of previous outliers such as the Sun Ra Arkestra and the Art Ensemble of Chicago. But the couple of musicians I asked about it liked it.

"The thing is," said Christian McBride, "once you've figured out that Emily has nothing to do with 'Esperanza Spalding,' quote, unquote—obviously it is Esperanza, but it's not what we're used to seeing her do with Joe Lovano, or whoever it is. Or even with her own group. But hey, I'm all for people experimenting and trying to express themselves in as many different ways as they can. I'm all for it. The first time I saw her do that project was actually on the Jimmy Kimmel show, and when I saw the braids and the electric bass, I thought, 'Oh, OK. Right away, this is going to be something different from what we're used to hearing.' I dug it!"

I'd spotted Vijay Iyer at the Schubert Theatre performance I reviewed, and when we spoke a couple of years later, I asked him what he'd thought. It turned out that Spalding had had the interview for her teaching job at Harvard that same day. The show that night clearly enhanced her prospect of getting Iyer's vote for hiring her.

"The way she played particularly the electric bass in that show, there was some kind of quantum leap from the last time I'd heard her," he told me. "There was a sense of groove and presence and strength there. She was always really talented, but in terms of what one needs from a bassist, which is a responsibility that is maybe deeper than for any other instrumentalist, because you're like moving people's internal organs around, you know? I felt like she had achieved something as a bass player that had really excited me.

"It's easy to get thrown by all the theatrics and everything else," Iyer added. "You start to forget that she's also making music. And I really appreciated the ambition of it, and the quirkiness—it's quite surreal, the whole thing. I just admire that somebody who had all this wind in her sails was out there taking all these chances. Not trying to please anybody, but just trying to be true to herself, no matter what the consequences. That to me was staggering. I never see people on that level taking chances like that. I had to give it up to her.

"That's the thing that I really admire about her: there's no bullshit, it's very uncompromising and very serious, what shall we say, deep-diving into the self and into the possibilities for expression. I hear her learning, and I hear the inquisitiveness, and there's a power to it that's really exciting to me."

The recorded version of the Emily material impressed Iyer as well.

"I really like that album," he said. "I thought there were some moments on there where the thing just really broke open in a new way for her. I've known her for ten years—truly following her as a bassist, and hearing her continue to push herself. That was one thing that came out in that interview. I don't mean to sound condescending, but a lot of people reach a certain prominence early on, and it's hard to keep pushing yourself. But she was obviously still studying. I have to say that when I first reached out to her about applying for a job at Harvard, I said, 'So there's this job opening. I think you'd be a pretty strong candidate for teaching in the music department. What do you think?' Her first question was, 'Can I take classes too?' That was literally her first question. So an eternal student—and to me, that's how to be a teacher."

Not surprisingly, Iyer played a role in bringing Spalding to Harvard. He served on a committee assigned to hire a contemporary performer, as part of Harvard president Drew Faust's desire to heighten the role of the arts at Harvard, and of the music department's plan to modernize its undergraduate curriculum. A broad initial candidate pool was narrowed to a short list of people mostly associated with contemporary classical or experimental music, and an offer was made to the brilliant flutist and MacArthur genius Claire Chase. Chase only wanted to accept a half-time position, however. The full-time position was split into two half-time appointments, and the search was reopened. Iyer suggested he ask Spalding to apply, along with other candidates from realms of music more diverse than those represented in the first pool. Spalding was hesitant initially, but came around to believing the job made sense for her.

"Once she applied it was a no-brainer, let's put it that way," Iyer told me. "It wasn't like I then had to convince anybody that this was a good idea. She had recommendation letters from Angela Davis, Herbie Hancock. She was pals with the Obamas, she had four Grammys, she was thirty years old. Who wouldn't want this person? And not only that, when she showed up for her interview, she was amazing. She wasn't resting on her laurels. She was actually very present, she had a lot to say. Academics talk about their projects in a large-scale sense—like you would talk about Edward Said's intellectual project, or something like that. But she comes across as having a project, having a sense of direction and underlying coherence to all the diverse things that she's involved in, and that really came across well. She met with President Faust, she met with Skip Gates—everyone was falling all over themselves to welcome her, and she hadn't even gotten the job yet."

For her first semester, Spalding taught two courses: Songwriting Workshop and Applied Music Activism. The latter was her opportunity to teach a course that merged music with political science, giving her the chance to couple those two lifelong interests. I observed her teach one session of it. The class had been divided into several groups, each of which had chosen a cause to find a way to support through music. That day a guest speaker had come from the marketing department at Emerson College to provide Spalding and the students some nuts-and-bolts pointers on how to mine social media research to focus their campaigns.

Politics and activism are important to Spalding. Her songs are often inspired by social issues, and she has donated her time and money to a variety of causes. These activities include organizing a benefit concert for the organization Free the Slaves in 2012, donating portions of tour income to the environmental group Earthjustice, and making a special video protesting imprisonment at Guantanamo that included cameos from Stevie Wonder and Harry Belafonte.[153]

She also speaks up for women's rights, including in the world of jazz. I asked her what she thought of the kerfuffle that took place over Robert Glasper's infelicitous remarks during an interview with Ethan Iverson.

"I didn't care that much," she said. "But it was funny to watch an individual take the downfall for a cultural phenomenon. Robert is very silly, and says dumb shit sometimes and brilliant shit sometimes. That felt like they were having a private conversation, but it was a public conversation, and I think it's easy to address all of our frustration to an easy target, and Robert was an easy target."

"It's a good reminder," she added. "It was like a hair trigger on this suppressed frustration amongst women in music, of being generally typecast as having a particular type of relationship to the music. So it could have been anything that set it off. And, you know, it literally could have been anything that set off that chain of events."

I noted that the interview had happened in February, before the #MeToo movement began in October.

"That's what I mean," she said. "It's like when you try to give subtle cues to somebody that you don't like what they're doing or saying, and if the subtle cues don't work, you work up to [less subtle warnings], and if those don't work, you're like, 'Get the fuck out of my face.' If the person was missing the subtle cues, that seems really out of left field. Understandably so. And I think a lot of unsaid and said frustration wasn't being heard."

"That reminds me," I said. 'You've got a song on *Exposure*, 'I Am Telling You,' that . . ."

"That happened before MeToo broke," she interjected. "That's funny. I was just talking about one of the record people doing that typical hand-on-the-lower-back thing to women. And they don't do it to men. It's not that deep. It's just like, 'What the fuck, dude? Don't!' I know that it doesn't come from a place of malice, but that's the problem—that when the behavior goes unaddressed, it becomes normalized."

I mentioned having attended the Jazz and Gender panel discussion Spalding had participated in a few months earlier at Winter Jazzfest, and that I'd been particularly struck by what the trumpet player Arnetta Johnson and Spalding had said about having to put on a sort of armor or mask to play with men in bands to keep the focus on music. (Spalding had added that her experience playing in an all-woman trio with Geri Allen and Terri Lyne Carrington had been liberating.)

"It's a thing," she responded simply.

"I'm Mr. Privilege here," I replied, feeling awkward about being unaware of the widespread nature of the problem. "I'm white, male, a straight guy. So this stuff was news to me."

"There's levels to the shit," she corrected me, becoming her mother's contrarian daughter once again, "because we're all safe Americans, too. I'm light-skinned, and a pretty woman. Privilege is operating everywhere, so how deep do you want to look for our own privilege? Think about our privilege—in contrast to another person in the same social hemisphere, who doesn't have access to that privilege, is being left out, because of the space we occupy—and then think about how we can use that privilege to make space, and not speed the very dynamics that prop up our privilege. It's fucking hard, man, and nobody's immune. No one is immune from privilege—not anyone that we know, anyway—but immune from the work of identifying, addressing, and deconstructing one's privilege. We're all Americans. We have the privilege of being on the launching side of the rocket, you know? That is a profound privilege that we don't ever have to think about."

That afternoon at the Jazz Standard was also my opportunity to discuss Spalding's more recent projects with her. *Exposure* had yielded impressive music now unavailable to anyone who didn't buy one of the 7,777 copies made of it.[154] The music was made with Matthew Stevens on guitar, Raymond Angry on keyboards, and Justin Tyson on drums, with Robert Glasper, Andrew Bird, and Lalah Hathaway dropping by for guest appearances. I had already spoken with Stevens and Vijay Iyer about the project before sitting down with Spalding.

When I asked Iyer if he'd caught any of the *Exposure* streaming, he confirmed that he had. "Yeah, I was all over that," he said. "I basically learned all the songs with her. I'd play in the band if I could." He laughed. "They're all learning in real time, and you find yourself kind of caught up in it. That was also like a revolutionary moment. I think people are not sure how to talk about her, because for one thing there's so much to say. But it's also that people get dazzled by appearances, and you might miss how profound innovation is taking place.

"That's how I felt about *Exposure*. It's a complete de-centering of the object, the object being the record. We've been trained to think that the music industry is predicated on these objects circulating, and when you tour it's to make sure that you can sell more of them. They always say that you're 'supporting your record.' I'm like, 'No, I'm here to make music for a thousand people in the room, that's what I'm here for. I'm not here to sell. They already bought a ticket.' I don't need to sell something else, you know? And also, the object is not music. I mean, it contains some trace of it, or some version of it, but music is about co-presence, and this is what she kind of laid bare to the world in that project. A couple of million people tuned into this real-time creative process, and that's what records are—traces of that process. I don't think most people really knew that. So I think something was revealed in that project that was new to the world, a reminder of something really special.

"And you know," Iyer added, "she assembled a pretty strong team. I enjoyed Raymond Angry and Matt Stevens as much as I did Esperanza.

"I was really impressed with her," he said, "and that—I told her this—I think it's a real testament to her willingness and desire to just dig deep and excavate her artistic self, and just bring it to bear as purely as she can."

Stevens echoed Iyer's point regarding how unusual it is for artists of Spalding's stature to take the sort of risks she took in both her *Emily* and *Exposure* projects.

"It's a legitimate quantifiable risk, and with serious potential consequences, both good and bad," he told me. "And that alone, I was like, 'Shit, if you are willing to put that much on the line, then it's nothing for me to put whatever misgivings or insecurities I may have, just hang those things up and go take the ride.' That was my take on it. I will remember that very fondly my whole life, I think. It was totally unique and unlike anything I'd ever done. There was a wonderful sense of community and togetherness, and a mutual sort of striving towards this tangible goal that we were just trying to collectively reach. And getting there, feeling pretty elated. It was really something also in the sense of feeling strengthened and empowered by the whole situation. Like, 'Man, maybe I can get to some of this stuff quicker than I thought, or maybe my ears are a little faster than I gave them credit for.' "

Spalding had streamed short bits of similar music on Facebook earlier that spring with Stevens, Angry, and Tyson that made me wonder whether that had been meant as a sort of rehearsal for *Exposure*. Stevens said that he believed so, and that a bonus disc sent with those limited copies of *Exposure*, titled *Unexposed* and consisting of entirely different songs, had been recorded at that spring get-together.

Spalding confirmed that she had indeed been training the musicians to trust their improvisational instincts at the spring session.

"Exactly," she said. "I have been in that studio many, many times practicing that process—'OK, you have two hours to write a song'—and what I discovered, in an unorganized way, [was that] if I didn't have time to go back and make something right, I would be forced to address whatever came out. And it was usually much more interesting than what I would have edited it into. So when Matt first came into the studio, and he played a few things, he was like, 'OK, let me go back and do that better,' and I didn't say anything, I said, 'Sure, do a few takes.'

"So he did some more takes, and he did some more takes, and he tried to get it even better, even more refined. So then I said, 'OK, Matt, can I interrupt you for a second? Can we just listen to the first thing you played?' And he was like, 'Why? It wasn't happening,' and I was like 'Let's just listen.' So we went back to the first thing he played when he didn't know it, and I was watching his face, and he was like, 'Oh shit, I did that?' And my response was, 'That's the point of *Exposure*, what just happened is the essence of this whole damn thing—that there's a part of you that gets activated when you don't have anything guaranteed to support you.'

"It's some sort of uninhibited, unhinged, uncornered mode of creative development, of improvisation, of spontaneous composition, response—it almost feels like honest dialogue, because you don't have a prepared response. You're telling the truth, and sometimes what you say without thinking about it often reveals what you really fucking think about the thing. It's more connected to intuition or true self. And I obviously, as the word *exposure* would imply, was really wanting to invite the true selves of everybody in that project to enter the recording studio and make an album together, all our true selves."

I asked if she planned to tour the songs that resulted.

"No," she said with matter-of-fact finality. "It was just a picture."

Noting that an executive from Concord Records had shown up for the surprise celebration that was aired at the end of the 77 hours of Facebook streaming, I asked if the company—which had purchased and made Heads Up a subsidiary in 2005—had been cool with limiting sales of the album to 7,777 copies.

"They were cool," she said. "As cool as they can be, because they're a record label. I really appreciate how far they stretched. It wasn't far enough for this project, but to their undying credit, and my full undying gratitude, they stretched as far as they possibly could. But it wasn't far enough, because the project, to be fair, has no place in a record label structure, because it wasn't for profit. It was an exchange that was operating outside the commodity exchange, because what it cost to make it was more than what we were going to earn selling it. That's not true: what it cost to make was exactly what we earned by selling all the copies, but there was no room for, like, income in perpetuity.

"So that's where the capitalism comes in," she elaborated. "There was no surplus of capital. There was no surplus of product. We just produced what we needed to make the damn thing. Now I sound like a socialist or a communist, and I'm not. It's just, that was a very revealing exercise in the limits of capitalistic structure, attempting to foster a gift exchange, essentially, where we may end up with one party giving more than the other. And that's OK, because the primary event is the giving of the gift. That's square one: you don't check what you're going to get out of it."

Spalding drank cups of English breakfast tea as we spoke, having worn herself out since I'd seen her on the train that Thursday. She had returned to Boston the next day to receive an honorary doctorate from Berklee. She watched and participated in the college's commencement concert on Friday night (performing her "Radio Song" with the student musicians), then improvised a short, inspirational commencement address on Saturday.[155] She returned home to New York that afternoon, and had a great date that night, she informed me, staying up all night talking and eating cashews. When I expressed admiration for musicians' ability to travel and get by without sleep, she demurred. "That's not my normal state," she said. "That's why I'm so tired, because usually I'm so much of a grandma." Hersch interrupted us at one point to go over some sheet music they'd be using that night.

Because this was my first chance to talk to her about her previous project, *Emily's D+Evolution*, I told her I'd been impressed by its theatricality. Her response led to her telling me about one of her projects in progress, which sounded every bit as experimental and three-dimensional as Emily had been.

"Yeah, we've been pretty hemmed up in the presentation format of this music," she replied. "I think it's the only music that grew out of the African diaspora that doesn't integrate dance. I mean, since swing dance ended anyway. Emily came through to move. Every time I would ask Emily, What are you doing here? What is this? Why are we doing this? The word that came, the message, the kind of modus

operandi, was like, 'I need to move. We need to move.' And I didn't have any association with dance at that point, so to me movement was narrative. It was bodies
just on the stage, just using three-dimensional space, and starting to move in that
space and animate the space, instead of having mic static picking up things in the
same plane. But now I do have some connecting points with dance."

I asked how so.

"You'll have to just wait and see," she answered, "because it's too epic—your
fucking iPhone would crack if I talk about it right now, because it's other entities
moving through. There are other entities that want this project to happen, and
I don't know who they are or where they come from, but they keep talking even
through other people—at me, to me, like through my feet."

She told a story about a woman who had been holding Spalding's feet at a Reiki
initiation ceremony coming up to her afterward and telling her what the new
project was about, though Spalding had never mentioned it to her.

"So I can't even sink my teeth into it yet," Spalding said. "I have to just start
reaching at it, and pulling it into this plane, and then following its progression,
and its gestation."

I told her it was interesting that she had mentioned dance, because the *New
Yorker* piece about her had said something about her music being more accessible
to some people than other modern jazz because it retained a sense of dance, as
opposed to emphasizing arty complexities such as weird time signatures.

Spalding liked the linking of her music to dance but not the implied criticism
of unusual time signatures.

"Weird time signatures and dance don't have to be mutually exclusive," she
pointed out, "and there's space for everything. I just am really feeling the absence.
I think we all, in a way we don't understand, are feeling the absence of movement
in this art form—on behalf of listeners, and on behalf of performers—and I think
actually the music itself wants us to move with it. It's so vibrant and human. I
mean, it's about spontaneous exploration and manifestation, and spontaneous
movement, and freedom to move in response to what you're hearing in real time
is so obvious and natural.

"Now every time I engage with a jazz performance, or think about performances
I've done for a sitting audience, feels totally counterintuitive to what the body would
want to do when you're really engaged in that heightened stage of performance. It's
visceral, and it's a lot of things that we probably don't have terminology—maybe
somebody does, but I don't—to address that's, like, moving through us in the music
in real time. And I wonder if the energy gets blocked as it tries to move through the
audience when they can't move their bodies, other than maybe tap their feet, move
their shoulders. Because we're alive with movement, you know?"

I contrasted two performances I had seen by Jason Moran of his Fats Waller Dance Party, one at the Berklee Performance Center, where the seats are bolted down and it's hard to move, the other at the Newport Jazz Festival, where audience members were happily on their feet and dancing in front of the stage.

"Exactly," she said. "Particularly now when we spend so much time seated in front of a machine. It's highly stimulating, so our body is engaging even less—we're not reaching for paper, we're not reaching for the phone. It's very static. All the energy is focused on the eyes and on the brain and on the mouth. And I feel like I keep running into people who are not engaged with music at all who are acknowledging how healing movement and dance is for them, as a balance and recalibration in our current lifestyles. Being in cars and in front of computer desks most of the time, or hunched over a phone. Again, we're in this contracted-lung position, with all the focus on our eyes and our brains. It feels like it's a prime landscape to activate movement again."

Spalding told me she would be focused on three major projects over the next few years alongside her job at Harvard.

"One of them's a *loooong* project around music and music therapy, and it's a long story, but I'm going to work with the school of Public Health at Harvard and really dig into some nitty gritty stuff about how . . ." She cut herself off. "It's not refined enough to give you a blurb. Essentially that, this theater-in-the-round piece, which again, it's a long thingy—this one that I'm talking about around movement and music, that's like coming from my feet, some spirit in my feet making me do it. And then of course the libretto, which is really great, because as soon as I hand in my final draft, it's like I can take my hands off of it, which is a luxury compared to every other project."

The libretto she referred to was for *Iphigenia*, the opera she had been working on the past few years with Wayne Shorter, to be directed by Penny Woolcock, whose previous credits include the operas *Doctor Atomic* and *The Pearl Fishers* and the film *The Death of Klinghoffer*. Shorter's music will be performed by his quartet with Danilo Pérez, John Patitucci, and Brian Blade, and a sixteen-piece chamber orchestra. Spalding will sing a part in it in addition to writing the libretto, but considers her opera duties to be a breeze compared to those of her other projects. "I will perform in it," she told me, "but again, that's not my work. I just show up and do my part, so it's like I don't have to worry about making it go." She laughed. "I can just write my thing and hand it in, edit as needed, and other people will make it go, and I don't have to be on those people about making it go. It's such a relief."

Scattered among her larger projects would be quick-hit collaborative ones: a handful of dates with the new TEN trio with Carrington and Payton; others in a quartet with Kenny Werner, Dave Liebman, and Carrington; a Spring Quartet reunion tour with Lovano, DeJohnette, and Genovese in spring 2019.

And her two sets with Fred Hersch later that night.

Spalding left her bass at home and limited herself to singing at the Jazz Standard, and her voice and Hersch's piano playing were marvelously in sync both sets. They performed some of the same music at each, including some Jobim (sung in Portuguese) and two of Hersch's collaborations with lyricist Norma Winstone, "Stars" and "A Wish." Three other repeated songs particularly stood out. Spalding sang wordless vocals on "Loro," the fleetly upbeat Gismonti piece she had included on her debut album. She sang Hersch's lyrics on his "Dream of Monk," a tribute to his hero.

Spalding announced her playful interpretation of "Girl Talk," written by Neal Hefti and Bobby Troup for the 1965 film *Harlow*, by noting that "This song was not written in the MeToo era." In Spalding's version, the tune's male chauvinism was transformed into gentle but pointed mockery of men's disinclination to talk, especially to women. At the second set, she added some extra fun by introducing the tune with an improvised comparison of rutting male animals to men hesitating to approach women at a bar, and returned to the theme by inserting bits of interior monologue into a break. "I can wait all night under this tree . . . I *know* your horn is bigger than his . . . If they wanted to get the girl, all they have to do is put their head on straight and open their mouths and talk." (An earlier bit of feminism had occurred in the first set, when Hersch introduced the Gismonti piece by saying, "All the jazz guys love him." Spalding shot him a look that included raised eyebrows. "And the jazz girls," he added. "Whoops.")

Leo Genovese and Francisco Mela showed up to watch the second set together as Spalding's guests, and as she walked past my table to get drinks for them, I told her she could have been a straight-up jazz singer if she wanted to be, but that I liked her own stuff even better. When she passed by again with the drinks, I told her about McBride remembering Pat Metheny showing him that early story of mine about her as they toured with Antonio Sánchez. "Now you're making me emotional," she said, and continued on her way.

Spalding lingered backstage after the second set, and I had a train to catch the next morning so I didn't stick around to say goodbye. But I did stop Hersch as he walked past my table and told him, "Please tell me you're going to record at least the Monk tune and 'Girl Talk' with her." He gave me a funny look and replied that he had been recording that night.

The next week Hersch emailed asking if it was OK with me for him to post a Sonny Rollins interview I had done for *Esquire* on his Facebook page. His email also included this: "I just listened to the recording of the first set Sunday with Esperanza—we may have a live record in there if she is down for it! Off the hook . . ."

Please visit the open access version of Make It New *to see a video resource for Chapter Eight. This resource can be viewed by visiting the chapter in the e-book:* https://doi.org/10.3998/mpub.11469938

EPILOGUE

On September 19, 2018, at the VIP opening of Jason Moran, a multimedia exhibit at Boston's Institute of Contemporary Art, the artist himself was onstage. Moran stood alone, a few strides from the Steinway grand piano at the center of the stage. He looked contemplative, his hands in his pockets as the huge dark screens behind the stage slowly rose up the theater's enormous glass walls to reveal Boston Harbor. He listened with the rest of us as the recorded voice of the conceptual artist and philosopher Adrian Piper began offering thoughts such as, "Artists ought to be writing about what they do."

After a few moments, Moran moved onto the piano bench and played along to the syllabic rhythms of Piper's voice until it faded away, then concluded the piece with his unaccompanied piano, as he had on his 2006 Blue Note album, *Artist in Residence*. He followed that with "Reanimation," composed for a collaboration with visual and performance artist Joan Jonas. (Moran later recorded the piece on his recent live solo piano album *The Armory Concert*.)

Moran paused after performing those first two pieces to address the audience, noting that women had been important influences on him as a young pianist. He began by describing his mother's habit of audibly, and annoyingly, taking notes during his piano lessons when he was not so sure he wanted to play piano (referenced by the sound of a scribbling pencil through most of Moran's elegiac "Cradle Song," also on *Artist in Residence*).

He later decided to attend college at the Manhattan School of Music so that he could study with the great Jaki Byard. "I like my peers," he said, "but they ain't got nothing on the masters."

"My partner in finding this out is in the audience," he then noted, referring to his wife, Alicia Hall Moran, whom he had met at the Manhattan School and whose own mentor there was the master mezzo-soprano Hilda Harris. He then offered brief encomiums for Piper and Jonas, "women I met after my mother passed," whom he credited as integral figures in helping him broaden his work beyond music around the time *Artist in Residence* was made.

To preface his final number, "Russian Rag," he sketched out a quick history of James Reese Europe, the focus of Moran's performances that fall.[156] Moran described how Europe had introduced jazz to France one hundred years earlier during World War I while fighting with the 369th Infantry Regiment (nicknamed the Hellfighters for their fierceness in combat), then returned to the United States, only to be murdered a few months later while touring with his band, fatally stabbed by his own drummer during a concert "right here in Boston"—at the old Mechanics Hall, which Moran noted for his audience of locals had been located where the city's Prudential Center now stands.

Moran's version of "Russian Rag" incorporated the busy left hand of jazz's early pianists while retaining his own impressionistic, up-to-the-moment approach to the piano. When the piece was through, he and Alicia made their way upstairs to mingle with audience members viewing his visual art.

The exhibit, which had opened at the Walker Art Center in Minneapolis that April and would move on to the Wexner Center for the Arts in Columbus, Ohio, in June 2019, and the Whitney Museum of American Art the following September, was dominated physically by sculptural recreations of three historical jazz venues: the Savoy Ballroom, the Three Deuces, and Slugs' Saloon. A wall label beside the Three Deuces began with Moran's explanation for having undertaken his STAGED series. (Piper's recorded voice, remember, had begun the night's performance by declaring that "artists ought to be writing about what they do.")

It read: "I love playing music from the past, but considering America's desire to raze cultural landmarks, why not fabricate those spaces as well. Architecture continues to inform music, from the big bands of the Savory Ballroom, to the small groups at the Three Deuces. From the vast ballroom to the tiny corner stage."

The Steinway Spirio player piano on the Three Deuces set would periodically launch itself into improvisations that Moran had loaded into it. His representation of the Savoy Ballroom, a major venue during jazz's swing era, was paired with contrasting samples of black work songs recorded by prisoners at Louisiana State Penitentiary (Angola). The Slugs' Saloon sculpture included a Wurlitzer Americana II jukebox whose programming included samplings of audience reactions to music at the Village Vanguard. There was also a tipped over chair a few feet from the

Wurlitzer, presumably an oblique reference to Slugs' having been the site of the fatal shooting of Lee Morgan.

There was a selection of drawings from Moran's Run series, which involves his taping paper to a piano keyboard, capping his fingertips with charcoal, and improvising music to create a visual image on the paper. A side room displayed the fluttery imagery of *The Death of Tom*, Moran's collaboration with visual artist Glenn Ligon,[157] on a continuous loop. In a similar room next door, Moran played a bandleader at a 1970s jazz-funk recording session at a recreation of the famous Columbia 30th Street Studio, a.k.a. "The Church." This was Stan Douglas's six-hour 2013 art installation film *Luanda-Kinshasa*. Moran and the other musicians in the film wore clothing and hair styles appropriate to the period. Among those I recognized were Jason Lindner, Kimberly Thompson, Marvin Sewell, and Burniss Earl Travis. One I didn't recognize was guitarist Liberty Ellman, whose beard, long hair, and glasses in the film made him look more like Al Di Meola in his Return to Forever years.

Other videos were projected on walls in the main room of the exhibit as a sort of evolving backdrop, featuring Moran in collaboration with Joan Jonas, Kara Walker, Theaster Gates, Julie Mehretu, and other visual artists.

The evening added up to a summation of the new places Moran has taken jazz beyond music, both physically and artistically. But he had been busy musically since I'd completed writing my chapter about him as well. A month before the VIP opening, I had watched him perform with Charles Tolliver and three other elder masters—Gary Bartz, Buster Williams, and Jack DeJohnette—in a performance at Marcus Garvey Park celebrating the fiftieth anniversary of the recording of Tolliver's classic album *Paper Man*, as part of the New York's annual Charlie Parker Jazz Festival. Three days before the ICA event saw the release of *Freebird feat. Jason Moran*, on which Moran joined the adventurous quartet Walking Distance for free-wheeling reinventions of the music of Charlie Parker. And a recording with Noah Preminger was in the can for release in 2019; titled *Preminger Plays Preminger*, it explores music from the films of the saxophonist's great uncle Otto Preminger. That was all in addition to the three albums of his own that he and his wife released on their Yes Records label between November 2017 and March 2018, *MASS {Howl, eon}*, *Here Today*, *Looks of a Lot*, and *Music for Joan Jonas*. The second issue of his *LOOP* magazine had not materialized in 2017 as planned, but the first issue was soon to be published online by the Walker Art Center.[158]

The tricky thing about writing snapshots of artists at the peak of their careers is that they keep moving. But as of October 2018, this is what the other musicians in this book had going on:

Vijay Iyer was fitting weekend touring around his teaching duties at Harvard, much of it with his sextet, with Jeremy Dutton filling in for Tyshawn Sorey on drums. There was also one performance scheduled with Sorey and violinist Jennifer Koh, and a *Blind Spot* performance at Bard College with Teju Cole, Stephan Crump, and Patricia Brennan. Iyer and Craig Taborn had recorded a duo piano concert in early 2018 at Liszt Academy in Budapest, which ECM would release in March 2019, titled *The Transitory Poems*.

Rudresh Mahanthappa had recorded a demo with bassist Eric Revis and Dave King for a new trio they were calling Movable Mirror, with plans to tour together and record a live album in 2019. In the meantime, he managed a two-week tour of Europe and Brazil with the Indo-Pak Coalition in fall 2018. He joined Henry Kaiser, Simon Barker, and Bill Laswell on the album *Mudang Rock*, released in September and described as music "inspired by rhythms and Spirit of the Korean shamanic tradition." And he and Terri Lyne Carrington had a project in the works for 2020 called Fly Higher: Charlie Parker @ 100.

Dave King and Reid Anderson had recorded and toured with saxophonists Tim Berne and Chris Speed in a group called Broken Shadows, focused on reworking classic pieces by Ornette Coleman, Julius Hemphill, Dewey Redman, and Charlie Haden, with an album scheduled for 2019 release from Newvelle Records. King also joined bassist Jorge Roeder on Julian Lage's third trio album, *Love Hurts*, which would come out from Mack Avenue that February. Their new Bad Plus bandmate Orrin Evans and his Captain Black Big Band released a new album, *Presence*, in September, and Evans told me that a new album with his Tarbaby trio mates Eric Revis and Nasheet Waits "should be out within the year." The Bad Plus itself continued touring steadily: an October tour of Europe would be followed immediately with an early November run at the Village Vanguard, and another stretch of US touring would commence Christmas Day in Minneapolis and wrap up in March in Chicago.

Ethan Iverson continued keeping busy after departing the Bad Plus. He was touring his *Temporary Kings* duo project with Mark Turner in September and October. (They played at the Regattabar a few days before the Moran event at the ICA, and Iverson stopped by the exhibit before leaving town and posted a couple of photographs from it on Facebook.) Iverson had formed a new quartet with Dayna Stephens, Ben Street, and Eric McPherson, but wrote in an email that much of his "quartet energy" would be devoted to the existing Billy Hart Quartet (also featuring Turner and Street), with plans for another ECM album in 2019 and much touring in celebration of Hart's eightieth birthday in 2020. Iverson had written appreciations of Carla Bley and Wayne Shorter for the *New Yorker*'s Culture Desk in May and August, the latter to honor Shorter's eighty-fifth birthday, and said that "a book certainly will follow in a few years." His classical music activities included the April premiere of his *Concerto to Scale*, commissioned by the American Composers Orchestra. He and the Mark Morris Dance Group would continue performing *Pepperland*, a work featuring original music by Iverson that debuted in 2017 for the fiftieth anniversary of the Beatles album *Sgt. Pepper's Lonely Hearts Club Band*.

In November 2018, Iverson would be in residence at the EFG London Jazz Festival, overseeing a three-night exploration of British jazz ranging from "Raising Hell with Henry Purcell" (Iverson and collaborators using the Baroque composer as a launching pad for new improvisations) to "Ethan and the British Composers" (explorations of pieces by Kenny Wheeler, Django Bates, and others) to "Ethan's Last Rent Party" ("How ragtime and early jazz found Britain, and what happened next"). And he would ring out 2018 in late December at the Umbria Jazz Winter Festival by premiering his big band suite *Bud Powell in the 21st Century*, a commissioned work that Iverson expects to bring elsewhere: "It requires a professional level core quintet (in Umbria I will have Ingrid Jensen, Dayna Stephens, Ben Street, and Lewis Nash) and a reasonably talented pick-up big band. I'm also doing it at New England Conservatory in February, and my idea is to try to place it in various performing arts venues in the future."

Miguel Zenón released his album featuring the Spektral Quartet, *Yo Soy La Tradición*, in late September, and was working with the SFJAZZ Collective through October and into November, with the new season's work devoted to celebrating Antônio Carlos Jobim. It would be the final year in the collective for Zenón, the lone remaining member of the original contingent of musicians assembled in 2004. To honor that long service, SFJAZZ released *Miguel Zenón Retrospective: Original Compositions 2004–2016*, a two-CD collection of Zenón's contributions to the collective's repertoire through the years. "It just seems like the right time to move on into other things," Zenón explained in an email. "Besides that (and many other things), I'm the artist in residence at the Conservatorio de Música de Puerto Rico this academic year (18–19), so I'll be spending some quality time there this coming year."

Anat Cohen returned to the Kennedy Center's Mary Lou Williams Jazz Festival[159] with her Tentet in May 2018. She performed twice that August at the 2018 Newport Jazz Festival, as a duo with guitarist Marcelo Gonçalves and with Artemis, an all-female all-star band. Directed by pianist Renee Rosnes, the band also comprises vocalist Cécile McLorin Salvant, trumpeter Ingrid Jensen, tenor saxophonist Melissa Aldana, bassist Noriko Ueda, and drummer Allison Miller. While Cohen was off preparing to hit the main stage with Artemis, Gonçalves was hanging out in the press tent and told me that Cohen had another Tentet project in the works. She confirmed later that her musical director and business partner, Oded Lev-Ari, had been commissioned by Carnegie Hall and Chicago's Symphony Center to compose a concerto, which the Tentet would perform at those venues in early 2019. The plan was to record the concerto and additional music for a second Tentet album, also early in the new year. And she had a steady stream of shows lined up with a variety of bands: three nights of duos with Fred Hersch at the Village Vanguard in October, and dates with the Tentet, Gonçalves, Trio Brasileiro, Choro Adventuroso, and her longtime quartet well into 2019. In September 2018, Cohen joined the faculty at New School University's School of Jazz and Contemporary Music.

Robert Glasper had an extraordinary monthlong residency at the Blue Note Jazz Club in October 2019, with an array of different bandmates as the month wore on: starting with Derrick Hodge and Chris Dave; Christian McBride and Nicholas Payton for a couple of nights mid-month; guest vocalists including Bilal, Anderson .Paak, and Yasiin Bey (a.k.a. Mos Def); and the all-star group R+R=NOW to wrap things up. Otherwise he kept busy touring, switching back and forth primarily between R+R=NOW and August Greene, but finding time to squeeze in a few nights at Chicago's Jazz Showcase in late September with his original acoustic trio mates Vicente Archer and Damion Reid.

For the second year in a row, Esperanza Spalding used Facebook for a spectacularly experimental project. While her peers all make extensive use of social media to promote their work, Spalding has been taking the next step of using those media to engage followers with the art itself. This new project saw her releasing one song every day between October 7 and October 18 (her birthday), each linked to a different body part (thoracic spine, mouth, eyes, hips, fingers, abdominal portal, feet, solar portal, arms, legs, mind, ears) and each accompanied by its own artful, strangely shamanistic video. The album itself, *12 Little Spells*, was made available for streaming on October 19 and had a March release date for CD and LP sales, after a twelve-date tour squeezed into November and December. The multimedia project was inspired by Spalding's study of the healing power of art and the book *Psychomagic*, by Alejandro Jodorowsky, according to an online preview on *Vanity Fair*'s website.[160] The same night the album began streaming, Spalding would begin *her* three nights of duos with Fred Hersch at the Village Vanguard, following Anat Cohen's duo sets with Hersch the previous three nights. And Spalding had other more straight-forward jazz sets since I had finished my chapter about her: with Terri Lyne Carrington and Nicholas Payton in the summer, and with Kenny Werner, Dave Liebman, and Carrington in the fall. And, as the chapter mentioned, she would also be reuniting with Joe Lovano, Leo Genovese, and Jack DeJohnette in early 2019 for performances by their Spring Quartet.

The jazz and creative music world remained fertile among other artists as well.

Women instrumentalists kept becoming more visible. Nicole Mitchell was artist-in-residence at New York's 2018 Winter Jazzfest (and on the cover of the British jazz magazine *Jazzwise* that September), with Meshell Ndegeocello announced as the festival's artist-in-residence in 2019. Mary Halvorson and Tia Fuller were each featured on a *DownBeat* cover in 2018 (Halvorson also appeared on the April 2018 cover of the British magazine *Wire*, and *Jazziz* magazine ran a feature that I wrote on Fuller).[161] Besides Artemis, the 2018 Newport Jazz Festival also featured the Canadian saxophonist Jane Bunnett and Maqueque, Bunnett's stellar band of Cuban women. And I saw an impressive performance by a new group that was mostly women at a Hudson Valley club called the Falcon later that same month; I went to that show already familiar with violinist Jenny Scheinman and drummer Allison Miller, but the group's superb pianist Carmen Staaf was new to me (the lone man in the group was bassist Tony Scherr). Miller and Staaf were also co-leaders on an excellent 2018 album, *Science Fair*, on which they were joined by Matt Penman, Dayna Stephens, and Ambrose Akinmusire.

Jazz's internationalism continued apace. Bunnett and her band all originated from outside the United States, after all, and Artemis encompassed international origins as well, with two members hailing from Canada (Rosnes and Jensen), one each from Israel (Cohen), Chile (Aldana), and Japan (Ueda), and a American-born member whose two parents are Haitian and French (Salvant). Linda May Han Oh, raised in Perth, Australia, returned Down Under for duo performances with her Cuban-born husband, Fabian Almazan, before she joined a fall 2018 tour with the Pat Metheny band, whose two other members, Antonio Sánchez and Gwilym Simcock, began life in Mexico and Wales, respectively. Nate Chinen's *Playing Changes: Jazz for the New Century*, published by Pantheon Books in August 2018, devotes several pages to describing the nascent jazz scene in China, and when I interviewed Aaron Goldberg for my book the pianist had just returned home from performing with Joshua Redman at the new Jazz at Lincoln Center Shanghai.

A thriving new British jazz scene was heralded in the *New York Times* and *Rolling Stone*, made up largely of first- or second-generation immigrants to the United Kingdom, several of whom performed at the 2018 Winter Jazzfest: saxophonist Nubya Garcia, trumpeter Yazz Ahmed, vocalist/guitarist Oscar Jerome, and two groups featuring saxophonist Shabaka Hutchings, the Comet Is Coming and Sons of Kemet. Hutchings later toured the United States with Sons of Kemet in fall 2018, playing music from his soca-charged first recording for Impulse! Records, *Your Queen Is a Reptile*.

Guitarist Lionel Loueke, Benin-born and now residing in New York and Luxembourg, had two albums coming out in late 2018 and 2019, the latter a record of standards with Charles Lloyd's rhythm section of bassist Rueben Rogers and Eric Harland. Loueke's 2018 album of original music, titled *The Journey*, featured a revolving cast of a dozen international musicians, among them Robert Sabin, Pino Palladino, Cyro Baptista, John Ellis, Étienne Charles, and Loueke's own longtime trio mates, Massimo Biolcati and Ferenc Nemeth (whom he'd met when they were all international students at the Berklee College of Music). Recorded for the French classical label Aparté Music, the album was inspired by the plight of the world's refugees. "The crisis of the refugees is a humanitarian crisis," Loueke was quoted in a press release distributed with the album. "Despite the nationalist politicians rising in the west, with their slogan that immigrants are the source of every problem, nothing can stop the migrants. When you are facing famine and civil or ethnic wars, you are not afraid to cross the Mediterranean in a small boat with no food and water. I believe there's a survival instinct in every human being."

The turbulent times continued to produce other protest music. Marc Ribot's *Songs of Resistance*, released in September 2018, consisted of songs, mostly originals, that the guitarist had performed at the 2018 Winter Jazzfest in January of that year. The album version added such vocalists as Tom Waits, Steve Earle, Fay Victor, and Syd Straw. A similar program of protest music had been presented at the previous year's Winter Jazzfest, with drummer/music director Ulysses Owen Jr. leading vocalists Dee Dee Bridgewater, Theo Bleckmann, and Alicia Olatuja through songs by Joni Mitchell, Abbey Lincoln, and Nina Simone. Owens's album version of the project, also titled *Songs of Freedom*, featured Bleckmann, Olatuja, Joanna Majoko, and René Marie singing songs by Mitchell, Simone, Randy Newman, Max Roach, and Oscar Brown Jr. and was released in March 2018 on Japan's Somethin' Cool label.

September 2018 also saw the release of Arturo O'Farrill's *Fandango at the Wall: A Soundtrack for the U.S., Mexico, and Beyond*. O'Farrill, of Cuban descent but born in Mexico City and raised there and in New York City, was joined on the album by Mexican American drummer Antonio Sánchez, whose Grammy-nominated solo album *Bad Hombre* had come out the year before and was titled to convey his loathing for Donald Trump.[162] In October 2018 came Ambrose Akinmusire's *Origami Harvest*, which blended classical (Mivos Quartet), hip-hop (rapper Kool A.D., of the defunct group Das Racist), and jazz (his own trumpet, drummer Marcus Gilmore, pianist Sam Harris, and others) into a brilliant musical examination of racial injustice, with an opening track referencing Trayvon Martin ("a blooming bloodfruit in a hoodie") and another featuring a whispered roll call of victims of police violence ("Free, White and 21").

The politics of Glasper's R+R=NOW project was more muted and upbeat, but the music the group made was another example of jazz musicians reaching beyond any strict definition of what qualifies as jazz—in this case to incorporate R&B and hip-hop. As Glasper was quick to point out, jazz was derived from other musics. So why should it now silo itself off from other genres? "Jazz is literally a mutt," he told me ahead of the band's performance at the 2018 Newport Jazz Festival. "Jazz is made from blues, jazz is made from classical music. It was made from religious music. And so it always was a music that was mixed together to make something. People say, 'Oh, well if you mix this, is it still jazz?' Yeah! Because it was mixed to begin with. That's how they made it."

Glasper's R+R=NOW bandmate Christian Scott has a historical perspective as well, having in 2017 released a trio of albums pegged to the hundredth anniversary of the first jazz recording. His stretch music concept involves jazz being mixed with other music from around the globe, and protest has been a part of Scott's music throughout his career—the final album in his Centennial Trilogy, released in October 2017 and titled *The Emancipation Procrastination*, includes such tracks as "Gerrymandering Game" and "Unrigging November."

Like Ezra Pound and the modernists, Scott knows that making things new often involves repossessing elements of the old and reanimating them.

"For me, it stems more from the West African concept called Sankofa," he told me. "The visual representation of Sankofa is a bird that is facing forward but its neck is turned backwards—so its body is facing forward, but its focal point is actually behind it. It sort of deals with the cyclical nature of everything we experience, not just our creative conscience but how the things that you go through and what you've endured affect how you move forward. I think we sort of see it as a conceptual element. I think to anyone that's listening it's pretty clear that we're intent on finding new modes of operating, a new vernacular, new ways of expressing ourselves, and to sort of sharpen and refine and reevaluate the way that we're communicating to listeners now."

This had come up in the context of Scott's use of a Pan-African drum kit on his album *Stretch Music* (2015), which mixed traditional West African drums with a standard twentieth century trap drum kit and electronic triggers, and of Jason Moran's use of stride piano technique in his music, most obviously on his cover of James P. Johnson's "You've Got to Be Modernistic" on his first solo piano album and his larger-scale projects honoring Thelonious Monk, Fats Waller, and James Reese Europe.

"Jason is saying people are listening to what he is doing and maybe conjecturing that what he is doing is completely fresh," observed Scott, but "because he has a stronger frame of reference, he understands that he is pulling that from something else. So I think a lot of what we are doing, the way we are putting things together is new, but to say that conceptually on a holistic level what any of the bands are offering at this moment is purely new—you're not accurately describing what is going on."

What *is* going on is that today's musicians help themselves to aspects of jazz's past while making art that reflects the present. For some, that means being open to mixing it with more current forms of pop music, something that has gone on for years. The difference is that, unlike in the peak years of jazz neoclassicism, it's now becoming more widely noticed.

Scott talked about how he and Glasper were credited with bringing a younger generation of listeners to jazz by blending it with hip-hop on their albums of the mid-2000s. "But my own uncle [alto saxophonist Donald Harrison] was releasing records ten years before that where he was mixing elements of hip-hop into what he was doing," he noted. "And so you listen to what is going on with nouveau swing[163] or M-Base, these are cultures of jazz that are our predecessors. They may not have gotten the same type of press that we got, but at the end of the day they were also doing those things."

"At this juncture," Scott continued, "in creative live music—or jazz music, or whatever you want to call it—we're embarking on the second century, and I think it's important to be clear about 1) where the music comes from, and 2) the trajectory that the music has the potential to have. But that's trajectory rooted in the music's actual history, and not the cleaned up and washed out history of what happens in this music."

He spoke of the advantages having grown up in New Orleans gave him in understanding that history, and of how grounding his own work in history—he mentioned the work of New Orleanians Alvin Batiste and Harold Battiste as references he could draw from—can help him sort out the best way to communicate to this generation.

"That through line of the same culture and the same—as you're putting it, '*Make It New*'—I think that exists heavily in this era of what we're doing musically," Scott said. "Because we're all reevaluating—like Jason, like myself—the way that we communicate so that we can figure out the best way to communicate in the future. It's like we're priming the canvas for the next generation of cats."

The generation of musicians still in their thirties and forties still have plenty of music to make of their own, of course. But there are others coming up fast behind them. Jon Batiste, of *The Late Show with Stephen Colbert* fame, barely into his thirties as of this writing, was making formidable albums such as *The Music of John Lewis* (2017, recorded with the Jazz at Lincoln Center Orchestra and Wynton

Marsalis) and *Hollywood Africans* (2018). Cécile McLorin Salvant, Christian Sands, Jazzmeia Horn, James Francies, Adam O'Farrill, Maria Grand, and Sasha Berliner were a few still in their twenties as 2018 neared completion who were already stars or seemed headed in that direction. Morgan Guerin, twenty, was about to hit the road with Esperanza Spalding for her 12 Steps tour, on which he would play bass, keyboards, drums, and tenor saxophone. Guerin had already performed as a member of Terri Lyne Carrington's band Social Science at the 2017 Winter Jazzfest. Piano phenom Joey Alexander turned fifteen in June 2018, a year that saw him release his fourth album (*Eclipse*), a digital-only holiday EP (*A Joey Alexander Christmas*), and perform an NPR Tiny Desk Concert with Reuben Rogers on bass and Kendrick Scott on drums.[164] They and others like them, like those featured in this book, can be counted on to keep refreshing the music.

Something like twenty-five years ago, I interviewed Sonny Rollins for a magazine profile at his home in New York's Hudson Valley. At one point, the question of jazz's future came up. This was in the early 1990s, toward the end of the music's neo-classical phase. Rollins noted that jazz didn't begin with bebop, the music he broke in with before moving through periods exploring hard bop, calypso, bossa nova, free jazz, and more. To prove the point, he stood up and led me to a print of the famous 1958 Art Kane photograph of a large group of elite jazz musicians posed on and beside the front steps of a Harlem brownstone that he had hanging on a wall of his practice studio. Rollins was the youngest musician in the photograph, and sixty years later, he and Benny Golson were the only two still alive.

"We must remember that jazz was happening in the '20s also," Rollins began that 1993 interview. "Right? I mean, Louis Armstrong was playing in the '20s, and then you had the whole period of the '30s, which had some great bands. So you can't just say the bebop era, because there was a lot happening prior to the bebop era."

Rollins motioned toward the photograph, in which nearly every era of jazz development through that time was represented.

"There's Monk," he said, pointing. "There's this guy here, see this little guy there? He's a great pianist called Luckey Roberts. He was one of the great stride pianists, and there was also—who was supposed to be there but walked out of the picture—a guy called Willie 'The Lion' Smith. You've heard of him. He was also there. So there's stride piano guys there, a lot of people. [Count] Basie, Lester Young, Dizzy [Gillespie], Gerry Mulligan, Roy Eldridge, Rex Stewart, Mary Lou Williams, Lawrence Brown, Mary McPartland, Oscar Pettiford, Coleman Hawkins, Stuff Smith. . . .

"Anyway," Rollins summed up, returning to his seat, "I was saying that to make the point that those guys represented a lot of the different periods throughout jazz. The stride guys—that was a great period of jazz development, stride piano. So will jazz survive? People could have asked the same question then. Jazz will go on a long time. As long as people give it a chance to be heard and guys want to play it, it will happen."

As long as men and women choose to study and create jazz, that is, it will continue to be made relevant and new.

—*Swampscott, Massachusetts, October 2018*

INTERVIEW SOURCES

The interviews done specifically for this book all took place between May 2012 and May 2018, with two additional phone calls to Robert Glasper (for a *Boston Globe* story) and Anat Cohen that both yielded information that appeared in the epilogue written that October. I've also doubled back to early interviews with Jason Moran, Glasper, and Esperanza Spalding in 2005 and 2006, a period when I was writing about jazz weekly for the *Boston Globe* and not keeping careful record of which specific date interviews took place. Those are listed here as well, as are master classes, lectures, and private lessons described in the chapters on Moran and Miguel Zenón. Where no location is specified the interviews were conducted by telephone.

Jason Moran: February 2005; May 14, 2012, his apartment, Harlem; March 17, 2016, Brasserie Jo restaurant, Boston; (Master class, Andrew Hill) January 28, 2016, New England Conservatory, Boston; (Master class, death) September 22, 2016, NEC, Boston; (Master class, Jaki Byard) March 2, 2017, NEC, Boston

Vijay Iyer: April 11, 2015, his apartment, Cambridge, Massachusetts; March 15, 2016; February 19, 2018

Rudresh Mahanthappa: October 24, 2014, rented practice space, Montclair, New Jersey; February 20, 2016; August 23, 2017

The Bad Plus

    Dave King: November 19, 2016, Doubletree Guest Suites, Boston; July 1, 2017, Starbucks, Montreal; August 17, 2017

    Ethan Iverson: April 1, 2016, his apartment, Brooklyn

Reid Anderson: June 8, 2017, his apartment, Brooklyn

Orrin Evans: August 8, 2017

Miguel Zenón: June 1, 2012, and May 17, 2013, Blue Revolution restaurant, Washington Heights; (Residency) May 22-25, 2014, SFJAZZ Center, San Francisco; (Lecture) August 24, 2014, Arroyo, Puerto Rico; April 3, 2015, Cabrini 181 restaurant, Washington Heights; June 30, 2016; (Lecture) August 21, 2016, Cidra, Puerto Rico; (Private lessons) September 13, 2016, New England Conservatory, Boston

Anat Cohen: November 5, 2015, Doubletree Guest Suites (where Scullers is based), Boston; June 24, 2016, friend's apartment, Brooklyn; June 20, 2017; June 21, 2017; September 29, 2018

Robert Glasper: January 2006; January 20, 2012, Blue Note Records, Manhattan; May 28, 2015; June 12, 2015; June 24, 2017, Solid Sound Festival, North Adams, Massachusetts; June 20, 2018

Esperanza Spalding: April 2005, Berklee practice room, Boston; April 10, 2017; May 13, 2018, Jazz Standard, New York City

Christian Scott aTunde Adjuah, Julian Lage, and Lionel Loueke each granted me repeated interviews thinking they would be featured in this book. Deadlines conspired to prevent that, but my new intention is to move them to a second volume. Several of Christian's observations appear in this one, however. Most or all of them were made on May 2, 2017, when we conducted a series of interviews on the fly in New Orleans—during sound check for a late afternoon concert in Lafayette Square, and in Uber rides that night to and from a recording studio in Algiers.

The following musicians graciously granted me interviews for the book despite not being featured in it. In some cases they weren't ultimately quoted in it, but in all cases they greatly enhanced my understanding of the musicians I was writing about.

Rez Abbasi: September 28, 2017

Darcy James Argue: October 27, 2017

Nels Cline: May 29, 2017

Henry Cole: December 15, 2016

Roman Diaz: May 5, 2017, New Orleans

Chris Eldridge: May 25, 2017

Aaron Goldberg: December 7, 2017

Billy Hart: June 28, 2017

Fred Hersch: April 25, 2017

Guillermo Klein: September 30, 2016

Steve Lehman: September 25, 2017

Oded Lev-Ari: December 1, 2017; February 1, 2018

Joe Lovano: February 20, 2017

Branford Marsalis: September 9, 2017

Tito Matos: August 2014, San Juan, Puerto Rico

Christian McBride: June 4, 2016, Boston

Alicia Hall Moran: May 31, 2017

Greg Osby: August 4, 2017

Danilo Pérez: December 19, 2016

Josh Roseman: November 17, 2016

David Sánchez: March 31, 2017

Matthew Stevens: April 19, 2018

A third category of interviewees generously allowed me to piggyback questions related to the book onto interviews they had granted for *Boston Globe* stories:

Geri Allen: March 28, 2017

Gary Burton: January 12, 2015

Terri Lyne Carrington: April 4, 2017

Jack DeJohnette: September 29, 2017

Dave Holland: April 26, 2017

Adam O'Farrill: February 25, 2016

Damion Reid: December 6, 2015

Wadada Leo Smith: March 19, 2016

Henry Threadgill: June 7, 2017, New York City

George Wein: July 18, 2016

Others had interviews repurposed from stories I wrote for the *Boston Globe* (Wadada Leo Smith again, in this case an earlier piece from April 2005), *JazzTimes* (Don Was, Mulgrew Miller, Derrick Hodge, Meshell Ndegeocello), or *DownBeat* (François Moutin), as described in the relevant chapters in the book. I interviewed Sonny Rollins for a magazine profile in fall 1993 at his longtime home in Germantown, New York, and wound up using part of what he told me that afternoon in this book's epilogue.

There were also many casual conversations with others that touched on the book's featured musicians and themes but generally didn't see print. The lengthiest and most enjoyable of these was with Teju Cole over dinner one night in Cambridge, after he'd accompanied me to duo performance of Vijay Iyer and Wadada Leo Smith at Harvard after having been featured in Emerson College's writers series that afternoon.

I read Cole's books *Open City*, *Every Day Is for the Thief*, and *Blind Spot* while researching and writing mine, and two other works of literature that inspired projects discussed in the Jason Moran and Miguel Zenón chapters: *Under the Glacier*, by Halldór Laxness, and *Hopscotch*, by Julio Cortázar. In the interest of including a short list of recommended reading in lieu of a full-fledged bibliography, here are twenty-six books about music that I found especially useful while researching my project:

Jazz Masters of the 50s, Joe Goldberg
Weather Bird: Jazz at the Dawn of Its Second Century, Gary Giddins
Thelonious Monk: The Life and Times of an American Original, Robin D. G. Kelley
A Power Stronger Than Itself: The AACM and American Experimental Music, George
    E. Lewis
Future Jazz, Howard Mandel
Speaking Freely, Nat Hentoff
Blues People: Negro Music in White America, LeRoi Jones (Amiri Baraka)
Digging: The Afro-American Soul of American Classical Music, Amiri Baraka
Four Lives in the Bebop Business, A. B. Spellman
But Beautiful: A Book About Jazz, Geoff Dyer
Miles: The Autobiography, Miles Davis with Quincy Troupe
Possibilities, Herbie Hancock with Lisa Dickey
Footprints: The Life and Work of Wayne Shorter, Michelle Mercer
Charles Lloyd: A Wild, Blatant Truth, Josef Woodard
Good Things Happen Slowly: A Life in and Out of Jazz, Fred Hersch
Cuba and Its Music: From the First Drums to the Mambo, Ned Sublette
The World That Made New Orleans: From Spanish Silver to Congo Square, Ned
    Sublette
The Rest Is Noise: Listening to the Twentieth Century, Alex Ross
*How Music Got Free: The End of an Industry, the Turn of the Century, and the
    Patient Zero of Piracy*, Stephen Witt
How to Listen to Jazz, Ted Gioia
Jazz 101: A Complete Guide to Learning and Loving Jazz, John F. Szwed
Why Jazz Happened, Marc Myers
Jazz: A Critic's Guide to the 100 Most Important Recordings, Ben Ratliff
Flyboy 2: The Greg Tate Reader, Greg Tate
*The New Face of Jazz: An Intimate Look at Today's Living Legends and the Artists of
    Tomorrow*, Cicily Janus
Playing Changes: Jazz for the New Century, Nate Chinen

The Chinen book was not published until everything in mine but its epilogue had been written. It covers the same era as mine does but with a different approach, and it was good to see that the current developments in jazz are finally getting attention in book form. Likewise, it was nice, and validating, to see the *New Yorker* profile Jason Moran and Vijay Iyer (and Esperanza Spalding before them) while my book was being researched. Those pieces, and Gary Giddins's critical appraisal of Rudresh Mahanthappa in the same magazine, are also worth checking out. So is John Zorn's multivolume book series of essays by musicians, *Arcana: Musicians on Music*.

Notes

1. In some cases, this newness involved refreshing old art to make it seem new again, à la Ezra Pound and other literary modernists such as James Joyce and T. S. Eliot. Examples include Jason Moran and others reviving stride piano techniques and employing them in their own contemporary work or Anat Cohen bringing the clarinet back into modern jazz in a high-profile way and playing neglected old tunes like "Tiger Rag" and "The Mooche" with her brothers in their band, the 3 Cohens. These types of historic jazz, ironically, were themselves all new when literary modernism was at its height in the first three decades of the twentieth century.

   Mining earlier music to produce something new didn't begin with this generation. Branford Marsalis, pooh-poohing the fetishizing of the new, called my attention to two examples of John Coltrane tapping into earlier works to create cutting-edge projects of his own. "I don't fault jazz writers and their limited musical understanding for not knowing that when John Coltrane wrote 'Impressions' in 1961 that it was basically lifted, melody and harmony, from a composition by Morton Gould in 1939, called 'American Symphonette No. 2, Pavane,'" he told me, "because they don't have that kind of expanded musical palette."

   Marsalis's other example was Coltrane's most famous work, *A Love Supreme* (1965). "Everybody says that that sound had never been heard before," Marsalis said. "Well, that sound had been heard in Pentecostal churches for a hundred years. It'd never been heard in jazz. The first time I went to a Pentecostal church, which was well before I listened to John's music, I came out of there sweating and shaking. And then when I finally started listening to what Elvin [Jones] and them were doing, I went like, 'Aw man, that's that Pentecostal stuff.' I'm hearing people saying no one has ever done this stuff before. It's not true. But it fits into this narrative that jazz musicians are singular geniuses, and that they fall out of their mother's womb with this cornucopia of ideas that just makes them so different from everyone else."

2. https://jazztimes.com/archives/bob-belden-riddle-me-this/

3. I'm thinking in the former case of work of such artists as Bob Dylan, Phil Ochs, Joni Mitchell, James Brown, Sam Cooke, Marvin Gaye, Aretha Franklin, Stevie Wonder, and others. Hip-hop itself is making inroads into jazz, with Jason Moran, Vijay Iyer, and Robert Glasper among the

many artists referencing it in their work. But it remains controversial. Wynton Marsalis launched his latest fusillade against it in a May 2018 *Washington Post* interview in which he called its more vulgar manifestations (in particular its frequent use of the N word) "more damaging than a statue of Robert E. Lee." Christian Scott posted a strong rebuttal to Marsalis soon afterward on Facebook.

4. Scott added the Ghanian names aTunde Adjuah to his given name in 2012 but is generally referred to by his original surname on second reference.

5. A work still in progress, the *Coin Coin* project explores African American history, including Roberts's own ancestry, through what she has called "panoramic sound quilting." The series is expected to comprise twelve "chapters," the first three of which were released as albums in 2011, 2013, and 2015. *Coin Coin Chapter Four: Memphis* was scheduled for release in October 2019.

6. http://www.a-great-day-in-harlem.com

7. The controversy is discussed in detail in chapter 7.

8. That's how I remembered that night for many years, but my memory could be off. Blakey was famous for proclaiming that "jazz washes away the dust of everyday life," and I may have inadvertently combined that saying of his with his encouraging that night's audience to buy albums to help keep jazz alive for young musicians like Marsalis.

9. https://nyti.ms/2ZkdjxL Hajdu would later collaborate with Hersch on Hersch's 2017 memoir, *Good Things Happen Slowly: A Life In and Out of Jazz.*

10. https://nyti.ms/2MrRNW8

11. https://nicholaspayton.wordpress.com/2011/11/27/on-why-jazz-isnt-cool-anymore/

12. www.esquire.com/entertainment/music/interviews/a30419/herbie-hancock-book-interview/

13. https://www.npr.org/2013/02/02/170882668/wayne-shorter-on-jazz-how-do-you-rehearse-the-unknown

14. Seale, a political activist, co-founded the Black Panther Party with Huey P. Newton and was later among the original Chicago Eight defendants charged with conspiring to disrupt the 1968 Democratic National Convention in Chicago.

15. "For Jason Moran, playing music is all relative," Boston Globe, February 18, 2005.

16. https://www.villagevoice.com/2001/10/16/heir-to-a-secret-history/

17. https://nyti.ms/33IsHaZ

18. https://www.youtube.com/watch?v=yNBv9nXSKPE

19. Tucker, a musician as well as a professor and scholar, wrote *Ellington: The Early Years* (Urbana: University of Illinois Press, 1991) and edited *The Duke Ellington Reader* (New York: Oxford University Press, 1993). He died of lung cancer in 2000. https://nyti.ms/2TT1ldl

20. Several months later, I had an opportunity to do so. Here is what Fred Hersch told me about studying with Jaki Byard at New England Conservatory:

"Jaki really showed me the lineage of solo piano in jazz. He was a master of all jazz styles, but he approached them in his own way. It showed me that I could play stride without trying to sound like Teddy Wilson or Fats Waller. I could do it in my own way. I think everything Jaki did, he did it in his own way, in his own particular style. And you know, Jaki should have had a bigger career than he did. For various reasons, he didn't.

"I wasn't his best student in terms of doing all the exercises and things that he wanted me to do and stuff like that. I've never been so good at that kind of stuff. But I definitely hear it in Jason's line playing. I hear Jaki's influence, in the way that he shapes lines. Like Jaki, [Jason] is a fairly commanding pianist, confident, and pretty much in the zone. He's very creative, as Jaki was.

I think the message of Jaki was (a) have some fun, (b) try some things you've never tried before. And there was a certain kind of both reverence and irreverence for the tradition that Jaki had. He had clearly studied and been around everybody. I mean, he's on some of the great jazz records of all time, and played with some of the most important figures in music. So there's that. And for a young kid from the Midwest who'd never had a jazz piano lesson, just being around somebody who'd been around all those great Dolphy and Mingus records, and just sort of hanging out and playing two pianos with him, was really an eye opener.

"I think Jaki is one of those pianists who, if you know his style at all, it's pretty easy to drop the needle and say, 'Oh, that's Jaki Byard.' And I think that's the goal. I mean, I'm really happy when somebody says, 'Hey, you know I was listening to the radio and there was a piano solo and I knew it was you.' I think that's what we are all trying to do—is to in some way be identifiable. Like, I never transcribe solos. That's very common practice now. Nobody told me I should. It was just not kind of a thing. Now a lot of these jazz studies programs, you have to transcribe solos."

21. Earl John Powell, as a young child, appeared looking over his father's shoulder on the cover of the 1959 Blue Note album *The Scene Changes: The Amazing Bud Powell (Vol. 5)*.

22. The episode, titled "At Ojai Music Festival, Vijay Iyer Showcases Improvisation," first aired in October 2017 and is available at https://n.pr/2ZhCHUS. Others interviewed about the intersection of jazz and classical music include George Lewis and Claire Chase, the latter discussing a 1962 Ojai performance by Eric Dolphy of the Edgard Varèse composition for solo flute, *Density 21.5*.

23. https://www.nextbop.com/blog/allthecooksinthismysticbrewacriticalanalysisofcovers

24. https://www.npr.org/templates/story/story.php?storyId=120089568

25. Iyer and Moran were born just over three years apart: Iyer on October 26, 1971, and Moran on January 21, 1975. A third pianist-composer friend of theirs of comparable stature and high-art leanings, Craig Taborn, was born February 20, 1970. Ethan Iverson and his successor in the Bad Plus, Orrin Evans, are also close contemporaries, born February 11, 1973, and March 28, 1975, respectively.

26. Abrams died on October 29, 2017, at age eighty-seven, four months after performing at Ojai Music Festival.

27. *Etudes* (1988), recorded with bassist Charlie Haden and drummer Paul Motian in 1987, was among Allen's most acclaimed albums.

28. Two other pianists Iyer often cites among his most important influences but didn't think to include here are Muhal Richard Abrams and Alice Coltrane.

29. The documentary *Thelonious Monk: Straight No Chaser*, directed by Charlotte Zwerin, was released in 1988.

30. Iyer explained to me how he came to adopt Iyer as his surname while in graduate school in California. "The name I grew up with is my father's given name—but it's not a surname, because we [his family's ethnic group] don't have surnames. That name is Raghunathan and gets misspelled at times—so, it turns out, does Iyer. Now, the word *Iyer* is a clan surname. It's kind of like the name Cohen. Like there's tons of Cohens in the world—you wouldn't necessarily say that they're all related, but any two of them might be." Some of Iyer's uncles also use the name Iyer, he said. "Iyer basically tags me as 'Tamil Brahmin who worships Shiva,' if you must know." California was a convenient place to take on the new name because of the state's "usage method," in which consistent use of a name on IDs and other documentation makes that name legally official. "There's no subterfuge," Iyer deadpanned. "I didn't kill anybody."

31. https://thewire.in/culture/vijay-iyer-jazz

32. The show aired March 28, 1987, with Charlton Heston as that week's guest host.

33. Szwed would go on to write biographies of Billie Holiday, Miles Davis, and Sun Ra as well as the superb primer *Jazz 101: A Complete Guide to Learning and Loving Jazz* (New York: Hyperion, 2000). He left Yale in 2008 to become a professor of music and jazz studies at Columbia University, where he directed the Center for Jazz Studies from 2011 until his retirement in 2014.

34. Toward its beginning, Iyer sets up the distinction between European classical music and the music he would focus on: "The inapplicability of these linguistics-derived models to other musics is quite glaring in the cases of West African and African-American musics such as jazz, rumba, funk, and hip-hop. In these cases, certain salient musical features, notably the concept of groove, seem to have no analogue in rational language. Although groove is a highly subjective quality, music that grooves can sustain interest or attention for long stretches of time to an acculturated listener, even if 'nothing is happening' on the musical surface. A prime example is James Brown's music [CD-2], which frequently has precious little melodic or harmonic material and is highly repetitive, but would never be described as static. The fact that groove carries weight to override other musical factors in certain kinds of musical experience suggests that the traditional linguistics-based viewpoint does not suffice in describing the entirety of music cognition.

    "A major reason for this mismatch between tonal-music grammars and most music of the world is not (as is commonly thought) differing levels of musical sophistication or complexity, but rather a major cultural disparity in approaches to rhythmic organization and musical form. I claim that an essential component of this disparity is the status of the body and physical movement in the act of making music. The role of the body in various musics of the world becomes clearer when one observes the function that music and dance assumes in these cultures, the common cultural/linguistic metaphors associated with musical activity. All of these observations have led us to study the role of the body in cognition in general."

    The entire dissertation is available at https://www.academia.edu/20277280/Microstructures_of_Feel_Macrostructures_of_Sound_Embodied_Cognition_in_West_African_and_African-American_Musics_Ph.D._Dissertation_University_of_California_Berkeley._1998_.

35. Other committee members included composer Olly Wilson, who established the first conservatory music program in electronic music at Oberlin Conservatory; the Nobel laureate physicist and neurobiologist Donald Glaser; and psychology professor Ervin Hafter.

36. The entire master class is viewable on YouTube at https://bit.ly/2Nlp6tx.

37. Morris defined "conduction" as "an improvised duet for ensemble and conductor." https://www.nytimes.com/2013/01/30/arts/music/butch-morris-dies-at-65-creator-of-conduction.html

38. Baraka, born LeRoi Jones, wrote the classic *Blues People: Negro Music in White America* (New York: Morrow, 1963) and was an early champion of Iyer. His review of *Memorophilia*, collected in Baraka's book *Digging: The Afro-American Soul of American Classical Music* (Berkeley: University of California Press, 2009), begins "Iyer is an oncoming phenomenon, already up to his fingers in the most advanced music of this wildly contradictory age, where we have got to since a whole generation of giants have swooped." It goes on to celebrate the "emotional and intellectual depth" of his compositions, and concludes: "Iyer brings a sensuous (i.e., reaching the senses) sensitivity to the instrument and a clearly stated intellectual aesthetic that seeks to organically link the infinite microtonics of Eastern music, not as a musical passport but with a precise congruence that flows into really lush harmonic constructions. A very stimulating and thoughtful presentation."

39. https://bit.ly/2KKpYGm

40. https://www.bostonglobe.com/arts/music/2016/03/31/convened-iyer-diverse-artists-con-verge-harvard/EFhUCmJj7WosV2LhOM1dHL/story.html

41. At the time, Iyer noted that Lehman, Sorey, and a third artist featured at the event, pianist Court-ney Bryan, were doctoral students in composition at Columbia University. They have each since graduated and moved on to teaching appointments: Bryan at Tulane University, Lehman at the CalArts School of Music (from which Wadada Leo Smith had retired in 2013), and Sorey replacing the retiring Anthony Braxton at Wesleyan University.

42. One notable later example, of course, was that quartet at Ojai, with Mahanthappa, Zakir Hus-sain, and vocalist Aruna Sairam.

43. "Blood Count" is by Billy Strayhorn; the first track on *Mutations* (2014) is one of Iyer's own, "Spell-bound and Sacrosanct, Cowrie Shells and the Shimmering Sea," which Iyer had first recorded on his debut album as a trio piece.

44. Titled *Solo*, the album was released in 2010 on the German label ACT Music + Vision.

45. That one, tantalizingly slow-moving and carried along by Crump's elegant bass, caused me to do a kind of auditory double take when it came up on my car stereo once. It sounded like something the Bad Plus might have come up with, perhaps owing to that bass work or Ethan Iverson having preceded his Bad Plus tenure as music director for the Mark Morris Dance Company.

46. The Giddins piece, titled "Purely Piano," appeared in the *Village Voice* in October 2002 and is reprinted in his collection *Weather Bird: Jazz at the Dawn of Its Second Century* (New York: Oxford University Press, 2004). Giddins noted the hip-hop beats that connected the three featured pia-nists. "Several times I wondered whether Ethan Iverson, Vijay Iyer, and Jason Moran were playing jazz at all," he wrote in the piece, "but I never really cared." He went on to describe their shared affinity for pianists who had been overlooked in the '60s and '70s. "Now we keep hearing talk of and works by Jaki Byard, Andrew Hill, and Muhal Richard Abrams, plus the earlier stride hierar-chy, not to mention Ellington, whose *Queen's Suite* evidently has a special resonance."

47. I saw Iyer perform live for the first time several months earlier, in December 2011. He was with his trio in a double bill with Miguel Zenón's quartet at the Berklee Performance Center, a show I reviewed for *JazzTimes*. https://jazztimes.com/reviews/concerts/miguel-zenonvi-jay-iyer-berklee-12911/

48. Trio 3 had recruited two other pianists to join them on albums prior to Iyer: Geri Allen and Jason Moran.

49. Esbjörn Svensson led the Swedish piano trio e.s.t. (for Esbjörn Svensson Trio) between 1993 and his death in a scuba diving accident in 2008.

50. The material cited above comes from a screen shot posted on a Reddit discussion of the Rosen-winkel post. https://imgur.com/a/xLdrz

51. https://bit.ly/2Zkt4Fj

52. Groundbreaking albums by John Coltrane, Miles Davis, and Ornette Coleman, respectively.

53. The program can be viewed at https://charlierose.com/videos/28350.

54. The Moran interview was conducted in October 2011, and the track played for him was the Thelonious Monk tune "Epistrophy" from Iyer's album *Solo* of the previous year: "That sounds like Vijay. Vijay has a distinct tone at the instrument. A lot of piano players go up; he likes to go down. He likes to crawl down this mountain into the bottom of the piano. He figures out these ways and shapes that kind of tumble down. He's kind of a brother in the sense we are coming from some of the same spaces. Andrew Hill is an influence; M-Base is an influence; the AACM is an influence—these creative musicians who approach music with a wide outlook. Vijay is a

player where you can't really say, 'I heard it, I got it.' He's still way in development. His technique thing is getting more precise. So he's always fun to listen to." https://bit.ly/2P8TEBa

55. "I like what David Weiss said, it's really not about 'complicated melodies or tricky time signatures, it's about playing music with conviction and passion and with a strong groove.' You're a perfect example of that Vijay. I'll be the first person to tell you that when it comes to composing complex music, I could never do it because I don't hear music being formed that way in my mind. I could try, but it wouldn't be an honest representation to anybody. HOWEVER, I can play it for days, for some odd reason, lol. That shit that you & I performed with Rich Brown, Jeff Watts, Steve Lehman & imani uzuri was HOT!!!!!!!!"

56. "I love Vijay, man. Vijay's incredible. One time we played this thing—I was working with him in Copenhagen or something like that, it was a festival, and he was hanging out backstage. I've always been a fan of his, and he's like, 'What are you guys going to play? What material are you doing?' I was like, 'Well, we're doing "Eye of the Hurricane," do you want to play?' And he was like, 'Yeah!'

"That was the most intense and beautiful 'Eye of the Hurricane' that I've ever played. I think he understood that part of what we were dealing with conceptually is that every man is his own reality. But he could really hear that, so he wasn't trying to follow the wave. He was trying to be in his own space within all these different perspectives, and it was one of the most palpable experiences of my life in terms of how much fervor was actually in the composition, which was crazy. So I had a great time playing with him on that. But I'm just a fan of his music. Obviously, you know? Marcus Gilmore is one of my best friends in the world. He started playing in our band when he was seventeen years old, and he's been with Vijay for years—so it's also like a mutual love because there's shared band-ness."

When I mentioned Iyer's detractors, Scott's response was blunt.

"The thing is, anybody that says that Vijay Iyer can't play is an asshole and a liar," he told me. "Please print that. Because on a conceptual level the guy is a genius. There's a reason that people love what he's doing in a lot of those spaces. But who knows? It might be a jealousy thing. That's what it feels like to me when you say that."

57. The saxophonist on the album, *Brain Dance* (2011), was Mark Shim, who is also the tenor saxophonist in Iyer's sextet.

58. "People usually take him for an accountant, he says," Alec Wilkinson had written of Iyer in the opening paragraph of his 2016 *New Yorker* profile (https://www.newyorker.com/magazine/2016/02/01/time-is-a-ghost). The stereotype is a recurring irritation for Iyer, who has brought it up in other interviews. In *Jazziz* magazine, for instance, Shaun Brady quotes him thus: "I feel like people tag me as cerebral, but don't tag anybody else that way. You know who's cerebral? Ethan Iverson. You know who's mathematical? Miguel Zenón. But no one ever says that, so it's actually about something else. That's the way people talk about Asian-Americans, which is that we're treated as soulless robots who do things with mathematical and technical efficiency but have no emotions." https://www.jazziz.com/vijay-iyer/

As for the recent Kaplan review Iyer was referencing, it occurred approximately three months before Iyer and I spoke, not one. But here's the entirety of what Kaplan wrote about *Far from Over* in his roundup of the best jazz albums of 2017: "Vijay Iyer, a virtuosic pianist and theoretical physicist, once came off a bit schematic in his compositions and improvs, but those days have been over for years, and his new album, which expands his usual trio into a sextet (with horns), is positively ebullient, a couple of tracks stepping into soulful." http://www.slate.com/articles/arts/music_box/2017/12/the_best_jazz_albums_of_2017_and_the_best_reissues.html

59. A Herbie Hancock composition from his classic 1965 album *Maiden Voyage*.

60. Iyer's brief liner notes for the album conclude: "As the arc of history lurches forward and backward, the fact remains: local and global struggles for equality, justice, and basic human rights are far from over. We hope that our music both reflects this truth and offers a useful residuum that might outlast it."

61. One of the band's two emcees was Mohammed Bilal, a minor celebrity at the time as a cast member on MTV's *The Real World*, which helped enable the band to get booked nationally. The other emcee, William "Wilpower" Wylie, now known as Will Power, has gone on to become an accomplished playwright and performer. "They played with a live band, and I played with them for years," Iyer told me. "We did all sorts of stuff together. We made hip-hop musicals about AIDS and the black community, and collaborated with choreographers. They were very open in their conception. It wasn't just about laying beats and rhyming. It was actually about—you've been using the term; what'd you use? something about engagement—'social engagement.' "

62. https://bit.ly/2Z6B2Xg

63. Crump was leading dates that weekend in Baltimore and New York with his group Rhombal. Gilmore had duo performances at Birdland with Savion Glover.

64. https://www.newyorker.com/magazine/2002/01/14/all-this-jazz-3

65. https://www.newyorker.com/magazine/2009/03/02/a-passage-to-india

66. "Music that defies category, music that very much fits with the times in which we live," Mahanthappa wrote in his album notes. "In my pursuits, each album represents a new investigation into the meaning and trajectory of global society and community."

67. The second series of concerts eventually led to Mahanthappa's collaboration with Ragamala Dance Company. Co-artistic director and lead dancer of the company, Aparna Ramaswamy, caught the performance at the Walker Art Center in Minneapolis and, after hearing Mahanthappa interviewed on *Fresh Air* and reading about the Giddins piece in the *New Yorker*, contacted him about working together on what became *Song of the Jasmine*. Mahanthappa wrote music and led a five-piece ensemble in performing it live to accompany the dancers in a handful of US performances; the work premiered at the Walker in spring 2014.

68. http://www.slate.com/articles/arts/music_box/2008/12/top_10_jazz_albums_of_2008.html

69. Thomas would resign from the Peabody Conservatory in October 2017.

70. Years later, while being interviewed onstage as the year's artist-in-residence at the 2016 New York Winter Jazzfest, King broke up an audience with a hilarious true story involving Prince. King was in a hip Minneapolis coffee shop talking with a French record producer who had just signed King's band Happy Apple when the record producer asked if King ever saw Prince around town. To their astonishment, Prince walked past them through the coffee shop at that precise moment. " '*He fuckin' walked right by us.*' I said, 'He's right there.' His face: He was like, '*Holy shit!*' I couldn't believe it. The timing was like I just ordered up Prince."

71. https://www.nytimes.com/2004/07/11/arts/music-let-s-play-the-music-and-dance.html?mtrref=www.bing.com&gwh=5DC1B19B50AB67315561DFE1DF81ABEE&gwt=pay

72. https://nyti.ms/2GV8V24

73. https://www.villagevoice.com/2003/03/04/trio-savvy/

74. https://jazztimes.com/archives/the-bad-plus-great-white-hypes/

75. https://jazztimes.com/archives/the-bad-plus-saying-it-proud-but-way-too-loud/

76. Klein is hardly the only one to raise this philosophical question: At what point does making the music new cause it to stray so far from its African American roots that it ceases to be jazz?

77. https://jazztimes.com/features/lists/before-after-with-billy-hart/

78. https://bit.ly/2uVO3Qp

79. "Hilarious! I remember that well," Mahanthappa emailed me when I passed along Evans's recollection. "The club is called the Neo Lounge right down the street from the Blue Note on West Third. I think I had been sitting in at another club earlier that evening. I also knew Darryl Hall already because we had met at a festival in Jamaica the summer before. So it wasn't quite as blindly as coming in off the street and asking to play, I definitely had an in. And I remember they were doing a really difficult arrangement of 'Body and Soul' in an odd meter."

80. The baseball star Roberto Clemente, a native of Puerto Rico, became the first Latin American and Caribbean player to be inducted into the National Baseball Hall of Fame in 1973. Clemente died in a plane crash on December 31, 1972, while attempting to deliver aid to earthquake victims in Nicaragua.

81. Short film clips from many of these, including the group playing "St. Thomas" at the Rollins tribute in Cidra, can be found on Zenón's website, https://miguelzenon.com/caravana-cultural/.

82. My review of the NEC show can be found at https://jazztimes.com/reviews/live/live-review-miguel-zenon-quartet-and-nec-jazz-orch-in-boston/.

83. The *Jazz Night in America* broadcast is available at https://bit.ly/2KKdluT.

84. Eugene Holley, "Import Duties," *DownBeat*, November 1996, 32–35.

85. Reich has more authority making this suggestion than most, having served on the committee that was the first to award the Pulitzer Prize for Music to a jazz musician: Wynton Marsalis for *Blood on the Fields* in 1997. https://www.chicagotribune.com/entertainment/music/howard-reich/ct-hyde-park-fest-review-ent-0926-20160925-column.html

86. https://jazztimes.com/reviews/live/concert-review-miguel-zenon-at-the-sfjazz-center-may-22-25/

87. https://www.nytimes.com/2013/05/05/arts/music/anat-cohen-and-her-jazz-clarinet.html

88. So had certain members of the AACM, albeit without a perch as prominent as Jazz at Lincoln Center for getting the word out. The trio Air (Henry Threadgill, Fred Hopkins, Steve McCall) featured two compositions apiece by Scott Joplin and Jelly Roll Morton on the 1979 album *Air Lore*, and Anthony Braxton and Muhal Richard Abrams gave Joplin's "Maple Leaf Rag" a remarkable update on Braxton's 1976 album *Duets*, a track included on *Jazz: The Smithsonian Anthology*, a six-CD historical compilation released in 2011.

89. https://www.npr.org/2015/02/26/387374023/anat-cohen-choro-aventuroso-at-jazz-at-lincoln-center

90. Flying Lotus is the stage name for Steven Ellison, a popular hip-hop experimentalist and grandnephew of John and Alice Coltrane. Cohen and her quartet cover his song "Putty Boy Strut" on her 2015 album *Luminosa*.

91. Israel requires military service of its citizens when they turn eighteen. Men serve three years, and women serve two.

92. Raised Arnold Lawrence Finkelstein in Brooklyn's Brownsville neighborhood, Lawrence spent five years as a featured band member on *The Tonight Show*, leaving when the program relocated from New York to California in 1972. In addition to several projects as a band leader, Lawrence

did sideman work with a wide range of musicians including Charles Mingus, Chico Hamilton, and the popular jazz-rock group Blood, Sweat & Tears.

93. Fort studied jazz at William Paterson College in New Jersey, built on that experience with private studies with Paul Bley after moving to New York City in 1996, and has since returned to Israel. She works primarily with her trio and records for ECM Records.

94. Hoffman moved to New York in the early 1990s after a year in Amsterdam, and spent time early on there busking in the subway with Art Blakey's vocalist daughter, Evelyn Blakey. He soon began performing in clubs with musicians including bassist Cohen and pianist Jason Lindner, and became a pioneer in fusing modern jazz with Middle Eastern music after seeing the audience reaction to his playing oud, recording with Cohen on both guitar and oud on the bassist's 1998 debut album, *Adama*.

95. https://www.tabletmag.com/jewish-arts-and-culture/music/56737/jazz-standards

96. The third educator Goldberg referred to was pianist Amit Golan, who studied at the New School before returning to Israel to start a high school jazz program.

97. A conspicuous exception to this was Tzadik, launched by John Zorn in 1995 to showcase avant-garde and experimental music. Cohen herself recorded on two Tzadik projects of the Brazilian percussionist Cyro Baptista, *Beat the Donkey* (2002) and *Infinito* (2009).

98. Impulse! returned to releasing new music in 2014 as a division of Universal Music France, with US distribution overseen by Blue Note Records.

99. https://www.nytimes.com/2007/05/11/arts/music/11anat.html

100. https://www.npr.org/templates/story/story.php?storyId=87773328

101. That Avital's name appeared repeatedly on both the Israeli and non-Israeli lists of Anzic artists on this page is no accident. Cohen considers him the link that first brought many of her key associates together in those early years at Smalls. "Daniel and Jason went to high school together," she told me, meaning LaGuardia High School of Music & Arts, Freedman commuting there from Soho and Lindner from Brooklyn. "In the '90s they were playing with Omer. Avishai knew Omer, started to play with them. I started, met Jason and all this new scene. Omer is a really serious musical force and social connector."

102. Johannes Brahms, 1833–1897.

103. Jean de Ockeghem, c. 1410–1497.

104. An excerpt from Glasper's apology:

"Jazz has been called a boys' club. That's not opinion, that's fact. I've played in jazz clubs across the world, and I have personally witnessed the absence of women at shows. That's an actual thing. And that's an actual problem. We can go further—why don't we see so many black people at jazz shows? It's our music—but audiences are white. White and male.

"My thing is, why?

"Personally, what I wanted to speak about was the idea that jazz has lost its connection with something fundamental. The groove, the dance, the soul that it was originally built off of. And yes, this is connected to sex—for men and women. I don't think it's a bad thing to mention sex. It's a real, natural human thing—and I'm paying attention to it. There's been too much shaming of women as sexual beings. And I truly feel that my music is inclusive. Women are my teachers, co-conspirators and collaborators. I learned music from a woman: my mom was a musician—she is the reason I do what I do.

"The reality is, I do over a hundred interviews a year—somewhere in there I'm gonna say something that may come out wrong. I apologize that this came out wrong and caused offense—or upset. I was speaking from my experience. The whole point is that I would love to see more women in jazz. In general I love to see people that aren't initially connected to jazz coming to it. My experience, with my music, is that this shift has meant audiences with more women and more young people, and I connected that to a return to a groove which just feels good—for everyone."

105. When I interviewed him about *Black Radio* for *JazzTimes* in 2012, Glasper boasted of having club owner Lorraine Gordon approach him at the Village Vanguard while his trio was performing there and telling him, "Don't take this the wrong way, but I've never seen this many young black people in here."

106. Kim Yvette Glasper Dobbs, forty-three, and her second husband, the minister Brian Keith Dobbs, thirty-seven, were murdered in their Stafford, Texas, home in 2004 by a man who had been staying with the couple, according to reports in the *Houston Chronicle*. In a plea arrangement, Richard Reynol White, twenty-one, confessed to fatally striking Dobbs on the head with an object during an argument and attacking Glasper Dobbs when she returned home soon afterward. White was sentenced to forty-six years in prison.

107. Glasper may have been exaggerating when he claimed six months. I asked him whether he had had classical training when I interviewed him in 2006. "No, I never really took classical lessons," he told me. "I tried to for like two months, but it didn't work out. I had to improvise. I couldn't just sit there and like read the notes off the paper that had been played over and over again through years and years. I want to make stuff brand new."

108. Glasper is a big, genial man who bears a physical resemblance, both in size and the shape of his face, to Thelonious Monk. He told journalist John Murph, in a 2010 *DownBeat* profile, that relatives of his then-girlfriend and future wife, Angelika Beener, a great niece of Monk, have told him that his mannerisms match Monk's as well.

109. "Resolution" is the second movement in John Coltrane's *A Love Supreme*, a four-part suite released in January 1965 and considered by many to be his greatest work.

110. Bristlenose Plecos, Siamese Algae Eaters, Black Mollies are some likely possibilities among fish known for helping keep tanks clean by eating algae (not fungus).

111. Known locally as CAPA, the school's notable music alumni include the prominent jazz musicians Christian McBride, Joey DeFrancesco, and Kurt Rosenwinkel as well as Ahmir "Questlove" Thompson and Black Thought (Tariq Trotter) of the Roots.

112. I also spoke briefly with Bilal about the making of the track. "I knew his mom well," he told me. "The music had so much emotion in it already, I just basically opened up my mouth and sang. I didn't want to get in the way of what was already there."

113. Hyman sings on Tyner's 1982 album *Looking Out*.

114. A combination drum machine and sampler, the MPC—for "music production center"—allows users to upload sounds and program them to serve as a sort of electronic drum kit.

115. "I just had to do that to create," Glasper told me, explaining his decision to enlist Blanchard and Questlove to carry out the prank. "I get that kind of stuff from listening to hip-hop records, because you have fun. Your average jazz recording, they're not having fun. It's fucking serious as hell. They have their songs, and that's all you're getting. You're not hearing any talking, you're not hearing any jokes. For the most part, it's just pretty boring."

116. https://jazztimes.com/features/profiles/robert-glasper-renegade-of-funk/

117. Miles Davis himself was another artist who refused to be left behind. Nor was he shy about

seeking a wide audience. As he and his co-author Quincy Troupe wrote in his autobiography, *Miles* (New York: Simon and Schuster, 1989): "As a musician and as an artist, I have always wanted to reach as many people as I could through my music. And I have never been ashamed of that. Because I never thought that the music called 'jazz' was ever meant to reach just a small group of people, or become a museum thing locked under a glass like all other dead things that were once considered artistic. I always thought it should reach as many people as it could, like so-called popular music, and why not? I never was one of those people who thought less was better; the fewer who hear you, the better you are, because what you're doing is just too complex for a lot of people to understand. A lot of jazz musicians say in public that they feel this way, that they would have to compromise their art to reach a whole lot of people. But in secret they want to reach as many people as they can, too. Now, I'm not going to call their names. It's not important. But I always thought that music had no boundaries, no limits to where it could grow and go, no restrictions on its creativity. Good music is good no matter what kind of music it is. And I always hated categories. Always. Never thought it had any place in music."

118. Even with "Stella by Starlight," Glasper's arrangement was meant to appeal to his newer fans, people he assumed to be unfamiliar with classic jazz. "It's more digestible to the average listener," Glasper explained. "You can nod your head to it. Does that make it not jazz, because you can nod your head? You know what pisses me off? How can you define a whole genre from one rhythmic pattern? People feel like if it doesn't go, *ting-ting-ta-ding ting-ta-ding*, if it doesn't swing, it's not jazz. That kills me. How can you define a whole genre of music from one rhythmic pattern? It makes no sense whatsoever. That's the music of expression. So if I put a backbeat to something, that doesn't make it not jazz. It's still African. Still coming from the same place, the same bloodline. You can't define any other music by drum beat. Not one. You can't say, 'OK, this pattern means that it's this type of music.' But jazz—which is supposed to be the freest music—for some reason has rhythmic chains on it. I've never understood that at all."

119. Glasper did, however, co-teach a course with author Ashley Kahn on the music of Miles Davis in fall 2016 at New York University's Clive Davis Institute of Recorded Music.

120. https://www.npr.org/sections/therecord/2017/03/09/519482385/sexism-from-two-leading-jazz-artists-draws-anger-and-presents-an-opportunity

121. http://www.sashaberlinermusic.com/political-and-social-commentary-1/2017/9/21/an-open-letter-to-ethan-iverson-and-the-rest-of-jazz-patriarchy

122. https://www.wbgo.org/post/sexism-jazz-conservatory-club-one-saxophonist-shares-her-story#stream/0

123. https://www.nytimes.com/2017/12/01/arts/music/year-in-jazz-women-musicians.html

124. Others have noticed women's indifference toward the music of the pioneering jazz-rock fusion bands. Branford Marsalis has a story about discovering the same thing at a Weather Report concert. Here's the version that came up when we spoke for this book: "I was going to Weather Report and Return to Forever and Mahavishnu. I would go to all these concerts. I'm like eighteen or nineteen. I noticed something that I just never really paid attention to before. It's that the entire room was filled only with men. So it started to be, for me, 'Whatever is in this music, there's something that is clearly missing, because the women ain't digging it.' And that kind of changed my idea about it. I started saying, 'I don't know if I'm going to hang around this too much longer.' Even though I still listen to some of those old records and I love it."

125. Iverson raised a related point in his wide-ranging, masterful debut piece for the *New Yorker*'s culture blog that summer. Titled "Duke Ellington, Bill Evans, and One Night in New York City," the

essay assessed how the two men's different approaches to performing Ellington's "In a Sentimental Mood" at different venues on August 17, 1967—Ellington at the popular upscale restaurant and ballroom Rainbow Grill and Evans at the Village Vanguard—illustrated what Iverson singled out as a key cause of jazz's diminishing popularity in the years since: "the *influence* of scalar thought at a introductory level." (A secondary culprit pinpointed by Iverson, prompted by Eddie Gomez taking a virtuosic one in the Evans set, was the increasing prevalence of bass solos.)

Iverson details the surprises Ellington unveils for the dancers uptown before moving on to Evans and the Vanguard. "In 1967, you could still get a hamburger or a turkey club sandwich at the Vanguard, but there certainly was no dancing." Evans's playing that night is found to be lacking in comparison to the richness of Ellington's, a problem greatly exacerbated since then when lesser talents are taught as students that scales are the basic building blocks for jazz improvisation. That Ellington, like Glasper after him, prioritized melody and rhythm over the ostentatious manipulation of scales is what kept his music so creative and impactful.

"It is so beautiful how radical and avant-garde [Paul] Gonsalves and Ellington can be while also playing for dancers," Iverson wrote. "It's a kind of avant-gardism that prizes melody and beat first. It also aligns with mystery and even pop sensibility, or at least a way to make something unusual within a confining commercial marketplace." https://bit.ly/2uVO3Qp

126. Iverson has begun to rectify that situation. As of March 2018, he had published an interview with Joanne Brackeen and had another in the works with Carla Bley. His interview with Glasper remained available online as well (though it appears to have been subsequently removed), Iverson having added these lines introducing it in December 2017: "This interview was widely criticized. I was also dumb as a post in a defensive reaction. Glasper apologized on Facebook and Sarah Deming [Iverson's novelist wife] offered a post-storm essay: 'My Husband, the Misogynist.'"

127. http://talkeasypod.com/artist/esperanza-spalding/

128. Spalding, Glasper, keyboardist Ray Angry, guitarist Matthew Stevens, and drummer Justin Tyson recording the final take together can be watched on YouTube at https://www.youtube.com/watch?v=966ZswEDkyw.

129. The performance is available online at https://bit.ly/2IsD6g7.

130. Participants included Jason Moran, Craig Taborn, Kris Davis, and Don Byron, among others, in addition to Spalding and her fellow symposium organizers Terri Lyne Carrington, Ingrid Monson, and Vijay Iyer.

131. Whether that included romantic heartbreak as in the song is unclear. But, in an article in the *Harvard Gazette,* Wingate described living out of the family van with his mother for fourteen months after Hurricane Sandy destroyed their home on the New Jersey shore. "I still had my schoolwork to do and was working as a manager at McDonald's," he told the *Gazette* of that experience. https://news.harvard.edu/gazette/story/2017/04/harvard-college-student-makes-the-most-of-harvard-after-close-encounter-with-hurricane-sandy/

132. https://www.youtube.com/watch?v=rFsVXdmwZoo

133. https://www.youtube.com/watch?v=oxfG-dJFbxc

134. https://www.youtube.com/watch?v=WNFf7nMIGnE

135. https://www.youtube.com/watch?v=CtaRwKJMVR8

136. https://www.youtube.com/watch?v=g-rWNAQxiZE

137. https://www.newyorker.com/magazine/2010/03/15/new-note

138. The performances took place on April 14 and 15, 2017, just over two months before Allen's unexpected death of cancer on June 27.

139. DeJohnette's off-the-cuff shorthand for Spalding's theatrical performances of the music from her 2016 album *Emily's D+Evolution*.

140. She and I share that birthday, as does Wynton Marsalis. When I reminded her of this at the Jazz Standard, Spalding told me of recently discovering that two members of her new quintet, saxophonist Myron Walden and drummer/vocalist Josh Dion, have that same birthday as well.

141. Russonello would five years later succeed Nate Chinen and Ben Ratliff in covering jazz for the *New York Times*. https://jazztimes.com/features/esperanza-spalding-star-time/

142. A private woman, she asked the *New Yorker* not to give her name in its profile of her daughter. I am honoring her desire for privacy here as well without being asked.

143. Spalding is one of four inductees associated with jazz. The others are Sonny Rollins, Quincy Jones, and Wynton Marsalis. https://bit.ly/3owLOmo

144. https://www.achievement.org/achiever/esperanza-spalding/

145. "I'm kind of like the poster child of Berklee, because I'm Latina and a girl and a minority," she told me early in the interview when I asked what she thought of being depicted on the wall. "From what I heard, it's kind of abstract. Unless you know it's me, I don't think you'll be like, 'That looks like that girl.' I don't think I'll be recognizable. So that's cool."

146. Spalding had been missing a lot of school, I later learned, because of autoimmune deficiency-related illnesses, which she blamed on the stress caused by the family's lack of resources.

147. Spalding and other star alumni returned to campus in 2016 to perform with Crook at a special retirement concert, which I reviewed. https://bit.ly/2TeAdWa

148. Genovese and Mela were with her a few months later when she made her debut as a leader at Scullers that October. My review of the set described her telling the audience she had just finished writing her piece "I Adore You" (which would appear a couple of years later on *Esperanza*) and how "killing" it was, and concluded: "That charmingly girlish enthusiasm, equal parts bubbly and hip, is something you don't see much of in jazz. One more reason that Spalding is a performer to watch." https://bit.ly/31vavzl

149. "She really knows what she's got," Mela had said, "but she doesn't know yet how to combine those two abilities that she has. She's a great singer, she's a great bass player, and so she's just trying to put all the things in her to go in one direction."

150. https://bit.ly/2KIVX9O

151. She was probably misremembering "revolving eye," a metaphor Eiseley used in his 1969 book, *The Unexpected Universe*.

152. *Ebony & Ivy: Race, Slavery, and the Troubled History of America's Universities* (New York: Bloomsbury, 2013).

153. https://www.youtube.com/watch?v=c68gcu3oMnA

154. An exception is one clip available on YouTube, in which Robert Glasper sits in on a run-through of the song "Heaven in Pennies." https://www.youtube.com/watch?v=966ZswEDkyw

155. https://www.youtube.com/watch?v=kIjGh-wsPEg

156. Moran would give four performances of his project *The Harlem Hellfighters: James Reese Europe and the Absence of Ruin* in the United Kingdom and Germany over several days beginning late that October. He told me he would also play material from the project with the Bandwagon at their annual Thanksgiving week residency at the Village Vanguard and that the American premiere of the full-scale *work* would take place at the Kennedy Center in December. https://jasonmoran-nharlemhellfighters.com

157. Ligon was scheduled to appear with Moran at another ICA event in November, at which Moran

would play piano and then discuss his artistic methods with Ligon afterward. Moran would also perform at the museum with his Bandwagon trio mates in October.

158. "Issue 2 is almost done," he explained in an email. "I keep procrastinating." https://walkerart.org/magazine/series/loop-issue-no-1

159. The festival's name had been changed from the Mary Lou Williams Women in Jazz Festival beginning in 2014, at Moran's urging. The *Washington Post* reported at the time that "Moran said his musical development was 'inspired by everyone,' including women such as the jazz pianist Geri Allen, so he did not place a stark emphasis on gender. In his mind, the Kennedy Center's festival would benefit by concentrating instead on the legacy left by Williams, who died in 1981 at 71." https://wapo.st/2YKlGXx

160. "I'm employing [magic] as a tactic," Spalding told the magazine. "I'm saying 'magic' in a way that's tongue in cheek." https://bit.ly/2AIUVFV

161. The vocalist Cécile McLorin Salvant was profiled by Fred Kaplan in the May 22, 2017, issue of the *New Yorker*, in a piece titled "Kind of New." https://www.newyorker.com/magazine/2017/05/22/cecile-mclorin-salvants-timeless-jazz

162. As Sánchez wrote in his album notes: "The rise of Donald Trump's candidacy and his xenophobic and racist rhetoric against Mexicans and other minorities had been in the news for a while and it troubled and angered me deeply because I'm originally Mexican and there was no other way to take that rhetoric but as an insult and a threat."

163. Harrison's website defines nouveau swing, which doubled as the title of his 1997 album for Impulse! Records, as "a style of jazz that merges it with modern dance music like R&B, hip-hop, soul, and rock."

164. https://www.npr.org/2018/11/29/671859112/joey-alexander-tiny-desk-concert

Acknowledgments

Heartfelt thanks to everyone who agreed to be interviewed for this book—without their cooperation it would not exist. Most obviously this includes those artists featured in the book's eight chapters, with an extra thank-you owed to Jason Moran for getting the ball rolling by being the first to agree to participate. Special thanks, too, to the interviewees who agreed to talk without having chapters devoted to them. Those who granted formal interviews are listed by name beginning on page 271. Others told me they were willing to talk, but time ran out before I was able to follow through. Even so, the interview requests themselves sometimes yielded memorable moments: George Lewis telling me he'd rather I not use the word *jazz* to describe what I was writing about; Teju Cole speaking casually about Vijay Iyer and his music over dinner after we'd watched Iyer and Wadada Leo Smith perform together at Harvard, having driven over from Emerson College after Cole had been a featured speaker there that same afternoon; Cassandra Wilson, upon my mentioning that I'd particularly like to ask her about Moran (who backed her on her album *Loverly* and credited her with having years earlier introduced him to the Son House song "Death Letter" during his master class on death music at New England Conservatory), flashing a beatific smile and saying, *Jason*. All of these good people, named or unnamed, enhanced my understanding of the ways in which this music continued to evolve as it entered its second century.

The book was written with the financial assistance of the Norman and Irma Mann Stearns Distinguished Faculty Award. I'm grateful to the Stearns family for establishing the award, and to Emerson College for choosing me as its recipient for the 2016–2017 academic year. The college's faculty development funding, which president Lee Pelton has increased since his arrival in 2011, also helped cover the travel costs involved in researching this project. And when my own allotment from this funding pool was tapped out in spring 2018 and I needed to make one final trip to New York to interview Esperanza Spalding, dean Rob Sabal redirected a bit more of it my way to underwrite the trip. Emerson also supplied me with a succession of graduate student research assistants, whose duties included transcribing interviews and checking facts. Thanks to Emerson for providing them, and to these researchers for their work: Kyle Dacuyan, Shane Aldridge, Annmarie Tompsen, JennyMae Kho, Bill Hatfield, Matthew Herzfeld, and Rick Bach. (Rick so dependably returned accurately transcribed interviews overnight, usually accompanied by a note zeroing in on something the interviewee had said that he found particularly profound or striking, that I continued paying him for such work myself after he graduated.)

Journalism also helped underwrite the book. At the *Boston Globe*, Steve Smith and Hans Schulz edited the newspaper's jazz coverage over the several years the book was being researched and written. Before them, Hayley Kaufman and Mark Shimabukuro edited me in the years I was getting to know the work of Jason Moran, the Bad Plus, Robert Glasper, Esperanza Spalding, and others I realized were making jazz new, and then executive editor Marty Baron and then arts editor Scott Heller—now at the *Washington Post* and the *New York Times*, respectively—both played roles in giving me the opportunity to do so. The late Jack Maher hired me at *DownBeat* in 1985, and decades later the same magazine's Frank Alkyer and Bobby Reed assigned me feature stories on Rudresh Mahanthappa and Julian Lage. Lee Mergner and Evan Haga of *JazzTimes* assigned me numerous album reviews and a 2012 feature story on Robert Glasper and his album *Black Radio*. Joe Keohane and Nate Hopper each assigned me an interview at *Esquire*, with Sonny Rollins and Herbie Hancock. In between my book manuscript being sent out for peer review and my writing its epilogue, David Pulizzi of *Jazziz* assigned me a profile of Tia Fuller.

Publicists, club managers, and others provided me with access to musicians and their music, both live and recorded. There are too many such people to name all of them, but an honor roll of the most helpful starts with the great Fred Taylor, Boston's legendary booker of jazz at Scullers, Paul's Mall and the Jazz Workshop (shuttered by the time I arrived in Boston), Tanglewood, and other venues. Fred's Scullers associates Dayla Santurri and Alexandra Yabrov were always accommodating, as have been Fred's successor Jan Mullen and her box office supervisor Marla Kleman. Fenton Hollander welcomed me to the Regattabar when I was getting started at the *Globe*; the succession of people the Charles Hotel has had overseeing the club since Fenton's departure, most recently Louis Heck and Molly Collins, have been similarly helpful. Stephanie Janes and Jack Wright of the Celebrity Series of Boston and Jennifer Fox of Global Arts Live have been generous about providing access to their organizations' many world-class events, and Margaux Leonard of ICA Boston approved press passes to two performances associated with Jason Moran's art exhibit there and a third to Teju Cole reading from his book *Blind Spot* while accompanied by Vijay Iyer and other musicians. Rob Hayes, Nick Balkin, Margot Edwards and others at Berklee College of Music have been consistently helpful, as has Sue Auclair of Sue Auclair Promotions.

Beyond Boston, thanks are owed to Carolyn McClair of the Newport Jazz Festival; Matt Merewitz of New York's Winter Jazzfest and his own PR agency, Fully Altered Media; Ann Braithwaite of the Montreal Jazz Festival, New England Conservatory, and her agency, Braithwaite & Katz Communications; Don Lucoff and Maureen McFadden of DL Media; Scott Southard of International Music Network; Jason Paul Harman Byrne of Red Cat Publicity; Ted Kurland of The Kurland Agency; Alex Kurland and Jordy Freed of the Blue Note Jazz Club in New York; publicist April Thibeault provided me press access to the Jazz Standard, floor manager Ivory McKay treated this out-of-town journalist like royalty when I got there, and artistic director Seth Abramson supplied me Ivory's last name when we crossed paths in the press tent at Newport; my former *Globe* editor Steve Smith, now of National Sawdust; and Marshall Lamm of SFJAZZ Center. Especially helpful folks associated with the recording industry include Cem Kurosman of Blue Note Records; Tina Pelikan of ECM (who aside from dispensing recorded music brought me to a Vijay Iyer/Wadada Leo Smith duo performance at the Met Breuer as her guest); Seth Rosner and Yulun Wang at Pi Recordings; Bret Sjerven of Sunnyside Records; Mike Wilpizeski of Concord Music Group; Julia Casey of Verve; Ken Weinstein of Big Hassle Media; and my Sonny Rollins contact Terri Hinte, who joined me at one of the Miguel Zenón performances I caught during Zenón's residency at SFJAZZ Center, Radiclani Clytus, Stephen Cohen, and Brenda Goldstein-Young provided special help securing the use of video files featuring Jason Moran, Vijay Iyer, and Anat Cohen, respectively, and Jenna Molster explained how NPR Music links could be substituted for the two artists for whom I wasn't able to obtain them.

All of this support would have been for nought if no one had agreed to publish the resultant book. The trade publishers I approached didn't see sufficient potential profit in a book documenting the current jazz scene—"on the rare occasion we do publish [a jazz book]," an executive editor at one explained, "we tend to stick with the tried-and-true classic artists." Fortunately, academic publishers showed more interest in the project. I'm delighted that Beth Bouloukos acquired the book for Lever Press, and am grateful to Mary Francis of the University of Michigan Press for steering me to her. It is a pleasant bonus that Amanda Karby, a graduate of Emerson's master's degree program in publishing and writing, is overseeing the book's production.

Emerson provided me moral support along with its financial assistance. Jeff Seglin chaired the search committee that initially hired me, his departure for Harvard's Kennedy School of Government a few years later opened a tenure line that I eventually filled, and his periodic nudging in the years after his departure helped ensure that I finished my book in time to secure tenure. John Skoyles also took an interest in my project and helped guide me through academia and the tenure process. My wife has accurately described each of them as a mensch for these efforts. Pamela Painter and Steve Yarbrough suggested I create a course on writing about music, and acting dean Dan Tobin and acting chair Bill Donoghue signed off on allowing the course to be offered. Jerald Walker and Maria Koundoura chaired the Writing, Literature, and Publishing department in the years the book was researched and written, and both gave my book project their enthusiastic support, as did provost Michaele Whelan and dean Rob Sabal. Pam Painter was a joy to have with me for a bunch of live music, always ready to stick around after a show to chat with the artists and snap photos with her iPhone. Other Emerson colleagues who joined me once or more at book-related concerts include Steve Yarbrough, Maria Koundoura, Kim McLarin, Pablo Medina, Florence Gonzalez, Ladette Randolph, Jabari Asim, Roy Kamada, David Emblidge, and John Rodzvilla. And my wife and I ran into Lisa Diercks and her husband, George Restrepo, at one of Jason Moran's performances at the ICA.

Journalism pals Joe Heroun and Joe Keohane also saw music with me, and served as valuable sounding boards as the book progressed. Fellow jazz writer Jon Garelick and his novelist wife, Clea Simon, showed interest in the project when I ran into them in clubs or at Newport, and sold my wife and me on making our first visit to the Jazz and Heritage Festival in New Orleans. Likewise, encounters through the years with Boston-based jazz writer Bob Blumenthal and radio hosts Eric Jackson, Steve Schwartz, and José Massó proved helpful. A jazz bassist who lives down the block from me, Joe Delia, joined me at several shows while the book was being researched as well. So did Dana Garvey, with Rich Wiley joining Dana and me a couple of times too. In addition to keeping me company at those concerts, Dana translated Miguel Zenón's Caravana Cultural lecture on Sonny Rollins for me from Spanish to English.

Dana and Rich were also among those who minded our kids and/or cats while my wife and I were away on reporting trips. The others were all relatives: Emily Abrams, Dan and Leonora Abrams, Nicole and Jerome Stern, Ally and Randall Yee, Kathy and Ken Kassner, and my mother. Danny and Leonora also lent me the use of their house on Cape Cod for a week in April 2017 so I could get away and write. My mother graciously tolerated my using her house in the Hudson Valley as a writer's retreat from time to time—*with her in it*—and/or using it as a staging post for quick research trips to New York City. Don Andrews introduced me to jazz before I turned sixteen by playing Mahavishnu Orchestra during a car ride; four decades later he and his wife, Rachel, put me up for a night in Connecticut as I was en route to New Jersey to interview Rudresh Mahanthappa.

Said kids (and cats) had to put up with a father who was too often distracted or cranky while laboring on the book and trying to interest agents and editors in publishing it. I missed many more of Abe's and Henry's basketball games than I wanted to, and vacation trips to Montreal and Los Angeles. Even during what the boys proclaimed our best family vacation ever, I slipped away from San Juan's Caribe Hilton for most of one day to watch Miguel Zenón give his Sonny Rollins lecture and concert in Cidra.

My wife, Kim, cheerfully picked up the parental slack that day in Puerto Rico as she always has at home—ferrying the kids to away games throughout Massachusetts, traveling with them to California and Florida while I stayed home and worked, and so forth. True, she traveled with me on some of my reporting trips. But that could entail spending the weekend before our ninth wedding anniversary in New York and keeping Jason Moran's four-year-old twins occupied across the room while he and I conducted the first interview specifically for the book, or meeting me in New York the weekend before our fifteenth so that I could meet with Esperanza Spalding for its final one. Kim not only tolerated my book-induced moodiness and divided attention, she pitched in and gave my manuscript a thorough first read, tidying typos and grammatical slip-ups as she went. I could never have written this book without her help. Now that it's done and I'm pondering the travails involved, I'm reminded of the bookmarks we distributed as party favors at our wedding reception and the last half of a quotation I'd chosen for them from Mark Twain's *Adam's Diary*: "After all these years, I see that I was mistaken about Eve in the beginning: it is better to live outside the Garden with her than inside it without her." I can only hope she feels the same way about me after all the book has put her through.

CPSIA information can be obtained
at www.ICGtesting.com
Printed in the USA
BVHW011440071019
560295BV00004B/3/P